Chorlaine
1991

WHAT IS PSYCHOTHERAPY?

Jeffrey K. Zeig
W. Michael Munion
Editors

WHAT IS PSYCHOTHERAPY?

CONTEMPORARY PERSPECTIVES

 Jossey-Bass Publishers

San Francisco • Oxford • 1990

WHAT IS PSYCHOTHERAPY?
Contemporary Perspectives
by Jeffrey K. Zeig and W. Michael Munion, Editors

Copyright © 1990 by: Jossey-Bass Inc., Publishers
350 Sansome Street
San Francisco, California 94104
&
Jossey-Bass Limited
Headington Hill Hall
Oxford OX3 0BW

Library of Congress Cataloging-in-Publication Data

What is psychotherapy? : contemporary perspectives / Jeffrey K. Zeig
and W. Michael Munion, editors.
     p.   cm. — (The Jossey-Bass social and behavioral science
series)
    Includes bibliographical references.
    Includes index.
    ISBN 1-55542-283-7
    1. Psychotherapy.   I. Zeig, Jeffrey K., date.   II. Munion, W.
Michael.   III. Series.
    [DNLM: 1. Psychotherapy—methods.   WM 420 W5545]
RC480.W45   1990
616.89'14—dc20
DNLM/DLC
for Library of Congress   90-5010
                                      CIP

All royalties from the book are the property of The Milton H. Erickson
Foundation, 3606 North 24th Street, Phoenix, Arizona 85016. Royalties
will be used to foster educational and scientific efforts that pertain to
psychotherapy and hypnosis.

Manufactured in the United States of America

JACKET DESIGN BY WILLI BAUM

FIRST EDITION

Code 9078

For information about our audio products, write us at:
Newbridge Book Clubs, 3000 Cindel Drive, Delran, NJ 08370

THE JOSSEY-BASS
SOCIAL AND BEHAVIORAL SCIENCE SERIES

Contents

CHAPTER SIX:
PHILOSOPHICALLY ORIENTED
PSYCHOTHERAPY   169

Section 1: Culturally Based Approaches

Section 2: Personal Meaning

Section 3: Transcendent Approaches

Section 2: Modalities

CHAPTER TEN:
HYPNOTHERAPY AND
ERICKSONIAN PSYCHOTHERAPY   353

Section 1: Ericksonian Approaches

List of Contributors

To all of Michael Munion's families: the one that raised and nurtured him (Munion), the ones that have been true friends to him (Felix, Miller, and Good), and most especially the one he is building with Amy. Family is everything.
W.M.M.

To Nicole — who likes playful definition.
J.K.Z.

Preface

What Is Psychotherapy? brings together eighty-one commentaries on the nature and practice of psychotherapy. The goal was to present a broad survey of the field that captured both its diversity and its richness. The authors of these selections are authorities who have contributed significantly to the development of the field. Almost all of the major schools of thought are represented in cogent, insightful compositions. The reader should regard this volume as a status report on the evolution of modern psychotherapy — a field that has demonstrated phenomenal growth since Freud first attempted the "talking cure" about one century ago.

As a collection of contemporary perspectives, written with the express intent of revealing each contributor's vision of his or her *practice,* this book provides the reader with an opportunity to discern the subtle interplay between theory and the individual practitioner's personality — and how they combine to produce a therapeutic stance. For graduate students and beginning therapists, this information can provide invaluable insight into the therapeutic process. The information here is not a substitute for an in-depth study of psychotherapeutic theory and method, but, as an adjunct to such study, it will help bridge the gap between theory and practice.

This volume is also intended for seasoned clinicians, who will find it a unique source of information about current practice within their discipline and who will garner insights into other approaches.

The initial impetus for this project was the editors' curiosity about the nature of psychotherapy, which is practiced in so many diverse ways. Although the sheer number of approaches in current practice defies exhaustive compilation, the editors believe that the primary goal of surveying the field has been well met — by writings that are informative as well as interesting to the reader.

Acknowledgments

The editors gratefully acknowledge the assistance of a number of people in making this project possible. First, all of the individual contributors who took the time and effort to submit responses: The psychotherapeutic community owes you a debt, and the editors are most grateful.

We also wish to thank the staff of the Erickson Foundation: Theresa Cords for her assistance in correspondence, Greg Deniger for his help in the mass mailings, Mary Helen Kelly for organizing all the incoming correspondence, and Lori Weiers for her unflagging effort at the computer (and her attention to detail).

We appreciate the efforts of Fritz Snider, who took the time to review and critique literary style. We would also like to thank Gracia A. Alkema, John C. Norcross, and Gerald Weeks for their feedback and direction in final revisions to this project.

Last, but not least, we would like to thank Amy Munion for her patience and for allowing a portion of her home to become, at various times, a mailroom, a library, and a literary sweatshop.

Phoenix, Arizona　　　　　　　　Jeffrey K. Zeig
August 1990　　　　　　　　　　W. Michael Munion

The Editors

JEFFREY K. ZEIG is founder and director of the Milton H. Erickson Foundation and conducts a private practice in Phoenix, Arizona. He is widely acclaimed for his work in the fields of hypnosis and psychotherapy and has conducted training workshops for professionals nationally and internationally. Zeig received his B.S. degree (1969) from Michigan State University in zoology, his M.S. degree (1973) from San Francisco State University in clinical psychology, and his Ph.D. degree (1977) from Georgia State University in clinical psychology. He studied intermittently with Milton H. Erickson for more than six years and is internationally recognized for his presentations of Erickson's work. Zeig organized the International Congresses on Ericksonian Approaches to Hypnosis and Psychotherapy held in 1980, 1983, 1986, and 1988, as well as the 1985 and 1990 Evolution of Psychotherapy Conferences. He received the Milton H. Erickson Award from the Netherlands Society of Clinical Hypnosis for outstanding contributions to the field of clinical hypnosis and the Milton H. Erickson Award of Scientific Excellence in Writing in Hypnosis from the American Society of Clinical Hypnosis. Zeig has edited, coedited, or authored twelve books and monographs, and he has written numerous professional articles.

W. MICHAEL MUNION has worked in the behavioral health system in Arizona for over ten years and has been associated with the Milton H. Erickson Foundation since 1980. In 1983, he began a private practice centered in Tempe, Arizona. Munion holds a B.A. degree (1976) from Miami University (Oxford, Ohio) in psychology and an M.A. degree (1981) from Indiana University of Pennsylvania in clinical psychology. Currently, in addition to conducting an individual and family therapy private practice, he is clinical director of Superstition Mountain Mental Health Center, Inc., in Apache Junction, Arizona; program consultant to Against Abuse, Inc., a domestic violence agency for Pinal County; and consulting therapist for Pinal County's Administration for Children, Youth, and Families. Through his ongoing work with East Valley Behavioral Health Association's (EVBHA) Peer Review Committee, Munion provides clinical supervision and quality assurance for EVBHA's provider agencies. He is also a member of the Arizona Association of Alcohol, Drug, and Mental Health Treatment Programs Quality of Care Committee through his role as a founding member of its Clinical Supervisors Subcommittee.

WHAT IS PSYCHOTHERAPY?

Jeffrey K. Zeig
W. Michael Munion

1

=

What Is
Psychotherapy?

Other men are lenses through which we read our own minds.
— *Ralph Waldo Emerson*

Consider the plight of John, an individual who experiences pain when turning his head. Depending on John's personal views and experiences, he may visit a series of specialists to find relief, beginning with the one he believes most likely to hold the answer.

However, John customarily will find that each specialist's perception and consequent response is highly dependent on the *specialist's* educational and experiential background. For example, his family physician may diagnose muscle tension and prescribe muscle relaxants; a spiritualist may diagnose spiritual imbalance and offer prayer and the laying on of hands; a psychotherapist may wonder who is being "a pain in the neck" and recommend assertiveness training; a chiropractor may find cervical misalignment and begin manipulation treatments; and a naturopath may diagnose an energy imbalance and prescribe acupuncture. Of course, John's next-door neighbor, who sells bedroom furniture, may diagnose worn inner springs and recommend a new mattress.

Each treatment may be effective, reinforcing John's beliefs, as well as the beliefs of the specialist. It is likely that both John and the consultant will tenaciously maintain their philosophy of treatment, unclear about how anyone could possibly treat the problem differently.

1

Mark Twain quipped about this phenomenon, "If the only tool you have is a hammer, an awful lot of things will look like nails." We will return to this issue of perception shortly, when we discuss "lenses."

This book is about perspective and practice in psychotherapy. Within the discipline of psychotherapy there are many entrenched notions about theory and treatment. This volume presents the perspectives of exemplary therapists in order to clarify these core issues, thus providing a context within which practitioners and students can scrutinize their own standards and perhaps develop some of the flexibility that is necessary to maximize therapeutic effectiveness.

In this chapter, we will review the development of the *What Is Psychotherapy?* project, describe the organization of the remaining chapters, and offer a paradigm that should be useful to the reader in the process of integrating this material.

The Development of the *What Is Psychotherapy?* Project

In 1985, through the Milton H. Erickson Foundation, the senior editor (Zeig) organized the Evolution of Psychotherapy Conference in Phoenix, Arizona. This was the first comprehensive gathering of master clinicians and theorists from major contemporary disciplines and featured twenty-six faculty: Aaron Beck, Bruno Bettelheim, Murray Bowen, Albert Ellis, Mary Goulding, Robert Goulding, Jay Haley, R. D. Laing, Arnold Lazarus, Cloe Madanes, Judd Marmor, James Masterson, Rollo May, Salvador Minuchin, Zerka Moreno, Erv Polster, Miriam Polster, Carl Rogers, Ernest Rossi, Virginia Satir, Thomas Szasz, Paul Watzlawick, Carl Whitaker, Lewis Wolberg, Joseph Wolpe, and Jeffrey Zeig. The schools of psychotherapy represented at the meeting were: behavioral, cognitive, Ericksonian, experiential, family, gestalt, humanistic, Jungian, multimodal, psychoanalytic, rational-emotive, psychodrama, Rogerian, and Transactional Analysis.

Each of the faculty was to present an address and was given a series of suggested questions to answer. Among these were: How do you define psychotherapy? What are its goals? What are the basic premises and underlying assumptions in your approach to facilitating change? What are seen as the benefits and limitations of your approach?

In the proceedings of the conference, *The Evolution of Psychotherapy,* Zeig (1987) indicated that although experts expounded extensively at the conference, the question "What is psychotherapy?" remained unanswered. Zeig suggested that there was no capsule definition on which any of the twenty-six presenters could agree. Therefore one could view the field of psychotherapy as being in disarray. Alternately, one could reframe the experts' inability to agree on a definition of psychotherapy as positive because it leaves practitioners free to devise their own definitions (Zeig, 1987).

The present *What Is Psychotherapy?* project was initiated to expand on the findings of the conference. In addition, this project is a continuation of the Milton H. Erickson Foundation's commitment toward being multidisciplinary.

Experts in various schools of psychotherapy were invited to participate. Each author was asked to provide: (1) a 75-word definition of psychotherapy as he or she practices it; (2) a 500-word qualification that makes any necessary clarifications and relates the definition to both its theoretical underpinnings and the goals of psychotherapy; and (3) a 500-word critique that addresses specfic criticisms, advantages, and disadvantages of the approach. We chose a flexible form so the authors would have the best opportunity to present their ideas clearly and concisely.

The responses to our invitation were both gratifying and enlightening. We regret that many insightful, informative contributions were not included in this volume, owing strictly to space limitations. During the final selection process, we endeavored to maximize diversity of perspective within and across treatment modalities. In many ways the included contributions reflect the variance within the field of psychotherapy. In addition to the expected differences in content and perspective, there were many variations in style and length. Some authors merely submitted definitions; others sent definitions and qualification statements without any critique. As in the therapeutic process, the author's persona shines through. For this reason, we have tried, as far as possible, to publish the writings as received.

Organization

For organizational purposes, the contributions were divided
into nine chapters: Psychodynamic Psychotherapy; Humanistic and Experiential Psychotherapy; Behavioral Psychotherapy;
Cognitive Psychotherapy; Philosophically Oriented Psychotherapy; Eclectic and Integrative Psychotherapy; Family and Systemic Psychotherapy; Group Psychotherapy; and Hypnotherapy and Ericksonian Psychotherapy.

The editors selected these divisions based on one of two
criteria: *theoretical orientation* (psychodynamic, humanistic, behavioral, cognitive, philosophical) or *treatment format* (family,
group, hypnotherapy). There is also one division that combines
both criteria (eclectic and integrative). The two main divisions
roughly correspond to input and output. Some therapies stress
the input to the therapist through a theoretical model. Other
therapies stress output by the therapist; these are more oriented
to treatment format and deemphasize the theoretical model. As
with any imposed system of distinctions, the criteria are uni-
dimensional and therefore accurate only in the most general
sense. That is to say, all of the theoretically based approaches
have a treatment format in practical application, and those approaches emphasizing a treatment format integrate theoretical
principles, as in group therapy that is psychodynamic in orientation. There are obviously other ways in which the material
might have been ordered (for example, chronologically), but
the divisions used here reflect the ways in which most of the
contributors identify their work.

In the introductory section of each chapter, salient features
of implicit or explicit theories of personality will be briefly discussed. A brief historical overview and description of the contributions will also be presented. As editors, we chose to present
the material using a classifying system — a taxonomy.

Taxonomy

To illustrate a taxonomy, consider a person's car: There are
specific attributes that classify the vehicle as an automobile;
certain additional attributes that classify it as a specific type of

car (for example, Ford or Mercedes); and some very specific attributes that make it *my* car.

The taxonomic system we have imposed upon the responses to the question "What is psychotherapy?" is loosely borrowed from the biological sciences. In biology, an animal can be classified according to its kingdom, phylum, class, order, family, genus, species, and subspecies. Each taxonomic level is clearly defined by specific attributes that determine membership or exclusion at that level. For the present project, one possible taxonomy for psychotherapy might read as follows: Kingdom is mammalian communication; phylum is human communication; class is communication directed at helping others; order is professional assistance; family is psychotherapy; genus is therapeutic discipline (for example, behavioral); species is modality (for example, implosive therapy); subspecies is the modality variant (for example, implosive therapy as practiced by an eclectic therapist versus a strict behaviorist). For present purposes, within each chapter we will present contributions addressing the species and subspecies. As editors, we will be able to comment on the genus and the family levels. Consideration of the genus also will be found in the chapter introductions.

The family level — namely, psychotherapy as a whole — will be discussed below, and in the concluding chapter. In each chapter that addresses a specific discipline of therapy (genus), those contributions that are more general (species) are presented first, followed by more specifically defined approaches (subspecies) within that discipline. This will allow the reader to observe some of the defining parameters, followed by some of the variations and adaptations possible within those parameters.

Each contributor declared his or her own theoretical orientation, and this, for the most part, determined where a given selection was placed. In some instances, a contribution legitimately belonged in two or more chapters, and the ultimate placement of the work was decided in the interest of producing a balanced perspective within each chapter.

Perspectives in Psychotherapy

At a general (family) level, three areas of convergence emerged from studying the submitted contributions: relationship, change, and theory. Each of these is necessary to define an interaction as psychotherapy. Because these facets are rather obvious, discussion of them will be limited. However, by further subdividing these distinctions, it is possible to present a method for differentiating the schools of psychotherapy. This will entail an examination of "lenses" and "units-of-analysis."

Relationship

Many of the contributors explicitly, and all of the contributors implicitly, reference the importance of the therapeutic relationship. After all, the therapy process occurs within the context of an empowering empathic relationship between a designated therapist and a patient. Larry Beutler, an eclectic practitioner, discusses the importance of therapist-patient compatibility. In his plea for thorough scientific validation, behaviorist John Furedy acknowledges the impact of therapist-patient rapport, which is a confounding factor in specific effects research but in no way extraneous to practical application. Approaches such as client-centered therapy and psychoanalysis assign the relationship a primary place in the creation of therapeutic change.

Change

A second element common to the approaches delineated in this book is change. Patients contract with their therapist to promote change. Bruno Bettelheim characterizes psychoanalytic therapy as an uncovering process that frees the patient from unnecessary suffering. The rational-emotive approach of Albert Ellis focuses on modifying the client's belief systems. Jeffrey Zeig suggests in his Ericksonian approach that any change, even a "negative" one, is essential.

Aspects such as beliefs, cognitions, behaviors, repressed experiences, and ongoing experience of self or the world are all targets for change. Change in one unit can produce a systemic snowballing effect. For example, Thomas Stampfl's implosive therapy for a patient who is fearful of flying produces not only a reduction of anxiety (affective change) but an increase in the incidence of flying (behavioral change) as well. James Framo asserts that his intergenerational family therapy usually results in positive change not only in the client's internal problems but also in the family of origin and in marital and parent-child relationships. Existential psychotherapy, according to Stephen DeBerry, manifests improvement that can be evaluated in at least three dimensions: behavior, affect, and cognition.

An additional implicit aspect of psychotherapeutic change is that it is durable: Change can be expected to last unless it is deliberately or circumstantially altered. This is true of both circumscribed and global change. Many behavioral approaches are based in extinction, the methodical permanent suppression of a specific response. The desired result of many psychodynamic psychotherapies is global change in the patient's character.

Theory and Lenses

Theory is a distinguishing factor among the various genera of psychotherapies. Each of the contributors has an implicit or explicit working model of the patient's personality and/or the therapy process. That working model structures the treatment and determines aspects ranging from duration of sessions and treatment, to number of individuals involved, to what portion of one's life is discussed and who does the discussing, to which techniques are employed. Theory explicitly defines the nature of the therapeutic relationship and/or the targets for change.

The implicit or explicit principles of theory and practice used by practitioners become perceptual lenses that organize data and make client behavior intelligible. In fact, one of the stated purposes of some therapies is to make client behavior, which is often quite idiosyncratic, more intelligible. The therapist's theoretical framework of personality and/or treatment is superimposed on the information (behavior, belief system, personal history, relational functioning, value system) provided by the client, providing an organized way of viewing the problem and, consequently, a logical intervention strategy.

As an illustration, consider a client who presents with anxiety. A behaviorist, of course, would look at behavior and likely conceptualize anxiety as a learned response, consequently eliciting a description of times and places (stimulus situations) where the client experiences the symptom (probably quantifying the strength of each response in the process). As it emerges that each experience of anxiety is either in, or in anticipation of, a social encounter, a diagnosis may be formulated (social phobia). Based on that diagnosis and any extant research on the disorder, an appropriate intervention is implemented. The same symptoms, imposed on a psychodynamic theoretical framework, would yield both a different conceptualization of the problem, and a different consequent intervention (perhaps with similar outcomes).

The perceptual lens of a given practitioner is "inserted" by a respected teacher at an early point in the student's professional development, often in graduate school. Depending on his or her own idiosyncratic makeup and predilections, the novice therapist gravitates to a particular model of personality or treatment and is expected to demonstrate orthodox adherence to that model. The model is not only a philosophy; it is also perceptual in that it becomes a lens. This lens tells the practitioner what to look for and respond to in the therapeutic encounter — but it is a double-edged sword in that it focuses and limits viewing simultaneously. The therapist then passes on the lens (like a family heirloom) to patients.

For example, a devotee of rational-emotive therapy looks for (and finds) the internal "shoulds" with which patients pester themselves, such as the demand, "I must be perfect." Treatment follows by exposing and correcting these irrational beliefs. Patients then find and self-correct their own irrational beliefs. Devotees of rational-emotive therapy insist that this is the essence of therapy. Other therapies have different lenses; however, in all therapies the lens focuses the practitioner on a particular unit-of-analysis, and the unit-of-analysis concomitantly determines the lens.

The next section offers a unit-of-analysis paradigm as a way of conceptualizing the complex interaction among model of intervention, practitioner, and patient. The unit-of-analysis determines the species of psychotherapy practiced by a particular clinician.

Units-of-Analysis

Psychotherapy is a rather idiosyncratic endeavor that is practiced in many guises. In a sense, it is a projective technique that says as much about the therapist's personality as it does about the patient's. This has to do with the fact that even within the confines of a given theory, therapists have idiosyncratic ways of viewing patients, problems, and the solutions that apply. In psychoanalytic parlance, this could be called "countertransference," a term that has negative connotations. Rather, we prefer to use the more neutral idea of units-of-analysis. Every therapist has units-of-analysis, which are bound to be idiosyncratic positions.

The idea of the unit-of-analysis can be elucidated by using a concept applied to patients by the Mental Research Institute (MRI) group, namely, "the position the patient takes" (Fisch, Weakland, & Segal, 1982). For example, a patient can take the position of being equivocal, angry, or overbearing. The practitioners at the MRI Brief Therapy Center stress the importance of determining the position that the patient takes so that therapy can be tailored to the individual. The patient can be addressed from within his or her own value system.

It also is valuable to look at the position the *therapist* takes; that is, what comprises the therapist's unit-of-analysis? What does the therapist consider to be the "quark" or essential unit in psychotherapy? Depending on one's background, a therapist may choose one of a number of things as the essential unit-of-analysis, for example, emotion, behavior, thought, or relationship. Also, some therapists emphasize the past, others the present, and still others, the future. Some therapists emphasize what goes on within the client; others emphasize the process between the therapist and the client. Others emphasize the process among clients. Some emphasize method, others theory. Some emphasize research; others eschew research. Some elevate the importance of growth. Others orient toward the symptom. Some emphasize conscious processes; others focus on unconscious processes. Some derive models of therapy from art, others from science.

The unit-of-analysis is often a fixed action pattern. As with animal instincts, a simple stimulus within a complex field releases a series of stereotyped behaviors. Fixed action patterns normally are self-motivating in that animals will seek out the stimulus that triggers the pattern (consider for example a cat playing with a mouse).

This is applicable to psychotherapy. For example, once a psychoanalyst finds an example of transference, a fixed action pattern results; namely, an interpretation, confrontation, or clarification. Once a behaviorist sees behavioral avoidance, a systematic desensitization may follow. If a gestalt therapist perceives poor contact boundaries, an awareness exercise may result.

Subsequently, the therapist develops a lens for finding the unit-of-analysis within a particular patient field. The therapist's perceptions can become rigidified. For example, Transactional Analysts start to see Parent, Adult, and Child ego states and perceive scripts and games. Jungians find "shadows" and "animus projections."

Patients often respond to therapist projections and manifest the phenomena their therapists seek. A simple example concerns dreams. Analytic patients will spontaneously report dreams in therapy, while behavioral or family therapy patients will not. One wonders if analytic patients respond by having more dreams than behavioral or family therapy patients.

The number of units-of-analysis and lenses is virtually endless. To better understand the position that the therapist takes, we will use a scheme devised to examine elements of human communication. The elements of communication are a convenient way of categorizing the unit-of-analysis, the position the person takes. Zeig (1987) has divided therapeutic communication into twelve discrete elements. The four primary elements that compose communication are behavior, feeling, thought, and a sensory component comprised of perceived sensations (for example, sight, sound, touch) and internally produced, imagined sensory experience. Concurrent with the primary elements of communication are eight secondary elements that modify the primary elements: attitudinal, ambiguous, symbolic, relational, qualitative (intensity and duration), contextual (happening in one time and one place), biological, and idiosyncratic (in that they are representations of the unique history of the person). (For more information, see Zeig, 1987.)

These elements of communication are manifested by both patients and practitioners of psychotherapy. In their theory and practice, various disciplines of therapy also emphasize particular elements of communication. For example, behavior therapists maintain that psychotherapy is about changing behavior. Rogerian schools emphasize feeling. Analytic schools stress thinking. Neurolinguistic programming focuses on sensory experience. Cognitive approaches emphasize attitudes. Ericksonians often are ambiguous (indirect). Jungians are symbolic. Family approaches emphasize relationship. There are schools labeled contextual and there are a number of idiosyncratic approaches. It is probable that a practitioner is drawn to approaches that reflect personal communication style.

An additional point is that any problem can be defined from the perspective of any element of communication or combination of elements. For example, depression can be defined as a behavior, a feeling, a relational pattern, or a biological event. This definition can be offered by the patient *or* the therapist, and sometimes the two have to fight it out to see whose definition will prevail because both patient and therapist alike tend to emphasize one element to the exclusion of others.

It is useful to recall that defined simply, communication is "the exchange (sending and receiving) of information." The elements of communication are types of information, and this information is present both explicitly and implicitly. Overtly or covertly emphasized elements and their content define the positions the patient and therapist take.

Consider a patient's anxiety (symptoms *are* communications) and the position he or she can take: "My problem is I've quit leaving the house." This is a behavioral definition. However, if the patient offers, "I've quit leaving the house *alone,*" this could be a relational definition. Alternately, the patient could say, "There is pounding in my chest and difficulty in breathing," a definition focused on sensation. But if the patient proclaims, "It's silly, really; there's nothing to be afraid of," the definition is more attitudinal.

The patient could say, "My problem is like a weight" (symbolic) or "a *heavy* weight" (qualitative). "It only happens at home" (contextual); or, "It comes from growing up in my particular family" (idiosyncratic). Additionally, the statement, "I am anxious," is ambiguous because it is inadequately specified.

The therapist's task is to explore both the expressed and unexpressed elements. For example, with depression there could be an underlying affect about the predicament although the feeling is unexpressed; for example, "I'm angry."

The implicit modifying elements often merit investigation by the therapist: "What function have these symptoms served in your social and family life (relational)?" However, as previously stated, the elements that the therapist pursues depend on the therapist's predilections. Oftentimes therapy becomes a process whereby the therapist meta-comments about a particular element of communication. For example, the Rogerian could meta-comment about feelings, the family therapist about relational patterns.

In transactions including therapy, the influence of the twelve communication elements is bi-directional: Communication is affected both from patient to therapist, and from therapist to patient. When patients present their complaints, they emphasize particular aspects of the communication complex, thus making available for examination the position the patient takes. When the therapist responds to the patient, he or she also emphasizes one or more of the elements thus defining the position that the therapist takes. If the therapy is to be successful, the therapist's unit-of-analysis must empathize with and confirm the position that the patient takes but in a way that influences change in that position.

The units-of-analysis emphasized by the therapist are projected upon the patient within the approach to psychotherapy offered by the therapist. The therapist's unit-of-analysis must dominate, and the patient must accommodate to it for therapy to proceed. Fortunately, problems are an amalgamation of the twelve elements. Each problem is made up of behavioral, affective, cognitive, sensory, and other components; thus, by making an intervention in one element, there can be a change throughout the system. For example, if one is successful at changing the behavior, the system of twelve elements that comprise the problem can change. The same can be true of a systemically significant intervention with feelings. If, by approaching a problem through one entry point systemic change can be affected, that's great. Otherwise, the therapist must have the flexibility to switch to another unit-of-analysis, or try another combination of units.

To summarize, the emphasized element or combination of elements can vary within an individual patient according to situational demands, but communication by that individual most often will be dominated consistently by a fraction of those twelve elements. Just as the patient brings his or her communication predilections to therapy, so does the therapist. As previously mentioned, some therapists stress behavior, some attitudes, some relationships, and so on. These predilections determine the unit of analysis, which is what the therapist considers the quark, the essential element requiring attention.

The units-of-analysis of any given therapist become theoretically determined, implanted lenses. Units-of-analysis are not merely intellectual; they become perceptual — quite literally a way of seeing a problem. Therapists view their patients according to the lenses that they acquire early in their training. (This is in addition to the lenses learned during the course of early personal development.)

Lenses focus the beginning therapist on the quark to be observed in the patient's problem. Oftentimes, lenses rigidify over time, which can hamper flexibility within the therapeutic encounter and lead to counterproductive results. Because many lenses are used by therapists to make clients' responses intelligible, there are many different definitions of the essential nature of psychotherapy at the genus and species and subspecies levels.

Psychotherapy Defined

Having examined areas of consensus about psychotherapy and explored the units of analysis of both patients and therapists, we arrive at a family-level (theory-nonspecific) definition of psychotherapy: *Psychotherapy is a change-oriented process that occurs in the context of a contractual, empowering, and empathic professional relationship. Its rationale explicitly or implicitly focuses on the personality of the client(s), the technique of psychotherapy, or both. Durable change is affected on multiple aspects of clients' lives. The process is idiosyncratic and determined by the interaction of the patients' and therapists' preconceived positions.*

In the concluding chapter, previously published family-level definitions will be presented. The editors will examine the state of development in psychotherapy vis-a-vis the domain within which it has evolved, and units-of-analysis will be reevaluated.

The contributions in this book are thoughtful and well written. With no further ado, we turn this book to you, the reader, so that you may become immersed in the persuasive logic of the contributors and, in so doing, clarify your own perspective on "What is psychotherapy?"

References

Fisch, R., Weakland, J. H., and Segal, L. (1982). *The tactics of change: Doing therapy brieflly.* San Francisco: Jossey-Bass.

Zeig, J. K. (1987). Introduction. In J. K. Zeig (Ed.), *The evolution of psychotherapy* (pp. xv–xxvi). New York: Brunner/ Mazel.

2

Psychodynamic Psychotherapy

In its broadest scope, according to Marmor (1968), psychoanalysis may be considered to be three things: a *method* of investigation of thoughts and feelings that are unconscious, a *theory* of human personality, and a *technique* of therapy. Psychoanalytic procedure developed prior to a comprehensive theory (Menninger and Holzman, 1973), and the theory has been continually evolving. Psychodynamic theory actually is a collection of theories about unconscious processing and personality development. Psychoanalytic theory holds that:

> Human behavior is determined by conflicts both within the individual and between the individual and society. The human being attempts to make an adaptation to these conflicts either by changing himself (autoplastic change) or his world (alloplastic change). The goal of the adaptation is to meet needs for pleasure and to avoid pain. The attempt at conflict resolution and adaptation results in a personality character-set of functions and traits, abilities and inhibitions that is characteristic for each individual. A degree of flexibility, comfort, control

of behavior, and ability to meet life's challenges and
relate to other human beings is a mark of good mental health. Discomfort, inhibition, isolation, lack of
success, rigidity, and failure to control behavior are
signs of disordered mental functioning. [Bernstein
& Warner, 1981, p. 1]

In that regard, Paolino (1981) specifies that the four goals
of psychoanalytic therapy are (1) to expose the patient to unresolved intrapsychic conflicts from the past that are causing
symptoms in the present; (2) to achieve an intense, regressive
transference neurosis; (3) to observe and resolve the transference neurosis through the therapeutic relationship so that the
unsolved unconscious intrapsychic conflicts are resolved; and
(4) to undergo constructive alterations of the psychic structures
as a result of the newly acquired emotional, physical, and cognitive awareness of the unconscious.

Freud's association with Josef Breuer in the final quarter of
the nineteenth century afforded him exposure to Breuer's work
with "Anna O." Under hypnosis she recalled previously suppressed conflictual information, and in the process, her symptoms yielded. Uncovering and understanding history has been
a cornerstone of the psychoanalytic method from its very inception.

The evolution of psychoanalytic theory from this beginning
is so rich in detail and diversity as to defy encapsulation. Milestones, or more accurately, influential contributors in the development of psychodynamic theory can only be mentioned here.
Within the Freudian school (that is, that group of individuals
who either expanded on Freud's theses or differed only in non-
significant ways—per Wyss, 1973), significant contributions
were made by Sandor Ferenczi in his expansions of Freud's foundations, Anna Freud in her work on the ego and defense,
Melanie Klein in her development of child analysis, and Wilhelm
Reich in his work on the orgasm; these comprise only a partial
listing.

Neo-Freudians, including Alfred Adler and his individual psychology, Karen Horney, who recognized the importance of cultural contexts, Erich Fromm and his focus on interpreting hu-

man development, and Harry Stack Sullivan and his psychiatry of interpersonal relations, all expanded the bounds of psychoanalytic thought. The philosophically oriented schools of depth psychology were founded by C. G. Jung, who described the structure of the psyche, Otto Rank, who examined both volition and birth trauma, and Ludwig Binswanger, whose existential analysis grew from phenomenology. Again, the listings here are incomplete and are meant to provide a broad context against which one may view the writings that comprise this chapter.

Dynamic psychology contains a number of incredibly complex theoretical systems that can emphasize many units-of-analysis in regard to the elements of communication. However, all the analytic schools have considered cognitions and idiosyncratic history to be primary. The therapist takes the position of promoting understanding and bringing hidden aspects into consciousness. These are the lenses for both therapist and patient. There is a commitment to charting the murky recesses of the unconscious and understanding its evolution.

The "Overview" section is comprised of contributions that address psychodynamic approaches and psychotherapy generally (the genus level in our taxonomy). Judd Marmor describes elements essential to all psychotherapeutic approaches. Harold Mosak offers a metaphor that describes the way in which neo-Freudian and other dynamic approaches derive from classical Freudian thinking. Gerald Albert discusses elements common to any psychodynamically oriented approach, and Joseph Kobos emphasizes the importance of relationship in the therapeutic process.

The "Classical Approaches" section includes approaches that most nearly approximate the work of Freud and his disciples Jung and Adler. Richard Chessick elucidates the distinction between supportive and uncovering psychotherapy and makes a strong case for the unique value of the psychoanalytic approach. Jungian thought is represented in Mary Ann Mattoon's contribution, and the Adlerian viewpoint is provided by Guy Manaster and Raymond Corsini.

The final section of this chapter, "Psychodynamically Based Approaches," demonstrates the degree of practical variation possible within the confines of psychodynamic theory. Richard

Robertiello articulates a dynamically based eclectic-integrative aproach. The biological nature of psychological processing forms the core of Donald Nathanson's therapy. Robert Langs emphasizes communication in his psychoanalytic approach. Freud's position that psychoanalytic therapy is a form of reeducation is the basis for Hans Strupp's time-limited dynamic psychotherapy. Robert Firestone's voice therapy focuses on internalized negative parental attitudes and damaging childhood experiences. The need for empirical validation and the possibility of achieving that end are illustrated by Peter Sifneos.

We conclude the introduction to this chapter in a special way; the late Bruno Bettelheim submitted the following statement for the *What Is Psychotherapy?* project. It expresses the ultimate goal of any psychodynamically based approach.

> Since I am committed to psychoanalysis, I view psychotherapy in its light; its purpose is, according to Freud, to help the patient to uncover what goes on in his unconscious through free association, dream analysis, etc. Its purpose, according to Freud, is that where there was id, there ought to be ego. Or in other words, to free the patient from having to suffer from the unnecessary hardships of life, so that he will have the strength to cope successfully with the unavoidable hardships of life. And to quote Freud once more, to become able to love well and to work well at work which is socially useful and personally meaningful to the patient.

References

Bernstein, A. E., & Warner, G. M. (1981). *An introduction to contemporary psychoanalysis.* New York: Jason Aronson.

Marmor, J. (1968). New directions in psychoanalytic theory and therapy. In J. Marmor (Ed.), *Modern psychoanalysis.* New York: Basic Books.

Menninger, K. A., & Holzman, P. S. (1973). *Theory of psychoanalytic technique* (2nd ed.). New York: Basic Books.

Paolino, T. J. (1981). *Psychoanalytic psychotherapy theory, technique, therapeutic relationship and treatability.* New York: Brunner/ Mazel.
Wyss, D. (1973). *Psychoanalytic schools from the beginning to the present.* New York: Jason Aronson.

Section 1
Overview

A Broad-Based Definition of Psychotherapy

Judd Marmor

Definition

Psychotherapy is a process in which a person who wishes to change symptoms or problems in living, or who seeks personal growth, enters into a contract, implicitly or explicitly, to interact verbally or nonverbally in a prescribed way with a person or persons who present themselves as helping agents.

Qualification Statement

The definition that I have given is a broad-based one, essentially covering all psychotherapeutic approaches. It corresponds to my conviction that there are certain basic common denominators in all psychotherapeutic approaches that account for behavioral change. The first and foremost of these common denominators is a sound patient-therapist relationship, resting on trust, rapport, and the therapist's genuine interest in, respect for, understanding of, and empathy with the patient. Given this basic matrix, other elements usually present are: release of emotional tension; development of cognitive insight; operant reconditioning (including a corrective emotional relationship with the therapist); identification with the therapist; and repetitive reality testing, or rehearsal, of the newly acquired adaptive techniques — all in the context of the therapist's consistent emotional support. The particular mix of these elements will vary with different problems, patients, and therapists, but they are usually

20

present to some degree in all forms of interpersonal psychotherapy. Despite claims to the contrary by partison supporters of
particular approaches, I do not believe that there is any specific technique or procedure, other than the basic matrix of a
good patient-therapist relationship, that constitutes a sine qua
non for successful psychotherapy.

My goals in therapy, like those of all therapists, I believe,
are to help my patients to obtain relief from their ego-dystonic
symptoms, to achieve satisfying interpersonal and sexual relationships, to work effectively, and to be socially responsible and
productive human beings within the limits of their potentials.
These goals, incidentally, are not unique to psychotherapy; they
represent normative standards in our culture. What is unique
in dynamic psychotherapy is not its objectives but its method
of attempting to help individuals become aware of all of the systemic factors underlying their intra- and interpersonal difficulties, and its deliberate and controlled utilization of the patient-
therapist relationship to further the patient's maturational and
adaptive potentials.

Critique Statement

In describing my way of working with patients psychother-
apeutically, I do so with a full awareness that there are other
approaches that work equally well for other therapists, and I
do not presume, therefore, that my technique is necessarily superior to the others in this volume. My approach obviously grows
out of my background and training. As a physician I am aware
of the many ways in which physiological and biochemical factors can influence behavior. In addition, my psychoanalytic
training has sensitized me to the intricacies of intrapsychic functioning, and to the significance of dreams, fantasies, and para-
praxes. Finally, a lifelong interest in anthropology and sociology has alerted me to the important influence of sociocultural
factors on the human substrate. Thus I approach every psychopathological problem as the outcome of a dynamic interaction
between the biological, psychological, and sociological vectors,

and the first challenge I face with my patients is the effort to unravel, with their help, how, when, where, and why the interaction of these vectors in their lives created their unique and specific difficulties.

In the process of doing that, the way in which I handle the quality and nature of my personal interaction with my patients at both conscious ("realistic") and unconscious ("transference and countertransference") levels is the key instrument in effecting psychotherapeutic change. The other elements involved in my approach are elaborated in my report to the Evolution of Psychotherapy Conference, sponsored by the Erickson Foundation in 1985.

Criticisms. The psychoanalytic approach has been widely criticized both on theoretical grounds and in terms of its time and cost demands. My own approach, however, is not a classical one; it neither rests on libido theory nor is bound by ritualistic concerns about use of the couch or frequency of visits. I see most of my patients face to face, adapt the frequency of visits to their clinical needs, and try to make my work focused and time-limited.

Advantages. A systemic bio-psychosocial approach gives me a broader than usual perspective on my patients' problems. If physiological or neurochemical factors are involved, I can deal with them pharmacologically when indicated, and in so doing can often facilitate the psychotherapeutic process. Similarly, a sensitivity to external environmental factors enables me (and the patient) to deal with reality stress factors constructively, when possible. At the same time, the ability to work with patients' unconscious defenses and resistances makes it possible for me to help them see how they may be contributing to the maladaptive problem.

Disadvantages. Admittedly, any therapy that focuses only on the individual patient has significant limitations. There are clearly situations in which conjoint marital therapy, family therapy, or group therapy are either primarily indicated or add an invaluable adjunctive dimension. Similarly, there are certain conditions, especially the phobias, in which hypnotherapeutic, behavioral, or combined behavioral-pharmacological approaches are generally more effective and quicker in resolving the patient's problem.

Ideally, a well-trained psychotherapist should be prepared to use such variant approaches when indicated, or else to make the appropriate referral in the best interest of the patient.

Biography

Judd Marmor is Franz Alexander Professor Emeritus of Psychiatry at the University of California, and adjunct professor of psychiatry at the University of California, Los Angeles. He received his M.D. degree (1933) from the College of Physicians and Surgeons, Columbia University. He is past president of the American Psychiatric Association, the American Academy of Psychoanalysis, and the Group for the Advancement of Psychiatry. Marmor is the recipient of numerous awards, including the Founders Award of the American Psychiatric Association, the Ittleson Award of the American Orthopsychiatric Association, the Bowis Award of the American College of Psychiatrists for Outstanding Achievements and Leadership, and the Silver Medal for Distinguished Contributions to Psychiatry from the College of Physicians and Surgeons, Columbia University. He is on the editorial board of ten journals, and has authored approximately 400 articles and book reviews as well as six books. Marmor is a strong advocate of a systems-theoretical approach to problems of mental illness. He played a leading role in the American Psychiatric Association's declassifying of homosexuality per se as a mental illness.

Recommended Reading

Marmor, J. (1974). The nature of the psychotherapeutic process. In *Psychiatry in transition: Selected papers of Judd Marmor, M.D.* (pp. 296–309). New York: Brunner/Mazel.

Marmor, J. (1975). The nature of the therapeutic process revisited. *Canadian Psychiatric Association Journal, 20,* 557–565.

Marmor, J. (1987). The psychotherapeutic process: Common denominators in diverse approaches. In J. K. Zeig (Ed.), *The evolution of psychotherapy* (pp. 266–282). New York: Brunner/Mazel.

For Whoever Believeth in It
Shall Have Everlasting Life

Harold H. Mosak

Definition

Psychotherapy, a "religious" conversion process that invites
people to eliminate, modify, or exchange old beliefs, perceptions,
and practices in the hope of achieving "salvation," is conducted
by "priests" and "deacons" (variously defined by universities,
professional organizations, and the law) and a lay ministry
(paraprofessionals and self-designated "ministers") who are versed
in the religion's tenets and rituals and trained to perform con-
versions. Adler concurred that "individual psychology makes
good religion if you are unfortuate enough not to have another"
(Rasey, 1956, p. 254).

Qualification Statement

It was an age of miracles! The "lame" were made to walk and
the "blind" to see. Freud went to France, learned how to perform "miracles," and founded a new religion—psychoanalysis.
This departure from existing orthodoxy invited calls for his
"crucifixion" but Freud persevered, and with the aid of his apos-
tles the new religion took root. The new religion became a "true"
religion; only those who had undergone conversion could legitimately question it, and they were hardly likely to do so. However, some original communicants, like Adler, Jung, Rank,
Stekel, and Ferenczi, challenged Freud's tenets, left the fold (or
were "excommunicated"), and founded their own sects. Despite
these defections psychoanalysis thrived, its gospel spreading to
the ends of the earth, becoming the dominant religion. While
Freud attempted to cast psychoanalysis into a scientific mold,

he recognized that he had merely modified the ancient religious belief in demons that controlled people's destinies (Freud, 1959; Mosak & Phillips, 1980).

As religionists often are enchanted with "the mysteries," so psychoanalysis captured people's imaginations with its new jargon and constructs such as the unconscious and the demons inhabiting it. Only those initiated into "the mysteries" could be full communicants and aspire to the priesthood of analysts who would later initiate others into "the mysteries." While Freud maintained that medical training was unnecessary for ordination, the American "church's" official view held that only physicians could become "secular pastoral workers" (Freud, 1950).

After World War II, with the emergence of Rogers's nondirective therapy, the "Reformation" began, attracting many adherents who could not aspire to priesthood in the older religion. Rogers's therapy laicized the priesthood, dispensed with the Freudian rituals, and replaced Freud's bad demons with good demons — the person's "growth forces." Suddenly the psychological world witnessed an explosion of religious movements, each with its own belief systems and practices. Among the newcomers were belief systems based upon cognition, upon affect, upon behavior, upon things spiritual, and upon relationship. Religious practices proliferated — some merely desirable, some required — including marathons, psychodrama, massage, implosion, paradoxical intention, and conditioning. Priests and supplicants were expected to conduct themselves in certain ways, and if the latter didn't, they might be accused of resisting their church's or priest's efforts. Faith in the priest was crucial.

Ultimately what these religions offered was salvation, variously defined in terms of symptom eradication, interpersonal functioning, the discovery of meaning, self-realization, and intrapsychic harmony. Some religions see the gates of heaven as open to all; others reserve entry to the elect; for example, people with good prognosis or a transference neurosis.

The road to salvation is paved with faith. People seek conversion after someone describes a "wonderful, miracle-performing therapist" or after reading an article extolling the religion. Perhaps a physician referred them, and their faith in the physi-

cian was transferred to the priest. Then the priest initiated a
faith-enhancing conversion process by being an oracle, by working through the resistance, by creating a therapeutic alliance,
by providing insight or a corrective emotional experience, or
by creating a climate conducive to growth. If faith can move
mountains, why can't people?

Critique Statement

While not describing their systems as "religions," many theorists—for example, Freud, Adler, Jung, Mowrer, and Frankl—
have noted the similarities between aspects of their theories and
aspects of religions. Psychodynamic therapists often hold out
the promise of the Truth, behavioral therapists demonstrate the
Way, and existential therapists point to the Life.

As an Adlerian therapist I am both "priest" and "missionary"
(Mosak & Shulman, 1963). I attempt to convert people to my
faith, to offer them one path to "salvation." In matters of faith
I adhere to the religion's tenets. Trained as a mathematician,
I regard these as "givens," the axioms and postulates of my system. As in mathematics I acknowledge the possibility of other
equally valid systems each with its "givens." My theory centers
about the holistic, the teleological, the phenomenological, the
social, the interpersonal, and individual responsibility. Its highest
ideal—what we attempt to instill in people, in life as well as in
therapy—is "social interest," a construct including such qualities as social cooperation, contribution to the common welfare,
courage, confidence in and liking of self, caring, and the obligation to lend one's efforts to changing society in those areas
where we see change to be desirable or necessary.

With respect to practice, however, my approach is more eclectic, flexible, and pragmatic, although my practice does not violate the basic assumptions of my system. This approach parallels
that of a religious believer. While it is possible, for example,
to be a Christian regardless of whether one believes in baptism
by sprinkling of holy water or baptism by immersion, it is not
possible to be a Christian without accepting that Jesus is the
Christ. The basic tenets are inviolate, but within this given

structure, there is latitude for acceptance of variation in certain practices, including deviation from certain practices, improvisation, and innovation. While I am an Adlerian and attempt to "indoctrinate" my patients in the religion, with respect to practice, both my patients and I possess the freedom to choose. My goals vary with the patient. I listen to confessions, extend hope, relieve guilt, "heal" the sick, raise the fallen, lift up the spirit, illuminate and unravel "the mysteries," propose new options and alternative behaviors, and promote faith. The patients' growth of faith in my religion promotes growth of faith in self—the feeling that they are worthwhile as they are. They learn the courage to be imperfect (Lazarsfeld, 1927/1966), and they learn that imperfection renders them merely human and therefore capable of belonging.

Salvation, for the Adlerian, is open to all. We do not engage in prognosis. We assume that all people can be better than they are, and the task of the therapy is to help the patient grow. What I do is not science. The therapist is an artist, often a charismatic one, who is proficient in matters of faith enhancement. While the "conversion process" is not science, it is nevertheless amenable to scientific investigation.

Biography

Harold H. Mosak currently teaches at the Alfred Adler Institute of Chicago, where he serves as chairman of the board of trustees. He received his Ph.D. degree (1950) from the University of Chicago in clinical psychology. He received his undergraduate training in behaviorism and did his graduate training with Carl Rogers and his internship under Freudian supervisors. His first postdoctoral position was with the Adolf Meyer psychobiologists. Almost four decades ago he converted to Adlerian psychology and has been in full-time private practice of psychotherapy since. Mosak is the author of many articles and books, among them *Ha Ha and aHa: The role of humor in psychotherapy, On purpose,* and "Adlerian psychotherapy" in Corsini's *Current psychotherapies.* His interests are catholic: Among his writings are papers on psychopathology, psychotherapy, religion, men's and women's issues, and classroom climate.

Recommended Reading

Adler, A. (1964). *Social interest.* New York: Capricorn Books. (Original work published 1929)

Mosak, H. H. (1984). Adlerian psychotherapy. In R. J. Corsini (Ed.), *Current psychotherapies* (3rd ed., pp. 56–107). Itasca, IL: Peacock.

Rogers, C. R. (1942). *Counseling and psychotherapy.* Boston: Houghton Mifflin.

References

Freud, S. (1950). *The question of lay analysis.* New York: Norton.

Freud, S. (1959). A neurosis of demoniacal possession in the seventeeth century. In *Collected papers* (Vol. 4). New York: Basic Books.

Lazarsfeld, S. (1966). The courage for imperfection. *Journal of Individual Psychology, 22,* 163–165. (Original work published 1927)

Mosak, H. H., & Phillips, K. S. (1980). *Demons, germs, and values.* Chicago: Alfred Adler Institute.

Mosak, H. H., & Shulman, B. H. (1963). *Individual psychotherapy: A syllabus.* Chicago: Alfred Adler Institute.

Rasey, M. I. (1956). Toward the end. In C. E. Moustakas (Ed.), *The self: Exploration in personal growth.* New York: Harper.

Uncovering Memories:
A Psychodynamic Approach

Gerald Albert

Definition

Psychotherapy is a combined developmental and remedial process applied to individuals suffering from inhibited emotional growth and/or distorted patterns of response to internal or external stimuli. The process involves uncovering hidden memories of trauma-causing experiences and the defensive mental mechanisms erected to protect against painful awareness of them, together with development of realistic perspectives on life experiences and constructive, rewarding management of present events.

Qualification Statement

Behavior exists as an implementation of mental processes and/or reflexive neurological events. To function well behaviorally, today and tomorrow, requires removal of the effects of yesterday's distortion-producing experiences.

Recognition must be given to the cognitive processes required to reach and unveil these defensively concealed memories. Awareness also must be sought of the self- or other-damaging consequences of behaviors learned in relation to these experiences.

Experimentation with new, more healthful response patterns, and experiencing of the rewarding consequences of these responses at the deepest emotional and instinctual levels, is essential to effectuate growth-producing and remedial change.

There can be no shortcuts to restructuring an impaired psyche. Short forms of psychotherapy can only palliate, not rebuild the personality to produce a coping, functioning, enjoying human being.

Critique Statement

The most frequent criticism of this approach centers on the length of time it usually requires, since it seeks deeper-level personality restructuring, and clear-cut behavioral change is often not immediately evident. But shorter therapies, focused on limited dynamics or specified behavior change, rightly may be charged with practicing band-aid psychotherapy, since they rarely produce the kind of basic change in existential perception that can help the patient cope effectively with the whole range of life stresses, rather than merely those specifically dealt with in the shorter forms of treatment.

Biography

Gerald Albert is professor emeritus of counseling and educational psychology at Long Island University's C. W. Post Center. He received his Ed.D. (1965) from Columbia University in counseling psychology. He has authored two psychological texts and more than thirty-five journal articles, booklets, and book chapters. He has served as editor-in-chief of the *Journal of Contemporary Psychotherapy* and has been named a fellow of the American Association for Marriage and Family Therapy, for "outstanding contributions to the field." Albert has been a clinic director of the Long Island Consultation Center and dean of training of the Long Island Institute for Mental Health.

An Interpersonal Psychological Approach

Joseph C. Kobos

Definition

Psychotherapy is a planned, purposeful treatment of an individual experiencing emotional distress and interpersonal conflict or ineffectiveness. The treatment is implemented by a trained professional with the explicit goal of helping the individual to deal with inner processes that interfere with effective personal functioning in work, play, and significant relationships. The core features of the treatment are the planned use of the interpersonal relationship, examination of impediments to candid emotional interchange, and a focus on internal processes manifested in the expression of thought, feelings, and attitudes toward the therapist and significant others.

Qualification Statement

The definition distinguishes psychotherapy from general conversation and other therapeutic activities. The qualifying characteristics are the following: (1) The goal is to remediate disturbed or ineffective functioning; (2) behavioral theory and relevant scientific knowledge guide the process and the outcome; (3) internal processes in the form of self-definition and interpersonal attitudes are key concepts; and (4) the therapeutic relationship is defined as a technically implemented learning model in contrast to social relationships, which are ends in and of themselves.

In this characterization, psychotherapy is defined by presence of illness or personal disturbance, assumed roles of therapist and client, implementation of techniques, and intended outcome of improved personal functioning. Each element — personal disturbance, role function, therapeutic technique, and outcome — is subject to scientific scrutiny. The definition also implies that inner process (including thoughts, feelings, and attitudes) and external behavior (in the form of activities, relationships, and human transactions) are intertwined.

The definition of psychotherapy is built upon the following assumptions regarding personality development: One, it is normal and expectable for people to mature and develop with a sense of optimism and confidence, with the ability to form trusting, collaborative relationships that are mutually dependent and respect individual autonomy. Two, a person's developmental history (including parental and family relationships, along with cultural institutions in interaction with constitutional factors) determines how the individual's sense of self, coping mechanisms, and interpersonal relationships are developed. Three, disturbances in self-confidence, personal relationships, and coping mechanisms in response to stress are experienced as a sense of being ill. Four, when constitutional factors can be excluded as the cause of the disturbance, psychotherapeutic intervention is the method of reparation. These assumptions clarify that psychotherapy has as its goal effective personal functioning.

The major task of psychotherapy is for the therapist to establish an environment and working relationship that encourage the client to deal with aspects of self, interpersonal relationships, and attitudes that interfere with spontaneous effective functioning. The relationship between therapist and client is the major vehicle through which the client learns how his or her sense of self, learned patterns of human interaction, and interpersonal attitudes interfere with current adapation.

Change in psychotherapy is the product of the client experiencing in the psychotherapy relationship how previously learned attitudes and expectations affect the therapeutic interchange, making conscious efforts to interact differently with the therapist, and initiating new or modified thoughts, attitudes, and behaviors toward significant others. Three separate stages are important in the development of the therapeutic work: One, forming the working relationship; two, establishing the therapeutic focus and following it to conclusion; and three, dealing with the termination of the therapeutic work and working relationship.

Biography

Joseph C. Kobos is director of the Counseling Service, Office of Student Services, and associate professor in the Department of Psychiatry, University of Texas Health Science Center at San Antonio. He received his B.A. degree (1964) from Benedictine College (Kansas), his M.S. degree (1967) from Ohio University, and his Ph.D. degree (1970) from the same university in clinical psychology. He completed residency and postdoctoral training at the University of Illinois Medical Center. Kobos is a diplomate in Clinical Psychology, American Board of Professional Psychology, and a fellow of the American Group Psychotherapy Association. He is a past chair of the Texas State Board of Examiners of Psychologists. He has published on a broad range of psychological issues and presented numerous workshops on psychological assessment, group psychotherapy, and brief psychotherapy. Most recently, he has coauthored the book *Brief therapy: Short-term psychodynamic intervention*, which was published by Jason Aronson in 1987.

Recommended Reading

Bauer, G. P., & Kobos, J. C. (1987). *Brief therapy: Short-term psychodynamic intervention*. Northvale, NJ: Jason Aronson.

Ford, D. H., & Urban, H. B. (1963). *Systems of psychotherapy: A comparative study*. New York: John Wiley and Sons.

Herron, W. G., & Rouslin, S. (1984). *Issues in psychotherapy* (Vol. 1). Washington, DC: Oryn Publications.

Section 2
Classical Approaches

Dynamic Psychotherapy

Richard D. Chessick

Definition

Psychotherapy is a paid professional relationship undertaken
by the patient for the purpose of the relief of mental suffering,
the various syndromes of which are delineated in *DSM-III-R*.
The patient pays for the treatment in good faith, assuming (1)
that the psychotherapist has had a thorough training in diagnostic and treatment techniques, and (2) that the psychotherapist has had a thorough personal psychoanalysis that will maximally ensure against countertransference acting out and enable
the psychotherapist to listen to what the patient is trying to communicate without being disturbed by the clamor of the therapist's
own needs. Only psychoanalytic psychotherapy can offer this
fundamental setting, in which the roots of the patient's pathology can then unfold for examination and working through. If
symptom removal is attempted, primarily under the influence
of some sort of relationship, this is known as supportive psychotherapy. If the focus is on allowing the transference to develop and interpreting it when it does so, then the usual uncovering techniques that define the psychoanalytic approach can
be used.

Qualification Statement

Heraclitus said that "character is the demon in many," by
which he meant that the driving force of our behavior, the motor

behind success or difficulties in living, is our basic characterological structure. This character or personality is formed in the
first few years of life in a series of epigenetic layers, beginning
with a unification of the sense of self and laying down of self-
soothing techniques or apparatuses, proceeding to the development and integrating of narcissistic structures, and consolidat-
ing upon the resolution of the Oedipus complex. After that, with
a renewed phase of flux and consolidation in adolescence and
a series of tasks and experiences that can be growth-promoting
later in life, such as marriage, parenting, and grandparenting,
further modifications of character are possible but less likely,
in a fundamental sense.

The findings of almost one hundred years of psychoanalytic
investigation have provided a solid base of understanding of at
least the outlines of character formation and personality functioning. Although several theories present alternate views on
the details, the usual assortment of elements — Freudian drive/
conflict/defense, object relations (whether Kleinian or neo-Klein-
ian), self psychology approaches, and theoretical formulations —
serve in practice to define the basis of our conceptualization of
what has happened to produce the individual we are trying to
help. Some investigators, like myself, also like to call on the
phenomenological and the interactive points of view, especially
when they are stumped. I have defined these "channels" of psychoanalytic listening in my forthcoming book, *The Technique and
Practice of Listening in Intensive Psychotherapy.*

This theoretical basis also defines our approach to the patient
in terms of setting goals, techniques, and practices. After careful listening to the patient, a decision needs to be made as to
whether the psychotherapy offered will be primarily for the purpose of uncovering or of support. The making of this decision
presupposes a thorough training of the kind set forth in my book
Why Psychotherapists Fail (1983) and a complete personal psychoanalysis so that the therapist can hear the patient without
distortion and present the patient with a setting in which proper
communication can occur.

If supportive therapy is the primary mode, then, providing
the two initial assumptions made by the patient are correct, any

technique that is pleasing both to the therapist and to the patient is acceptable. This includes a whole variety of group, family, and individually oriented therapies that are described in any standard psychotherapy textbook, sometimes with the founder's name attached and sometimes not. The point of support is to improve the cohesion of the patient's sense of self through mirroring techniques or by offering an idealizable figure for identification, validation, permission, education, and so forth. Regardless of the technique used, from the point of view of psychoanalytic psychotherapy manipulation of the transference is the method employed to bring about change.

If uncovering psychotherapy is the primary mode, then only the psychoanalytic method offers an escape from conscious or unconscious collusion with the patient to avoid facing the truth. This method requires special techniques and capacities in the psychotherapist in order to let the material emerge in a relatively undisturbed fashion and to facilitate the development of transference manifestations. Ultimately, once a proper empathic relationship has been established, it is primarily in the interpretation of these transference manifestations that the patient gains insight into the roots of his or her mental suffering and the basic functioning of his or her character. Transference interpretations, beginning with contributions from both the therapist and the patient, eventually allow valid reconstructions of the patient's early relationships and character formation.

The alteration of character that results from transference interpretations and reconstructions of the past is then tested out by the patient, first on the therapist and then on others in the outside world. Through new experiences a gradual modification and correction takes place on the basis of this testing, known as "working through." In uncovering psychotherapy, due to limitations of time, we often deal with derivatives of the basic or nuclear transferences and as a result we must be satisfied with partial results or improvement in only certain sectors of the patient's living; usually these are the sectors the patient has identified as needing immediate treatment. In psychoanalysis we hope for a more general and deeper change in the patient's character, which also leads to a greater capacity to deal with problems that arise in the future.

Critique Statement

As of this writing (June 1988), psychoanalytic psychotherapy and psychoanalysis are regarded in the United States as unfashionable, unpleasant, and economically questionable, and are attacked in the media at every opportunity. A certain level of sophistication is required for a patient to be able to rise above the popular culture; usually this develops only after the patient has tried a variety of other simpler, cheaper, and more enjoyable techniques, of which there seem to be no end. Karl Jaspers, philosopher and psychiatrist, said, "The doctor is the patient's fate" (Jaspers, 1969, p. 156). A lot depends on the "doctor" to whom the patient is referred, and the referral often in turn depends more on the capacity of the "doctor" to develop and nourish referral sources than on the validity of his or her technique. Patients able to accept only supportive psychotherapy are not harmed by this unless the two assumptions mentioned above are not met — and they often are not met. Hence the advantage of beginning with a psychoanalytically trained and oriented psychotherapist.

Uncovering psychoanalytic psychotherapy has many pitfalls. It is long, time-consuming, and expensive. There are not many good studies either validating or invalidating it, which works to the advantage of insurance companies and business corporations who wish to minimize employee benefits for mental illness; they claim it is not proven to be cost-effective. This uncertainty and lack of coverage causes many problems for the patient and his or her family. Yet such therapy often prevents much more expensive hospitalization and collapses, as demonstrated in a number of studies beginning with a 1958 study by Hollingshead and Redlich. The assessment of a long-term uncovering psychotherapy is extremely difficult for an outside party since it is primarily a two-person relationship, and stands or falls on the basis of what happens in that relationship. Even audio- and videotape recording of such therapies has proven unsatisfactory for two reasons. First, it profoundly interferes with the treatment itself; no matter how much collusion there is to pretend it does not matter, it represents an unempathic invasion of privacy. Second, so much data is gathered that it is extremely difficult to develop criteria and techniques to analyze the data for anything really relevant, although advanced computer techniques hold at least the theoretical hope that this problem could be overcome.

Training of psychotherapists is at present in a poor state, with all sorts of training programs scattered over the various medical, nonmedical, and paramedical professions that offer psychotherapy to the public. There is no coordination and no agreed-upon standards of training. To do effective, intensive psychoanalytic psychotherapy requires the most meticulous and difficult training in addition to shouldering the expense of one's own psychoanalysis. Therefore, most psychotherapists today avoid the whole thing. Yet these very psychotherapists violate the two key assumptions made by the patient. As a result a whole variety of acting out goes on, leading to many messy situations in which the patient runs the risk of being exploited or retaliated against or forced into dependent compliance.

Psychoanalytic psychotherapy in an uncovering mode carried out by an untrained psychotherapist poses the greatest risk to the patient; it is analogous to brain surgery carried out by a barber. Therefore, the major disadvantage of my approach is in the demands it makes on the therapist. In an age that values fast-fast-fast relief above all, the tendency is to bypass these slower techniques or to present a mine of misinformation or "wild analysis" to the patient, sometimes even over the telephone or on a radio talk show. It is easy to distort or make a mockery of intensive psychoanalytic psychotherapy, and there is always a patient who is eager to enter into collusion with such "therapists" in order to avoid facing the truth.

Furthermore, a serious problem also manifests itself among psychoanalytic psychotherapists, even those with proper training. There is a longstanding tradition, beginning with Freud's experience, of professional schisms and theoretical disagreements degenerating into the formation of opposing groups who proceed to mistreat and malign each other in a most immature fashion. There is no commonly accepted truth among psychoanalytic systems at this time, although some clearly have greater clinical validity and capacity to be empirically tested in the psychoanalytic consulting room than others. A lack of tolerance among opposing theoreticians for each other personally, and a lack of civilized dialogue and exchange of ideas on an academic plane makes it harder to examine and resolve apparently irreconcilable theoretical stances, which adds to the chaos in the field for no acceptable reason. In some instances, angry litigation has even been initiated between opposing schools or professional groups, to the cost and detriment of everybody.

Biography

Richard D. Chessick is professor of psychiatry, Northwestern University, Evanston, Illinois, and senior attending psychiatrist, Evanston Hospital. He received his M.D. degree (1954) from the University of Chicago and his Ph.D. degree in philosophy (1977) from California Coast University. He is the recipient of numerous awards, including the Sigmund Freud Award from the American Society of Psychoanalytic Physicians in 1989. He has served on the editorial board of several journals, including *Dynamic Psychotherapy* and the *American Journal of Psychotherapy,* and has published in scientific journals more than 200 papers since 1953 in the fields of neurology, psychiatry, and philosophy. He is a fellow of the American Psychiatric Association, the American Orthopsychiatric Association, the Academy of Psychosomatic Medicine, and the American Society for Adolescent Psychiatry; a corresponding member of the German Psychoanalytic Society; and a member of eighteen other professional societies. Chessick has an international reputation as lecturer and educator, having conducted teaching activities in many countries, including Germany, Kenya, Japan, and Israel. The author of ten books, Chessick has concentrated on the epistemological premises and the meta-psychiatric and philosophical implications of modern psychiatry and psychotherapy. His work also focuses on the technique and practice of psychoanalytically based psychotherapy and the psychoanalytic treatment of pre-Oedipal disorders of all varieties.

Recommended Reading

Chessick, R. D. (1980a). *Freud teaches psychotherapy.* Indianapolis, IN: Hackett Publishers.

Chessick, R. D. (1980b). *How psychotherapy heals.* Northvale, NJ: Jason Aronson.

Chessick, R. D. (1983a). *A brief introduction to the genius of Nietzsche.* Washington, DC: University Press of America.

Chessick, R. D. (1983b). *Technique and practice of intensive psychotherapy.* Northvale, NJ: Jason Aronson.

Chessick, R. D. (1985a). The frantic retreat from the mind to the brain: American psychiatry in *mauvaise foi. Psychoanalytic Inquiry, 5,* 369–403.

Chessick, R. D. (1985b). *Intensive psychotherapy of the borderline patient.* Northvale, NJ: Jason Aronson.

Chessick, R. D. (1985c). *Psychology of the self and the treatment of narcissism.* Northvale, NJ: Jason Aronson.

Chessick, R. D. (1987). *Great ideas in psychotherapy.* Northvale, NJ: Jason Aronson.

Chessick, R. D. (in press). *The technique and practice of listening in intensive psychotherapy.* Northvale, NJ: Jason Aronson.

References

Chessick, R. D. (1983). *Why psychotherapists fail.* Northvale, NJ: Jason Aronson.

Jaspers, K. (1969). *Philosophy* (E. Ashton, Trans.). Chicago: University of Chicago Press.

Jungian Psychotherapy

Mary Ann Mattoon

Definition

Psychotherapy is a process of psychological development necessitated by suffering—emotional and sometimes physical. The therapist is less a physician treating a patient than a companion on the way. Symptoms, dreams, emotions, and behaviors reveal unconscious contents that indicate what attitudes and actions are needed for such development. Healing results from the mutual respect of therapist and client, their openness to the challenges and resources of the psyche, and their devotion to the client's wholeness.

Qualification Statement

A premise of this definition is that the psyche is self-regulating and has an innate tendency toward healing and growth. Pathology distorts that tendency. Yet pathology is purposeful; it motivates self-reflection and openness to psychological development.

Self-regulation means that when the psyche is out of balance (the condition that brings a person into therapy), compensatory contents are mobilized in the unconscious. These contents manifest themselves in dreams, symptoms, memories, emotions, instinctual urges and fantasies, and behaviors. When these manifestations are recognized and acted on, they modify the one-sided attitude of the sufferer's consciousness, changing that person's attitude, behavior, and emotional state.

Contents emerge from the unconscious psyche to compensate conscious attitudes and emotions. Awareness of these contents is necessary but not sufficient; to be conscious, the content must be brought under the control of the ego.

The components of the unconscious psyche are the complexes —
interrelated clusters of mental contents that are emotionally
charged, usually unacceptable to consciousness, and therefore
repressed. They act autonomously, causing emotional conflict,
embarrassment, and other suffering. Complexes are valuable,
however, because they offer access to the resources of the unconscious psyche.

The relationship of therapist and client — transference — is a
special case of the projections that occur in all human interactions. The client sees in the therapist qualities, positive and negative, that have been experienced in parents, siblings, and other
significant persons in the client's life and which have been incorporated as complexes.

Behind all these figures, qualities, and complexes stands the
figure of the Self — the integrating force at the center of the
psyche. It contains healing resources on which the process of
development draws.

Therapeutic method varies with the individual, the range of
the therapist's capabilities, and the psychic material that the client
brings into the process. Thus, there is no set sequence in the
process and no preestablished number of sessions. Some of the
therapeutic work is reductive — separating, examining, and interpreting the complexes. Much of the work, however, is constructive, focusing on the purpose of the pathology and the potential for growth. The therapist must be alert to a client's readiness
to deal with specific problems and unconscious images and must
eschew preconceived notions about the process. In the analysis
of dreams, the focus of the work is less an intellectually satisfying interpretation than experiencing of the dream and assimilating it emotionally.

Some of the therapy proceeds outside the designated sessions;
for example, the client may write and reflect on dreams and
emotional contents as well as draw, paint, sculpt, or dance images from the unconscious, or engage in imaginary conversations with such images.

The goal of therapy is individuation according to Jung's definition: a continuing process of recognizing one's uniqueness, struggling with complexes, and accepting what has been unac-

ceptable within oneself. Through this process, consciousness is enlarged and engages in a healthier interaction with the multitude of unconscious contents that impinge on the client's everyday life. Thus, the person becomes freed to live more creatively in the inner and outer worlds.

Critique Statement

The Jungian approach to psychotherapy is a cooperative one between therapist and client and is tailor-made for each client, within the range of the therapist's capabilities. The therapist encourages the client's uniqueness, respecting that person's inner wisdom and potential for wholeness. The goal of the process is transformation of personality.

The therapeutic process does not rely on intellectual insight but seeks out the emotional roots of the client's problems, complexes, and symptoms. The therapist, who has undergone extensive personal analysis, is engaged deeply in the struggle for wholeness, as well as in providing a point of reference and objectivity to which the client can cling while making major attitudinal and behavioral changes.

The sessions with the therapist are only a part of the client's therapeutic work. Between sessions, the work can proceed by means of reflection, recording of dreams, and the use of imaginal techniques. After cessation of the therapy sessions, the process continues as the former client makes further use of these means.

The disadvantages to Jungian therapy are largely the obverse of the advantages. Among these is its relative ineffectiveness for short-term work. Although there are instances when a few sessions effect the desired change, most clients must engage in a long process that is expensive in terms of both time and money.

The process aimed at transformation makes Jungian therapy often unsuitable for persons whose problems require quick action, such as addiction and family violence. This limitation and the intense attention to individual development spill over into Jungian therapists' being less likely to work with children, couples, families, and other groups.

The attention to dreams and other imagery can be a disadvantage. It is possible for a client to become so enamored of imagery that the waking-life problems are neglected—by the therapist as well as by the client.

The advantages and disadvantages of the Jungian approach to psychotherapy are thus interrelated. The insight producing intensity of the inward focus may subvert attention to outer reality. Dealing with the depths of the psyche, the soul, and with the external world in a balanced way requires strong motivation for the process to be carried to any fruition.

Biography

Mary Ann Mattoon is a Jungian analyst in private practice and a clinical professor of psychology at the University of Minnesota. She received her Ph.D. degree (1970) from the University of Minnesota in personality psychology and is a diplomate (1965) of the C. G. Jung Institute, Zurich, Switzerland. She is the author of *Understanding Dreams,* a comprehensive, systematic, and well-illustrated presentation of Jung's theory of dream interpretation. Her second book, *Jungian Psychology in Perspective,* is the only extant textbook of Jungian psychology. It was developed out of her first ten years of teaching a University of Minnesota course on Jungian psychology. This course is one of only a few such courses accredited by a department of psychology in a major university. Mattoon has lectured to Jungian groups and training institutes in the United States and in Europe. She has authored articles published in Jungian journals and is a frequent reviewer of Jungian books in journals of psychology, both academic and Jungian.

Adlerian Psychotherapy

Guy J. Manaster

Definition

Psychotherapy is a learning process, in four phases: (1) the establishment of a formal relationship of friendly equality; (2) analysis, or uncovering, of the patient's life-style, personal goals, and private logic; (3) interpretation to develop self-knowledge, to understand and recognize personal goals in thought, feeling, and behavior; and (4) reorientation and reeducation through encouragement to change goals; avoid basic mistakes; develop self-confidence; improve social functioning, social feeling, and social interest; and eliminate symptoms.

Qualification Statement

Adlerian psychotherapy is distinguished from many other psychotherapies by the nature of the therapeutic relationship, by the form and content of the assessment of personality through life-style analysis, by the social emphasis on life-style interpretation, and by the eclectic techniques used to encourage reorientation and reeducation in the social interest, all of which are directly related to Individual Psychology theory.

Individual Psychology may be defined as "a holistic, phenomenological, teleological, field-theoretical, and socially oriented approach . . . based on the assumption of the uniqueness, self-consistency, activity, and creativity of the human individual (style of life); an open dynamic system of motivation (striving for a subjectively conceived goal of success); and an innate potentiality for social life (social interest)" (Ansbacher, 1973).

Thus the psychotherapeutic relationship stresses the issue of equality, in order to illustrate and offset the patient's issues of inferiority-superiority, and the issue of sociability (the wish to belong or to fit in) in order to reinforce the social nature of the patient's goals and behavior. Adlerian psychotherapy is a face-to-face, cooperative learning endeavor with, it might be said, two experts—the patient, the expert on himself or herself; and the therapist, the expert on helping the patient to relate to the theory and its emphasis on social interest.

Analysis, or assessment, of personality in Adlerian therapy is by means of a life-style interview. This method is built directly on every point of the theory definition. Therefore, life-style assessment uncovers the individual's goals, as the individual created them in the family of origin and as they are interpretable through family constellation, early recollection, and dream analysis, which are the core of the life-style analysis procedure. Life-style analysis demonstrates the consistency of the person's goals in social situations through life and the mistakes, exaggerations, and extremes of these goals as understood by the client—that is, in the client's private logic. The uncovered goals and associated behaviors may then be seen as more or less dysfunctional, not in keeping with the common sense of social living, social equality, and social interest.

This analysis is fine-tuned through discussion with the clients until it is agreed on by both therapists and clients, at which time the interpretation process commences. In this process the clients come to recognize their life-style and goals in all aspects of life—in thought, feeling, and action, both past and present.

With this recognition and an understanding by clients of their responsibility in creating the life-style and the situations through which they have lived and are living, the fourth phase of therapy is built on encouraging clients to change goals through improved social functioning, and vice versa. These aims are intertwined, or reciprocal, such that lessened feelings of inferiority lessen the striving for superiority and allow functioning *with* others rather than against others and, again, vice versa. To further these aims, Adlerian theory allows, if not demands, that therapists use any and all techniques that hold promise and can be understood as in keeping with the theory.

Critique Statement

Adlerian psychotherapy has a long history as a target of criticism since it developed, in part, as a criticism itself and thus must be seen both in its historical and present contexts. A not insignificant portion of Adler's theoretical developments, begun prior to and continued well after working with Freud, were in reaction to excesses and errors he saw in Freud's theory. Their bitter split and Freud's continuing efforts to thwart Adler focused the attention of Adlerians on both the separation from and the criticism by the Freudians. The resulting defensiveness limited the spread of the Adlerian approach. However, as the major movements in psychotherapy both emerged from and developed toward Adlerian theory and practice, attention has become more equally focused on both similarities and differences in the Adlerian and Freudian approaches.

The historic criticisms of Adlerian therapy had to do precisely with its theoretical basis in Adlerian theory, which made it distinct from the behaviorist and analytic therapies based on natural science or on reductive, instinctual-biological, demystical, or mystical models. Adlerian therapy was criticized primarily for its holism, as well as for being too cognitive, too socially embedded, and too simple — too commonsensical. The evolution of psychoanalysis and the development of neoanalytic and cognitive behavioral therapies, as well as the inclusionary trends in practice of Adlerian therapy, have reduced discrepancies between some other theories and practices of psychotherapy, and Adlerian theory and practice. Thus, today Adlerian therapists are being included in analytic societies, and cognitive behaviorists are among the more humanistic Adlerians, although some important and basic differences in theory and technique remain.

The crowning advantage of Adlerian therapy rests on the completeness and comprehensibility of Adlerian theory and the direct relationship between the theory and psychotherapeutic practice. The theory may be seen as simple and makes good common sense. Clients understand that and can immediately see themselves in the unique interpretations of their life-styles. The concept of teleology may be difficult to comprehend in the abstract, but seeing what you are after (your goals) in day-to-day situations — especially ones you are having trouble with — is not difficult.

According to Adlerian theory, the most basic human wish is to belong, to fit in, to have a place in the human group. It is to that end, albeit with concerns about adequacy and misconceptions about human living, that individuals develop their goals — their sense of what they have to do or be to fit in. Clients can, with relative ease, recognize what they are after and then see themselves striving for those goals in various settings. Adlerian therapists are then free to encourage their clients with any techniques that adhere to the basic theoretical tenets. Adlerian therapists have long helped their clients to set realistic situational goals and develop interpersonal and coping skills. As part of this process, they have confronted their clients' irrational beliefs, even allowing their clients to free associate, although within limits that bring their clients to recognize their responsibility in being what they are and for doing what they do.

Adlerians have no preconceptions about the length of therapy and therefore practice brief therapy whenever the case permits. Without jargon, with a sense of camaraderie, as equals in a world that is comprehensible only to the degree that it is, Adlerian therapists effectively and efficiently encourage their clients to be responsible, contributing members of the human community.

Biography

Guy J. Manaster is professor of educational psychology at the University of Texas at Austin. He is the former director of the Counseling Psychology Training Program there and teaches in that program and in the Developmental-Social-Personality Psychology Program as well. He received his Ph.D. degree (1969) from the Committee on Human Development, University of Chicago. Manaster is past president of the North American Society of Adlerian Psychology and has been editor of the *Journal of Individual Psychology* (now titled *Individual Psy-*

chology) for fourteen years. He has authored books on Individual Psychology, adolescent development, and cross-national research and has written numerous articles in these areas as well as in social psychology, gerontology, and education. The holistic view characteristic of Adlerian theory and therapy is used by Manaster in his developmental, social, personality, and educational work, much as he uses knowledge and perspectives from these fields to extend his work in Adlerian theory and practice. In his research and writing he attempts to integrate this view and move from nomothetic research to ideographic understanding, from the macroscopic to the microscopic and back, in the fashion he has explained as illustrative of the Adlerian psychotherapeutic approach.

Recommended Reading

Dreikurs, R. R. (1953). *Fundamentals of Adlerian psychology*. Chicago: Alfred Adler Institute.

Dreikurs, R. R. (1967). *Psychodynamics, psychotherapy and counseling*. Chicago: Alfred Adler Institute.

Manaster, G. J., & Corsini, R. J. (1982). *Individual psychology: Theory and practice*. Itasca, IL: Peacock.

Wexberg, E. (1970). *Individual psychological treatment*. Chicago: Alfred Adler Institute. (2nd edition, originally published 1929)

Reference

Ansbacher, H. (1973). In General Information section of the *Journal of Individual Psychology, 29*.

Adlerian Psychotherapy

Raymond J. Corsini

Definition

Psychotherapy cannot be defined with any precision. A dictionary definition might read as follows: Psychotherapy is a formal process of interaction between two parties, each party usually consisting of one person but with the possibility that there may be two or more people in each party, for the purpose of amelioration of one of the two parties' distress relative to any disability or malfunction (or a combination thereof) of the following areas: cognitive functions (disorders of thinking), affective functions (suffering or emotional discomforts), or behavioral functions (inadequacy of behavior); with the treatment party having some theory of personality's origins, development, maintenance, and change; some modality of treatment logically related to the theory; and, generally, professional and legal approval to act as a therapist.

Qualification Statement

Adlerian psychotherapy, in my judgment, is the most eclectic of all systems. While Adlerians have a common philosophy and a minimalist theory, both of which have survived intact since the death of Alfred Adler in 1937, the actual methodology of Adlerian psychotherapeutic and counseling practice has varied considerably. For example, in my edited book *Handbook of Innovative Psychotherapies* (1981), five of the forty-six chapters were written by Adlerians, each explaining quite different systems of treatment. So Adlerian psychotherapy may be said to be based on a simple philosophical principle (*Gemeinschaftsgefühl*, or social interest) and on a relatively simple set of twelve basic theoretical principles well discussed in the Ansbacher and Ansbacher text, *The Individual Psychology of Alfred Adler* (1956).

The goals of psychotherapy in a sense are two: helping an individual to be more comfortable (phenomenology) and helping that individual to become more successful (social interest) — operating better in terms of self-interest and other-interest.

My own approach is a blend of what I have learned from others: psychodrama from Moreno, confrontation from Ellis, analysis of individuals from Dreikurs, and general approach from Rogers — and I dare say that if any of them were to watch me as I operated at any time, each would be disappointed to some extent. My concern is always of a tripartite nature: First comes *understanding* (Adlerian psychotherapy is based on the cognitive learning model), then comes *behavioral changes,* and then comes the consequences of *better feelings* as a result of better understanding and better behavior.

From an Adlerian point of view, my major goal is to attempt to try to find out what the individual really wants — since Adler stressed the importance of the perceived future to behavior. And this is difficult to discover since often clients don't know it themselves. A procedure of great value to me, which should be better known to clinicians, is the analysis of early recollections.

Critique Statement

I have no criticisms of my approach to psychotherapy, and I doubt that practitioners who have knowledge of a number of systems and are intellectually honest can have any criticisms of their own approaches since I believe all psychotherapists, by the very nature of their work, attempt always to do their best.

What bothers me are people who were led into some specific path and who continued for years in that path because they knew nothing else or were afraid to change. I think, for example, of the situation that some Catholic priests are in: joining a religious order (usually prompted in part by their mothers' wild enthusiasm), spending years in training, and then perhaps at age thirty-five or so (after actually being priests), suddenly finding that they can no longer believe what they were taught for so many years. In other words, my primary concern is not about myself, but about others, such as those who, having adopted what I consider to be mistakenly exclusive views of classical behaviorism or psychoanalysis, are now locked in and can't get out.

The advantage of the Adlerian method is that it is based on two simple things: The *philosophy* of *Gemeinschaftsgefühl* or social interest, which can serve as the essence of a value system (such as the golden rule, which it resembles) and its relatively simple and common-sense *theory*. The theory, incidentally, is mysterious to, and mistaken by, most therapists of other orientations, since it appears there has been almost a concerted effort on the part of writers in psychology and psychotherapy to give incorrect impressions of Individual Psychology.

I happen to have, I believe, a considerable knowledge of other systems due to the various books in this field that I have edited, primarily *Current Psychotherapies* (1983) and *Handbook of Innovative Psychotherapies* (1981). I have moved from Rogers to Moreno to Adler, and so have never been locked into any system. I have not given up on any, and still use Rogers's and Moreno's insights, but I am primarily Adlerian — quite satisfied and have been for some thirty years now.

Biography

Raymond Corsini is on the affiliate graduate faculty of the Department of Psychology of the University of Hawaii, now retired from private practice of psychology, having been a psychologist for over fifty years. He received his Ph.D. degree (1955) from the University of Chicago. He has received a number of awards for his contributions to psychology and education and is on the editorial board of a number of journals. He has authored more than 100 articles and has either written or edited 25 books, including a best-selling text in psychotherapy and four-volume encyclopedia of psychology.

Corsini, who sees psychotherapy essentially as a form of teaching, has developed the Corsini Four-R School System, in which mental health aspects are essentially incorporated. The Four-R School System is currently in use in a dozen schools in the United States, Canada, Holland, and Israel.

Recommended Reading

Olson, H. A. (1979). *Early recollections: Their use in diagnosis and psychotherapy.* Springfield, IL: Thomas.

References

Ansbacher, A., & Ansbacher, R. (Eds.). (1956). *The individual psychology of Alfred Adler.* New York: Basic Books.

Corsini, R. J. (1981). *Handbook of innovative psychotherapies.* New York: Wiley.

Corsini, R. J. (Ed.). (1983). *Current psychotherapies* (3rd ed.). Itasca, IL: Peacock.

Section 3
Psychodynamically
Based Approaches

Dynamically Based Integrative Approach

Richard C. Robertiello

Definition

My approach to psychotherapy incorporates the theoretical underpinnings of a psychoanalytic approach with a technical difference from the usual psychoanalytic mode; I view the therapy as a corrective emotional experience. My psychoanalytic orientation is eclectic and involves the use and the work of diverse psychoanalytic thinkers. My stance with the patient is one of being warm, human, and emotionally available—not using the couch or the blank-screen neutral stance of many classical psychoanalysts.

Qualification Statement

My theoretical stance is based on the idea that to be anything but eclectic is equivalent to being narrow-minded. In any other field of science it is important to be familiar with all the contributions from various sources. Why should this not apply to the field of psychotherapy? Freud was the founder of psychoanalysis, and his contributions were major ones and have been useful to me in my work. But Freud died forty years ago. To infer that the science stopped growing then is ridiculous.

There have been many therapists, including some who were not psychoanalysts, whose ideas have added greatly to my therapeutic armamentarium. These would include Milton Erickson, Aaron Beck, and Fritz Perls. I use their ideas when they seem to fit the mode of the patient's communication and can help me clarify what is going on. Among some of the psychoanalysts whose ideas I use consistently are Freud, Jung, Adler, Melanie Klein, Winnicott, Kohut, and Kernberg. An analyst should be flexible and use the theoretical frame of reference that best applies to the patient's verbalizations. This frame can shift from session to session and even within one session. Being anything but eclectic and flexible in the use of different theoretical frames is greatly limiting to the therapeutic possibilities and results.

Even more than in the area of theory I am extremely flexible in the area of technique. But this hardly means that I advocate wild psychoanalysis. Every therapeutic intervention should have a firm theoretical base, so the technique that a particular therapist uses must be a function of his personality. A private, closed therapist will not feel comfortable using a technique that is self-revealing and interactive. Personally, I eschew the word "technique." I believe in being open, authentic, self-revealing, and very much interactive. I never use the couch; for me it impedes communication and greatly reduces the corrective emotional experience of therapy.

I see most of my patients once, never more than twice, a week. Some of my patients are also in group therapy. I think the combination of individual and group therapy is often, but not always, ideal. I am flexible about changing appointments. I rarely charge for missed appointments. I not infrequently have sessions over the telephone. I often will visit patients who are physically ill in the hospital. I attend weddings, bar mitzvahs, plays, or art openings. Under certain conditions I might have dinner or attend sports events or other gatherings with patients. I draw the line sharply at any sexual contact with patients. I am flexible about fees. When a patient is legitimately financially disadvantaged, I may see him or her without charge. I believe the therapist should be a human being first, a doctor second, and a therapist third.

Critique Statement

One of the advantages of my approach is that it is very flexible. The patient has a real relationship with a real person who is authentic and not presenting a mask. I believe that most of our problems are caused by difficulties in a dyadic relationship. So curing them also must take place within a genuine dyad rather than a very artificial frame. One of the legitimate criticisms of my approach is that it may slow down or impede the patient's emotional separation. A sterile impersonal atmosphere might force the patient into a more separate position. I acknowledge the validity of this criticism without totally agreeing with it. I think an interactive therapist may be able to help the patient go through the separation-individuation process better than a remote one.

Another criticism that is frequently leveled against my approach is that it impedes the patient's getting into the deepest levels of exploration of his unconscious. Once again, I can acknowledge the possible validity, but I have not found this to be true. Many analysts believe that the more real the analyst is, the less the patient will be able to transfer past figures onto him. There is another school of thought that says the more able the patients are to trust the real person of the analyst, the freer they are to enter into transference neuroses. Perhaps the most valid objection to my approach is that it opens the door to potentially destructive countertransferences in the analyst. On this issue I must agree. I think my approach should be restricted to an analyst who is experienced, has had extensive analysis and supervision, and can trust him- or herself not to have major countertransference reactions.

Biography

Richard C. Robertiello has been in private practice of psychiatry and psychoanalysis for forty years in New York. He received his B.A. degree (1943) from Harvard University and his M.D. degree (1946) from Columbia University's College of Physicians and Surgeons. He received his psychoanalytic training at the New York Medical College. He is the chairman of the board of trustees at the Long Island Institute for Mental Health and on the advisory board and faculty of the American Institute for Psychotherapy and Psychoanalysis. He is a life fellow of the American Psychiatric Association, a fellow of the American Academy of Psychoanalysis, and a member of the Society of Medical Psychoanalysts and the National Psychological Association for Psychoanalysis. He has written over fifty articles and twelve books, including *Voyage from Lesbos, A Psychoanalyst's Quest,* and *101 Common Therapeutic Blunders.* His work has always taken a strong stand against orthodoxy in theory as well as technique.

Emotion-Based Psychotherapy

Donald L. Nathanson

Definition

Psychotherapy is a formal, structured process by which a professional therapist addresses the needs of those who request assistance in dealing with their emotional life. *Emotion-based psychotherapy* derives from a developmental theory based on an understanding of *affect,* the physiological basis of emotion. In addition to the self-observation encouraged by all psychodynamic therapies, it creates a shared lexicon of emotions, allowing both members of the therapeutic dyad new understanding and greater opportunity for change.

Qualification Statement

Despite the fact that we claim to treat emotional illness, psychotherapists rarely address the specific emotions expressed by those who seek their aid, or understand those emotions in terms

of a developmental scheme. Freud traced all emotion to drive
forces shunted away from their proper aim; notwithstanding the
failure of contemporary science to demonstrate these hypothetical forces or the pathways along which such energy travels to
produce emotion, psychoanalysts (and those therapists who base
their work on psychoanalytic theory) continue to avoid questions about the nature of emotion.

There is another way to view emotion. Drawing on Darwin's
earlier observation that the newborn infant is capable of all the
emotional expressions that will ever be seen on the face of the
adult, Tomkins (1962–1963) suggested that the innate affects
are part of our genetic heritage, a group of built-in, prewritten
subcortical programs initially responsive to the shape and intensity of neural stimulation and later triggered by learned
stimuli. Integrating Tomkins's affect theory with psychoanalysis, Basch (1976) asks that we reserve the term *affect* for physiological events, *feeling* for our awareness of an affect, and *emotion*
for the combination of an affect with our associations to previous experiences of that affect. Emotional experience involves
five levels of operation: *Structural effectors* and *chemical mediators*
affecting various *sites of action* (most notably the face, but including the voice and a host of odors, postures, and behaviors) triggered initially by subcortical *organizers of innate affect* and assembled into adult emotions by *complex neocortical functions* (Nathanson,
1988). Experience can trigger emotion, and each expression of
emotion is itself an experience involving all five of these levels;
thus we tend to interpret as "true" emotion the feelings resulting from disordered biology. "Anxiety" from caffeine or excessive thyroid hormone, and our "depressive" response to anti-
hypertensive medication represent attempts on the part of the
neocortex to explain chemically mediated feelings on the basis
of prior emotional experience.

The emotions expressed during any therapeutic encounter
may be analyzed along the lines sketched above. Where emotion has been amplified or released by damage to neural structures, attention may be paid to repair of those structures or
amelioration of the effects of such damage; the emotions of disordered biology need biological attention. Yet in the normal

human innate affects must be modulated by learning, away from their all-or-none presentation in the infant toward the sophisticated elaboration of the adult. Each of us has grown up in both macroscopic and microscopic cultures requiring highly specific patterns of emotional expression — we are stamped by our development. Although we share a common biological heritage and therefore essentially identical affect mechanisms, we cannot know what another person is feeling until we have learned about the experiences from which that individual has developed a personal lexicon of emotion.

When patient and therapist share a language for emotion, they are capable of empathic interaction allowing significant change at whatever depth is required. Emotion-based psychotherapy is an evolutionary development allowing integration of all prior therapeutic modalities in terms of the full range of knowledge available today.

Critique Statement

Much therapeutic inefficacy may be attributed to our failure to study emotion as such. Noting the remarkable disparity between the ubiquity of shame within our culture and the regularity with which it has been ignored in psychotherapy, I gathered many of those identified with significant work on "the hidden emotion" to produce a multiauthor book called *The Many Faces of Shame* (Nathanson, 1987). As long as the psychodynamic therapist accepted Freud's dictum that shame does not appear until the infant has renounced its "normal narcissism" during the Oedipal phase of development, long after most other psychic structures have been firmly established, shame was considered vastly less important than guilt. In our culture shame is defined as an internal punishment for narcissism, a defect in the structure of the self, while guilt is a related internal punishment for an action that has harmed another or violated some code of behavior. In the adult, shame is about the self, while guilt is about action.

Yet the study of innate affect reveals the presence of shame as an affect mechanism from the earliest postnatal period. Tom-

kins (1962–1963) suggested that the innate shame affect operated to limit the affects of interest-excitement and contentment
(enjoyment-joy) whenever the organism was unable to do so
voluntarily. In an extension of this theory for innate shame, I
have postulated that in such situations an error-correcting feedback mechanism (Basch, 1988) triggers the subcortical affect
center to release a neurohumoral vasodilator substance elaborated upward (both structurally and phylogenetically) to cause
the cortical shock associated with the experience of shame (see
"A Timetable for Shame" in Nathanson, 1987). Shame affect
involves an acute loss of tonus in the head and neck, accompanied by aversion of gaze from the now problematic triggering
situation and a variable degree of blushing. As the infant grows
into maturity each experience of innate shame affect is assembled into a larger vocabulary of emotional experiences, producing the complex group of cognitions accompanying the various
adult experiences called embarrassment, humiliation, mortifica-
tion, or shame and resulting from such noxious interpersonal interactions as betrayal, contempt, and disdain. With
each leap in maturation the organism accumulates new triggers
for shame.

Wurmser (1981) points out that adult shame emotion is a
response to exposure, the uncovering of highly personal data
about the self, something the individual would have preferred
kept hidden. Psychodynamic psychotherapy is usually called uncovering therapy; by its nature such treatment must produce
shame. If the therapist is unaware of the visible expressions of
innate affect, the patient's communication of shame by gaze aversion, shyness, silence, and withdrawal may be misinterpreted
as resistance and made the source of further embarrassment.
Much or most of what people in therapy describe as their anger
is a defense against shame.

When patient and therapist are free to discuss emotions as
such and to place emotional experience within a framework encompassing all known data about the human condition, therapy itself is seen to lie on a continuum somewhere between art
and science.

Biography

Donald L. Nathanson is senior attending psychiatrist at the Institute of Pennsylvania Hospital and clinical associate professor of psychiatry at Hahnemann University in Philadelphia. He received his M.D. degree (1960) from the State University of New York, Syracuse. He is a fellow of the American Psychiatric Association and the College of Physicians of Philadelphia and a member of numerous other professional organizations. He is a leader in the movement to integrate the affect theory of Silvan Tomkins into the mainstream of psychodynamic theory and practice. His own clinical practice concentrates on the psychotherapy of psychotherapists. Nathanson has authored more than twenty-five articles, book chapters, and reviews and edited two books. He is completing one of his own delineating his approach to the treatment of shame in psychotherapy and is working on a major text to be called *The Nature of Human Emotion.* He has lectured all over the world on these topics. Nathanson's recent work suggests ways that psychotherapy must be changed in order to incorporate data from neurophysiology, psychopharmacology, infant observation, and endocrinology into the language and practice of psychodynamic psychiatry and psychoanalysis.

References

Basch, M. F. (1976). The concept of affect: A re-examination. *Journal of the American Psychoanalytic Association, 24,* 759–778.

Basch, M. F. (1988). *Understanding psychotherapy: The science behind the art.* New York: Basic Books.

Nathanson, D. L. (Ed.). (1987). *The many faces of shame.* New York: Guilford.

Nathanson, D. L. (1988). Affect, affective resonance, and a new theory for hypnosis. *Psychopathology, 21,* 126–137.

Tomkins, S. S. (1962–1963). *Affect/imagery/consciousness* (Vols. 1 and 2). New York: Springer.

Wurmser, L. (1981). *The mask of shame.* Baltimore: Johns Hopkins University Press.

Communicative Approach to
Psychoanalysis and Psychotherapy

Robert J. Langs

Definition

Psychotherapy is constituted by all types of endeavors involving a purported expert and acknowledged patient/client to ameliorate or to resolve an emotionally founded dysfunction—whether physical, psychological-emotive, or interpersonal in nature.

Qualification Statement

Psychotherapy is an effort to heal, regardless of theoretical basis. Its goal is the resolution of an emotionally based dysfunction. Its processes and mode of relief are almost entirely unknown at this time. My own approach is grounded in decoding the transformed meanings unconsciously conveyed in the patient's material. These encoded messages reveal the most substantial basis of madness (that is, all emotionally founded symptoms). They reflect the operation of a *deep unconscious system,* which is distinct from the conscious system of direct experience and direct recall (from its own *superficial unconscious subsystem*). The perceptions and malfunctions of the deep unconscious system account for psychopathology.

Psychotherapy heals adaptively through the creation of a sound therapeutic holding environment (as dictated in encoded messages from the patient's deep unconscious system) and through validated interactional interpretations that reveal the true unconscious meanings of the patient's derivative (encoded) expressions. Inevitable, ego-strengthening, positive, unconscious identification with a therapist capable of securing the ideal frame of therapy and of offering confirmed interactional interpretations also plays a role in the healing process.

It is to be noted, however, that symptom relief may also derive from patient-therapist systems in which proper holding, sound insight, and well-founded unconscious, constructive identifications do *not* play a role. Relief may come from a therapist's sanctioning of the patient's madness; from an unconscious process of comparison between patient and therapist in which the patient appears healthier than the therapist (the so-called cure through nefarious comparison); or from comparable means. The communicative technique described above offers relief at the least possible detrimental cost to both patient and therapist.

Biography

Robert J. Langs is the visiting clinical investigator at the Nathan S. Kline Institute for Psychiatric Research, Orangeburg, New York, and clinical professor of psychiatry at Mt. Sinai School of Medicine in New York City. He received his M.D. degree (1953) from the Chicago Medical School. Langs is also executive director of the Center for Communicative Education and Research at Beth Israel Medical Center in New York City. He has authored fifty-five papers and twenty-six books, including *Rating Your Psychotherapist, Decoding Your Dreams,* and *A Primer of Psychotherapy.*

Time-Limited Dynamic Psychotherapy

Hans H. Strupp

Definition

Psychotherapy is an interpersonal process designed to bring about modification of feelings, cognitions, attitudes, and behavior that have proven troublesome to the person seeking help. The psychotherapist, as ordinarily understood, is a trained professional. People who seek such help desire change, and the therapist agrees to work with them toward particular goals. Psychotherapy is a learning process and a collaborative endeavor that involves both a human relationship and techniques for bringing about personality and behavior change.

Qualification Statement

In broad terms psychotherapy is a psychological treatment designed to achieve beneficial personality and behavior change. Patients who seek help for a psychological problem desire such change — they want to feel or act differently, and the psychotherapist agrees to assist the patient in achieving that goal. Major questions in the study of psychotherapy relate to what is to be changed and how change can be brought about. The first part of the question entails definitions of the problem for which the patient is seeking help (for example, depression, marital difficulties, shyness, nail biting, sexual dysfunctions); the second refers to the process and techniques by means of which change is achieved (support, ventilation of feelings, insight through interpretations, systematic desensitization, assertiveness training, and so on). Distinctions are also made with respect to schools, or theoretical orientations, of therapists and to such variations as individual, group, couples, or family therapy.

Psychotherapy bears a closer relationship to an educational model than to a medical one. As early as 1905, Freud asserted that psychoanalytic therapy is a form of reeducation or "afteredu-cation," a position he maintained throughout his life. It was clear to him, as it has been to most therapists since, that psychother-apy above all else is a form of psychological influence, a col-laborative endeavor in which the patient, from the beginning, is expected to play an active part. From this point of view, the majority of neurotic and personality disorders — the prime con-ditions for which psychotherapy is used — are the products of maladaptive learning dating from early childhood and result-ing in low self-esteem, excessive dependency, social inhibitions, and other forms of maladjustment. To overcome these impedi-ments, patients are typically helped to become more autono-mous, self-directing, and responsible. In order to feel better about themselves, their relationships with others, and their be-havior in general, patients must learn to make changes within themselves and in their environment. The process of therapy is not designed to impose change on patients but to create con-ditions that allow internal changes to occur.

Therefore, psychotherapy is essentially a learning process, and the role of the therapist is somewhat analogous to that of a teacher or mentor. If troublesome feelings, ideas, attitudes, and patterns of behavior have been learned, it is possible, within limits, to effect unlearning or relearning. When learning is im-possible (for example, in conditions primarily attributable to genetic or biochemical factors), psychotherapy has relatively little to offer. Similarly, if the disturbance is solely due to factors in the person's social milieu (poverty, oppression, imprisonment), or if patients themselves do not desire change but change is man-dated (for example, by a court of law or school system), psy-chotherapists encounter great difficulties. Thus psychotherapy works best if patients wish to overcome their problems, are moti-vated to work toward change, live in an environment that toler-ates change, and do not have insurmountable inner obstacles to learning (defenses and rigidities of character). Since all indi-viduals show a tendency to resist personality or behavior change, psychotherapeutic learning is usually beset with difficulties.

Vanderbilt University's approach to time-limited dynamic psychotherapy is based on modern psychoanalytic and interpersonal principles. It views patients' problems in living as a function of disturbances in interpersonal relationships, both past and present. These difficulties are unwittingly enacted by the patient in relation to significant others, including the therapist. Through the creation of a viable therapeutic alliance and through focus on the transactions between patient and therapist in the here-and-now, the therapist seeks to bring about a corrective emotional experience. The experiential insights gained by the patient in this context lead to ameliorations in the patient's interpersonal and intrapsychic functioning.

Time-limited dynamic psychotherapy is appropriate for adult patients who have reasonable personality resources, who are psychologically minded and well motivated, and whose difficulties are not excessively serious or pervasive. The goal is not total cure (which may be impossible under virtually all circumstances) but a significant improvement of the patient's current interpersonal difficulties, including symptoms and maladaptive interpersonal behavior.

Psychotherapists and patients need to become increasingly realistic about the kinds of changes to be expected from psychotherapy and the results that can be achieved, both in time-limited and in time-unlimited forms of psychotherapy. While therapeutic skills are absolutely essential, important—and often insurmountable—limitations of therapeutic results are dictated by the patient's personality structure, past experience (notably in early childhood), and a host of socioenvironmental factors. While existing and yet to be developed technical innovations may augment therapeutic change, it seems unlikely that they can totally override the limitations in patients, therapists, and their interaction. This view is not a statement of therapeutic nihilism but rather a manifesto that strives to acknowledge reality factors, including importantly the severity of many intrapsychic and interpersonal problems that bring a sizable majority of patients to the attention of psychotherapists.

Biography

Hans H. Strupp is Distinguished Professor of Psychology at Vanderbilt University, Nashville, Tennessee. He received his Ph.D. degree (1954) from George Washington University in psychology. He is a recipient of numerous awards, including the American Psychological Association's Distinguished Professional Contributions to Knowledge Award, the Society of Psychotherapy's Distinguished Career Contribution Award, and Vanderbilt University's Earl Sutherland Prize for Research. He has served as president of the Society for Psychotherapy Research and of the Division of Clinical Psychology of the American Psychological Association. He has received an honorary M.D. degree from the University of Ulm (West Germany) and serves on the editorial boards or as consulting editor for numerous journals. Strupp has authored approximately 250 articles, book chapters, and reviews. He has written, coauthored, or edited eight books.

Recommended Reading

Strupp, H. H. (1987). The science and art of psychotherapy. *1988 Yearbook of science and the future* (pp. 221–248). Chicago: Encyclopaedia Britannica.

Strupp, H. H., & Binder, J. L. (1984). *Psychotherapy in a new key: A guide to time-limited dynamic psychotherapy.* New York: Basic Books.

Strupp, H. H., & Hadley, S. W. (1977). A tripartite model of mental health and therapeutic outcomes: With special reference to negative effects in psychotherapy. *American Psychologist, 32,* 187–196.

Strupp, H. H., Hadley, S. W., & Gomes-Schwartz, B. (1977). *Psychotherapy for better or worse: An analysis of the problem of negative effects.* New York: Jason Aronson.

Voice Therapy

Robert W. Firestone

Definition

The psychotherapeutic alliance is a unique human relation-ship, wherein a devoted and trained person attempts to render assistance to another person by both suspending and extending himself. Nowhere in life is a person listened to, felt, and ex-perienced with such concentrated sharing and emphasis on every aspect of personal communication. As in any other human rela-tionship, this interaction may be fulfilling or damaging to either individual. To the extent that a new fantasy bond or illusion of connection is formed (for example, doctor-patient, therapist-client, parent-child), the relationship will be detrimental; whereas in a situation that is characterized by equality, openness, and true compassion, there will be movement toward individuation in both parties. Our therapy helps a person to expose and chal-lenge dependency bonds and destructive "voices," remnants of negative childhood experiences that seriously impair his or her sense of self, spirit, and individuality.

Qualification Statement

My theoretical approach to psychotherapy represents a broadly based, coherent system of concepts and hypotheses that inte-grate psychoanalytic and existential views, yet should not be considered eclectic. The theory explains how early trauma leads to defense formation and how these original defenses are rein-forced as the developing child gradually becomes aware of his own mortality. My orientation focuses on an individual's search for self and personal meaning in the face of internalized inimi-cal processes and ontological anxiety.

Our concepts are congenial with certain constructs in object relations theory (for example, the concept of the "antilibidinal ego"). They provide a cogent explanation of the psychodynamics involved in dysfunctional family constellations that have been described phenomenologically in the work of Alice Miller, R. D. Laing, and others. The emphasis on exposing negative thought processes in our work overlaps cognitive theories and therapies, yet our approach is very different in that we deal more with feeling than analysis of logic or illogic.

My specific orientation and approach to psychotherapy has come to be known as "voice therapy." It is so named because it is a process of giving language or spoken words to the negative thought process at the core of an individual's maladaptive or self-destructive behavior. Its central purpose is to separate and bring out into the open elements of the personality that are antithetical to self resulting from the internalization of negative parental attitudes and damaging childhood experiences. Voices may be conceptualized on a continuum ranging from self-critical or self-depreciating thoughts or attitudes to self-attacks or actual suicidal ideation.

The specialized techniques of voice therapy are composed of three components: (1) The process of eliciting and identifying negative thought patterns, rendering them more accessible and susceptible to control; (2) the feeling release component; recovering repressed emotions and releasing the affect associated with destructive thinking; (3) counteracting maladaptive behaviors regulated by the voice through the collaborative planning and application of appropriate corrective experiences.

The process of identifying the voice can be approached intellectually as an analytical or cognitive technique, or more dramatically, using cathartic methods. Patients learn to verbalize their self-critical thoughts in the second person, as though another person were addressing them; for example, in the form of statements *toward* themselves, rather than statements *about* themselves. Expressing the voice in this format facilitates the process of separating the patient's own point of view from alien, hostile thought patterns assimilated from without. Patients immediately connect voices with parental attitudes and interactions that defined them either explicitly or implicitly. Our conclusions were not the result of an a priori hypothesis on the therapist's part; rather the patients themselves spontaneously developed insight and made the necessary connections. By exposing negative thoughts and antecedents, they disrupted a basic defense and idealization of the family and altered their self-concept in a positive direction.

It is necessary to emphasize that we consider the basic theory underlying voice therapy to be more important than the methodology, and our therapy approach is not restricted or limited to specialized techniques.

My theoretical position is based on a thirty-year study of resistance to change or progress in psychotherapy and a conceptualization of the neurotic process derived from that study. I have defined the neurotic process as "an inward, protective style of living that leads the individual to seek satisfaction more in fantasy than in the real world. It is the process of reliving rather than living, choosing bondage over freedom, the old over the new, the past over the now. It is the attempt to recreate a parent or parents in other persons or institutions, or even, if all else fails, in oneself" (Firestone, 1985, p. 36).

The basic tenet of my theoretical approach is the concept of the *fantasy bond.* The term refers to an illusion of connection with another person, formed originally with the mother as a compensation for what was missing in the infant's early environment. Later, this self-parenting process or fusion is transferred to significant others in adult associations. The term is not meant to describe bonding or positive attachment. It is a fantasy process that compensates for a lack of genuine love, a core defense that to varying degrees comes to be preferred over satisfactions in the real world.

Secondary defenses, including predictions of rejection, self-critical thoughts, negative anticipations, and cynical views of other people function to protect the fantasy bond. These views are maintained by voices that regulate behavior and cause the individual to reject positive experiences.

Abnormal defenses are formed as a result of primal hunger caused by emotional deprivation and separation experiences in childhood. Later, these defenses are compounded by death anxiety—the ultimate separation. We conceive of man's universal neurosis as a reaction to a real fear based on denial and dread of death, and we examine the evolution of this defense in a sociocultural framework. We describe society as a social process that represents a pooling of the individual defenses of its members. In exploring the relationship between core psychological defenses and man's retreat from feeling, we emphasize the importance of each person maintaining the capacity to experience his or her unique existence.

The goal of psychotherapy, as implied in the earlier discussion, is to help individuals achieve a free and independent existence, remain open to experience and feelings, and maintain the ability to respond appropriately to both positive and negative events in their lives. To this end, the process of identifying the voice and its associated feelings of self-hatred and rage toward self, combined with corrective strategies of behavioral change, significantly expand the patient's boundaries and bring about a more positive sense of self.

Critique Statement

Because my theoretical position implicitly challenges conventional views of the family, the principal opposition to my work has been expressed by individuals who adhere strictly to an idealized conception of the family. However, the accumulating evidence of the widespread incidence of emotional disturbance and child abuse in "normal" family constellations caused me to question the essential structure of the nuclear family. Despite my own personal biases and protective attitudes toward parents, I have been unable to resist the compelling nature of the clinical material that links psychopathology and personal limitation to destructive family bonds. Similarly, my approach does not deny the importance of biochemical or constitutional factors in the etiology of neurosis, but in most cases, I have found patients' maladaptive attitudes and behavior to be directly related to, and overdetermined by, environmental components.

Advantages. A major advantage of voice therapy lies in the patient's rapid achievement of personal awareness and insight, independent of therapists' interpretations. Thus, with fewer inter-

vening variables, our approach has important potential as a research tool for studying the negative thought patterns associated
with self-destructive behavior.

Voice therapy procedures uncover core defenses that directly
affect repetitive behavior and the compulsive reliving of the past
with new objects. Our conclusions are based on data obtained
from both disturbed and normal individuals and involve limited
speculation. The overall evaluation of our therapeutic results
is positive, as most individuals became less defensive, accessed
deeper feelings, improved relationships, felt a stronger identity,
and progressed beyond prior limits, both personally and voca-
tionally.

Disadvantages. Because voice therapy procedures are relatively simple and easily applied, the specific techniques can be
potentially harmful in the hands of an inadequately trained or
personally immature therapist. The methods deal with deep-
seated character defenses and crucial psychological issues; therefore, their application requires the skill of an expert professional,
sensitive to the guilt and anxiety involved in breaking away from
habitual defenses and symbiotic relationships. As is true in most
psychotherapies, at the point where the patient becomes aware
that present-day limitations are closely related to early experiences in the family, intense feelings of anger, grief, and out-
rage are aroused, and there is a strong tendency to turn this
rage against the self. At this stage, serious regressions may occur,
and there may be a corresponding breakdown in the therapeutic relationship. It is important that therapists working with these
specialized techniques have a complete understanding of the underlying theory in order to effectively help patients through critical phases in their development.

Conclusion. In recent years, voice therapy techniques have
been applied to problems of parenting and preventive mental
hygiene. In utilizing these techniques, we have helped parents
uncover the source of their ambivalent attitudes toward themselves and their children, enabling them to gain control over
destructive child-rearing practices. In this new format, we have
made an effort to interrupt the intergenerational cycle of child
abuse. The choice to break away from restrictive bonds and

deadening habit patterns is partially an ethical one, given the inherent damage caused by defenses that effectively limit a person's capacity for living and feeling, causing corresponding damage to his or her loved ones. The therapeutic venture, by counteracting the dictates of the voice and disrupting fantasies of connection, offers people a unique opportunity to fulfill their human potential, thereby giving life its special meaning.

Biography

Robert W. Firestone is affiliated with the Glendon Association in Los Angeles, a nonprofit corporation dedicated to the development and dissemination of innovative concepts and practices in psychotherapy. He worked with John N. Rosen, the founder of direct analysis (a specialized form of psychoanalytic therapy with schizophrenic patients), completing his doctoral dissertation, *A concept of the schizophrenic process,* in 1957 and receiving his Ph.D. degree in clinical psychology from the University of Denver that same year. From 1957 to 1979, Firestone was engaged in the private practice of psychotherapy as a clinical psychologist, working with a wide range of patients, amplifying his original ideas on schizophrenia, and applying these concepts to a comprehensive theory of neurosis. In 1979, he joined the Glendon Association, which has made possible a longitudinal study that provided supporting data for his theory of schizophrenia and an understanding of the fantasy bond as manifested in normal couples and family relationships.

Firestone's major works, *The Fantasy Bond: Structure of Psychological Defenses, Voice Therapy: A Psychotherapeutic Approach to Self-Destructive Behavior,* and *Compassionate Child-Rearing: A Psychotherapy Model,* describe how couples form destructive bonds that seriously impair their psychological functioning and have a damaging effect on their child-rearing practices. Firestone has also been involved in the study of negative thought processes and their associated affect and has developed an innovative therapeutic methodology to uncover and contend with aspects of destructive cognition. In his most recent book, he explores the problem of parental ambivalence, develops an exceptional philosophical and creative approach to child rearing, and describes a method of preventive mental hygiene involving the treatment of parents in a group therapy context utilizing voice therapy techniques.

Recommended Reading

Firestone, R. W. (1984). A concept of the primary fantasy bond: A developmental perspective. *Psychotherapy, 21*(2), 218–225.

Firestone, R. W. (1986). The "inner voice" and suicide. *Psychotherapy, 23*(3), 439–447.

Firestone, R. W. (1987a). Destructive effects of the fantasy bond in couple and family relationships. *Psychotherapy, 24*(2), 233–239.

Firestone, R. W. (1987b). The "voice": The dual nature of guilt reactions. *The American Journal of Psychoanalysis, 47*(3), 210–229.

Firestone, R. W. (1988a). *Compassionate child-rearing: A psychotherapy model.* Manuscript submitted for publication.

Firestone, R. W. (1988b). *Voice therapy: A psychotherapeutic approach to self-destructive behavior.* New York: Human Sciences Press.

Firestone, R. W., & Catlett, J. (in press). *Psychological defenses in everyday life.* New York: Human Sciences Press. (Revised edition of *The truth: A psychological cure,* published originally by Macmillan, 1981)

Firestone, R. W., & Seiden, R. H. (1987). Microsuicide and suicidal threats of everyday life. *Psychotherapy, 24*(1), 31–39.

Reference

Firestone, R. W. (1985). *The fantasy bond: Structure of psychological defenses.* New York: Human Sciences Press.

Short-Term Anxiety-Provoking Psychotherapy

Peter E. Sifneos

Definition

Short-term anxiety-provoking psychotherapy (or STAPP) differs from other forms of dynamic therapies of brief duration by having the strictest criteria for selection of appropriate candidates and by researching extensively with patients in cases where the focus of the treatment involves unresolved Oedipal issues. Furthermore, in contrast to time-limited psychotherapy, STAPP is open-ended, and it does not presuppose a strict adherence to a specific number of therapeutic sessions.

Qualification Statement

Short-term anxiety-provoking psychotherapy was developed during the middle 1950s at the Psychiatric Clinic of the Massachusetts General Hospital in Boston, the largest outpatient clinic in the Boston area at that time. Young students complaining of circumscribed symptoms such as mild depressions, phobias, obsessive preoccupations, anxieties, and interpersonal problems seemed to be able to resolve the emotional conflicts underlying their psychological difficulties when they were offered a focal dynamic psychotherapy of brief duration. Encouraged by these observations, an attempt was made to see as many patients as possible in follow-up interviews, one to one and a half years after the termination of their treatment. Although only twenty-one patients out of fifty were seen, their ability to report some symptomatic alleviations and a marked improvement in their interpersonal relations and self-esteem was striking. They also emphasized that they had learned a great deal about themselves. It was decided on the basis of these results that a more extensive study was necessary.

Between 1960 and 1964, more than 500 patients were given treatment utilizing the STAPP model. The criteria for selection of appropriate candidates were more liberal than those employed initially: a circumscribed chief complaint, identification of a meaningful relationship in childhood, a flexible interaction with the evaluator, psychological awareness, above-average intelligence, and motivation for change rather than symptom relief. Patients who met the criteria and who were assessed as being in a state of emotional crisis were not given STAPP, but received crisis intervention instead.

The next step—a controlled research study of STAPP—was actually achieved by 1968. The findings of this investigation were reported in a three-day symposium in London and published in a book titled *The role of learning in psychotherapy*. This study, in addition to matching patients according to age and sex and dividing them into experimental and control groups, involved assessments by independent evaluators of both the initial patient selection and the follow-up findings. One of the most striking discoveries involved the patients' statements that they had learned a great deal about themselves. Even more important was the fact that they were utilizing what they had learned in order to solve new emotional problems in their everyday lives without requiring the assistance of a therapist.

By the end of the 1960s, it became imperative to demonstrate convincingly the validity of the patient evaluation, the process of the therapy, and the outcome findings. Fortunately, the advent of videotaping helped to achieve these objectives, as STAPP could then be observed and evaluated directly by professionals.

Two more research studies were performed during the 1970s at the Beth Israel Hospital, and their results were published. The last study involved selection of a homogeneous patient population consisting of individuals who fulfilled all the criteria for selection, who had as the focus of their therapy an unresolved Oedipal problem, and who agreed to work intensively with their therapist on its resolution. The outcomes of these studies demonstrate unequivocally the value of STAPP as a treatment approach for this specific population.

Critique Statement

What then are the advantages of STAPP? What criticisms could one make about this form of brief dynamic psychotherapy? Let us first deal with potential criticisms. It has been stated that STAPP selects only patients who would improve with any kind of therapy, dynamic or nondynamic. At present, however, I know of no study that compares patients treated with STAPP to patients treated with another form of psychotherapy. Such a study is indeed necessary and should be undertaken.

The suggestion has been made that the patients chosen for STAPP would be good patients for psychoanalysis. Although this is true, one must ask why a patient should undergo a lengthy and expensive form of therapy when comparable results can be obtained in a shorter time at less cost.

Another criticism has to do with the relative health of the STAPP patient population, the implication being that one should spend time only with seriously disturbed patients. Although it is true that STAPP patients are relatively healthy, they nevertheless suffer a great deal from the symptoms or interpersonal difficulties they have been unable to resolve. Furthermore, they cause considerable problems to individuals close to them. These STAPP patients, however, are in many ways the productive pillars of our society. They deserve, therefore, every effort to help them resolve their psychological problems so they can continue contributing as much as possible to the welfare of their community.

Finally, it has been said that the results of a brief psychotherapeutic approach can never be compared with the more global results of a longer treatment process. There is simply no evidence that this is the case. Even if it is true that in-depth psychoanalysis yields a more far reaching change in the patient, this advantage in terms of change becomes marginal when one considers the savings in time and money when STAPP is employed.

It is much easier to discuss the advantages of STAPP. First and foremost, it is a type of treatment that has been investigated extensively with a large number of patients and that compares favorably with similar kinds of brief dynamic therapy. Above and beyond these considerations, STAPP evaluations, therapeutic sessions, and follow-up interviews have been videotaped extensively. Possibly the most important finding about STAPP is the similar statements made by many patients, to the effect that what helped them most was gaining insight about their emotional problems and being able to utilize this insight in order to solve new emotional problems. They were therefore free and independent and did not require a therapist to help them resolve new problems. In this sense, STAPP can be viewed as a true preventive psychiatric intervention.

Biography

Peter E. Sifneos is a professor of psychiatry at Harvard University and editor in chief of *Psychotherapy and Psychosomatics*. He received his M.D. degree (1946) from Harvard Medical School and was certified as a psychiatrist (1954) by the American Board for Psychiatry and Neurology. He is a life fellow of the American Psychiatric Association, fellow of the Royal Society of Medicine, honorary member of the Hellenic Society for Psychiatry and Neurology, and member of several other medical psychiatric associations. He has authored three books—*Ascent from Chaos: A Psychosomatic Case Study* (1964), *Short Term Psychotherapy and Emotional Crisis* (1972), and *Short Term Dynamic Psychotherapy (Evaluation and Technique)* (1979)—as well as 105 journal articles.

3

Humanistic and Experiential Psychotherapy

This chapter on humanistic, affective psychotherapy is intended to represent a major portion of the "third force," which developed in response to behaviorist and psychodynamic paradigms that were viewed as overly deterministic and inattentive to individuality. The commonality among the approaches represented here and in Chapter Six is an attitude that prizes the individual, his or her uniqueness and phenomenology. Approaches represented in this chapter are more firmly rooted in a theory of personal functioning that focuses on the individual's response to his or her own emotions. Humans are viewed as naturally growing and evolving in a positive manner within a supportive emotional culture, as long as that growth is not hampered by intrapersonal obstruction. The common principle is: Know yourself (or discover yourself) and you will grow in a healthy, healing way. Approaches in Chapter Six are less affective and more external, focusing on the individual's relation to the cosmos and to his or her immediate world.

According to Carl Rogers (1951, p. 510), "Psychological maladjustment exists when the organism denies to awareness significant sensory or visceral experiences, which consequently are not symbolized and organized into the gestalt of the self-structure." Healing then demands that these experiences be

brought into awareness. In this theoretical framework, phenomenology, experience, and perception are viewed as the authentic
substance of the individual's reality, not the artifacts of psychodynamically determined processes or learned response sets. The
theoretically determined units-of-analysis are, primarily, feelings that have been unexpressed. The therapist and patient work
to promote natural growth-oriented forces.

Historically the approaches represented here have multiple
roots. Client-centered therapy grew out of Rogers's nondirective therapy, which was technique-based and provided a climate
of empathic, unconditional, positive regard in which a client
could grow past his or her problem. Abraham Maslow conceived
of healthy individuals as being naturally growth directed, while
Fritz Perls added dramatic technique to promote awareness, contact, and emotional expression.

This chapter is divided into sections on client-centered therapy, experiential approaches, and gestalt approaches. In the first
section, Ruth Sanford elaborates the philosophy of the client-
centered approach.

The second section contains three distinct variations of the
experiential approach. In their contribution, Thomas and Patrick
Malone distinguish between counseling and psychotherapy,
describing the experiential relationship as a learning process.
Alvin Mahrer details another experiential process, one that focuses on the transformative potential of the therapy session.
James Iberg's experiential approach, which relies heavily on the
work of Carl Rogers and Eugene Gendlin, strives for enhanced
self-symbolization.

The gestalt approaches section contains contributions that
elaborate the theory and philosophy of Fritz Perls. Erving and
Miriam Polster discuss the conceptual foundations of gestalt therapy. A theoretical formulation for embodied gestalt therapy is
put forth by Edward W. L. Smith.

Reference

Rogers, C. R. (1951). *Client-centered therapy.* Boston: Houghton
    Mifflin.

Section 1
Client-Centered Therapy

Client-Centered Psychotherapy

Ruth Sanford

Definition

Psychotherapy is a process in which two persons enter into a relationship for the purpose of assisting the client to make positive changes in attitudes toward self and others and to find increasingly satisfying ways of coping with life situations. In client-centered psychotherapy the therapist aims, without intervention of personal values, to create a climate conducive to the release of the innate potential for growth and self-realization within the client. The therapist is able to trust the client to empower him- or herself and to move toward becoming a fully functioning person with an inner locus of evaluation. If the therapist genuinely respects and accepts the trustworthiness of the client as an autonomous human being, then traditional medical models of diagnosis, labeling, prognosis, interpretation, and externally conceived plan of treatment become irrelevant to the process and purpose of the therapy.

Qualification Statement

I wonder if it is really possible to define psychotherapy as if it were a coherent whole. In my opinion, the value of this exercise is for each of us to define what psychotherapy means to us, in the hope that we shall thereby be performing a service for ourselves, for our colleagues, and for the users of our services, present and future. The first step, for me, was to sort out the essentials of the way I have chosen to be with others who come to me for assistance in discovering how to make their lives more effective and satisfying. The next step is to communicate my findings to my colleagues, together with the philosophical, ethical, scientific, and personal bases for my choice.

There are many different ways in which persons having difficulty coping with the complexities of life can be helped. After many years of working one-to-one and in groups with young people and adults who either recognized their own need or were referred, I have found a clearly defined way of relating with them, regardless of the labels placed upon them by some members of our profession. My approach is effective and rewarding for me, and I believe for most of them. I choose to work in this way because it is compatible with my philosophy, my sense of responsibility, my respect for other human beings, and my respect for science. It has been greatly enhanced through ten years of working closely with Carl Rogers, from whose life and work it has evolved — first as client-centered therapy and later as a person-centered approach to significant relationships, including that of therapist with client.

I have chosen this approach rather than those for which I was initially trained because it calls upon my whole person, not just my intellect, my professional skills, or my pride in achievement. Client-centered therapy, as defined by Carl Rogers, is a way of being with a client based on the premise that within each human organism there are vast resources for self-understanding and constructive change in ways of being and behaving, and that these resources can best be released and realized in a climate with certain definable psychological conditions. When the therapist experiences and communicates his or her own realness, caring, and deeply sensitive, nonjudgmental understanding, such release and change are most likely to occur. In other words, the quality of the therapist-client relationship is central to the purpose of the therapeutic process, which is to enable the client to experience *self*-empowerment.

The traditional medical model of diagnosis, prognosis, interpretation, plan of treatment, and cure within a hierarchical relationship is irrelevant to the inherent human potential for self-directed change in which client-centered therapy has its roots. Rather than an externally conceived strategy, system, or technique, client-centered therapy is a deep response to the innate tendency of the human organism to reach toward fulfillment of its own potential—a tendency that persists as long as the organism is alive. It is an expression of the therapist's conviction that client behaviors destructive of self and others are indications that the natural tendency to healthy growth has been thwarted by a destructive environment; and that the client will respond to a safe and nurturing climate.

Critique Statement

Some questions raised by the originator of this approach have not been answered and can be answered only by extensive research. One that has become increasingly important is, In a repressive society, does a focus on personal growth and community spirit reduce the likelihood of social change? (In South Africa we were asked, "But will it defuse the coming revolution?") Another unanswered question raised in the same venue was, Is this approach doomed to be overcome by those who believe in aggressive domination by power? We will learn the answers only with time and persistent inquiry, the kind of rigorous research that Carl Rogers has always invited and used to test his hypotheses. A third question—Is stress on the self and on individual freedom and choice merely a Western or American cultural phenomenon, or is it interculturally basic?—has been answered in the positive in part as a result of work in Japan, South Africa, and the Soviet Union.

In the 1970s, critics tended to complain that the client-centered approach encouraged narcissism by its emphasis on self-realization and was thus influential in creating the "me generation" (with a resultant decline in social values). The truth is that freedom, responsibility, and the sharing of power are all central to the concept. According to the hypothesis on which client-centered therapy is based, the person who is listened to learns to listen to him- or herself and to others; the person who is trusted and respected learns to trust and respect him- or herself and others; and the person who is accepted as responsible for himself becomes more responsible as a person and as a member of society. As a more fully functioning person, he or she will be less likely either to follow someone blindly or to impose personal values on others.

Another criticism of this approach is that no provision has been made for the existence of evil in human beings or the world. Evil, violence, and destructiveness, much of it senseless, are not only in the world but threaten to destroy it. The real question is the source of evil. Trust in the human organism grows from the belief that—contrary to much of what is taught in religion, education, and business in our culture—the human being is not born evil, a being who must be watched, punished, and tamed, but rather is inclined to the positive and constructive and, in a climate conducive to natural growth, will reach toward its full potential. If the climate is destructive, the natural tendency will be thwarted and the organism damaged so that it may grow in distorted ways that lead to violent behavior. The self-actualizing tendency persists, however, and the organism, although severely damaged, will seek to grow in positive ways, given certain definable psychological conditions.

Two other criticisms of this approach to therapy are that it places unreasonable demands on the therapist and that the therapist pampers the client. It is true that a therapist who chooses to work in this way accepts a demanding discipline: to be congruently aware of self and the feelings flowing within from moment to moment; to be genuine and open enough to reveal them to the client at an appropriate moment; to be deeply empathic and secure enough to enter the world of the client, move comfortably about in it, and then return to his or her own world; and to do all this without judgment and with respect for another human being. When all of these attitudes are present, significant positive change is most likely to take place. There is no expectation that any therapist can assume all of these attitudes, all of the time, with all clients—or with any particular client. Therapist and client are two imperfect human beings on a journey together, getting better and better at what they are doing; the therapist more experienced, more emotionally or psychologically mature, but still human and fallible.

Biography

Ruth Sanford is adjunct professor at Hofstra University, Long Island University, and the Union Institute, Cincinnati, Ohio. She received her M.A.T.C. degree (1938) from Columbia University. She is the recipient of awards for outstanding contributions to education in schools and universities in New York State and for excellence in her profession. Sanford was cofounder and codirector of the Learning Program in the Person-Centered Approach on Long Island, New York. She initiated workshops in the person-centered approach on the East Coast with local staff and has worked with Carl Rogers on many workshop, institute, and seminar staffs since 1977. She helped to initiate and cofacilitated work with him in Mexico in 1981 and 1982, in South Africa in 1982 and 1986, and in the USSR in 1986; returning after Rogers's death to South Africa (1987) and the USSR (1988). Sanford is the author of papers that have been published in professional books and journals and is coauthor with Carl Rogers of several professional reports and papers, including "Client-Centered Psychotherapy," a chapter in *The Comprehensive Textbook of Psychiatry*.

Recommended Reading

Rogers, C. R. (1959). A theory of therapy, personality and interpersonal relationships, as developed in a client-centered framework. In *Psychology: A study of a science: Vol. 3. Formulation of the person and the social context* (pp. 184–256). New York: McGraw-Hill.

Rogers, C. R. (1977). *Carl Rogers on personal power: Inner strength and its revolutionary impact.* New York: Delacorte Press.

Rogers, C. R. (1980). *A way of being.* New York: Houghton Mifflin.

Rogers, C. R., & Sanford, R. C. (1988). Client-centered psychotherapy. In H. I. Kaplan and B. J. Sadock (Eds.), *Comprehensive textbook of psychiatry: Vol. 5.* Baltimore: Williams and Wilkins.

Sanford, R. C. (1985). *An inquiry into the evolution of the person-*

centered approach to significant relationships. Unpublished paper based on an invited address to the Evolution of the Psychotherapies Conference, Phoenix, Arizona.

Sanford, R. C. (1986). Unconditional positive regard: A misunderstood way of being. *Revista de Psiquiatria y Psicologia Humanista, 17*(4), 27–35.

Section 2
Experiential Approaches

Experiential Psychotherapy

Thomas P. Malone
Patrick T. Malone

Definition

Experiential therapy is neither a technique nor a school of therapy. Rather, it attempts to describe the nonlinear process that underlies any and all approaches to therapy. Its fundamental assumptions are that personal growth occurs only in the relational experience and that the movement of the experiential therapeutic relationship depends mainly on the person of the therapist, be he or she behaviorist, analyst, or humanist. In the intimate relationship, the client learns to learn and redevelops a natural capacity to explore and grow. He loses his dependence on either his history or his therapist.

Qualification Statement

Experiential psychotherapy suggests that there is a difference between *psychotherapy* and *counseling,* two components of any professional therapeutic experience. Psychotherapy promotes personal growth. Counseling directs that growth but does not promulgate it. Therapy is any experience that awakens, sustains, or directs personal change and growth. Described so, most therapy occurs in everyday human experience, not in the artifice of the therapist's office. Whenever a human being intimately connects with something or someone, change and growth occur.

Professional psychotherapy is part of that universal process. Unlike the natural serendipity of personal growth that simply occurs, psychotherapy on a professional level is an intentional and contractual agreement between a therapist-healer and one or more people, variously called clients, students, or patients, who are seeking healing, change, and growth.

Counseling concerns itself with learning to live with who you are rather than who you could be. Psychotherapy, on the other hand, promotes a healthy and constant discontent. Therapy, when effective, makes counseling and psychotherapy work together. When we counsel, we basically teach. Our instruments are teachable and are thus techniques. Such techniques may involve insight, affirmation, catharsis, confrontation, suggestions, working through, understanding, behavioral modification, structuring, scripts, analysis, and so on. When we "do" psychotherapy, we promote learning. We are nonintentional and non-goal-directed.

Experiential psychotherapists believe that the particular techniques and systems of treatment are less important than the congruence of these techniques and systems with the person of the therapist. Technique does not bring integral change in the patient. It can bring the patient to the point where such change may occur, but integral personal change and growth occur only in the therapeutic experience, not simply in the counseling-educative relationship.

The growth experience involves an interpersonal process, largely unintentional and nonverbal, occurring in the relationship between the therapist and the person seeking psychotherapy. It resembles the ways growth naturally occurs in the early stages of life in the family or in a person's everyday life. Relational experience is the agency of growth, for growth can only occur in the intimate moment. The importance of unconscious communication, affective connection between therapist and client, and congruence among therapist, client, and system is that these elements foster the relational experience, much as is true in functional families.

The experiential relationship allows the client to learn how to learn, increases her capacity to learn, and enables her to continue her personal growth on her own. It fosters independent growth, not dependence on the therapist or some encapsulated system of living. Self-learning, in contrast to tutorial learning, significantly increases personal freedom, spontaneity, authenticity, reciprocity, congruence, and presence, as well as self-discipline and self-responsibility. The core experience in self-learning is the increased capacity for being intimate in relationship, that is, being oneself expressively and being open to new experience when in relationship with others to whom one is close. Experiential therapy enhances that capacity for the intimate experience and thereby fosters growth and change.

Critique Statement

Experiential psychotherapy has been criticized mainly on three basic grounds. First, that it is not teachable, that is, it cannot be didactically taught (as can technique) or described in a simple how-to text. Second, that it represents not a school of psychotherapy but a life position or a personal philosophy and thus cannot be scientifically measured or calibrated. It lends itself more to art than to science. Third, that the process is primarily unconscious and thus not only is unteachable and indescribable but cannot be consciously initiated.

The first criticism is, of course, a true disadvantage. Experiential psychotherapy is not teachable because it is not oriented to technique or strategy. Experience cannot be packaged or transferred to others directly for them to apply. An experiential psychotherapeutic relationship cannot be concretely described as a set of therapeutizing behaviors, intentional approaches, appropriate maneuvers, or concrete strategies and goals. Experiential psychotherapy is, however, learnable. It has the distinct advantage that the therapist learning his art is involved in essentially the same process of self-learning that the people he will see are involved in. He learns to learn, and so he constantly learns from those he sees in psychotherapy. He grows with his clients, and thus burnout is less likely to occur.

A characteristic of novice experiential therapists is that they often complain of feeling that they are not doing anything. Any "being"-based therapy — that is, one emphasizing experience in relationship and growth and deemphasizing problems — will initially result in this subjective dilemma. This seems particularly true in a behavior- and goal-driven society. Another source of difficulty for some is that experiential psychotherapy is essentially countercultural. It values individual experience, personal relationships, and family life more than it does the culturally defined system. It is oppositional to a culture addicted to prepared answers, outside-generated cures, and describable "molding maneuvers." To insist that the inner relational experience is the source of human change and growth is bound to be disconcerting to both the people seeking help and the therapists offering it in the context of our mechanistic and outer-directed culture.

A cultural advantage of experiential psychotherapy is that since it is based on being, relationship, and intimate experience with the other, there is little likelihood that the individuals seen in psychotherapy will be controlled, used, abused, seduced, coerced, or punished. It makes psychotherapy a more symmetrical relationship rather than a purely teacher-student one. A basic assumption in experiential psychotherapy is that if the person sitting in the opposite chair is not more like you than different from you, you have no moral or professional right to treat him or her.

Another potential advantage of experiential psychotherapy is the value of the therapist learning to learn as a preparation for being an experiential therapist. This is somewhat different from the old adage that "to do therapy, you have to have had therapy." The experience of self-learning is process-oriented, not personally oriented. That process — that is, experience in relation and connection — is more important than the personal particulars involved. That process is the core of experiential psychotherapy. The process is there regardless of the subject matter, regardless of our conscious awareness. Most technique-oriented therapy relies on the facts of human experience. Experiential psychotherapy relies on its involvement with the pattern of human experience — the process of motion and growth on a deeper and more essential level.

Biographies

Thomas P. Malone is one of the cofounders of the Atlanta Psychiatric Clinic and presently in practice there. He received his M.D. degree (1953) from Emory University School of Medicine and his Ph.D. degree from Duke University. He served as a clinical psychologist in the army during World War II. He taught at Duke University and was on the faculty of the Department of Psychiatry at Emory for some years. He has written over 300 articles in professional journals and coauthored nine books. He has mainly been involved with the development of the literature on experiential psychotherapy, the psychotherapy of schizophrenia in the context of families, and, more recently, exploration of the qualities of intimate experience itself.

Patrick T. Malone is currently in practice at the Atlanta Psychiatric Clinic. He received his M.D. degree (1968) from the University of North Carolina School of Medicine and served in the U.S. Navy from 1964 to 1976. He is the author of a number of articles and coauthor with his father of *The Art of Intimacy*.

Recommended Reading

Felder, R. E. (1967). The use of self in psychotherapy. In D. S. Arbuckle (Ed.), *Counseling and psychotherapy: An overview*. New York: McGraw-Hill.

Felder, R. E., Malone, T. P., Warkentin, J., & Whitaker, C. (1961). Rational and non-rational psychotherapy: A reply. *American Journal of Psychotherapy, 15*(2), 212–220.

Felder, R. E., Malone, T. P., Warkentin, J., & Whitaker, C. (1963). Experiential psychotherapy: Evaluation of relatedness. *The Journal of Existential Psychiatry, 3*(2), 247–254.

Malone, K., Malone, T., Kuckleburg, R., Cox, R., Barnett, J., & Barstow, D. (1982a). Experiential psychotherapy: Basic principles, Part I. *Pilgrimage, 10*(1).

Malone, K., Malone, T., Kuckleburg, R., Cox, R., Barnett, J., & Barstow, D. (1982b). Experiential psychotherapy: Basic principles, Part II. *Pilgrimage, 10*(2).

Malone, T. P. (1980). Self in psychotherapy. *Pilgrimage, 8*(2), 93–104.

Malone, T. P., & Malone, P. T. (1987). *The art of intimacy.* New York: Prentice-Hall.

Malone, T. P., & Whitaker, C. (1969). Experiential or non-rational psychotherapy. In W. S. Sahakian (Ed.), *Psychotherapy and counseling: Studies in technique.* Chicago: Rand-McNally.

Malone, T. P., & Whitaker, C. (1980). *Roots of psychotherapy.* New York: Brunner-Mazel.

Warkentin, J., & Whitaker, C. (1967). The therapist as prototype. In A. Burton (Ed.), *Challenges of humanistic psychology.* New York: McGraw-Hill.

Experiential Psychotherapy

Alvin R. Mahrer

Definition

Experiential psychotherapy is defined by four steps that occur in *each session.* First, by attaining a level of strong feeling, the client accesses an inner, deeper experiencing and brings it a little closer to the surface. Second, this inner, deeper experiencing is appreciated, welcomed, received. Third and fourth, the patient undergoes a qualitative transformation by entering into this inner, deeper experiencing and then by sampling what it can be like to be and behave as this new personality in the extratherapy world.

Qualification Statement

Picture an experiential therapist and patient reclining in adjacent chairs, quite close to one another. Their eyes are closed throughout the entire session, which ends when both agree that work is finished, generally after one and a half to two hours or so. We go through the same four steps in each session, whether or not this is the initial session or a subsequent one.

We begin with whatever feeling is here right now, like feeling anxious or helpless or annoyed or excited or tearful. Or we begin with anything that is immediately front and center on the patient's mind, any attentional center, event, incident, concern, or problem that evokes or is connected to a feeling. Whether or not we begin with a feeling or feeling-related attentional center, the patient is shown how to let the feeling increase. We may stay with the same feeling or feeling-related attentional center. We may unfold into new ones. The process is flexibly accommodating, as long as we keep moving in the direction of increasing depth and breadth of feeling.

As the feeling level increases, the patient is shown how to attain a level of strong feeling that is gripping, saturated, intense. This is the goal, for this is when an inner, deeper experiencing is accessed. Strong feeling is the crucible that allows the inner, deeper experiencing to emerge.

Once the inner, deeper experiencing is accessed, sensed, felt, the purpose of the second step is to appreciate this inner experiencing by welcoming it, accepting it, enveloping it with an appreciative reception, letting its presence be felt.

The purpose of the third step is for the patient to undergo radical and transformative disengagement from the ordinary everyday personality and enter fully into "being" the inner experiencing. This is a profound shift in the very personality of the person, a metamorphosis into being the inner experiencing. Accordingly, a special premium is placed on the patient's absolute readiness, willingness, and choice.

The patient is to "be" the inner experiencing within the context of a key scene or incident from the patient's earlier life. Therefore, the first task is to locate the appropriate and useful earlier scene or incident, and then for the patient to step out of the ordinary, everyday personality and into the very being of that inner experiencing, all within the context of the vividly real earlier incident or scene.

The final step is the culminating goal of therapeutic work in each session. The patient is provided with an opportunity to have a taste of what life can be like as this new and different personality. The context is the extratherapy world of today, tomorrow, and beyond, and the person literally undergoes what it is like to be and behave as this new personality in actual scenes and incidents in the prospective world. Concrete new ways of being and behaving can be rehearsed and evaluated, modified and refined, declined or allowed to occur. The session ends when both are satisfied that work is over.

Critique Statement

This existential-humanistic theory of human beings and this experiential theory of psychotherapy open the way for virtually unlimited and radical changes in each session. The changes evolve from the particular inner deeper experiencing that is accessed in a given session. Yet the challenge is for the patient to leave the session as a qualitatively new personality with new ways of being and behaving in a world that is seen and lived in whole new ways. I am convinced that each session *can* yield utterly transformative changes that *can* be virtually permanent — once we free ourselves of truncatingly restrictive "truths" about human beings and about what we believe can be accomplished in each psychotherapeutic session.

Two features differentiate this approach from others in terms of patient and therapist roles, and in the ways they interrelate. One is that they both have their eyes closed throughout the session. The other is that the patient's momentary choice, readiness, and willingness are the prime determinants throughout the session. Accordingly, the therapist's major roles are to show the patient what to do and how to do it and to join with the patient in undergoing each step of the process. Not only are these challengingly new roles and ways of being together, but they leave essentially no place for the traditional therapist and patient roles and relationships.

In each session, the precious jewel is whatever inner, deeper experiencing is accessed. This determines what is to be achieved in the session and what the patient can be and become. It is the criterion template for the session's success. Accordingly, there is no place for traditional ways of categorizing patients, initial evaluations or assessments, psychodiagnostic classifications, target problems or problematic behaviors, therapeutic programs, or treatment goals.

The purpose of attaining a level of strong feeling is to access an inner, deeper experiencing — rather than merely affect expression, emotional release, abreaction, or catharsis. Strong feeling is a technical means of accessing what is inner and deeper. Furthermore, once this inner, deeper experiencing is accessed, therapeutic change occurs through appreciating this experiencing, welcoming and lifting it up, entering into it and being it, and experiencing behavior changes as this new personality in the imminent extratherapy world. Therapeutic change does not occur through insight or awareness, self-exploration, therapist-patient relationships, altering behavioral contingencies, or other traditional means.

We determine if experiential psychotherapy is useful for this patient at this time by simply trying out a session and seeing if we proceed through the steps. The axiom is that this therapy is useful for people provided they are ready and willing at this time. Accordingly, usefulness and appropriateness have essentially nothing to do with what is often referred to as the patient's presenting complaint, problem, target behavior, personality characteristics, psychopathology, or psychodiagnostic classification. As long as the patient is ready and willing to go through the steps, experiential psychotherapy is fitting.

Biography

Alvin R. Mahrer is professor of psychology in the School of Psychology at the University of Ottawa, Canada, where he teaches doctoral students, directs a psychotherapy research team, and supervises interns and postdoctoral fellows in experiential psychotherapy. He received his Ph.D. degree (1954) from Ohio State University. He is a fellow of the American Psychological Association, on the editorial boards of numerous psychotherapy journals, and has been in the private practice of experiential psychotherapy for the past thirty-four years. Mahrer has edited three books, authored seven books, and published over 125 chapters and articles, all within three interrelated themes. One theme is the formulation of an existential-humanistic theory of psychology and psychiatry. The second is uncovering the secrets of psychotherapy through discovery-oriented psychotherapy research. The third is the clinical architecting of the theory and practice of experiential psychotherapy.

Recommended Reading

Mahrer, A. R. (1985). *Psychotherapeutic change: An alternative approach to meaning and measurement.* New York: Norton.

Mahrer, A. R. (1986). *Therapeutic experiencing: The process of change.* New York: Norton.

Mahrer, A. R. (1989a). *Experiencing: A humanistic theory of psychology and psychiatry.* Ottawa: University of Ottawa press. (Original work published 1978)

Mahrer, A. R. (1989b). *Experiential psychotherapy: Basic practice.* Ottawa: University of Ottawa Press. (Original work published 1983)

Mahrer, A. R. (1989c). *How to do experiential psychotherapy: A manual for practitioners.* Ottawa: University of Ottawa Press.

Mahrer, A. R. (1989d). *The integration of psychotherapies: A guide for practicing therapists.* New York: Human Sciences Press.

Mahrer, A. R. (1989e). *Dream work: In psychotherapy and self-change.* New York: Norton.

Person-Centered
Experiential Psychotherapy

James R. Iberg

Definition

Experiential psychotherapy aims to create and sustain interactional conditions that foster self-examination involving a natural but distinctive opening up of feelings and emotions for new
and further authentic articulation (Gendlin, 1979). The resulting *change* in feelings moves the client toward an experience of
self which is better in that (1) it feels "more truly me," with increased self-acceptance and self-understanding, and (2) it permits easier, more interpersonally viable, less conflicted action
that more effectively serves personal values and objectives in
life situations.

Qualification Statement

This definition minimizes specification of precisely what the
therapist may and may not do. Rather, the emphasis is placed
on the effect for the client—the therapist does whatever helps
the client to open up troublesome feelings such that they may
change. The client is the ultimate judge of whether the desired
change occurs. The experiential therapist is free to apply (and
better off knowing) a variety of theories of therapy. The central
principle is that *whatever* theory is applied, one applies it in the
service of facilitating the opening and changing process for the
client, rather than adhering dogmatically to the theory. This
emphasis alerts the therapist to avoid becoming wedded to any
particular approach or theory or routinely applying certain techniques. What works experientially will be different from client
to client, as well as for a given client at different times.

This approach relies heavily on the axiom that *people are moti-vated and guided toward healthy change from within themselves, if given experiential interaction.* Empirical testing of this axiom is encouraged. Theoretically we posit the *actualizing tendency* (Goldstein, 1939; Rogers, 1959). This is the tendency, found in any living organism, to behave in ways that fulfill and further perfect the capacities, according to its nature, of the organism as a whole.

From pioneering research on the process of psychotherapy, Carl Rogers concluded that three conditions tended to be especially facilitative of the actualizing tendency. These conditions are empathy for the client, congruence or genuineness on the part of the therapist, and positive regard for the client (Rogers, 1957). When these exist, the encounter between the two people is more person-to-person than person-to-professional authority. This quality of encounter lessens defensiveness and promotes self-exploration.

Gendlin's research and writings about "focusing" (1964, 1981) collect much knowledge regarding the opening and changing kind of self-exploration. Gendlin's philosophical work (for example, 1962) places focusing in the context of a number of different human processes. Two key features of it are a "bodily felt sense" and friendly, gentle, receptive attitudes toward one's feelings.

"Bodily felt sense" refers to the way in which experiencing is felt in the body as well as symbolized in concepts, emotions, images, and behaviors. No matter how well symbolized a given area of experiencing is, it is never captured completely by the symbols. The meaning of what is symbolized can also be had as an inner sense that is there apart from any outward expression of meaning. It is such a "body sense" *from which* we can form words or pictures or actions to convey the meaning to someone else. A bodily felt sense always can be further symbolized and could be quite differently yet accurately symbolized. A distinct feeling of satisfaction comes with symbols that adequately symbolize meaning as it is felt.

Especially pertinent to psychotherapy is the way in which an area of experiencing can be inadequately symbolized. Emotionally significant or self-esteem-related experiences may be squeezed into symbols that leave out or distort important aspects, with implications that make living burdensome, socially problematic, and/or personally painful. In this situation, the symbols that would more accurately represent experiencing and provide the machinery necessary for more satisfying and authentic living (this defines better or improved symbolization) are only implicit in the bodily felt sense. Such implicit meanings need a process of self-exploration and expression that will allow the creation of symbols more effective for living in the world.

Improving self-symbolization is a delicate business. Changing the symbols for experiencing involves a variety of subjective threats: first, what has worked about existing symbols could be lost. If living is difficult as it is, such an additional loss may be quite threatening. A second threat is that something awful and ugly about the self could be revealed, and the therapist, others, and even oneself might then be too repelled to sustain a good relationship. Problematic existing symbols often imply that something undesirable must be concealed or controlled to avoid punishment or shame. Third, symbolizing experiencing anew inevitably involves exploring unknown inner territory. The unknown is, for many, a source of anxiety. Thus, holding friendly and receptive attitudes toward one's feelings related to serious problems is not a trivial matter and often requires support.

A body sense is a delicate phenomenon, easily chased away. The condition of having a body sense available for new symbolization is one of vulnerability: One feels one may reveal dirty laundry or flaws, or even spill one's guts. Thus one is especially vulnerable to negative judgments, signs of rejection, and misunderstanding. And in the first place, a body sense is only perceptible at a lower level of sensory intensity than a loud social conversation. To detect a body sense, we must attune to a level of sensitivity markedly more subtle than we are adjusted to for normal daily living. This attunement may take some minutes of quiet time in a safe setting to accomplish.

Adding to the delicacy of the situation, we wish for clients to recognize their ownership of the power and the means to improve. Sometimes only so much new material from poorly symbolized experiencing can be taken before the client would prefer to stop to examine the effects. In supporting such regrouping, this approach contrasts greatly with hypnotherapies which assume the existing set of concepts can be circumvented and dramatically changed without the conscious collaboration of the client. We believe that deeper and more lasting resolution of poorly symbolized experiencing occurs through the conscious, step-by-step collaboration of the client. On the other hand, the condition of the client in which improved symbolization of experiencing can be created shares some characteristics with hypnotic trance: It is a condition of inwardly focused, highly concentrated, heightened sensitivity to feelings and inner experiences. But where the hypnotist attempts to distract the conscious mind so that the "unconscious mind" can come to the fore with its attitudes of nonevaluation and objectivity, for the purpose of utilizing the resources within the client's experience, in experiential psychotherapy we aim to facilitate the client's *conscious* assumption of these attitudes through the empathy and congruence of the therapist, and by teaching the focusing process. When this is successful, the client is thereby less dependent on the therapist to achieve these change-productive attitudes in future times of need.

We trust the client's urge to press on with the exploration rather than assuming, as do practitioners of many forms of therapy, that the therapist must keep the client pressing on. The therapist fosters the client's urge by preserving (1) respect for the wisdom of the client's preferred pace, (2) an attitude of confidence that the experiencing underpinning symbols is to be trusted and explored to advantage, even though problems, pains, and difficulties can be sensed in it, and (3) a keen attentiveness to and empathic reflection of all expressive clues of experiencing felt but not expressed verbally. If this third quality is lost, the interaction may degenerate into an intellectual discussion of the client's material with little if any experiential effect for the client.

Critique Statement

Perhaps the major disadvantage or weakness of experiential theory is that it offers, within itself, little guidance as to types of client problems. The experiential therapist strives to avoid preconceptions about clients, preferring to know each person in great detail. In some cases, particularly when the therapist has little personal experience with what the client struggles with, this may be a slow and inefficient way to true empathic understanding of the client, without which effective experiential interaction is less likely. Thus there is a burden on the experiential therapist to remain alert and open to further training and information that could deepen empathic understanding of the specific clients with whom he or she works at any given time.

Effective experiential interaction results in that unique condition in the client in which the actualizing tendency is stimulated and a process of change can occur. The wisdom in experiencing then eclipses existing concepts and symbols to produce new and more effective symbols with which to live. From witnessing this happen repeatedly, a basic trust of, and optimism about, organismic feeling and striving arises that sets us apart from theories that view the unconscious as basically antisocial and in need of restraint or control. Thus, this approach respects the *conscious* mind more than hypnosis, and the *unconscious* mind more than psychoanalysis.

What is consciously unknown of experiencing is really not at all foreign or forbidding when properly approached. Rather it turns out to be recognizable as a most familar and abundant territory: who you really were all the time, but in richer, deeper detail. Walking the terrain with the right companion, at the right pace, with your feet planted solidly step by step, far surpasses relying on your map to know the territory. The walk reveals features not shown on the map. Especially valuable are those features *enfolded in* but *resolving of* pains and difficulties. The source of evil and antisocial behavior lies much more in factors that prevent full, accurate, ongoing symbolization of experiencing than it does in the individual personality.

Biography

James R. Iberg is an associate faculty member at the Illinois School of Professional Psychology. He received his M.B.A. degree (1971) and his Ph.D. degree (1979) from the University of Chicago in personality processes and social psychology. He is in private practice in Evanston and Chicago, Illinois, and has lectured on psychotherapy, experiential focusing, empathy, and communication skills in seven countries. He writes and teaches about the antiempathic, growth-stifling effects of evaluative, diagnostic thinking and communication.

Iberg's research interests are in intensive process analysis aimed at identifying interpersonal and intrapersonal variables associated with personal change and the empowerment of the individual as a creative, responsible citizen of the world community. He is especially interested in forms of research that can be done by the individual practitioner on a small budget to inform the practitioner directly as well as contributing to the body of general knowledge. In 1989, Iberg launched a writer-centered reading and publication network intended to stimulate writing and revision guided by writers and readers, rather than controlled by a few specialized editors.

References

Gendlin, E. T. (1962). *Experiencing and the creation of meaning.* New York: Free Press of Glencoe.

Gendlin, E. T. (1964). A theory of personality change. In P. Worchel & D. Byrne (Eds.), *Personality change.* New York: Wiley.

Gendlin, E. T. (1979). Befindlichkeit: Heidegger and the philosophy of psychology. *Review of Existential Psychology & Psychiatry, 16,* 44–71.

Gendlin, E. T. (1981). *Focusing* (2nd ed.). New York: Bantam.

Goldstein, K. (1939). *The organism.* New York: American Book Company.

Rogers, C. R. (1957). The necessary and sufficient conditions of therapeutic personality change. *Journal of Consulting Psychology, 21,* 95–103.

Rogers, C. R. (1959). A theory of therapy, personality, and interpersonal relationships, as developed in the client-centered framework. In S. Koch (Ed.), *Psychology: A study of a science* (Vol. 3, pp. 184–256). New York: McGraw-Hill.

Section 3
Gestalt Approaches

Gestalt Therapy

Miriam Polster
Erving Polster

Definition

Gestalt psychotherapy is a specialized interaction between therapist and patient directed toward the resolution of troublesome aspects of the patient's life. The life experiences of the patient are spotlighted through a variety of procedures, including dialogues and exercises, that are designed to make vivid those behaviors and feelings which, either through presence or absence, are contributing to dissatisfaction. The arousal and perspective that accompany these illuminations are springboards to making necessary changes.

Qualification Statement

The work of a Gestalt therapist is based on three major concepts: *contact, awareness,* and *experiment.* The first of these, contact, takes account of the obvious fact that each person *must* meet the world outside himself in order to survive. His psychological well-being depends on the quality of these contacts. Contact is established through a number of natural functions; seeing, hearing, touching, moving, talking, smelling, and tasting. Good-quality contact varies considerably among different people and may even vary considerably from time to time in the same individual.

Awareness, the second concept, refers to the specific experiences that inform each person about what is going on internally or environmentally. Awareness arouses the individual to action and provides a sense of the completion and the consequences of action. It is a fluid process, consisting of a sequence of figures that are focally compelling and perceived against a less articulated ground.

Neurotic interruption of the flow of awareness results from the individual's mistrust of himself or his environment. The individual interferes with the flow of awareness because he is unwilling to risk experiencing what appears dangerous—even though the familiar is already unsatisfying and the unknown might actually prove nourishing.

The Gestalt therapist works to reawaken the rhythm between awareness and engagement by attending to the individual's awareness at any of a number of levels: sensation, wants, actions, feelings, or values. She focuses the patient's attention on these ingredients of experience—accentuating and amplifying them until expressive interaction occurs and the patient's native surge toward completion of previously unfinished situations asserts itself. Throughout this process, attention must be paid to the ability of the patient to support himself in such interactions.

The Gestalt experiment, the third concept, seeks to redress the imbalance between fixity and action by integrating the possibilities for action into the therapeutic process. The experiment creates what Perls called a "safe emergency" where tentative exploration can be governed and supported. Dialogue, movement, body work, fantasy, and enactment are all valuable techniques that, when used appropriately, promote the transcendence of restrictive past experience. In the relative safety of the therapist's office, the patient is free to improvise ways to move from awareness to appropriate action and contact. This sequential process constitutes good function.

The experiment is not simply a facile technique to be applied indiscriminately, irrespective of person or timing. The reciprocal components of safety (support) and emergency (risk) call for careful attention, so the patient is neither blasted into experiences that are too threatening nor allowed to stay in safe but infertile territory.

In sum, these three major concepts — contact, awareness, experiment — provide the Gestalt therapist with a broad spectrum of therapeutic options. These options range from the creation of a diverse repertoire of techniques, based on the specific needs of each individual patient, to the exercise of simple human engagement. Underlying all of these therapeutic alternatives is the intent to restore the vitality of the interaction between the patient and his world.

Critique Statement

Gestalt therapy has made a unique contribution to psychotherapy in the areas of technique versus simple humanity, content versus process, and experience versus meaning. Although the positions taken in Gestalt therapy with respect to these dimensions served to counteract particular areas of neglect and abuse evident by the late 1940s, they spawned neglects and abuses of their own.

Technique Versus Simple Humanity. People in psychological trouble have found ordinary human engagement inadequate to solve their problems. It lacks both the precision and the impact to develop the powerful leverage required for psychological change.

Psychoanalysis demonstrated that certain techniques — such as hypnosis, free association, and interpretation — were useful instruments for deepening and enlarging experiences beyond encounters. The next breakthroughs in technique came much later, and Gestalt therapy was one of the greatest innovators with its technique-rich concepts: the experiment, the emphasis on the awareness continuum, and the focus on immediate contact. These techniques dramatically extended technical opportunities. Talking to empty chairs, practicing speech and language styles, doing breathing exercises, confronting people pointedly — these and many other keys to new experience were geared to enter the core of personhood. But the core of personhood is tantalizingly elusive — and these same techniques often deflected individuals from harmonizing psychotherapeutic realizations with everyday naturalness. Although these Gestalt techniques were powerful instruments, they often became trite gestures of premature change. This is a risk that all techniques run — and Gestalt therapy was no exception. Its techniques often were applied indiscriminately, and too often they lost connection with the methodology as a whole.

Content Versus Process. Influenced by Wilhelm Reich's recognition that *how* people behaved was at least as important as *why,* Gestalt therapy became absorbed in the *process* of therapy. Concern with process factors — such as expressive mannerisms, authenticity, relevance, and effectiveness of communications — overshadowed *what* the patient was actually talking about. Gestalt therapists became wary of saying things the wrong way or going on fruitlessly about troublesome life experiences. Although these concerns helped to speed up therapy and make communication more relevant to the total process, in the final analysis one cannot ignore the content of people's lives.

Experience Versus Meaning. Psychoanalysis emphasized the meaning that people assigned to their experiences as a crucial factor in their well-being. Once the sources of their behavior and the distorted implications they had given childhood events were explained, people would be able to accept and incorporate these understandings, freed of the repressive barriers that disabled them.

Gestalt therapy reacted against that bias and opted to highlight experience rather than meaning. The Gestalt view did not exclude meaning but preferred meaning to evolve spontaneously as the patient's unfinished business was reengaged and could move organically toward completion. Nevertheless, this restructuring of priorities tended to divert the Gestalt therapist's attention from meaning. Since meaning is indisputably a central organizer of behavior and feeling, this shortcoming requires correction by a fuller respect and recognition of the meaning the patient makes of experience.

Biographies

Miriam Polster is codirector of the Gestalt Training Center in San Diego and assistant clinical professor in the Department of Psychiatry, School of Medicine, University of California, San

Diego. She received her Ph.D. degree (1967) from Case Western Reserve University in clinical psychology. She is coauthor with her husband, Erving Polster, of *Gestalt Therapy Integrated* (Vintage), an important text in Gestalt therapy. Miriam Polster has recently offered a perspective on the sequences through which the patient integrates discoveries made in psychotherapy into everyday experience outside the therapeutic setting. She calls this process the "integration sequence" and describes how it draws from basic Gestalt principles.

Erving Polster is codirector of the Gestalt Training Center in San Diego and associate clinical professor at the School of Medicine, University of California, San Diego. He received his Ph.D. degree (1950) from Case Western Reserve University. He recently published a new book, *Every Person's Life Is Worth a Novel* (Norton), in which he spells out the therapeutic applicability of the kinship between the novelist and the psychotherapist. Erving Polster is recognized for his emphasis on the conjunction between ordinary engagement and therapeutic technique. Humor, incisiveness, fleshing out of storyline, instruction, and explanation are among the everyday ingredients that must be transformed into the high focus that therapeutic technique requires.

Embodied Gestalt Psychotherapy

Edward W. L. Smith

Definition

Psychotherapy in the Embodied Gestalt practice is a way of personal growth. As a path of growth it focuses on the embodiment of experience, the living out of that embodied experience, and the choice for growth through a change in the way one has embodied an experience. This is existential phenomenology applied. It is also applied Taoism. Personhood is highly respected, as the subtle, delicate process of awareness is facilitated in its unfolding in the here-and-now.

Qualification Statement

The philosophical underpinnings of Embodied Gestalt practice are existentialism and its Eastern analogue, Taoism. Both address basic ontological issues — the experience of the lived moment, freedom, choice, meaning, responsibility, value. Existentialism suggests the "I-Thou" relationship for the psychotherapy encounter. Taoism suggests the discovery of "what is" as the starting point for change. It also emphasizes the coming into harmony with what is natural by removing impediments and allowing the flow that is intrinsic.

Gestalt and Reichian therapy provide the theoretical underpinnings. The basic idea is that the human being functions through homeostatic need cycles. There is a natural rhythm whereby a need arises from the background of needs and the person proceeds to satisfy that figural need, then letting it recede again to ground and allowing a new figure to emerge. Thus, there is a cycle of contact and withdrawal. A *contact episode* involves several states of development:

Need → Excitement → Emotion → Action → Interaction → Satisfaction
Following satisfaction comes the *withdrawal episode.*

Personal dysfunction can be viewed as self-interruption in the natural flow through the contact withdrawal cycle. Because of "toxic introjects" (verbal and nonverbal messages received in childhood that prohibit natural aliveness), a person may choose to avoid allowing the next step in the cycle to develop. These avoidances (or inhibitions) are existential choices of diminished aliveness, and they may occur at any combination of the seven junctures of the cycle, with specific mechanisms that operate at each of these loci. Thus, by clouding, dulling, and/or confusing awareness, one may avoid awareness of a need, of a differentiated emotion, of satisfaction, and of appropriate withdrawal. One may avoid organismic excitement by means of restricted breathing (through tension in respiratory muscles). Action may be avoided by chronic contractions in those muscles that are antagonistic to the muscles that would perform the action forbidden by the toxic introject. Potentially satisfying interaction can be avoided by several tactics.

The main goal is to facilitate clients' awareness of *where* in the cycle they self-interrupt, *how* they do so, and *what* the underlying toxic introject is that demands this. A second goal is to support their taking responsibility for their choice. By confronting the toxic introject in a psychodramatic manner, an organismic choice may be made to reinstate a natural contact/withdrawal cycle. The toxic introject is embodied in a manner that diminishes natural flow and aliveness; thus, the psychodramatic acting out of the new choice is the quintessence of a change in that embodiment. Growth occurs through experiences under conditions of heightened awareness.

As arcane as the philosophy may seem, and as complex as the theory, the methods are simple. The procedure is to observe phenomenologically, tracking the client through the cycle. At the point of self-interruption, the client is facilitated in awareness and choice. The methods include role playing, experimenting with postures and movements, direct body contact, focused breathing, sensory awakening techniques, and functional questions (for example, What are you aware of? How are you doing that?). The dictum is "Be aware, experience, express."

Critique Statement

It is both its advantage and its limitation that Embodied Gestalt practice is growth-oriented. As its advantage, this allows the practice to focus keenly on the development of the human potential. Thus the practice is suitable for facilitating movement from an ordinary level of functioning to an extraordinary level, as well as from a level of dysfunction to the level of ordinary functioning. Growth, in this approach, involves awareness both as a method and as a criterion. However, awareness takes time to develop. In some situations symptomatic cure and behavioral change may be accomplished more quickly by other means. In some other therapies, awareness is not required for effective outcome with symptoms and undesirable behaviors.

In Embodied Gestalt practice issues of transference and countertransference often are left in the background. By the nature of the practice, attention tends to be on the client's personal process, with the practitioner as facilitator at points of self-interruption. This does not tend to bring forth transference and countertransference in as obvious or blatant a manner as is the case with certain therapies. Many would see this as a frequently lost opportunity in this practice.

A related limitation is that this practice does not encourage client regression for reparenting. Regressive reparenting may be a procedure of choice in the case of some severe characterological disorders. In this practice the role is more that of a guru than that of a parent.

In the group format, this practice focuses on the individual-in-environment process rather than on group process. Group process remains ground, unless a group issue reaches the threshold of interruption to the individual process. Thus, the potential benefits of group process work and analysis of group dynamics often are lost.

Embodied Gestalt practice is noncoercive. It may be confrontational, at times, but only in terms of firmly pointing out an avoidance. It does not offer either the pressure for change or the powerful backup that is needed in many cases of criminal behavior and substance addiction. If someone needs a period of external locus of control, this practice is not a good choice. It does not offer a high degree of structure.

This practice requires a commitment to growth-oriented experiencing. The client who benefits most is one who has at least a modicum of self-curiosity, values intraception, and enjoys working on herself or himself through experiments and disciplined activities. When these qualities are not present in the client, this practice will be of limited value.

Embodied Gestalt practice eschews advice giving, interpretation, and strategic manipulation. To many this would be seen as severely limiting. Learning is viewed in the practice as self-discovery. To paraphrase Fritz Perls, personal truth can best be tolerated if you discover it yourself, because then the pride of discovery makes the truth palatable.

Biography

Edward W. L. Smith is an independent practitioner in Atlanta, Georgia, specializing in adult psychotherapy, psychotherapy training, and case consultation. He holds an adjunct professorship in clinical psychology at Georgia State University. He received his Ph.D. degree (1969) from the University of Kentucky in clinical psychology. He has served as an external committee member for Antioch International, Fielding Institute, and the Union for Experimenting Colleges and Universities. He is a fellow of the American Psychological Association through the Division of Psychotherapy and a member of the American Academy of Psychotherapy, the Association for Humanistic Psychology, and the Southeastern and the Georgia Psychological Associations. Smith has published more than fifty professional articles and book chapters. His books include, as editor, *The Growing Edge of Gestalt Therapy* (1976) and, as author, *The Body in Psychotherapy* (1985), *Sexual Aliveness* (1987), and *Not Just Pumping Iron: On the Psychology of Lifting Weights* (1989). He has served on the editorial boards of the *Journal of Couples Therapy, Pilgrimage,* and *Voices.*

Recommended Reading

Smith, E. (1985). *The body in psychotherapy.* Jefferson, NC: McFarland.

4

Behavioral Psychotherapy

In its broadest scope, behavioral approaches conceive of all behavior as learned responses, characterizing even emotional responses as behaviors. Classical conditioning, per Pavlov's famous work, asserts that a novel or conditioned stimulus (a bell)
acquires a learned or conditioned response (salivation) when experienced contiguously with a previously known, unconditioned
stimulus (food) that elicits a natural, unconditioned response
(salivation). Instrumental conditioning reinforces behavior that
increasingly approximates the desired behavior during the learning process. Extinction is, inelegantly stated, the unlearning of
a response through one of several learning-based methods. The
units-of-analysis, then, are primarily the target behavior and
its characteristics (duration, strength, frequency). Also emphasized are contexts in which the behavior does (or does not) occur, reinforcers (positive and negative), and the backlog of research most relevant to the problem as conceived.

Behavior therapy has a rich history that is largely empirically
based. Its origins are found in animal research in Russia (Pavlov's work on the conditioned reflex) and in America (E. L.
Thorndike's puzzle box). John B. Watson's objectivism, a reaction to consciousness-oriented functionalism and structuralism,
favored research based in controlled scientific observation and

is a cornerstone of modern behaviorism. E. L. Thorndike, C. L. Hull, O. H. Mowrer, and B. F. Skinner all built upon Watson's work, developing principles and theories of learning and behavior that ultimately spawned behaviorally based treatments.

Two fundamental principles have carried through from the earliest developments in behavioral thinking: (1) that an emphasis on science and empirical validation is essential in expanding knowledge; and (2) that directly observable behavior is a focus preferable to reported subjective experience and the all-too-abstract concepts of "conscious" and "unconscious" minds. The current chapter addresses these two principles in two sections, one focusing on empirical thought and one on practical application.

The section on empirical thought examines three perspectives stressing the importance of empirical validation in any psychotherapeutic endeavor. E. Lakin Phillips reviews some of the more salient research on therapy outcomes and emphasizes the impact of the service delivery system. John J. Furedy echoes traditional behavioral values in elaborating the need for specific effects research in any therapeutic approach. Similarly, Paul Emmelkamp espouses a quasi-eclectic approach that allows for varied treatment modalities provided the primary behavioral imperative (validation of efficacy) is observed.

In the section on practical application three specific behavioral interventions are reviewed. Joseph Cautela and Albert Kearney discuss covert conditioning, a learning-based intervention utilizing imagery. Thomas Stampfl describes implosive therapy, which relies on the Pavlovian principle of experimental extinction. Steven Hayes presents a method that deals with mediating cognitive systems as conditioned behaviors.

This chapter is far from complete, both in detailing the evolution of behavioral thought and in describing the variety of interventions that have resulted from developments within the discipline. Technically, treatments currently range from purely behavioral (systematic desensitization) to a blend of cognitive and behavioral formulations. The goal of this chapter is to illustrate how behavioral theory functions in one of the only arenas where psychotherapy can truly be termed a science.

Section 1
Empirical Thought

The Delivery System as
Prime Therapeutic Determinant

E. Lakin Phillips

Definition

Psychotherapy is an interactive, interpersonal process most cogently defined by the *conditions* under which it occurs. Emphasis is not on process but on how the interaction is arranged (or encouraged). Psychotherapies largely yield similar results, hence commonalities reside in the conditions, not internally in the patient or therapist. Individual aspects yield to conditions of therapy presentation. Traditionally therapy definitions depend upon personal characteristics; this one resides in the *circumstances*.

Qualification Statement

The vast literature on psychotherapy (and its evaluation) can be summarized, in part, as follows. First, all therapies produce about the same results with minor exceptions; for instance, behavior therapies excel with at least minor phobias (Smith, Glass, and Miller, 1980). Second, short-term therapies appear to equal or better long-term ones (Koss & Butcher, 1986). Third, no therapies show a wide or decisive advantage for any type of complaint or diagnosis (Parloff, 1980). Fourth, therapies have concentrated on YAVIS (young, attractive, verbal, intelligent, single) types and not addressed the whole population of needy people in society (Bloom, 1981; Parad, 1971; Veroff et al., 1981).

115

Fifth, the attrition curve defining how people use psychotherapy services is a negatively accelerating, declining decay curve,
heretofore ignored or not discerned (Phillips, 1985), and this
curve forces new demands on psychotherapy theories and practices. Sixth, no variables assigned to *individual* clients (among
depth theories) have shown acceptable validity (Garfield & Bergin, 1971, 1978, 1986), but these concepts have dominated the
literature without being robust enough to account for more than
about 10–20 percent of the variance in outcome (Luborsky,
Singer, & Luborsky, 1975; Shapiro & Shapiro, 1983). Seventh,
the profession of psychotherapy has shown a dearth of research
on client outcome ratings and emphasized professional ratings,
which often dismiss important data from evaluation and propa-
gate sizeable patient-therapist discrepancies in evaluation, thereby
reducing the generality of findings (Strupp & Hadley, 1978; Phillips, 1985). Eighth, no hypotheses about relevant *psychotherapy*
(or interaction) variables have accounted for more than 10–20
percent of the outcome variance (Luborsky et al., 1975; Shapiro
& Shapiro, 1983). Ninth, short-term therapies are seldom theory-
driven, whereas long-term therapies have a theory overload lacking empirical support (Koss & Butcher, 1986; Parad, 1971;
Bloom, 1981), although psychotherapy has been mostly guided
by depth notions. Tenth, outcome predictions of psychotherapy (all variables, all participants) are unable to account for more
than 10–20 percent of the variance, a set of facts most therapists
seem to disregard. Eleventh, nearly all training for therapy—
all professions—has emphasized the depth model and eschewed
alternative hypotheses. Twelfth, the delivery system has been
almost totally neglected as a contributor to psychotherapy theory and practice (Phillips, 1985).

These twelve points summarize most features of traditional
therapy; they call for a new model that integrates research, theory, training, and policy. The delivery system defines the circumstances in which therapy occurs from intake to termination.
These circumstances are atheoretical and their natural limits
(for example, the attrition curve) suggest that any approach,
irrespective of theoretical origin, must recognize and operate

within those limits. Research agendas therefore should begin with examining the delivery system.

The main theoretical posture here is behavioral. Behaviors, normal or otherwise, are either learned or inherited and are integrated into functional relationships by the culture. Cultures produce thousands of personal traits, some of which are in conflict with others and with cultural values (standards, morals, mores, ethics). Psychotherapy is one way in which persons can address these conflicts and help overcome their effects. If there is no conflict, there is no problem; psychopathology derives only from conflict.

The twelve-item literature review above indicates that the thousands of characteristics people exhibit are related to their problems in some ways, are in constant flux, and always interact with each other and with the culture. None of these characteristics has been shown to be dominant. People (theorists, philosophers, moralists) select now one, now another characteristic or combination of characteristics as pivotal (Ellis's belief system, Freud's complexes); hence we now have some 400 theories of therapy. Most theorists emphasize *content*. Others largely avoid content (Rogers, the behaviorists). Most treatment theories arise from a personality-oriented or content-oriented base and in turn are fueled by personality therapy. The majority of client cases are fertile ground for content theories of motivation, personal characteristics, and the like.

The present position asserts that none of the hundreds of theories — or their personality theory base — has a corner on knowledge; that short-term therapy approaches yield as good results as do long-term efforts; that few — if any — techniques hold decisive potential for behavior or personality change; and that most therapists treat people mostly like themselves (the first four qualification points).

Once people are in therapy, the therapy delivery system is best described as an attritional system that people leave in a predictable pattern. This point replaces the traditional emphasis on client-therapist dyadic relationships, motivations, and so on (points five and six). Following these points, the clinic should

treat as many people as possible, emphasize the client's evaluation of outcome (tempered by social consequences), and keep
open the nature of psychotherapy used (points seven and eight).
Theories are not important and, given problems with selection,
attrition, and outcome, are not now even possible; they have
shown no heuristic benefits with respect to case selection, process,
or outcome (points nine and ten). To paraphrase Thomas Kuhn,
therapy proliferation points to confusion, not fruitfulness (points
eleven and twelve).

Clinic policies, therapist training, and research emphasis
should all derive from the characteristics of the delivery system.
We may well view all therapy as depending upon how it is *arranged*
(for example, the time limits), and this is best described by the
delivery system in action. Individual characteristics submit to
the system, which accounts for most of the variance and is more
amenable to change than client-therapist characteristics. Process
reduces to flow-through-the-system and control of the asymp-
tote. Outcome derives mainly from client satisfaction and subsequent social adjustment. Alternative short-term therapy efforts
are encouraged. Research on the whole delivery system will identify the best therapies. Therapy will become democratic, objective, open, nondoctrinaire, more easily researched, and more
ably connected with physical health problems and medicine.

Biography

E. Lakin Phillips is professor of psychology emeritus, George
Washington University, Washington, D.C. He received his
Ph.D. degree (1949) from the University of Minnesota. He is
a fellow of the American Psychological Association (American
Board of Professional Psychology, Clinical Psychology, Division
29, Psychotherapy) and a fellow in the American Association
for the Advancement of Behavior Therapy. He has published
seventeen books and approximately 200 papers and professsional
association presentations. Phillips started the School for Contemporary Education (and remains its executive director), a
school for all types of handicapped children that follows behavior
modification programs.

References

Bloom, B. L. (1981). Focused single-session therapy: Initial development and evaluation. In S. H. Budman (Ed.), *Forms of brief therapy.* New York: Guilford.

Garfield, S. L., & Bergin, A. E. (Eds.). (1971). *Handbook of psychotherapy and behavior change.* New York: Wiley.

Garfield, S. L., & Bergin, A. E. (Eds.). (1978). *Handbook of psychotherapy and behavior change: An empirical analysis* (2nd ed.). New York: Wiley.

Garfield, S. L., & Bergin, A. E. (Eds.). (1986). *Handbook of psychotherapy and behavior change* (3rd ed.). New York: Wiley.

Koss, M. P., & Butcher, J. N. (1986). Research on brief psychotherapy. In S. L. Garfield & A. E. Bergin (Eds.), *Handbook of psychotherapy and behavior change* (3rd ed.). New York: Wiley.

Luborsky, L., Singer, B., & Luborsky, L. (1975). Comparative studies of psychotherapy. *Archives of General Psychiatry, 32,* 995–1008.

Parad, L. G. (1971). Short-term treatment: An overview of historical trends, issues, and potentials. *Smith College Studies in Social Work, 41,* 119–146.

Parloff, M. B. (1980). Psychotherapy and research: An anaclitic depression. *Psychiatry, 43,* 279–273.

Phillips, E. L. (1985). *Psychotherapy revised: New frontiers in research and practice.* Hillsdale, NJ: Erlbaum.

Shapiro, D. A., & Shapiro, D. (1983). Comparative therapy outcome research: Methodological implications of meta-analysis. *Journal of Consulting and Clinical Psychology, 51,* 42–53.

Smith, M. L., Glass, G. V., & Miller, T. I. (1980). *The benefits of psychotherapy.* Baltimore: Johns Hopkins University Press.

Strupp, H. H., & Hadley, S. W. (1978). Specific vs. nonspecific factors in psychotherapy: A controlled study of outcome. *Archives of General Psychiatry, 36,* 1125–2236.

Veroff, J., Kulka, R. A., & Douvan, E. (1981). *Mental health in America.* New York: Basic Books.

Biofeedback and the Case for Pure Empirical Validation

John J. Furedy

Definition

Psychotherapy is a psychological procedure that results in an improvement in the functioning of the patient. The procedure may involve nonpsychological aspects, but it is the psychological component that is the essential component. To the extent that the procedure is to be considered to have a scientific basis, it must be specifiable as a set of repeatable operations that can be transmitted cognitively, and evidence must be adduced that it is the procedure and not other unspecifiable (placebo) factors that have produced the improvement. So, for example, biofeedback therapy has to be shown to be beneficial in terms of its specific effects, that is, an improvement produced at least partly through the provision of biofeedback information to the patient. On the other hand, there is no requirement that the *mechanism* through which the beneficial effect operates be of a certain type (for example, cognitive processing, voluntariness, conditioning, or self-actualization).

Qualification Statement

The theoretical basis of my position is that all therapies (be they psychological, physiological, or, as is most common, a complex interaction of the two) should be evaluated in terms of the same specific-effects logic. This logic is illustrated by the methods used in pharmacological medicine to evaluate the specific effects of drugs by double-blind arrangements that separate the placebo effects (which are not themselves studied or manipulated) from the drug's specific effects.

It is important to stress that the distinction between placebo and specific effects is not an absolute one, but rather is *relative* to what is being evaluated. In the pharmacological example, it is pharmacological effects that are being evaluated, and hence the psychological effects are placebo, even though these psychological effects are just as real, are equally worthy of study in another context, and may even be more powerful than pharmacological effects in particular situations.

Similarly, if it is biofeed*back* that is being evaluated, then we are concerned with the increase of control over involuntary functions that is gained through the feed*back* information delivered through the instrumentation to the patient. Other factors such as feed*forward* information, relaxation techniques, and therapist-patient rapport may be very powerful but, for the purposes of evaluating biofeed*back,* are part of the placebo.

The mark of a science-based technology is that it relies on specific rather than placebo effects, and that its efficacy is evaluated in terms of the former rather than the (evanescent and culture-bound) latter effects. In the case of biofeedback, the alternative, snake-oil approach is evidenced by a refusal to define the term biofeedback with any specificity and by a reliance on placebo effects in evaluating biofeedback treatments. The no-feedback, the best-alternative treatment, and even the bidirectional control conditions are instances of the implicit use of such unscientific, snake-oil logic, and it bears emphasis that these pseudo-control conditions are employed not only by clinicians but by the majority of basic researchers who, for other phenomena, employ much more sophisticated control methodologies. This means that even in the basic-research literature, there has been little or no progress in understanding the phenomenon of biofeedback. However, it is also important to recognize that the *clinical* evaluation of biofeedback can only be done in the clinic. The laboratory can merely provide hypotheses about clinical methods, which then have to be evaluated in terms of a science-based approach.

The failure to adopt a science-based approach to biofeedback technology means that behavioral medicine is unable to evaluate whether biofeedback of a particular system works. Moreover, even in cases where biofeedback does seem to have marked effects (for example, treatment of muscular dysfunction), it is not possible to evaluate the relative merits of *alternative* biofeedback treatment modes. This is a serious problem, because biofeedback is by no means a standardized procedure as regards such aspects as feedback density, sensory modality (auditory versus visual), and so on. On the other hand, many clinicians believe that science-based, pharmacology-type, double-blind, specific-effects (that is, noncontingent or so-called false-feedback) control is unfeasible. However, it is possible to adapt the specific-effects control to yield procedures that are practical, yet still allow the clinical community to evaluate biofeedback treatments in a scientific way.

Critique Statement

In addition to the criticism that it is unfeasible, the specific-effects control for biofeedback has been criticized by clinicians for being unethical, inasmuch as it withholds the treatment from some patients. But this ignores the fact that the conditions can be compared *within* subjects, so that the ethical problems involved when one adopts a specific-effects orientation are, in connection with biofeedback training, quite negligible. On the other hand, I would argue that for groups of professionals who wish to present their technology as based on scientific principles, it is ethically important to adopt modes of evaluation that are scientific.

As to feasibility, we have recently provided (Furedy, Shulhan, & Levy, 1989) a discussion of five concrete, clinically relevant areas (alpha feedback, heart-rate deceleration, muscular control, headache control, and myopia control via accommodation feedback) in which specific-effects-oriented evaluative research is being done or planned so that the evaluation of treatments will be based on knowledge rather than opinion.

It is also important to recognize that when I argue for the *elimination* of placebo factors in the evaluation of a particular therapy, I mean elimination in the experimental-control sense. So, in a pharmacological control test of a drug, it is the *differential* effect of placebo that is eliminated by the double-blind procedure, and not the placebo factor itself. A caricature of my position is that version which demands that nonbiofeedback factors like enthusiasm should be absolutely eliminated from therapy for the evaluation of biofeedback. But this caricature is plainly absurd. I am all for the enthusiasm on the part of the therapist, but it must be shown that the beneficial effect of biofeedback is due to more than this enthusiasm, which must be kept equal between the biofeedback (experimental) and non-biofeedback (control) conditions, a requirement which seems to imply a double-blind arrangement.

Another distinction that is important is that between the *administration* of a therapy by the *individual* practitioner (which is an art, and for which anything that the practitioner feels is useful may well be employed), and the *evaluation* of a particular sort of therapy by the clinical *community* (which must be scientific). It is only by scientific evaluation that we can continue to improve particular therapies with respect to the parameters involved both in them (for example, duration, intensity, and so on) and in the patient population (for example, determining which sort of patients are most likely to benefit).

In the short term, it may seem expedient to base positions on placebo factors like enthusiasm. It may even be that the voices of the few unpopular advocates for the most scientific approach are drowned out by those of the enthusiasts in the profession. In the long haul, however, the enthusiasm-based approach is counterproductive for the therapeutic profession. This is both because there are more quacks than true psychotherapists out there, and because the demagogic political skills of the quacks are superior to those of qualified psychotherapists.

Biography

John J. Furedy is professor of psychology at the University of Toronto, Canada. He received his Ph.D. degree in psychology (1966) from the University of Sydney, Australia. He is the recipient of numerous awards, including the Award for Research Excellence from the Pavlovian Society of North America. He has lectured on visiting appointments in Australia, Hungary,

Israel, Japan, Norway, the United Kingdom, the United States, West Germany, Sweden, and Switzerland and serves as associate editor on three journals and as occasional consulting editor on twenty-five others. Furedy has authored approximately 300 articles, book chapters, reviews, and letters to the editor in scientific publications concerned with psychophysiology, classical conditioning, motivation, and philosophy of science. Recently he has authored several conceptual papers concerning two applications of psychophysiology: biofeedback and lie detection. He argues for a specific-effects approach in the evaluation of these and other applications of psychology.

Recommended Reading

Furedy, J. J. (1980). Conditioning of phasic but large-magnitude heart-rate decelerations in humans: Methods and applications. In *Biofeedback and Meditation: Proceedings of the Biofeedback Research Society Meetings, 1977* (in Japanese), K. Ishakawa (Ed.), Seishin Shobo, Japan.

Furedy, J. J. (1983). Attaining autonomic calming through behavioral control: A response-learning approach. In A. Krakowski and C. Kimball (Eds.), *Psychosomatic medicine: theoretical, clinical, and transcultural aspects* (pp. 765–772). New York: Plenum.

Furedy, J. J. (1987a). On some research-community contributions to the myth and symbol of biofeedback. *International Journal of Psychophysiology, 4,* 293–297.

Furedy, J. J. (1987b). Specific versus placebo effects in biofeedback training: A critical lay perspective. *Biofeedback and Self-Regulation, 12,* 169–182.

Furedy, J. J., & Riley, D. M. (1981). Review of A. J. Yates, *Biofeedback and the modification of behavior. Biological Psychology, 14,* 149–152.

Furedy, J. J., & Riley, D. M. (1982). Classical and operant conditioning in the enhancement of biofeedback: Specifics and speculations. L. White and B. Tursky (Eds.), *Clinical biofeedback: efficacy and mechanisms.* New York: Guilford. Invited paper for closed-sessions research symposium on Clinical Biofeedback-Efficacy and Mechanisms, State University of New York at Stony Brook, May 1980.

Furedy, J. J., & Scher, H. (1985). On the decline of audience participation at SPR: The unexamined session is not worth attending. *Psychophysiology, 22,* 369.

Furedy, J. J., & Shulhan, D. (1987). Specific versus placebo effects in biofeedback: Some brief back-to-basics considerations. *Biofeedback and Self-Regulation, 12,* 211–215.

Riley, D. M., & Furedy, J. J. (1982). A reply to Mulholland. In L. White and B. Tursky (Eds.), *Clinical biofeedback: Efficacy and mechanisms.* New York: Guilford.

Riley, D. M., & Furedy, J. J. (1982). The theoretical and practical importance of making distinctions in psychophysiology. Paper presented at the International Organization of Psychophysiology meeting, Montreal.

Reference

Furedy, J. J., Shulhan, D., & Levy, B. (1989). The specific-effects logic of evaluation: Some examples analyzed. *Medical Psychotherapy, 2,* 103–113.

An Experimental Clinical Approach

Paul M. G. Emmelkamp

Definition

Psychotherapy is the application of scientifically evaluated procedures that enable people to change their maladaptive behaviors, emotions, and cognitions themselves.

Qualification Statement

It is my firm belief that psychotherapy would best proceed unencumbered by parochial adherence to one specific theory.

In my view, psychotherapy should be based on experimental evidence with real clinical patients rather than on orthodoxy or faith. Among the hundreds of varieties of psychotherapy, few have a strong empirical base to support their claims, with behavior therapy having the best record (Garfield & Bergin, 1986).

Behavior therapy is marked by its adherence to scientific methods in evaluating its results. While in the early days behavior therapy was defined as "the application of established laws of learning," more recently behavior therapy has become broader in its conceptualization. The claim that established behavior therapy procedures are exclusively based on learning paradigms seems nowaways to be no longer tenable. The experimental literature does not support such a claim; rather, it shows that additional factors such as cognitive processes play an important role (Emmelkamp, 1986). Some behavior therapists now rely heavily on mediational concepts in explaining the effects of the therapeutic procedures.

At present at least four schools of behavior therapy can be distinguished. There are first, those therapists who still view behavior therapy as the application of "learning theory" (for example, Eysenck); second, those who rely heavily on mediational concepts (for example, Bandura); and third, a school comprised of technical eclecticists or multimodel behavior therapists, who use whatever technique seems to work (for example, Lazarus). Finally, there is a category of workers (I am one) who view behavior therapy as an experimental-clinical process. The latter group does not adhere to one specific theory but stresses the necessity of testing theories and evaluating treatment with real clinical patients as subjects. Thus, this behavioral approach is characterized by its emphasis on methodology instead of a specific theoretical orientation. This is not to say that learning theories or cognitive theories have been abandoned by the proponents of the experimental-clinical approach; rather, they hold that their status as principles that explain the development and treatment of disorders must be empirically verified with clinical patients instead of taken for granted.

As stated in my definition, psychotherapy should not be restricted to one specific modality (such as behavioral). For example, research has now shown that focusing on the cognitive modality alone is of little or no value in the treatment of agoraphobics, while obsessive-compulsive, social phobics, and major depressives have been found to respond well to procedures dealing with both the cognitive and behavioral modalities.

The final clause of my definition refers to my subjective value system. I don't believe in a behavioral technology with therapists as superhuman technicians who change behavior, cognitions, and moods of patients more or less automatically. As emphasized in my definition, the client's role is that of a collaborator in (rather than an object of) the therapists' technology: The most potent of techniques is useless without the cooperation and motivation of the patient.

Critique Statement

1. *Criticism:* Broadening the scope of psychotherapy beyond a specific theoretical framework would lead to more or less random trial and error in treatment.

   Rebuttal: Therapies may be derived from a variety of theoretical sources, but the proof of the pudding is the accountability of treatment with specific, well-defined clinical populations.

2. *Criticism:* Such research is an expensive undertaking, and given the many forms of psychotherapy that are available today, evaluating them all would be an impossible task.

   Rebuttal: It is obvious that an attempt to evaluate all psychotherapies currently on the market is not a feasible project, and in my view not necessary at all. At the moment relatively few approaches already have sufficient accountability to justify a more rigorous evaluation. These few partially validated approaches need to be more thoroughly evaluated, and preliminary research should be begun on approaches that appear to be most effective but are, as yet, unvalidated. It is curious that society requires that the effects of drugs be thoroughly evaluated before they are prescribed but does not apply the same standards with respect to the prescription of psychotherapy.

3. *Criticism:* Many if not most problems that arise in therapy cannot be addressed at all by specific findings from laboratory research.

    Rebuttal: There is some truth in this statement. Indeed, laboratory research with *non*clinical subjects is often irrelevant with respect to therapy with real patients. Subject samples consisting only of slightly distressed individuals are quite susceptible to experimental demand and decrease the chances that the results of such studies will generalize to actual clinical populations. This does not imply that evaluative research is worthless; rather, it underscores that such studies have to be conducted with clinically distressed populations.

4. *Criticism:* The therapist tends to become only a technician, mechanically applying a variety of procedures without individual prescription.

    Rebuttal: This is a naive position with respect to what actually occurs in therapy. While research may indicate which procedure or combination of procedures may best be prescribed in particular cases, psychotherapy research already has demonstrated that such procedures are most likely to be successful when applied in a warm, understanding, therapeutic context. Thus, the therapeutic techniques to be used, whatever they may be for a given person, must be embedded in a therapeutic relationship.

5. *Criticism:* The experimental-clinical approach of psychotherapy is the same as electicism.

    Rebuttal: This is clearly untrue. The fact that two therapists are eclectics does not mean that their therapeutic work is comparable. As shown by Garfield (1988) and Lazarus (1988), individual eclectic therapists have different opinions about which procedures or methods they think will work best with specific patients. In contrast, the experimental-clinical approach results in identical treatment procedures across individual therapists, since decisions are based on research data rather than on clinical hunches or personal preferences.

Biography

Paul Emmelkamp is professor of clinical psychology and psychotherapy and heads the Department of Clinical Psychology at the University of Groningen, the Netherlands. He received his Ph.D. degree (1975) from the University of Utrecht, the Netherlands. He serves on the editorial board of seven journals and is past president of the European Association for Behaviour Therapy. Emmelkamp has written and edited ten books and has authored numerous articles and book chapters. His research interests include anxiety disorders, depression, marital distress, parental rearing style and psychopathology, and (failures in) behavior therapy.

References

Emmelkamp, P. (1986). Behavior therapy with adults. In S. L. Garfield & A. E. Bergin (Eds.), *Handbook of psychotherapy and behavior change*. New York: Wiley.

Garfield, S. L. (1988). Towards a scientifically oriented eclecticism. In P. M. G. Emmelkamp, W. T. A. M. Everaerd, F. Kraaimaat, and M. van Son (Eds.), *Annual series of European research in behaviour therapy: Vol. 3. Advances in theory and research in behaviour therapy*. Amsterdam, the Netherlands: Swets.

Garfield, S. L., & Bergin, A. E. (1986). Introduction and historical overview. In S. L. Garfield & A. E. Bergin (Eds.), *Handbook of psychotherapy and behavior change*. New York: Wiley.

Lazarus, A. A. (1988). Eclecticism in behavior therapy. In P. M. G. Emmelkamp, W. T. A. M. Everaerd, F. Kraaimaat, and M. van Son (Eds.), *Annual series of European research in behaviour therapy: Vol. 3. Advances in theory and research in behaviour therapy*. Amsterdam, the Netherlands: Swets.

Section 2
Practical Application

Covert Conditioning

Joseph R. Cautela
Albert J. Kearney

Definition

Psychotherapy is the process of assisting the individual in learning more adaptive behavioral patterns to increase the effectiveness of functioning within the culture. These changes in behavioral patterns take place through the process of learning and are not limited solely to overt behavior but also include covert and physiological behavior.

Qualification Statement

An individual's behavior is constantly being modified by interaction with the physical and social environment according to principles of learning. In the therapeutic context the behavior therapist plans systematic, efficient activities, with the client's knowledge and consent, to help modify behavior in the manner desired by the client.

The client's behaviors that are subject to this influence can be considered as occurring on three levels: (1) overt behavior, such as walking, talking, or hitting a golf ball, (2) covert physiological behavior, such as the activity of internal organs, and (3) covert psychological behavior, such as thoughts, images, and feelings. Behaviors of each of these classes are functionally equivalent, interact with each other, and can influence each other. The process through which these behaviors are influenced or modified is learning. Therefore, the role of the therapist is largely that of teacher. That is, assessment of what the client has already learned and needs to learn next; planning the most practical, efficient, and effective treatment for helping the client acquire new skills; implementing the therapeutic instructional program; and evaluating the learning that has taken place and the effectiveness of the program.

A general goal of psychotherapy should be to help the client acquire self-control procedures that will be useful in dealing with problems, thereby decreasing dependence on the therapist and increasing the client's competence, independence, self-control skills, and self-confidence. A second general goal should be to help the client to increase the general level of reinforcement (Cautela, 1984) in his or her life.

The process of behavior therapy often involves the use of therapeutic interventions based on imagery such as covert conditioning (Cautela & Kearney, 1986), systematic desensitization (Wolpe, 1982), and implosive therapy (Stampfl & Levis, 1967). These interventions are based on principles of learning (such as operant conditioning, reciprocal inhibition, extinction, and modeling), with both target behaviors and consequences experienced by the client in imagery. Learning that takes place on the covert psychological level transfers to the overt and covert physiological levels as well.

The client's covert psychological behaviors can be a target for change both in and of themselves and also because of their effect on overt and covert physiological behavior. Just as learning is constantly occurring on the overt level in random, unplanned, nondirected ways with subsequent impact on other classes of behavior, learning similarly occurs on the covert physiological and covert psychological levels. This process has been referred to as nondirected covert conditioning (Cautela & Kearney, 1986). The systematic, planned experience of covert events, either self-directed or therapist directed, is referred to as covert conditioning. The covert conditioning model has led to the development of several covert conditioning procedures based on their overt operant counterparts. These include covert positive reinforcement, covert negative reinforcement, covert sensitization, covert extinction, covert response cost, and covert modeling.

Additional assumptions, methods, and procedures used both in the covert conditioning approach in particular and in behavior therapy in general are treated in greater depth elsewhere (Cautela & Kearney, 1986; Cautela & Kearney, 1990).

Critique Statement

Criticisms of the covert conditioning model encompass those that are made of behavior therapy in general and those that are specific to covert conditioning. General criticisms have included charges that behavior therapy does not work; that it only treats symptoms, not the real problem; that it is no more effective than other more traditional approaches; and that it works, but only for a limited range of problems. These general criticisms have been dealt with by others elsewhere (for example, Wolpe, 1982).

Criticisms specific to covert conditioning have come primarily from the cognitive community in recent years. Criticisms are often similar to those made of behavior therapy in general: Covert conditioning does not work; it may work but is no more effective than cognitive therapy; it works, but because of cognitive principles not learning principles; and employing it in a manner consistent with learning principles adds nothing to it.

Some research has been offered in support of the criticisms made above. Cautela and Kearney (1986) have examined these criticisms and the research purporting to support them in detail. A close examination of that research reveals two major faults. First, the treatments labeled as covert conditioning were not really covert conditioning because of misapplication or a failure to employ them as learning-based procedures in a manner consistent with and compatible with the learning operations on which they are based. Second, results were interpreted in ways consistent with the authors' biases but not called for by their own data. In general the research indicates that when covert conditioning is properly employed, it is nearly always as effective as other approaches and frequently more effective.

A major advantage of covert conditioning is the strong empirical foundation supporting the operant conditioning principles on which it is based. This provides guidelines for its proper use, ideas for novel applications, and a framework for research.

A second advantage is the reliance on imagery. This of course permits the client to engage in an almost limitless range of behaviors and experience a variety of consequences on the covert level. Clinical uses are not limited by the practical availability of relevant circumstances or the client's physical limitations. Clients with poor visual imagery skills can usually be taught to use imagery skills more effectively, and/or other sense modalities (for example, auditory imagery) may be employed with those having other learning styles.

A third advantage is the ready availability of covert conditioning procedures for self-control uses. Clients can often be taught to employ many of these procedures on their own, thereby hastening their improvement, allowing them increased independence of the therapist, and giving them a greater sense of control over their own destiny.

Biographies

Joseph Cautela is the director of the Behavior Therapy Institute, Sudbury, Massachusetts. He received his Ph.D. degree (1954) from Boston University. Cautela is a past president of the Association for Advancement of Behavior Therapy and has authored seven books and more than ninety articles in the field of behavior therapy. Cautela has been professor of psychology and director of the Behavior Modification Program at Boston College. In addition, Cautela has been the primary developer of the field of covert conditioning. This approach bridges the gap between applied behavior analysis and cognitive therapy. Whereas many proponents of traditional behavior-analytic approaches are reluctant to deal with private events and most cognitivists have been reluctant to apply operant principles to private events, the covert conditioning model successfully extends therapeutic and prosthetic applications of the laws of learning to the realm of private events.

Albert Kearney is in private practice at the Behavior Therapy Institute in Sudbury and in Newton, Massachusetts, and is the school psychologist for the Maynard, Massachusetts, public schools. He received his Ph.D. degree (1976) from Boston College. He is a past president of the New England Society of Behavior Analysis and Therapy. Among other publications, he has coauthored a book on covert conditioning and has a second in progress. Kearney's professional interests include the application of behaviorological principles to clinical practice, education, and sport psychology.

References

Cautela, J. R. (1984). General level of reinforcement. *Journal of Behavior Therapy and Experimental Psychiatry, 15,* 109–114.

Cautela, J. R., & Kearney, A. J. (1986). *The covert conditioning handbook.* New York: Springer.

Cautela, J. R., & Kearney, A. J. (1990). Overview of behavioral treatment. In M. E. Thase, B. A. Edelstein, and M. Hersen (Eds.), *Handbook of outpatient treatment of adults.* New York: Plenum.

Stampfl, T., & Levis, D. J. (1967). Essentials of implosion therapy: A learning theory based psychodynamic behavioral therapy. *Journal of Abnormal Psychology, 72,* 496–503.

Wolpe, J. (1982). *The practice of behavior therapy* (3rd ed.). New York: Pergamon.

Implosive Therapy:
A Behavioral-Psychodynamic
Avoidance Model of Psychotherapy

Thomas G. Stampfl

Definition

All psychotherapeutic approaches seek to change overt or covert behaviors that represent problems for the client. Typically, changes are sought with various listening-talking techniques reflecting the theoretical position of the therapist. Strict adherence to a learning-conditioning model suggests that the major problem behaviors are related to avoidance phenomena observed in laboratory animal research. Problem behaviors are conceptualized as variants of avoidance responding — a product of the aversive conditioning history. A complex associative network of stimuli (internal and external) is seen as the controlling agent for the problem behaviors to be modified. The Pavlovian principle of experimental extinction is employed as the main change-agent to remove or attenuate the aversiveness of the controlling stimuli. The goal of the therapist is to identify the critical aversive stimuli in the personal conditioning history. Experimental "subzero" extinction of the aversive stimuli by exposure to imaginal or real-life approximations of the relevant cue categories comprising the controlling associative stimulus network is an extremely effective means of treatment for a wide range of psychopathological disorders (problem behaviors).

Qualification Statement

Early avoidance models of psychopathology failed to fully exploit the implications of laboratory research for treatment. In general, early models deferred to what was accepted in the human

clinical literature whenever deviations existed between the laboratory model and the "facts" of the clinical literature. Implosive therapy is a consequence of simply asking what treatment
strategy would be like if one rigorously followed the principles
generated over decades of research in the animal laboratory.

The therapeutic strategies are best described by drawing a
parallel between avoidance conditioning models of the laboratory and human psychopathology. The core of human psychopathology is seen as a product of aversive conditioning events
that result from specific experiences of punishment, pain, and
frustration. A range of affective states are conditioned to the
stimuli representing the aversive events. The affective states (for
example, anxiety) provide the motivation for the various maladaptive behaviors of the client. Defenses, symptoms, and other
maladaptive behaviors function as instrumental avoidance (escape) responses that reduce or minimize the amount of anxiety
(negative affect) experienced. A complex, sequentially organized
associative network then reflects the products of the personal
conditioning history as acquired because of parental child-rearing
practices, peer group events, and naturally occurring aversive
events. Implosive therapy simply asks the following questions
of each client's problems. What might the client be avoiding?
What might the client be afraid of? What might the client be
angry about? Each of these is reduced to their stimulus equiva-
lents and interpreted in terms of the personal (or likely) conditioning history of the client. Progressive exposure to each sequential stimulus segment underlying the critical aversive events
of the personal conditioning history is then introduced. This
is accomplished by having the client engage in a vivid imaginal
fantasy enactment of stimulus themes that include the defended-
against (avoided) stimuli. Stimulus themes may include many
conflicts and other avoided or repressed material commonly
described in the traditional clinical literature (sex, aggression,
hostility, rejection, abandonment, inferiority, sibling rivalry,
and so on). Visual, auditory, and other sensory modalities form
the structure of the scenarios presented by way of fantasy enactment. Impulses or urges to act are response-produced stimuli.
They comprise a significant stimulus component in the mate-

rial experienced by the client. A wide range of cognitive and noncognitive conditioned aversive stimuli are progressively experienced in a hierarchical arrangement that spans symptom-contingent, reportable, and hypothesized cues. Such cues are experienced in the absence of primary reinforcement. Pavlovian extinction decreases the affective responses to the critical controlling stimuli. Marked behavioral changes for a wide range of psychopathological disorders (problems) are thus achieved.

Critique Statement

Evaluation of any psychotherapy requires answers to the following questions: Does the therapy generate successes in the defined populations for which it is intended? What specific techniques and procedures flow from the theoretical foundation underlying the therapy? How adequate is the theoretical foundation? What problems are associated with the use of the therapy? To what extent does the therapy conform to conceptions of the human condition as they relate to dominant therapies in current use?

Implosive therapy is a laboratory-dependent procedure relying heavily on animal experimentation for its therapeutic strategies. An unusual feature of validation of the basic theoretical structure involves unique predictions with animals derived from observations of humans treated by the therapy (Levis & Boyd, 1979; Stampfl, 1987). A substantial number of experimental outcome studies provide validation for the effectiveness of the therapy (Boudewyns & Shipley, 1983).

There are several commonly stated objections to theory and practice. To start with, the two-factor fear-avoidance model that provides the theoretical structure supporting the therapy is no longer considered a viable theory by many theorists even on the level of animal experimentation. The dissatisfaction with the two-factor theory relies mainly on a limited number of analyses made years earlier. Such analyses do not include recent advances made in the burgeoning learning-conditioning literature. Additionally, a number of undetected deficiencies were present in the early critical analyses. In brief, the critics cited "facts" that were inaccurate. They omitted key references that provide experimental answers to their objections. They failed to recognize Skinner's dictum on the necessity of combining principles to account for complex behaviors (Stampfl, 1987).

Another form of objection especially prominent among clinicians is that the human condition is so unique that any derivation from rat or pigeon research must necessarily fail to capture the essence of therapy conducted with human subjects. Such objections overlook the marked therapeutic successes already achieved with laboratory-derived principles of learning and conditioning. They also do not recognize the distinction between basic principles and form and content separating human and nonhuman animals. Basic principles may be identical for the two conditions although marked differences exist in external manifestations of the phenomena observed.

Some real difficulties exist on the level of practice. Appreciable clinical experience combined with laboratory familiarity with subtleties in avoidance responding is essential in developing fully the stimulus themes used in the fantasy enactments. This is a relatively rare combination for most therapists. Some degree of dramatic ability also is desirable to foster realism in scenes incorporating the critical stimuli. An especially important but difficult aspect of the treatment is obtaining key information in the diagnostic interviews that pinpoint the connections between symptomatic behaviors and specific aspects of the personal conditioning history. Also, many clinicians are uncomfortable with the relatively high level of emotionality that frequently accompanies the presentation of aversive stimulus themes. The objection is also made that clients would not return for further treatment. This is controverted by the low attrition rates reported by those using the therapy. In any case, reduction in emotionality usually proceeds quite rapidly with repetition within the treatment session.

Biography

Thomas G. Stampfl is professor of psychology and director of clinical training at the University of Wisconsin, Milwaukee.

He received his Ph.D. degree (1958) from Loyola University, Chicago. Stampfl developed implosive therapy as a means of linking laboratory research with problems of therapy. He is the author of many articles and chapters and strives to integrate learning principles with clinical practice and specific issues in psychopathology. He received John Carroll University's Gold Medal Award for his psychological contributions and was a nominee for the American Psychological Association's Distinguished Psychologist Award for Contributions to Psychology and Psychotherapy. He is convinced that basic principles of laboratory research combined with clinical formulations will provide solutions to other significant problem areas of human experience. An example is the development of "psychoeconomics"— a simple but powerful economic system based on the use of learning principles and clinical strategies that represents a radical departure from conventional economic theory.

Recommended Reading

Stampfl, T. G. (1970). Implosive therapy: An emphasis on covert stimulation. In D. J. Lewis (Ed.), *Learning approaches to therapeutic behavior change* (pp. 182–204). Chicago: Aldine.

Stampfl, T. G., & Levis, D. J. (1967). Essentials of implosive therapy: A learning-theory-based psychodynamic behavioral therapy. *Journal of Abnormal Psychology, 72,* 496–503.

Stampfl, T. G., & Levis, D. J. (1976). Implosive therapy: A behavioral therapy? In J. T. Spence, R. C. Carson, and J. W. Thibaut (Eds.), *Behavioral approaches to therapy* (pp. 189–210). Morristown, NJ: General Learning Press.

References

Boudewyns, P. A., & Shipley, R. H. (1983). *Flooding and implosive therapy.* New York: Plenum.

Levis, D. J., & Boyd, T. L. (1979). Symptom maintenance: An infrahuman analysis and extension of the conservation of anxiety principle. *Journal of Abnormal Psychology, 88,* 107–120.

Stampfl, T. G. (1987). Theoretical implications of the neurotic
paradox as a problem in behavior theory: An experimental
resolution. *Behavior Analyst, 10,* 161–173.

Contextual Behavior Therapy

Steven C. Hayes

Definition

In psychotherapy clients learn willingly to make contact with
the thoughts, feelings, and other behavioral reactions that emerge
in a situation; to see them as they are; and to do what works
behaviorally in that situation. Its goal is effective living in work,
play, and relationships (as process, not outcome) — not the repair
of "ill" human beings. Effective living involves both the abandonment of emotional avoidance and the development of effective action.

Qualification Statement

My therapeutic work is organized around a contextualistic,
radical, behavioral world view. All psychological phenomena
are acts in context, to be understood in terms of that relation
(that is, in terms of contingencies). The position is monistic,
functionalistic, and deterministic in a nonmechanical and prob-
abilistic sense.

Verbal rules can produce a marked insensitivity to direct contingencies of reinforcement (see, for example, Hayes, Brownstein,
Haas, & Greenway, 1986). I assume when working with clients
that their own self-verbalizations about what a situation requires
may produce an insensitivity to what the situation really requires.
The "solution" has made them insensitive to a real solution.

Work in the area of "stimulus equivalence" (by, for example, Devany, Hayes, & Nelson, 1986) reveals that human beings (but not nonhumans) readily form networks of bi-directional relations among stimuli, and that stimulus functions can transfer among these stimulus networks (Wulfert & Hayes, in press). I take this to mean that through the verbal organization of events, clients may be responding in a current situation to experiences that bear only the most remote connection to the present context. To put it directly, I view human language as the source of most psychopathology.

My goal, then, is to confront directly the edifice of human language. My allies in this effort are paradox and confusion. The goal is the loosening up of literal meaning so that a client can think a thought *as a thought,* not as an act that organizes the stimulus environment. Rather than try either to change or to ignore thoughts and feelings, I attempt to recontextualize the relation between thought or feelings and overt action.

Much of psychopathology involves the avoidance of behavioral reactions, driven by literal meaning. Some feelings are taken to be "bad" (for example, anxiety or depression). Their "badness" is taken to be in the feelings, not in the clients' relation to them. The goal of successful living is taken to be the avoidance of "bad" reactions. The problem is this: If anxiety is bad, then anxiety is something to be anxious about. Depression is something to be depressed about. However, emotional reasoning prevents effective action (for example, "I can't do 'x' because I am too anxious.").

We have developed a procedure, called comprehensive distancing, that is designed to attack this system (Hayes, 1987). The procedure undermines the attempt to control emotions by creating a state of creative hopelessness (that is, a sense that the system will never work). It uses paradox; for example, in the area of thoughts and feelings, if you are not willing to have it you've got it. It attempts to train a monistically and behaviorally sensible sense of spirituality (Hayes, 1984). All of this is combined to encourage emotional acceptance as a basis for committed living. Finally, upon this foundation are placed the more usual behavioral procedures of exposure, behavior change commitments, and homework.

Critique Statement

Our work is generally understood by radical behaviorists (that is, Skinnerians) but has received a cooler reception by cognitive-behavior therapists. They are confused by a radical behavioral interpretation of such topics as spirituality and are hostile to the notion that successful living can occur without first changing thoughts (for the cognitive therapists) or feelings (for the desensitizers).

Old-line behavior analysts said, "Ignore feelings; change behavior and the feelings and thoughts will change." Clients themselves universally resisted that idea, and it left in place the massive social support for a kind of emotional reasoning that can paralyze effective action.

Behavior therapists and cognitive behavior therapists said, "Change the feelings and thoughts and the overt behavior will change." This approach has led to a new, scientifically rationalized form of emotional repression.

Our view is that feelings and thoughts are never the enemy, and they are not ignored. The destructive relation between thoughts and feelings on the one hand and overt behavior on the other is, we believe, produced by social-verbal contexts (contexts of literality, reason giving, and emotional control). Thus, we focus on changing the context itself, not the thought or feeling (Hayes & Brownstein, 1986). This can then permit the client to feel a feeling *as a feeling* without having to have it structure overt action of any kind.

Another criticism has been that we spend too much time on thoughts and feelings and not enough on overt behavior change. Our experience has been that once the system producing such marked insensitivity to the natural contingencies is altered, behavior change can begin with much less effort and resistance. After a period of three to four months of this kind of work, we begin to move forcefully into direct behavior change.

A final criticism has come from nonbehavioral therapists who feel that the ideas our work encompasses are not behavioral. In a sense, they resent behaviorists claiming their territory. This reaction is generally based on an ignorance of the true nature of contemporary behaviorism. The work definitely *is* behavioral in the sense that it is integrated with behavioral theory and philosophy. The techniques, however, are drawn from many traditions. One advantage of a behavioral approach to these topics is that it can lead readily to the development of data, both basic and applied, that bear on them (see reference list as an example). Much of clinical psychology is desperately in need of a strong empirical base, especially for the theoretical concepts used. Behaviorists may be of real assistance in this area to clinicians of a variety of persuasions.

Biography

Steven C. Hayes is a professor of psychology at the University of Nevada, Reno, and is director of clinical training of the university's doctoral program in clinical psychology. He received his Ph.D. degree (1977) from West Virginia University. Hayes is the author of nearly 150 articles and several books on the philosophy, theory, and method of behavior analysis and its application to adult clinical work. He also does basic research on language processes, including rule-governed behavior and semantic meaning. Hayes is the immediate past president of Division 25 (The Experimental Analysis of Behavior) of the American Psychological Association, is secretary-treasurer of the Assembly for Scientific and Applied Psychology, and serves on APA's Council of Representatives. He is presently on the editorial board of nine journals.

References

Devany, J. M., Hayes, S. C., & Nelson, R. O. (1986). Equivalence class formation in language-able and language-disabled children. *Journal of the Experimental Analysis of Behavior, 46,* 243–257.

Hayes, S. C. (1984). Making sense of spirituality. *Behaviorism, 12,* 99–110.

Hayes, S. C. (1987). A contextual approach to therapeutic change. In N. Jacobson (Ed.), *Psychotherapies in clinical practice: Cognitive and behavioral perspectives* (pp. 327–387). New York: Guilford.

Hayes, S. C., & Brownstein, A. J. (1986). Mentalism, behavior-behavior relations and a behavior analytic view of the purposes of science. *The Behavior Analyst, 9,* 175–190.

Hayes, S. C., Brownstein, A. J., Haas, J. R., & Greenway, D. E. (1986). Instructions, multiple schedules, and extinction: Distinguishing rule-governed from schedule controlled behavior. *Journal of the Experimental Analysis of Behavior, 46,* 137–147.

Wulfert, E., & Hayes, S. C. (in press). The transfer of conditional control through conditional equivalence classes. *Journal of the Experimental Analysis of Behavior.*

5

Cognitive Psychotherapy

Cognitive psychotherapy approaches attend to the manner in which life events are processed by the patient. Cognitive theory posits an interreactive relationship among life events, beliefs about those life events, and consequent affective, behavioral, and physiological responses. Because cognitive theory recognizes the fact that there are multiple determinants of pathology, such as behavior, physiology, and attitude, there has been effort within the cognitive community to integrate other modalities. This accounts for the rapid development of hybrid cognitive-behavioral interventions. Cognitive therapies involve the careful examination and reevaluation of thought and perception and often are much less emotionally laden than implosive or affective-oriented interventions. The primary units-of-analysis, then, are thoughts and attitudes. The therapist and patient examine and modify the self-evaluations and cognitions that block effective living.

There is no consensus regarding the origins of cognitive psychotherapy. Both Albert Ellis and Aaron Beck have credited the therapeutic models of Alfred Adler and Karen Horney as being influential in the development of their cognitive approaches (Freeman, 1987). Others view cognitive approaches as stemming from behavior therapy.

145

The present chapter defies division into discrete sections; each contribution embodies the theoretical base delineated above, and each, within that context, is unique. Rational-emotive therapy is described by Albert Ellis; it is a directive, concrete paradigm. Kenneth Gutsch presents an elaboration on cognitive theory, illustrated by the flooding technique. Richard Wessler's approach reframes unconscious processing as conscious algorithms that are replaceable. Robert Neimeyer's approach, based in George Kelly's work, defines psychopathology as failure to modify reality constructions to accommodate invalidating feedback. Michael Mahoney reframes therapy as an exploratory behavior (implicitly growth directed) deliberately undertaken by the patient in order to facilitate development.

Reference

Freeman, A. (1987). Cognitive therapy: An overview. In A. Freeman & V. Greenwood (Eds.), *Cognitive therapy: Applications in psychiatric and medical settings* (p. 20). New York: Human Sciences Press.

Rational-Emotive Therapy

Albert Ellis

Definition

Rational-emotive therapy holds that effective psychotherapy helps people not only to *feel* better but also to *get* better. It assumes that clients largely disturb themselves by adding to their rational beliefs (preferences and desires) irrational beliefs (absolutist musts and commands). Effective psychotherapy, therefore, consists of helping clients to clearly see and strongly dispute their conscious and unconscious imperatives, using a number of cognitive, emotive, and behavioral methods, and to thereby make themselves less disturbed and less disturbable.

Qualification Statement

Rational-emotive therapy assumes that symptom removal is highly desirable but that efficient psychotherapy helps people to get better (rather than merely feel better) by showing them how to minimize their presenting symptoms; how to maintain these gains; how to acknowledge and minimize other symptoms; how to become less prone to create new symptoms; and how to quickly overcome recurring or new symptoms when they arise.

To accomplish these ends, rational-emotive therapy assumes that thoughts, feelings, and behaviors are interactional and transactional, and that emotional-behavioral problems mainly (but not exclusively) arise from powerful irrational beliefs. Disturbed people first have rational beliefs, which consist of *preferences* and *desires* (for example, "I want to succeed and be approved by significant others"), and when these are thwarted, they feel appropriately and self-helpingly sad, disappointed, and frustrated — *if* they only stick with these rational wishes and accept alternative solutions to their goals. But they also frequently add irrational beliefs — *musts, demands,* and *commands* (for example, "Because I strongly *prefer* to do well and be approved, I always *must* get these results!"). When their dogmatic imperatives are blocked, they then feel *in*appropriately and self-defeatingly panicked, depressed, and enraged.

Rational-emotive therapy holds that the goal of effective therapy is to use cognitive, emotive, and behavioral methods to clearly show clients (1) that they are largely creating their own disturbances by their dogmatic shoulds and musts; (2) that they can actively dispute and surrender these imperatives by scientifically challenging them; (3) that they can make a profound philosophical change by using forceful, dramatic methods of acknowledging and working against their disruptive feelings; and (4) that they can persistently and insistently act against their irrational beliefs.

Some of the main cognitive methods that rational-emotive therapy employs to help people feel better and get better include empirical and logical disputations of clients' dogmas and inferences; the use of coping statements or rational self-statements; referencing the advantages of change and the disadvantages of not changing; reframing self-sabotaging attitudes about life's problems; changing semantic usage; filling out self-help cognitive homework sheets; using psychoeducational methods (such as reading and listening to audio- and videocassettes); proselytizing others with rational philosophies; listening to tape recordings of therapy sessions; modeling of rationally behaving individuals; acquiring a philosophy of unconditional acceptance of oneself and others; and working at rating only one's traits and performances and not one's self or being.

Emotive-evocative techniques favored in rational-emotive therapy include forceful self-statements and self-dialogues; shame-attacking exercises; rational emotive imagery; unconditional acceptance by the therapist; the use of humor, parables, analogies, poems, and dramatic stories; and role playing.

Some of the behavioral techniques favored in rational-emotive therapy include in vivo desensitization; the deliberate courting of uncomfortable situations until they become comfortable; reinforcement and penalization methods; implosive techniques of desensitization; response prevention; and skill training.

The goal of using these many methods, again, is not merely to remove symptoms but to effect a profound philosophical change that will hopefully last and improve for the rest of the client's life.

Critique Statement

Some specific advantages of rational-emotive therapy include the following:

1. It consciously and actively aims to help people *get* better and *stay* better, rather than merely help them to *feel* better.
2. It particularly investigates and helps people to change the basic philosophic assumptions by which they create self-defeating feelings and behaviors.

3. It quickly gets to the most important cognitive, emotive, and behavioral aspects of people's disturbances and shows them how to actively uproot and change their self-sabotaging tendencies. It is consequently an intrinsically brief form of psychotherapy; and it emphasizes self-help procedures.

4. It always emphasizes profound cognitive, emotional, and behavioral change, almost invariably uses a number of thinking, feeling, and action techniques, and is therefore a pioneering mode of integrative (and to some extent eclectic) therapy.

5. It takes an unusually psychoeducational approach to therapy, routinely using pamphlets, books, audiovisual cassettes, charts, and other educational methods, which serve to hasten and intensify the course of therapy, and which are also quite helpful to many individuals who rarely or never come for treatment.

Specific criticisms of rational-emotive therapy and some of its disadvantages include these:

1. It is supposedly too intellectual for some clients, particularly for less intelligent and educated ones.
2. It is too direct and active.
3. It is supposedly too digital and not sufficiently analogical.
4. It does not deal sufficiently with clients' past history and early childhood experiences.
5. It does not have, as yet, a comprehensive theory of personality.
6. It does not thoroughly explore the relationship between the therapist and his or her clients.
7. It does not emphasize deep unconscious thoughts and repressed feelings.
8. It may easily show clients what their irrational beliefs are without necessarily inducing them to change these beliefs.

Biography

Albert Ellis is executive director of the Institute for Rational-Emotive Therapy, New York City. He received his Ph.D. degree

(1947) from Columbia University. He is the recipient of numerous awards, including the Humanist of the Year Award from
the American Humanist Association, the Distinguished Contributions to Professional Knowledge Award of the American
Psychological Association, the Professional Development Award
of the American Association of Counseling and Development,
and the Distinguished Psychotherapist Award of APA's Division
of Psychotherapy. He has held offices in many professional societies, including president of APA's Division of Consulting Psychology. Ellis has published over 600 articles, book chapters,
and reviews and has authored or edited over fifty books. He
has served as consulting editor of twelve professional journals.

As a result of seeing over 15,000 clients and publishing many
research, clinical, and theoretical papers, Ellis has become the
founder of rational-emotive therapy and the grandfather of cognitive-behavioral psychotherapy. He is also a pioneering integrative therapist, since he has used and advocated a variety of cognitive, emotive, and behavioral methods since 1943. He is also
known as one of the main promulgaters of modern sex therapy
and of marriage and family therapy. He argues strongly for a
"double systems" approach to therapy, wherein the therapist helps
people change both themselves (while living within a structured
system) and the systems in which they exist.

Recommended Reading

Ellis, A. (1962). *Reason and emotion in psychotherapy.* Secaucus,
    NJ: Citadel Press.
Ellis, A. (1973). *Humanistic psychotherapy: The rational-emotive ap-
    proach.* New York: McGraw-Hill.
Ellis, A. (1985). *Overcoming resistance: Rational-emotive therapy with
    difficult clients.* New York: Springer.
Ellis, A. (1988). *How to stubbornly refuse to make yourself miserable
    about anything — yes, anything!* Secaucus, NJ: Lyle Stuart.
Ellis, A., & Dryden, W. (1987). *The practice of rational-emotive
    therapy.* New York: Springer.
Ellis, A., & Grieger, R. (Eds.). (1986). *Handbook of rational-emotive
    therapy.* New York: Springer.

Ellis, A., & Harper, R. A. (1975). *A new guide to rational living.* North Hollywood, CA: Wilshire Books.

Schwartz, R. M. (1982). Cognitive-behavior modification: A conceptual review. *Clinical Psychology Review, 2,* 267–293.

Smith, T. W., & Allred, K. D. (1986). Rationality revised. In P. C. Kendall (Ed.), *Advances in cognitive-behavioral research and therapy, Vol. 5* (pp. 63–87). New York: Academic Press.

Cognitive Psychotherapy

Kenneth U. Gutsch

Definition

Psychotherapy is a psychologically based treatment process through which a professionally trained person, a psychotherapist licensed by the state in which he or she practices, uses well-researched psychological knowledge and intervention strategies to understand, influence, and modify the behavior of an emotionally troubled person, the client. It is a process based primarily on the art of relating and the science of understanding behavior change. Its ultimate purpose is to reduce cognitive distortions.

Qualification Statement

The cognitive model of therapy is based on the idea that emotional disorders result from predispositional factors (that is, genetic endowment plus early childhood experiences) and situational factors (that is, current stimuli to which people respond). Thus, cognitive theory finds some of its roots in both *dynamic theory,* which attends to explanations of psychopathology and the trait characteristics by which emotional disorders can be identified, and *behavioral theory,* which attends to the ways by which people have learned to respond to specific stimuli.

Cognitive theorists, for example, believe that emotional disorders are the basic consequence of mood disturbances and that a primary disturbance in thinking causes the development of a disturbed mood state. Further, it is their contention that when a client conceives of an experience as unpleasant, there will be a corresponding unpleasant affective response. Ultimately, cognitive sets (that is, the readiness to respond in a given way to specific thoughts and ideas) are transposed to behavioral sets (that is, the readiness to act out in a given way to situational stimuli). Thus, when clients experience depression, it can be identified through definitive cognitive sets (for example, expressed feelings of despair, futility, rejection, hopelessness, and remorse) and/or definitive behavioral sets (for example, physical expressions of nervousness, fatigue, withdrawal from responsibility, and/or attempts at suicide). To this extent, it might be said that cognitive structure (that is, the organizing aspects of our thinking that modify and direct the strategy of our thoughts) becomes the basis for how a person will respond behaviorally. Both of these contingencies must be considered in treatment planning.

Because the thought processes of emotionally disordered clients are seldom, if ever, reality based, such clients must learn how to draw appropriate and realistic conclusions from arbitrary inferences, overgeneralizations, and grossly magnified distortions. To accomplish this objective, they are challenged to become aware of their present patterns of thinking (their sets) and to analyze philosophically those ideas within the patterns that may be easiest for them to change. The client is then encouraged to imagine these ideas thematically as the therapist floods the patient with potentially emotional difficulties related to change. The use of flooding helps the therapist to desensitize the patient to the threat of change and helps the patient to understand the need to build a stable backup system (viable alternative courses of action) should such strategies be needed to divert failure. This cognitive therapeutic action also helps patients to develop a philosophical understanding of how to deal with life in a personally acceptable way.

The method by which behavior change takes place incorporates a two-step design in which the patient first explores the cognitions that are faulty and then scrutinizes the basic risks involved in change. Since the risk of change can be moderated through such things as skills acquisition training, appropriate restructuring, and the development of a good backup system, patients who have learned to use such contingencies are in a position to reduce their cognitive distortions.

Critique Statement

Although cognitive theory probably suffers from a number of weaknesses, the criticism that appears to concern therapists of other vintages the most is the presumption by cognitive theorists that cognitive structuring determines how experiences are processed and thus how clients will draw from them in the future. Psychologically, the idea is somewhat like the concept of thematic extrapolation. It is based on the belief that sets—those personal patterns of thinking and/or behaving that provide people with a readiness to respond in a given way—extend themselves from people's past into their future. Some theorists consider the idea deterministic. They feel that it is theoretically unsound to carry on therapy with a preconceived notion that the client's cognitive structures appear somewhat irreversible. Obviously, some of these same theorists consider an immediate change in behavior the ultimate criterion of therapeutic effectiveness; they seem to confuse the *process* of thinking and behaving with the *outcomes* derived from such a process. Ultimately, the impression they convey is that therapists who do not produce immediately observable behavior changes are not effective.

Perhaps the real strength of cognitive theory comes from its systematic application. By first helping clients to modify their thought processes and then helping them to test the reality of those processes through concrete, behavioral activities that complement their new ways of thinking, the therapist serves as a catalyst between the client's past and his or her future. The advantage to such an approach is that clients can test their changed cognitions against reality and convert them into a reality with satisfaction to themselves and benefit to society.

A second criticism is that the cognitive approach lacks personal sensitivity — that is, feelings of empathy and warmth between therapist and client. Those who are opposed to it suggest that clients who are not exposed to empathy and warmth as part of their treatment have only limited ways of learning about such things. They consider this a serious disadvantage in therapy.

On the other hand, cognitive theorists argue that the advantage of their approach is that it is reality based. The therapist does not have to ponder empathy or personal warmth (which are difficult to define) but can deal primarily with the application of psychological principles to the problem at hand. Cognitive theorists recognize that what one person considers kindness another may well consider cruelty. They argue that the extent to which one person can participate in another's feelings or vicariously experience such feelings is questionable. At best, the concept of empathy is too subjective; at worst, it seems to confound the process of effective therapy.

Biography

Kenneth U. Gutsch is a diplomate in counseling psychology of the American Board of Professional Psychology, a fellow of the American Psychological Association, and the former director of training for the Department of Counseling Psychology at the University of Southern Mississippi. He received his Ed.D. degree from Florida State University. He is the author or co-author of eight books and more than seventy articles.

Cognitive Appraisal Therapy

Richard L. Wessler

Definition

"Psychotherapy" refers to the use of psychological principles to favorably alter distressed individuals' emotional and interpersonal patterns. Each form of psychological therapy has limited application. We developed our approach—cognitive appraisal therapy—because we could not treat certain personality disorders with conventional cognitive psychotherapy. Cognitive appraisal therapy makes three distinctive assumptions: (1) Social information is processed by nonconscious algorithms; (2) motivation is provided in part by a need to reexperience familiar feelings that confirm one's sense of self; and (3) shame has a significant role in maintaining cognitive, affective, behavioral, and interpersonal patterns.

Qualification Statement

Psychotherapy is the application of psychological principles to favorably alter patterns of emoting and interacting with others. There are many varieties of psychological principles and therefore many varieties of psychological therapy. Each has limited application. For example, behavioral and cognitive approaches based on conditioning and social learning principles are suitable for some anxiety and affective disorders. However, they require clients who are willing to carry out the tasks assigned as homework, and the completion of the homework is necessary for the treatment to be effective.

The decision not to cooperate in one's treatment is itself subject to understanding using psychological principles. The search for such understanding led us first to realize the significance of the personality disorders (Axis II of *DSM-III-R*) in the treatment of Axis I symptoms for which cognitive and behavioral methods were devised and then to rethink the so-called neurotic paradox; that is, why people continue to exhibit self-defeating patterns of behavior that seem to defy the hedonistic assumptions of reinforcement theory. Little in conventional cognitive-behavior therapy applied to the disorders of personality, for we were no longer dealing with anxiety and depression but with aspects of personality itself.

Our understanding was aided by developments in cognitive psychology, specifically research in support of nonconscious processes — an alternative to the psychodynamic unconscious. A nonconscious algorithm is a stored routine for the automatic processing of social information. Such algorithms, which are typically learned early in life and perpetuated by the person's biased interpretations of data, are implicated in affective processes and in value-based responses. In our approach — cognitive appraisal therapy — they are called personal rules of living, and as such they function as guides for affective and behavioral responses to situations. Thus, one aspect of our approach is to uncover these rules and consciously adopt alternatives.

The second distinctive feature of cognitive appraisal therapy concerns motivation. Cognition provides the map and affect provides the motivation. The child uncritically absorbs distinctive patterns of knowing, acting, and emoting from its family and receives reinforcement within the family subculture. We call these distinctive patterns of emoting "personotypic affect" and hypothesize that people develop characteristic ways of feeling that they consider natural and, to some extent, use to confirm their own sense of self. Indeed, people derive a sense of security from these familiar feelings and seek (even contrive) to pull responses from others that confirm their cognitive self-concept and cause familiar feelings to be experienced. These security-seeking maneuvers explain what seems mysterious from a rational and hedonistic point of view: that people may act in ways that increase rather than decrease negative affect to reexperience familiar feelings. These maneuvers are discovered and explained in cognitive appraisal therapy, and the person is coached in how to act against them. Setbacks in psychotherapy are seen as the individual's nonconscious attempt to restore familiar negative affective states.

Finally, shame is recognized as a ubiquitous emotion not only by itself but also in tandem with rage. Shame and/or rage are components in most of the disorders of personality. Shame is not only defended against and avoided; if it is part of an individual's personotypic affect, it is sought as well.

The goal of cognitive appraisal therapy is to alter self-defeating patterns and to increase a sense of emotional well-being. This is accomplished through therapeutic dialogue in which the client's cognitive, affective, and interpersonal developmental patterns are described and plans are made to act on these insights and to work against the tendencies thus uncovered.

Critique Statement

The majority of distressed people change without the help of psychotherapists. They must be doing something right, and we could learn from them. Instead, we learn from people we treat who do not change. Therapists of different orientations learn different lessons from their clients; their orientation prepares them to assimilate certain information. Assimilating discrepant information or making accommodative shifts is more difficult. And yet, one often has to look outside one's orientation to get information about dealing with emergent issues — just as we did when working with disordered personalities. The cognitive and behavioral literature was silent, with a few exceptions, and the literature of psychoanalysis had to be consulted.

One result is the creation of an integrated approach that is less cognitive and more affective than conventional cognitive-behavioral therapy, with an explicit acknowledgment of nonconscious processes and an unconventional view of motivation. Unlike other cognitive-behavioral approaches, ours developed from experiences with clients in a treatment setting not in a university research program. Thus, direct empirical support is weak, but there is a great deal of indirect evidence consistent with our main hypotheses. Research on nonconscious processes has been reported by Lewicki (1986), a detailed exploration of self-confirmation theory with supporting literature review has been done by Andrews (in press), and the role of shame was researched by Lewis (1987). Although our work began with conventional cognitive-behavioral approaches, it soon extended into other realms.

Cognitive appraisal therapy is limited to certain disorders of personality and is not intended to treat symptoms of depression and anxiety except as they are the result of aspects of personality. Because we explore motivational patterns, there is an obvious similarity to psychodynamic theory; because we emphasize self-appraisal and affect, there is an obvious similarity to Rogerian principles; because we urge conscious alterations in relations with other people, there is an obvious similarity to interpersonal therapy.

Cognitive appraisal therapy is not so systematic that its procedures can be carefully specified and recorded in a treatment manual. Nor is it possible to remain client-centered and ignore the concerns people raise that do not directly bear on the concepts of our approach. We might spend weeks or months building a therapeutic alliance and discussing anything the person thinks important. No rigid, preconceived agenda will do; it is a question of the client first, our approach second.

Biography

Richard L. Wessler is professor of psychology at Pace University, Pleasantville, New York, and in private practice at Cognitive Psychotherapy Associates in New York City. He received his Ph.D. degree (1966) from Washington University. He has written numerous articles and book chapters and coauthored two books on psychotherapy. He reviews articles for several psychotherapy journals and has conducted training workshops on various forms of cognitive-behavior therapy throughout North America and Europe.

Initially trained in rational-emotive therapy, Wessler found that it could not be used with diverse clients without significant modifications in the approach. These modifications became so extensive that the result could no longer be called rational-emotive therapy. He found that no single therapeutic approach can be used with all clients, or as he once wrote, "If it's not eclectic, it's not ethical."

Recommended Reading

Wessler, R. L., & Hankin, S. (1988). Rational-emotive and other cognitively oriented therapies. In S. Long (Ed.), *Six group therapies*. New York: Plenum.

Wessler, R. L., & Hankin, W. R. (1986). Cognitive appraisal therapy. In W. Dryden and W. Golden (Eds.), *Cognitive-behavioral approaches to psychotherapy*. New York: Hemisphere.

References

Andrews, J. D. W. (in press). *The active self in psychotherapy*. New York: Gardner.

Lewicki, P. (1986). *Nonconscious social information processing*. Orlando, FL: Academic Press.

Lewis, H. B. (1987). *The role of shame in symptom formation*. Hillsdale, NJ: Lawrence Erlbaum.

Personal Construct Therapy

Robert A. Neimeyer

Definition

Human beings live their lives on the basis of personal, and sometimes problematic, explanatory systems that represent the main themes of their pasts and permit them some degree of security in anticipating their future. Psychological disorder occurs when these *personal construct systems* are unable to accommodate to changing events and when a particular construction continues to be used in spite of its consistent invalidation. The utilization of technical assistance in devising and testing out more viable constructions of life is the special transaction we call psychotherapy.

Qualification Statement

Human beings are essentially interpretive, always in the process of attributing meaning to their ongoing experience. In a construct theory view, individuals are like incipient scientists who attempt to devise hypotheses (or constructs) that render the events of their lives understandable, and to some degree predictable. Thus, unlike theorists who view human behavior as determined by past traumas or present reinforcement contingencies, construct theorists consider people's behavior as ways of testing their beliefs about the future, given the limits imposed by their current understandings. When individuals become stuck in the process of elaborating their personal theories, so that important events in their lives appear chaotic, contradictory, or meaningless, they sometimes seek professional assistance from a psychotherapist. Together, in the safe laboratory of the therapy room, the therapist and client collaborate in articulating, testing, and revising those personal constructions that are most bound up with the client's current distress. Thus, the essence of therapy is the psychological reconstruction of life.

Personal construct therapy is distinguished from traditional forms of cognitive therapy by its commitment to *constructive alternativism,* the philosophical view that all of our constructions are subject to revision or replacement; none can make a claim to absolute truth. This constructivist view contrasts with the dominant rationalist view that reality is something "out there" and that psychological distress results when our beliefs about the world are irrational, distorted, or unrealistic. Instead, construct theorists view reality as largely a personal or social invention and disorder as the development of a construct system that is no longer *useful* for anticipating events and channelling one's behavior toward them. Moreover, "negative" emotions (such as depression or anxiety) are not so much problems to be eliminated by logical thinking as important signals of impending transition in our construct systems.

From this constructivist view, it follows that therapy is more a *creative* than a *corrective* enterprise. Rather than directly challenging the validity of the client's existing beliefs, the therapist helps the client invent new and perhaps more viable alternatives (particularly through the use of role-played enactments of different approaches to life). Thus, personal construct therapy is typically more invitational and exploratory than it is directive and disputational. This strategic preference follows from the explicit model of personality that undergirds the therapy approach, which assumes that our construct systems constitute integral wholes rather than cognitive ticker tapes of isolated self-statements. If our personal theories do indeed have systemic properties, then the simple deletion of "faulty" constructs by even a well-intentioned therapist can upset the delicate ecology of self, much as the elimination of a species of animal or plant can disrupt the viability of a natural ecosystem. For this reason, personal construct therapists tend to respect the integrity of the client's current construing and carefully collaborate with the client in experimenting with new behavior that is not at odds with core identity constructs in existing systems.

Critique Statement

Personal construct theory has been criticized for being philosophically solipsistic, theoretically insular, empirically infertile, and therapeutically impractical. While each of these criticisms may seem legitimate at first glance, on closer inspection each is grounded in an incomplete appreciation of construct theory and its continued evolution over the past thirty-five years.

Some critics have accused construct theory of philosophical solipsism, contending that its emphasis on the personal construction of meaning denies the reality of an objective world and leaves the person lost in his or her own subjectivity. However, most construct theorists are *critical constructivists;* they acknowledge the existence of an external reality but argue that we only can come to know it by construing it in human terms. Moreover, most psychological distress results not from a mismatch of our construing with hard physical facts, but from conflict of our construing with *that of other people,* which is equally as subjective as our own. In a sense, construct theory is far *less* solipsistic than traditional rationalist versions of cognitive therapy, in that it places far greater emphasis on the construction and disruption of role relationships with others than do more individualistic approaches.

Construct theorists also have been criticized for being theoretically insular, maintaining a tight in-group pattern of communication rather than drawing upon ideas developed by theorists in other traditions. In fact, this criticism has even been voiced by a number of personal construct theorists! In retrospect, this criticism is an apt summary of the theory's past, though not its present. When George Kelly first introduced construct theory in the early 1950s, psychology was dominated by a psychoanalytic tradition that gave precedence to unconscious dynamics and by a behavioral tradition that emphasized strict environmental determinism. Obviously, neither left much room for a constructivist view of individuals as personal scientists actively devising and testing their own models of reality. In view of this sociohistorical context, the insularity of early construct theorists was both defensive and defensible. On the other hand, the contemporary personal construct literature promotes a much more open exchange with other traditions, a point that will be elaborated below.

A frequently heard criticism is that the personal construct approach is long on theory and short on research. Ironically, this view is only supportable if one ignores the 1,677 personal construct publications that have appeared since the appearance of Kelly's original work in 1955, 65 percent of which consists of empirical research. However, unlike the literature generated by other psychotherapy traditions, much of this empirical work pertains directly to the basic theory of personality and its social psychological applications, in addition to its clinical and treatment implications per se.

Finally, while critics typically acknowledge that personal construct therapy is conceptually intriguing, they maintain that it is too abstract to implement on a practical level. In part, this is because construct therapy has resisted the temptation to define itself in terms of an approved list of acceptable techniques and instead has sought to provide a framework within which virtually any technique can be orchestrated, regardless of its theoretical pedigree. Thus, by providing a well-developed theory of personality that details the *process* of construing, the *structural features* of our construct systems, and the *social embeddedness* of our anticipatory efforts, construct theory coordinates the use of a wide variety of techniques, selected on a case-by-case basis. As a result, while it continues to generate novel interventions, its technical eclecticism helps promote the integration of different psychotherapy traditions. The integrative thrust of current personal construct work is reflected in the attempts of numerous writers to explore the interface of construct theory with cognitive-behavioral, psychoanalytic, and especially family systemic approaches to therapy. In the face of the sometimes bewildering variety of approaches to psychotherapy, this effort to identify constructivist themes that help bridge different traditions may prove to be one of the most enduring contributions of personal construct therapy.

Biography

Robert A. Neimeyer is an associate professor of psychology at Memphis State University, Tennessee. He received his Ph.D. degree (1982) from the University of Nebraska. An active contributor to personal construct theory since his undergraduate years at the University of Florida, Neimeyer has published seven books, including *Personal Meanings of Death: Applications of Personal Construct Theory to Clinical Practice* (coedited with Franz Epting in 1984), *The Development of Personal Construct Theory* (1985), and a *Personal Construct Therapy Casebook* (coauthored with Greg Neimeyer in 1987). As the author of over 100 articles and book chapters, he is currently conducting research on depression, constructive approaches to psychotherapy, and the development and breakdown of close relationships. In collaboration with his brother,

Greg, he coedits both the *International Journal of Personal Construct Psychology* and the biennial series *Advances in Personal Construct Psychology* and also organized the Seventh International Congress on Personal Construct Psychology in Memphis, Tennessee.

Recommended Reading

Dunnet, G. (1988). *Working with people: Clinical uses of personal construct psychology.* New York & London: Routledge.

International Journal of Personal Construct Psychology. New York: Hemisphere.

Kelly, G. A. (1955). *The psychology of personal constructs.* New York: Norton.

Neimeyer, R. A. (1987). Personal construct therapy. In W. Dryden & W. L. Golden (Eds.), *Cognitive-behavioural approaches to psychotherapy.* New York: Hemisphere.

Neimeyer, R. A., Baker, K. D., & Neimeyer, G. J. (1989). The current status of personal construct theory: Some scientometric data. In G. J. Neimeyer & R. A. Neimeyer (Eds.), *Advances in personal construct psychology.* Greenwich, CT: JAI Press.

Neimeyer, R. A., & Neimeyer, G. J. (1987). *Personal construct theory casebook.* New York: Springer.

Developmental Cognitive Therapy

Michael J. Mahoney

Definition

Psychotherapy is a culturally relative special *relationship* between a professional helper and individual or group clients. Working from a *theoretical rationale* that includes basic assumptions about human nature and the processes of psychological *development,* the psychotherapist works with the client to create a safe, stable, and caring alliance in and from which the client can explore — often via ritualized techniques — past, present, and possible ways of experiencing self, world, and their dynamic relationships.

Qualification Statement

This definition derives from a perspective that addresses *lifespan development,* as well as from *evolutionary epistemology,* the study of knowing systems and their ongoing development. Pioneered by the writings of philosopher Karl R. Popper and psychologist Donald T. Campbell, evolutionary epistemology has demonstrated that organisms are (1) embodied theories of life that (2) actively participate in the natural selection processes that shape and constrain their adaptation and development (Mahoney, in press; Radnitzky & Bartley, 1987). An important distinction is drawn between passive Darwinism, which gives primary power to the selection pressures of the environment, and active Darwinism, which recognizes the active and proactive involvement of the organism in selecting and modifying its environment. In sapient life forms, most notably humans, selection pressures become extensively internalized and symbolically transmitted, allowing a wide range of conscious and unconscious mentation that may serve adaptive functions. The assertions of developmental cognitive therapy are consistent with many of the tenets of the major schools of psychotherapy.

The key activity in successful adaptation and progressive development is exploration, generally expressed in humans as novel variations and creatively different styles of being in the world. The initiation of psychotherapy is a clear expression of such exploratory activity. The therapist may be initially sought in hopes of finding solutions to acute or chronic problems, but — if my analysis is correct (Mahoney, in press) — the client may ultimately be best served by a therapist who encourages and facilitates general exploratory activities. This is most often accomplished by means of what Jerome D. Frank has aptly termed the "3 Rs" of psychotherapy: An emotionally charged and trustworthy *relationship* in and from which individualized *rationales* and *rituals* are used to encourage the client's explorations of self, world, and their developing relationships. All significant psychological change (in or out of therapy) involves change in the *personal meaning* that comprises each individual's private reality. Changes involving the individual's sense of self, reality, values, or power (control) are seldom rapid, easy, or comfortable. When an individual is pushed (by a therapist, significant other, or life circumstances) to move too far or too quickly beyond current personal reality, *self-protective resistance* processes will be activated in the service of maintaining his or her integrity and viability as a living system. Working *with,* rather than *against,* such resistance is generally more successful in facilitating therapeutic change. Thus practiced, psychotherapy is inherently developmental, client-centered (phenomenological), and both inter- and intrapersonal, with explicit emphases on experiential processes, dynamic complexity, and the powers of emotional intensity and active (behavioral) experimentation.

Critique Statement

The primary advantages of the definition and elaboration I have offered include their acknowledgments (1) that psychotherapy is a socially sanctioned *special relationship* with a helping professional; (2) that this relationship constitutes the base camp or context in and from which clients can explore and experiment with old and new ways of experiencing; (3) that the *developmental processes* involved in psychological change require the active participation of the clients; and (4) that significant psychological change is often difficult, slow, and associated with self-protective processes that resist such change. Moreover, I believe that the foregoing features respect and reflect the contributions of the major traditions in psychotherapy (for example, psychodynamic, behavioral, humanistic, cognitive, and systems-strategic). What I have outlined may therefore encourage deeper integration of these diverse traditions, as well as dialectical exchanges that may generate novel developments in our conceptualization and practice of psychotherapy.

Possible criticisms of the perspective outlined here will necessarily reflect alternate assumptions about human nature, the essence of human helping, and/or the formal requirements of theories and models of psychological change. The approach I have outlined does not, for example, emphasize or encourage the type of prescriptive and piecemeal interventionism popular in some forms of behavior therapy (although it does advocate active behavioral experiences). Likewise, my emphasis on the power and importance of the therapeutic relationship is at variance with perspectives that prioritize techniques (even though, I would argue, my emphasis is in accord with the extant evidence on psychotherapy process and outcome).

The perspective I have outlined might also be criticized for its acknowledgments of resistance, unconscious processes, the difficulty of some forms of change, the operation of natural self-protective mechanisms, and the importance of experiential processes in change. Rationalist perspectives (which would include some of the cognitive psychotherapies) might fault my rendition for its failure to highlight "rational disputation" and "corrective cognitions" procedures (whose relative contributions I do, indeed question). And finally, traditional (orthodox) psychoanalysts might challenge the highly engaged (interactive, expressive, affectionate) role I have written for the helping professional.

Overall, I see the major disadvantage of developmental cognitive therapy as its abstractness. In the interest of comprehensive integration, it is couched in terms and concepts that can offer only scaffoldings — but no explicit blueprints — for the conceptualization and conduct of psychotherapy. At a time and in a culture where concrete, pragmatic, how-to-do-it models of helping are most popular, the approach here outlined may not appeal to some practitioners. In presentations of developmental cognitive therapy over the past few years, I have also encountered remarks that this perspective is nothing but a reformulation of the school of thought most or least respected by the commentator (for example, psychoanalysis, humanistic, gestalt, and so on). This again suggests that our human preference for neat, distinct, and unchanging categories may militate against the appreciation of integrative and/or emergent viewpoints. Finally, if practiced and examined in the evolutionary spirit, the approach I have outlined will necessarily change in the crucibles of the future — leaving it open to both criticisms and kudos for its plasticity. We shall see.

Biography

Michael J. Mahoney is professor of counseling psychology at the University of California, Santa Barbara. He received his Ph.D. degree from Stanford University. The author of twelve books and numerous scientific articles, Mahoney helped pioneer the "cognitive revolution" in psychology and is a continuing contributor to the growing interface between the cognitive and clinical sciences. Honored as a fellow by the American Psychological Association, he was chosen to be a master lecturer on psychotherapy process in 1981 and a G. Stanley Hall Lecturer in 1988. Dr. Mahoney has received several professional awards, including a Fulbright Award in 1984, the Faculty Scholar Medal from Pennsylvania State University in 1982, and a 1985 Citation Classic from Science Citation Index in recognition of the influence of his 1974 book, *Cognition and Behavior Modification.*

Mahoney has served on the editorial boards of twelve scientific journals and has worked with the U.S. Olympic Committee since 1978 in the area of sport psychology. His research interests include basic processes in psychological development and psychotherapy, theoretical and philosophical issues, psychology of science, and health and sport psychology. His forthcoming book, *Human Change Processes: Notes on the Facilitation of Personal Development,* attempts to integrate the research literatures from several disciplines as they bear on the conceptualization and facilitation of psychological change.

References

Mahoney, M. J. (in press). *Human change processes: Notes on the facilitation of personal development.* New York: Basic Books.

Radnitzky, G., & Bartley, W. W. (Eds.). (1987). *Evolutionary epistemology, theory of rationality, and sociology of knowledge.* LaSalle, IL: Open Court.

6

Philosophically Oriented
Psychotherapy

Finding meaning in life, both intrapersonally in terms of values
and spirituality and extrapersonally in terms of one's role in relation to peers, culture, and the cosmos, traditionally has been
the domain of philosophy and religion. A functional philosophy
can be a prerequisite to a balanced emotional life. The present
chapter examines contemporary philosophically based approaches
to psychotherapy.

As suggested in Chapter Three, the approaches described here
and those that focus on affective awareness share both a common historical bond and a profound respect for the client's
phenomenology and individuality. Broadly stated, the central
theory here is that the quality of an individual's life experience
results from his cultural beliefs, his philosophy and ethical values,
and his spiritual development as they affect life events. In that
regard, the primary units-of-analysis are idiosyncratic aspects
of the client and the client's relationship to his culture and the
cosmos.

In terms of historical development, the approaches represented
here have multiple roots, including inquiry into man's initial
quest for meaning. As psychotherapeutic modalities, none were
formally practiced until the humanistic "third force" developed
through the work of pioneers such as Carl Rogers, Fritz Perls,
and Abraham Maslow.

Viktor Frankl, Rollo May, and James Bugental are among those who initially attended to philosophical considerations in the context of therapy. The transpersonal approaches meld spirituality (traditionally the domain of age-old religions) and healing or growth. When we examine the context within which an individual operates (that is, the culture), mores and history emerge as primary determinants.

This chapter is divided into three broad categories: culturally based approaches, personal meaning, and transcendent approaches. The section on culturally based approaches examines the relation of man to his society. Thomas Szasz discusses psychotherapy and psychopathology in light of society's (perhaps prejudicial) definition. Jefferson Fish examines the larger phenomenon of psychotherapy and discusses how social context can provide a framework within which to conduct psychotherapy. Stanley Krippner discusses native healing as a form of psychotherapy, pointing out marked similarities in the healing process as it occurs in radically different cultures.

The personal meaning section examines therapies that are less culturally determined and that focus on meaning at an intrapersonal level. Rollo May, James Bugental, and Stephen De-Berry each discuss their existential humanistic approaches, and Keith Hoeller presents a concise view of existential psychotherapy. George S. Howard examines the search for meaning as an essential life task in each individual's construction of his or her personal story.

In the transcendent approaches section, aspects of nonordinary functioning are discussed. Allan Chinen's transpersonal psychotherapy examines the spiritual aspect of man as a factor in healing. The late R. D. Laing presented a psychotherapeutic approach that relies on unconscious communication, and David Feinstein examines the role of personal mythology in an individual's spiritual functioning.

Section 1
Culturally Based Approaches

The Myth of Psychotherapy

Thomas S. Szasz

Definition

The question "What is psychotherapy?" presupposes that psychotherapy exists. I contend that it does not. Like mental illness, psychotherapy is a metaphor and, as an extended metaphor, a myth. Metaphor being the use of a term literally denoting one thing in place of another, its meaning must be inferred from its use. The term *psychotherapy* may function as a phenomenal metaphor — for example, advising a person how to manage his marriage, which looks like advising him how to manage his diabetes; or a strategic metaphor — for example, calling imprisonment "treatment" not because it actually looks like any medical treatment, but in order to make it look like a treatment and thus justify it medically, morally, and legally.

Qualification Statement

For me, psychotherapy is listening and talking. Moreover, since psychotherapeutic conversations concern the question of how people should live, it is axiomatic that psychotherapy is a ministerial-existential rather than a medical-therapeutic enterprise. However, this is not the way psychotherapy is viewed. It is now official dogma — in science, medicine, psychology, law, politics, journalism, everyday life — that psychotherapy is "therapy." This belief is similar to the belief in transubstantiation. Asserting that transubstantiation is a myth does not mean that consecrated bread and wine do not exist; it means only that, to the non-Catholic, they are not the body and blood of Jesus, but (only) consecrated bread and wine.

Similarly, asserting that psychotherapy is a myth does not mean that the behaviors of persons called patients (or clients) and psychotherapists do not exist; it means only that, to the person who rejects the literalization of metaphoric treatments, they are not therapies, but (only) the claims and conduct of people identified as patients and therapists.

In short, the term *psychotherapy* denotes various principles and practices of (secular) ethics. Every method or school of psychotherapy is thus a system of applied ethics couched in the idiom of treatment; each reflects the personality, values, and aspirations of its founder and practitioners.

When I practice (what others call) psychotherapy (a term I reject whenever necessary), I regard the patient and myself as being engaged in an intimate human relationship. The patient is not ill, and I do not treat him. The ends and means of our relationship ("autonomous psychotherapy," if it need be named) are mutually reinforcing. The goal is to increase the patient's knowledge of himself, others, and the world about him and hence his freedom of choice and responsibility in the conduct of his life. The means are subtle and cannot be summarized; they center on the contract between patient and therapist and are best defined by specifying the limitations on the therapist's power. Thus, autonomous psychotherapy is incompatible with any compromise of confidentiality; with interference by the therapist in the patient's life; and, generally, with the use of force or fraud; that is, the therapist cannot, under any circumstances, coerce the patient, nor can he deviate from his contractually defined role in response to the patient's coercion.

Critique Statement

Because there is great diversity among individuals, and because psychotherapy is a type of human relationship, people have fashioned many different forms of psychotherapy in the past and will continue to fashion different forms of it in the future. Because I value individual liberty and human diversity, I favor pluralism in psychotherapy—much as I favor pluralism in religion, politics, and family relationships. Different people seek (and provide) different kinds of (psychotherapeutic) help for problems in living, just as different people practice different kinds of religions and construct different forms of government.

From such a perspective, it is meaningless to compare various psychotherapies and pronounce one better or worse than the other—just as it is meaningless for an atheist to say that one religion is better than another. People tend to form the sorts of associations that satisfy their needs. As a particular marriage is good or bad depending on whether the partners meet each other's needs, so also is a particular psychotherapeutic relationship good or bad depending on whether patient and therapist harmoniously collaborate toward a common goal. (And the only way to ascertain whether they do so is by observing whether they are together or have separated.)

I like to practice "autonomous psychotherapy," and the people who choose to come to me for "therapy" are usually pleased with what they get in return for the money they pay me. But I know people ("psychotherapists") who like to commit people, give them electric shock treatment and drugs, and advise them how to live; and I have known people ("patients") who have asked to be committed, electroshocked, drugged, and advised. As the saying goes, "It takes two to tango."

Because psychotherapy is intimately connected with medicine and psychology as well as with religion and law, there are powerful forces in every society toward making psychotherapy the servant of the dominant ethic and of the state. Inevitably, this has happened in the United States too. However, because of our laissez faire tradition toward religion and speech, epitomized by the First Amendment; and because of the transparent similarities between what used to be called the "cure of souls" and what is now called "psychotherapy," it was and still is possible for diverse types of psychotherapists to practice diverse types of therapy here, and for diverse patients to patronize diverse types of therapists. We are now witnessing the increasing medicalization of psychotherapy in tandem with the increasing economic, legal, and political control of medicine by the state.

Whether, in the economic-political climate thus created, it will be possible for diverse forms of psychotherapy to survive, much less flourish; and whether the state will approve, prescribe, and pay for one or a few types of psychotherapy and disapprove, prohibit, and penalize practicing and patronizing those not so recognized — all that remains to be seen.

Biography

Thomas Szasz is professor of psychiatry at the State University of New York, Upstate Medical Center in Syracuse. He received his M.D. degree (1944) from the University of Cincinnati. He is the recipient of numerous awards, including the Humanist of the Year Award from the American Humanist Association and the Distinguished Service Award from the American Institute for Public Service. He has received a number of honorary doctorates and lectureships and serves on the editorial board of or as consulting editor for ten journals. Szasz has authored approximately 400 articles, book chapters, reviews, letters to the editor, and columns. He has written nineteen books.

Recommended Reading

Szasz, T. S. (1970). *Ideology and insanity: Essays on the psychiatric dehumanization of man.* Garden City, NY: Doubleday.
Szasz, T. S. (1984). *The therapeutic state: Psychiatry in the mirror of current events.* Buffalo, NY: Prometheus Books.
Szasz, T. S. (1987). *Insanity: The idea and its consequences.* New York: Wiley.
Szasz, T. S. (1988a). *The ethics of psychoanalysis: The theory and method of autonomous psychotherapy.* Syracuse, NY: Syracuse University Press. (Original work published 1965)
Szasz, T. S. (1988b). *The myth of psychotherapy: Mental health as religion, rhetoric, and repression.* Syracuse, NY: Syracuse University Press. (Original work published 1978)

Social Context Therapy

Jefferson M. Fish

Definition

The term *psychotherapy* is a misnomer that denotes an incredible range of practices deriving from a wide variety of mutually contradictory theoretical rationales. As a social phenomenon, it reflects an increasing division of labor in complex industrialized societies, creating new roles from part-time functions of practitioners of religion and, to lesser degree, medicine. Psychotherapy can best be understood as involving social influence processes continuous with those of education, hypnosis, the placebo effect, brainwashing, and religious healing. It achieves its stated goal most efficiently when knowledge from the social sciences is deliberately employed to change explicitly identified problem behavior in its social-interactional context.

Qualification Statement

The need for a book-length project to define something both common and important suggests that it doesn't really exist. No such difficulties would be encountered in defining "chair" (though reality is socially constructed, and there are cultural variations — including some small societies without a chair concept). Psychotherapy, like beauty — or pornography — exists in the eye of the beholder; and a careful reading of this book will reveal that there is no element common to all definitions.

The attempt to define psychotherapy is reminiscent of Kroeber and Kluckhohn's project (1952) to define culture; and while both provide intellectual stimulation in considering the issues involved, both are ultimately doomed to failure for the same reason. Depending on one's theoretical orientation, there is much that can be pointed to as cultural, or psychotherapeutic; but the terms have been made to serve so many differing purposes that any internally consistent definition would exclude or contradict reasonable meanings.

Once one has dispensed with the attempt to delineate psychotherapy as a thing and then decided how to do it, it is possible to ask the related question of how to understand and change behavior (including thoughts and feelings) in its interpersonal context. From this perspective, there is much information in psychology, sociology, and anthropology concerning education, persuasion, hypnosis, the placebo effect, brainwashing, religious healing, and similar forms of social influence that therapists can apply directly (e.g., Fish, 1973; Frank, 1973). In addition, since behavior exists within an interactional context, theoretical approaches such as symbolic interactionism, social learning theory, and systems theory offer useful conceptual guides to understanding and changing behavior.

One way of looking at people's problems and the change process is that individuals find themselves caught up in dissatisfying and self-perpetuating patterns of interaction within a significant social context—usually family or work. They come to therapy with more or less vaguely defined misery, as well as beliefs about their misery (for example, "I'm a hopeless case") and a pattern of failed attempts by themselves and/or significant others to do something about their misery and beliefs (for example, "cheer up"). Often the very attempts to solve the problem are what perpetuate it; and interfering with these attempts, or with dissatisfying patterns of social interaction, is sufficient to lead to significant change.

This view of therapy raises an important ethical issue. A recognition that behavior is interwoven with its social context implies that when a client's behavior changes others will be affected. Thus, in contracting to do therapy, therapists must be aware that nonconsenting others may wind up changing in ways undesired by them.

Critique Statement

There are many disadvantages to adopting a critical stance toward the concept of psychotherapy, the various social organizations involved with it (for example, university departments, training institutes, journals, mental health centers), and the prestige, money, power, and enthusiastic adherents associated with any given variety. By eschewing alignment with a particular approach, one loses potential allies, a career ladder, and ultimately the ability to influence institutions and thus affect the official definition of the field. On the contrary, by accepting a given approach, together with its definition of reality, social support system, and referral sources, one gains the comfortable assurance of being able to understand oneself and others, knowing how to treat their problems, and receiving institutional affirmation of one's correctness.

There are also a few advantages to a critical stance. It can be intellectually satisfying to allow one's thoughts to roam to whatever area of knowledge may shed some light on understanding and changing behavior, unencumbered by a given school's intellectual blinders. (There is no guarantee against making other — most likely culturally based — inaccurate assumptions, but searching for these is part of the intellectual journey.) In addition, by not affiliating oneself with an official version of truth, one can avoid the internecine conflict within a given camp (for example, Freudians versus Jungians, or Skinnerians versus cognitive therapists).

Here is an example of a problem. The general case for therapy involves the therapist and client(s) coming from different cultures. When they come from the same culture (for example, all Americans), many variables will appear to be constants, and culture-specific behavior will form part of their unquestioned shared reality. *What unquestioned assumptions about American culture interfere with the change process? Which such assumptions promote change and could be used more effectively if only they could be identified?* These are examples of useful questions that can be asked by questioning rather than defining the nature of reality. Years ago, an Indian psychologist I knew criticized psychoanalysis as ethnocentric because it provided no role for the grandparents in the Oedipus complex. Somehow, I find this observation more compelling than the ways in which analysts I knew assimilated it to their theoretical schema.

Biography

Jefferson M. Fish is professor of psychology at St. John's University, New York City, where he served previously as director of the Ph.D. Program in Clinical Psychology and as chair of the Department of Psychology. He received his Ph.D. degree (1969) in clinical psychology from Columbia University. He was a visiting professor in Brazil for two years and recently returned there as a Fulbright scholar. A fellow of the American Psychological Association, Fish has published two books, is the author of more than forty articles, book chapters, and other works, and currently serves on the editorial boards of four journals and an international newsletter. He is a diplomate in clinical psychology, American Board of Professional Psychology, and a diplomate in marital and family therapy, American Board of Family Psychology. Fish is treasurer of the International Council of Psychologists and has served as president of the Academic Division of the New York State Psychological Association and chair of the psychology section of the New York Academy of Sciences.

References

Fish, J. M. (1973). *Placebo therapy: A practical guide to social influence in psychotherapy.* San Francisco: Jossey-Bass.

Frank, J. D. (1973). *Persuasion and healing: A comparative study of psychotherapy* (rev. ed.). Baltimore, MD: Johns Hopkins University Press.

Kroeber, A. L., & Kluckhohn, C. (1952). *Culture: A critical review of concepts and definitions.* Cambridge, MA: Harvard University Press (Peabody Museum Papers).

Native Healing

Stanley Krippner

Definition

Psychotherapy is a deliberate attempt to modify behaviors and experiences that clients and/or their social group deem to be dysfunctional, that is, that inhibit interpersonal relationships, stifle competent performance, and/or block the actualization of one's talents and capacities. Native healing attempts to modify dysfunctional behavior and experience through a structured series of contacts between a socially sanctioned practitioner (or process) and distressed, but compliant, clients who acknowledge the status and/or the ability of that practitioner (or process).

Qualification Statement

Native healing (that is, folk healing, indigenous healing, traditional healing) must be included in any comprehensive survey of current psychotherapies because, in its various forms, it is relied upon by a larger percentage of the world's population than any other form of psychotherapy. Native healing qualifies as psychotherapy because it deliberately attempts to modify dysfunctional behavior and experience through human transactions that involve an implicit or explicit contract or agreement.

Failed relationships, flawed performance, and faulty self-actualization are all problems common to the human condition. When distressed individuals are motivated to make changes and decide that neither their own resources nor those of their family and friends are sufficient, they often look for assistance elsewhere. Industrialized cultures sanction psychotherapists to perform this function: traditional cultures provide a similar sanction for shamans, medicine men, priestesses, spiritualists, and so on.

The practitioners approved by a particular culture (or subculture) to engage in psychotherapy, balancing enlightenment, exorcism, and so on, reflect the world view and guiding mythology of that culture, utilizing techniques and establishing goals consistent with that world view and its attending cultural myths. What is considered dysfunctional in one culture (for example, hearing voices, seeing ghosts, engaging in competitive behavior) may not be considered problematic in another culture. Problems that are widespread in some cultures (for example, suffering from the evil eye, demonic possession, anorexia nervosa) may be virtually unknown in other cultures.

A cross-cultural comparison of the basic components of psychotherapy reveals that there are more similarities than differences between the psychotherapists found in industrialized nations and the native healers found in traditional societies (Torrey, 1986). The modification of dysfunctional behavior and experience by a socially sanctioned practitioner tends to be more effective (1) if the client and the practitioner share a diagnosis based on a common world view; (2) if the practitioner's personal qualities elicit beneficial responses from the client; (3) if the client enters into treatment with positive expectations; and (4) if the transactions evoke a sense of mastery that empowers the client. The few comparative studies that exist indicate that native practitioners are equally effective (or ineffective) as Western psychotherapists (Torrey, 1986). Therefore, traditional practitioners deserve both the respect and the interest of their fellow psychotherapists.

In some instances, the culture will prescribe a process rather than a practitioner (for example, affirmations, magical rituals, meditation, prayer, talking into a tape recorder, embarking on a vision quest or walkabout). To be effective, that process needs to reflect the client's (as well as the culture's) world view, contain elements that stimulate and maintain change, induce a constructive anticipation of change, and develop the client's ability to affirm and preserve his or her new life direction. Modification is more likely if a practitioner or a process manifests all four of these components. However, positive expectation alone has been known to facilitate personal empowerment; highly motivated clients may travel to a foreign country, pay an incompetent practitioner handsomely, and return symptom-free. The intense concern of the practitioner (and often of the client's community), in conjunction with emotionally stirring music and rituals, can make the cultural values explicit and can arouse a client who was originally skeptical and apathetic. On the other hand, the sores and discharges accompanying some sexually transmitted diseases rarely yield to the chants and rites of a charismatic practitioner even if the client's expectations are high; a shot of penicillin may be all that is needed to restore the client's sense of well-being. Even here, however, a naive practitioner's disregard for a native culture's world view may leave the client puzzled, anxious, and suspicious of sorcery, despite the obvious cure.

Critique Statement

Taking a cross-cultural perspective, psychotherapy could be described as an attempt to change clients' mythologies. A culture's myths explain natural phenomena, facilitate social harmony, expedite transitions, and provide a meaningful structure in which the culture's members can exist. Personal myths perform similar functions for the individual. When someone becomes confused, isolated, alienated, or overcome with anomie, one or more of his or her guiding myths have become dysfunctional. In monistic societies, native healers provide assistance on the assumption that the cultural mythology is correct and that the client needs to reconnect with his or her social web and cosmic fabric. In pluralistic societies, the psychotherapist is likely to emphasize personal myths, identifying which patterns of behaving, thinking, and feeling are not working to benefit a client's best interests (Feinstein & Krippner, 1988). The goal of psychotherapy becomes replacing dysfunctional myths with myths that provide for interpersonal and intrapersonal integration, for work and play satisfaction, and for an enhanced sense of meaning in life. Even if the psychotherapist does not realize that he or she is engaging in myth making and myth mending, this is one way in which both Western psychotherapy and native healing can be conceptualized and compared.

Placing psychotherapy in a mythological framework helps us to more fully understand the four components of effective psychotherapy listed above (Torrey, 1986). For instance, the causal mythology of industrialized societies attributes dysfunction to biological events (for example, genetics, infection, physical trauma, the aging process) and/or experiential events (for example, stress, unconscious conflicts, psychological trauma, errant child-rearing practices). Rarely considered are the metaphysical events that often permeate traditional healing systems (for example, conditions brought about by violating a taboo, by the intrusion of material from a client's former life, or by sorcery, soul loss, fate or karma). As a result, some diagnostic categories in other cultures do not interface with those constructed by psychotherapists in industrialized nations. There is no exact equivalent for *susto,* a malaise in much of Latin America thought to have been engendered by breaking a sacred rule. Even among industrialized nations there are cultural differences; *wagamama,* a behavioral condition found in Japan, has no exact counterpart in North America. Even within specific cultures there usually are differences in world views that interfere with diagnosis and treatment; for example, between upper-class and lower-class clients, or between practitioners and clients whose gender or ethnic background differ. For example, the pluralistic nature of the United States makes it necessary for psychotherapists to have some acquaintance with the world views of their potential clients from Native American, African-American, Asian-American, Hispanic-American, and Mexican-American backgrounds.

The personal qualities of effective practitioners may differ in cultures with different mythologies. Native American shamans claim to communicate with spirits and engage in what might be considered hysterical behavior; the mythos of the dominating North American culture considers both to be symptoms of mental illness. Yet these behaviors are highly valued in their own tribes; even on psychological tests standardized on non-Indian cultural groups, Apache shamans have received healthier scores than other members of their society (Boyer, 1961). It has taken social scientists several decades to retract their descriptions of shamanic behavior as "pathological"—allegations made on the basis of competing and conflicting cultural myths.

Personal myths can be thought of as explanatory cognitive structures. As such, the faith, hope, trust, and positive expectations brought by clients to sessions with their therapists can play an important role in stimulating behavior change. In much the same way, one can explain the effectiveness of native plants, roots, and berries that have no known psychotropic properties but have worked well for centuries, apparently because clients expected them to ameliorate their conditions. Herbal medicine has its critics among allopathic psychiatrists; however, these critics rarely cite studies that indicate that some 20 percent of hospitalized psychiatric patients suffer harmful side effects (including death) from prescribed drugs (Schimmel, 1964).

A client's emerging sense of mastery equips him or her with knowledge about what to do in the future to cope with life's adversities. Again, prevailing mythologies provide the framework for the client's empowerment. He or she may have learned the proper prayers that counteract malevolent spirits, the dream interpretation techniques that provide for harmony with nature, the rituals that will call one's power animal from the other world to be of assistance in time of trouble, the type of mental imagery exercise that will halt or reduce the growth of tumors, or the relaxation response procedures that counteract stress. There is no major psychotherapeutic technique that does not have its counterpart in one or more native healing systems; in my visits with native healers on six continents, I personally have witnessed what amounts to behavior modification, cognitive therapy, family therapy, milieu therapy, dream interpretation, and the use of psychotropic substances (Krippner & Colodzin, 1981). At its worst, I have found native healing to reflect superstition, ethnocentrism, and sexism. At its best, I have found native healing to be integrative (seeking to restore unity between body and mind, individual and community, humanity and nature) and cost effective and its practitioners amenable to dialogue with allopathic physicians and Western psychotherapists (Villoldo & Krippner, 1987).

Personal myths explain the world, provide social direction,

guide individual development, and address spiritual needs in a manner analogous to the way cultural myths carry out these functions for entire societies. Both types of mythologies are constellations of beliefs, feelings, and images that are organized around core themes. Native healing retains a close connection with its mythic roots. Other forms of psychotherapy neglect these roots at their peril.

Biography

Stanley Krippner is professor of psychology at Saybrook Institute Graduate School, San Francisco. He received his Ph.D. degree (1961) from Northwestern University. He is the past president of the Association for Humanistic Psychology, the Parapsychological Association, and Division 32 (Humanistic Psychology) of the American Psychological Association and is a fellow of the APA, the Society for the Scientific Study of Sex, and the American Society of Clinical Hypnosis. Krippner has authored or coauthored over 500 articles, book chapters, and reviews, as well as a dozen books, including *Dream Telepathy, Dreamworking, Human Possibilities, Healing States,* and *Personal Mythology.* Krippner has given invited colloquia for the USSR Academy of Pedagogical Sciences, Moscow, and the Chinese Academy of Sciences, Beijing, and has lectured extensively throughout Latin America.

Recommended Reading

Krippner, S. (1980). Psychic healing. In R. Herink (Ed.), *The psychotherapy handbook* (pp. 503–506). New York: New American Library.

References

Boyer, L. B. (1961). Remarks on the personality of shamans. *Psychoanalytic Study of Society, 2,* 233–254.
Feinstein, D., & Krippner, S. (1988). *Personal mythology: The psychology of your evolving self.* Los Angeles: Jeremy P. Tarcher.

Krippner, S., & Colodzin, B. (1981). Folk healing and herbal medicine: An overview. In G. G. Meyer, K. Blum, & J. G. Gull (Eds.), *Folk medicine and herbal healing* (pp. 13–29). Springfield, IL: Charles C. Thomas.

Schimmel, E. M. (1964). The hazards of hospitalization. *Annals of Internal Medicine, 60,* 100–110.

Torrey, E. F. (1986). *Witchdoctors and psychiatrists: The common roots of psychotherapy and its future.* New York: Harper & Row.

Villoldo, A., & Krippner, S. (1987). *Healing states.* New York: Simon & Schuster.

Section 2
Personal Meaning

Existential-Humanistic Therapy

Rollo May

Definition

Psychotherapy is the human relationship sought when a person is blocked in some form of his or her psychological and emotional existence. The person, then *unable* to have constructive human relationships (friendship, love) and work (creativity, productivity), becomes *able* through understanding of him- or herself with the help of another person who is typically called a therapist. The terms *therapy* and *client* are inadequate, but they are the best we have at the moment.

Qualification Statement

Therapy is a form of behavior that needs to be seen in its historical context. Ours is not the first age of therapy. There were similar periods in history; for example, in Greece in the second century B.C., or Europe in the fourteenth century A.D. The ages of therapy occur when the culture is in radical transition and the vicissitudes of the culture no longer give the individuals the security they need to perform their work and develop their friendships and loves. We see forebears of this situation in our nineteenth and twentieth centuries in the writings of Kierkegaard, Nietzsche, and Freud. The last named of these launched the present age of therapy. Those of us who are not Freudians are nonetheless post-Freudians, and we need to understand his writings as pivotal in the later development, which includes our various kinds of therapy.

The twentieth century has rightly been called the age of anxiety, the century when the sense of existence has been largely lost. Hence the similarity of psychotherapy to the movement called existentialism, which defined the age as one in which large numbers of people had lost their sense of existence, and therefore their capacity to love and to work.

The present-day forms of therapy are similar to religion in that they generally consist of one person (known as therapist or counselor) relating in a helping attitude to another person who is blocked in love and work (called the client or patient or counselee). Freud's posture was very much like that of the priest in the Catholic confession, since he, as the one listening, was mainly hidden by sitting behind the person doing the confessing. The goals of psychotherapy are to assist the person who is blocked in his or her capacity to love and to create (which I use as a synonym for constructive work) by means of a therapeutic relationship. This is done primarily by drawing out blockages in loving and creating. The ability to do this generally comes in natural human sensitivity plus special therapeutic training.

The major relationship in psychotherapy is empathy between the two persons (or more in group therapy). This consists of a sensitivity bearing a relationship to telepathy and is a form of transference and countertransference. We do not have accurate words for these significant aspects of psychotherapy. I believe the term *intervention* is not accurate or useful, inasmuch as the relationship is already begun when the patient has his first thoughts about the therapist, and the same with the thoughts of the therapist concerning the patient.

The concept of anxiety, a central symptom of the blocked capacities for love and work, is central in therapy of all sorts but especially in humanistic-existential psychotherapy. Until about 1950 (the year my volume *The Meaning of Anxiety* was published), mental health was defined as "living without anxiety." But since that time we have seen that there are constructive aspects to anxiety; for example in art, literature, and creativity of all sorts. Anxiety is now accepted as constructive as well as destructive. The existential movement, in its influence upon psychotherapy, seeks to reduce *irrational* anxiety, helping the patient transfer anxiety to the normal form. Normal anxiety has these four characteristics: It is proportionate to the threat; it does not involve intrapsychic conflict (repression); it does not require defense mechanisms; and it is productive of new insights.

Critique Statement

The criticism that humanistic-existential psychotherapy is philosophical is beside the point, since all therapy is based on some philosophy and our only choice is whether we will repress our philosophy or use it constructively.

The criticism that humanistic-existential therapy is pessimistic is simply untrue. This criticism comes generally from people who themselves do not believe in human evil or tragic aspects of human existence. Tragedy may produce the most loved of works — *Hamlet,* for example. Humanistic-existential therapy is based on the assumption that overcoming blockages in work and human relationships can reveal potentialities in the patient that can be used creatively. The value of humanistic-existential therapy is that it transfers the energy that has previously gone into neurotic symptoms, so that it now goes into creative activity in love and work.

Biography

Rollo May is currently in private practice in Tiburon, California. He received his M.Div. degree (1938) from Union Theological Seminary and his first Ph.D. degree (1949) in clinical psychology from Columbia University. The author or coauthor of fourteen books, he is the recipient of many awards and honors for distinguished contributions and humanitarian work. He is one of the main proponents of humanistic approaches to psychotherapy and is the principal American interpreter of European existential thinking as it can be applied to psychotherapy. He is currently supervisory analyst at the William Alanson White Institute of Psychiatry, Psychology and Psychoanalysis.

Existential-Humanistic Psychotherapy

James F. T. Bugental

Definition

Psychotherapy is the process of two people struggling with the issues of being alive in this world at this time. Both confront these issues, but the interests and needs of one, the client, have priority at all points. Psychotherapy attempts to disclose to the client the ways in which he keeps himself from the potential fullness of living and to ensure that he make choices that are as aware as possible of these patterns.

Qualification Statement

To be existential is to take the miraculous fact of being as one's starting point for conceptualizing and for practice. That fact is variously interpreted by different observers, and it is uniquely and implicitly defined by each person's lived life.

I find it useful to think of five basic givens of being alive as a human: We are each embodied, finite, and capable of acting, we each have a measure of choice, and we are each both separate from and yet related to all others. Each of these conditions of being confronts us with a circumstance with which we must deal in some way — respectively, these are change, contingency, responsibility, relinquishment, and "a-partness" (being a part of and apart from). These confrontations engender (existential) anxiety, and so each person finds ways of seeming to evade them, but those evasions then breed new (neurotic) anxiety.

As the client comes to us, she presents a diminished vitality in being that is the product of these evasions of authentic being in the world. This lessened fullness of living takes many forms, of course, including the familiar patterns that in our usual language are termed "symptoms" or the "neurotic syndrome." But they may also take forms less usually recognized as pathological, such as over-conscientiousness, self-negation, excessive ambition, compulsive need to please, and similar displacements of energy to the service of one's image or other externals. These are not illnesses; they are the resistance to full being that the client has learned to use to ward off what seemed to her to be overwhelming threat.

In an extremely over-simplified form, we may say that the main tasks of psychotherapy are three: first, to recognize the ways in which the client is less than fully present in the work of therapy itself and, recognizing these, to bring her to see how these patterns also limit her more generally in her life; second, to support the client in confronting the anxieties which she has so long sought to avoid (for only by doing so can she reclaim her lost authenticity); and third, to help the client redefine herself and her world in ways that foster greater genuineness of engagement with life and that result in an enlarged sense of being and potency in life.

It is crucially important to an understanding of this view to recognize that these tasks cannot be accomplished as cognitive exercises. Rather they must be organismic perceptions through which the client comes to a deep inner recognition of the ways in which she has been constricting her life. Perceptions of this order are transverbal, affectively charged, and uniquely personally relevant. Verbal insights are to such perceptions as the cereal box packaging is to nutrients in the food itself.

Implicit in this view is the recognition that both one's self-definition and way of conceiving the nature of the world are creations. This constructional view of being does not deny the reality of the given world, but it insists (with George A. Kelly) that "the key to a person's destiny is the ability to reinterpret what cannot be denied."

Critique Statement

Central to this conception and practice is the notion of presence (*Dasein*). While many therapeutic orientations will acknowledge the value of client attention and motivation, most existentialists insist it is not merely desirable; it is an absolute necessity of true depth psychotherapy.

A person is present to the degree that his cognition, affectivity, and intentionality are mobilized and focused in the immediate situation. This is not an all-or-none state, and the ability to be as fully present as one can be requires extensive commitment and dedicated practice. Both client and therapist are to seek such full presence continually. This requirement subsumes what is usually referred to as taking the work seriously, being highly motivated, and developing the therapeutic alliance. The last is produced by the intensity of their mutual presence: Two people fully present in their shared work are inevitably genuinely accessible and responsive to each other.

However, as noted, presence is not an either-or matter. Thus from moment to moment the presence of each therapeutic partner varies. The therapist monitors the client's presence as a primary source of cues about the progress of the work (content, nonverbal communications, affectivity, and so on). And note this: The therapist's major resource for this monitoring is her own presence and its fluctuations and content, which provide the bases of therapist intuition.

Client difficulties in being fully present are termed *resistances,* and, as such, they reveal as well the (neurotic) processes that limit the client's life outside the therapy. The client needs to become conscious of these intrusions on his efforts to be wholly engaged in self-exploration (that is, fully present to the therapeutic situation). This awareness must be organismic and transverbal rather than a psychodynamic explanation.

This is a point of sharp contrast with many other perspectives, which regard verbal formulations about causes and dynamics as the purpose of the work. Such formulations are called insights and thought to be curative. When they are arrived at in a nonpresent and cognitive way, they prove disappointing and transitory. Inner vision or awareness is only achieved through deep presence and extends far beyond the reach of the verbal.

Such inner vision means the client is more fully aware of his own alive-being-in-life and thus of his deeper intentions and the ways in which he has been unwittingly blocking those purposes. With this greater awareness, the client discovers that alternative possibilities exist where none were recognized before and that he has the capacity to make changes in his way of being in the world, changes that result in greater fulfillment and less distress.

Biography

James Bugental is semi-retired and devoting himself to teaching and writing; he is also a member of the adjunct faculty, Saybrook Institute, and an emeritus clinical lecturer (formerly, associate clinical professor), Department of Psychiatry, Stanford University Medical School. He received his Ph.D. degree (1948) from Ohio State University. In 1987 he was the recipient of the first annual Rollo May Award of the Mentor Society "for contributions to the literary pursuit," and in 1986 he received a certificate "in recognition of the distinguished contribution to the discipline of clinical psychology" from the Division of Clinical Psychology, American Psychological Association. He has been invited to give many addresses and keynote speeches for professional organizations and universities and serves or has served on the editorial boards of eight professional journals. Bugental has authored six books and edited another and has written approximately 150 articles, reviews, comments, and chapters in books edited by others.

Recommended Reading

Bugental, J. F. T. (1976). *The search for existential identity: Patient-therapist dialogues in humanistic psychotherapy*. San Francisco: Jossey-Bass.
Bugental, J. F. T. (1978). *Psychotherapy and process: The fundamentals of an existential-humanistic approach*. Reading, MA: Addison-Wesley.
Bugental, J. F. T. (1981). *The search for authenticity: An existential-analytic approach to psychotherapy*. (enlarged ed.). New York: Irvington.

Bugental, J. F. T. (1987). *The art of the psychotherapist.* New York: Norton.

Kelly, G. A. (1955). *The psychology of personal constructs.* New York: Norton.

Humanistic Existentialism

Stephen T. DeBerry

Definition

Psychotherapy can be defined as the delicate and purposeful utilization of a structured relationship to improve a person's state of being. The therapeutic relationship must be primarily an authentic encounter between therapist and patient(s) and secondarily the employment of therapeutic strategies and techniques. The structure provides a necessary and critical set of ground rules and parameters. A patient's improvement should be manifested in his or her entire being and thus can be evaluated in terms of interpersonal and intrapersonal changes in at least three dimensions: behavior, affect, and cognition.

Qualification Statement

This definition of psychotherapy has its theoretical roots in humanistic existentialism (Ofman, 1985) and object-relations theory (Horner, 1984). Humanistic existentialism stresses the importance of accepting responsibility in the present for all that a person is. Existentialism emphasizes existence (what I am) as opposed to essence (what I might like to be). Object-relations theory emphasizes the importance of the inner world; that is, my intrapsychic structures as they manifest themselves in my relation to the outside world of others and things. Combined, these theoretical orientations provide a relational model of psychotherapy in which the inner world of therapist and patient, as reflected in the here and now of the therapeutic encounter, is of paramount importance.

Within this model, psychotherapy is basically conceptualized as having two essential components: the authentic relationship and purposeful utilization. An authentic relationship implies the potentiality of being able to express anything, of not having to hide aspects of oneself; in short, of just being able to be oneself. Ideally, the therapeutic encounter is a meeting, for the benefit of the patient, of the therapist's and the patient's real selves (DeBerry, 1987; Masterson, 1985). The patient, regardless of symptoms, always experiences a problem in personal integration; that is, the ability to be oneself. An authentic relationship (Laing, 1969) or an I-Thou relationship (Buber, 1970) is always necessary to alleviate this position of ontological insecurity. However, the relationship must not be used by psychotherapists as an arena for the expression of their own needs. The relationship must always be used in the patient's best interest. An authentic relationship is not enough to qualify as psychotherapy.

There must also be a purposeful utilization of the relationship toward a desired goal. This provides the therapeutic encounter with a focus; for example, anxiety reduction, an improved marriage, a decrease in depressive symptomology, or a reduction of phobic behavior.

The relationship and the focus are the necessary factors of psychotherapy. (A necessary factor is a condition for the occurrence of a specified event in whose absence the event cannot occur.) Life is full of relationships and focused encounters, yet most are not defined as psychotherapy. However, when a relationship and a focus are combined within the context of psychotherapy, a sufficient condition known as the therapeutic alliance is created (Zetzel, 1970). (A sufficient condition for the occurrence of an event is a factor in whose presence the event must occur.)

Once a therapeutic alliance is established, specific techniques such as interpretation, clarification, systematic desensitization, or hypnosis can be employed to help the patient. Therapeutic strategies — for example, paradoxical intention or behavioral contracting—may likewise be introduced as a means of effecting change. It is within the therapeutic alliance that the patient's struggle to change takes place. If there is no therapeutic alliance (the sufficient factor), there can be no psychotherapeutic change. If the relationship and focus (necessary factors) are not skillfully managed, there can be no therapeutic alliance.

Critique Statement

A recent article in the popular press identifies 250 schools of psychotherapy. More scholarly journals distill the figure down to twelve main orientations.

A principal dilemma faced by practitioners of psychotherapy is that it has been defined so broadly as to become virtually meaningless. In extending the boundaries of practice we have lost sight of some basic therapeutic principles. One of these principles is that psychotherapy is not just an open relationship but a relationship with defined rules and specific purposes. Being in love or in a genuinely authentic relationship may certainly be personally therapeutic yet does not qualify the relationship as psychotherapy. Part of our dilemma stems from the fact that we often confuse what is therapeutic with psychotherapy (Herron & Rouslin, 1984). The value of the present model is that it forces the psychotherapist to be constantly aware of necessary ground rules and parameters for psychotherapy, such as confidentiality, abstinence from personal gratification, and consistency of time and location of sessions, to name but a few.

Following this model ensures that there will be an ongoing dynamic balancing of relationship and focus (the necessary factors) as a means of regulating the therapeutic alliance. Awareness of the necessary factors can prevent psychotherapy from degenerating into an open, loose relationship or its opposite, a dogmatic and static authoritarian employment of techniques and strategies. Furthermore, evaluating the patient's progress in terms of interpersonal and intrapersonal changes in behavior, affect, and cognition avoids murky meta-theoretical speculations of improvement while providing mutually observable guidelines for measuring change.

Finally, an existential framework ensures that the person's existence takes precedence over the dogmatic inclusion of his or her symptoms within any specific theoretical model (including this one). The danger of theoretical models is that we sometimes follow them literally and forget that they are metaphors. Theoretical models, like good maps, are necessary and useful; however, it is extremely important not to confuse the map with the territory. Existence and the human mind will always be far greater than any map is able to indicate.

Theoretical models and philosophical orientations belong to the world of essences and in this sense are wholly predictable and self-consistent. It is important to remember that people are not either wholly consistent or completely predictable. Remembering this will help maintain psychotherapy as what it should be: one of the most healthy and helpful of human encounters.

Biography

Stephen T. DeBerry, a clinical psychologist, is currently an assistant clinical professor of psychiatry at the Albert Einstein College of Medicine. He received his Ph.D. degree (1979) from Long Island University in clinical psychology.

References

Buber, M. (1970). *I and thou.* (W. Kaufman, Trans.). New York: Scribner.

DeBerry, S. (1987). Necessary and sufficient factors in psychotherapy: A model for understanding iatrogenic disorders. *Contemporary Psychotherapy, 17,* 235–249.

Herron, W. G., & Rouslin, S. (1984). *Issues in psychotherapy: Vol. 1.* Washington, DC: Oryn Publications.

Horner, A. J. (1984). *Object relations and the developing ego in therapy.* New York: Jason Aronson.

Laing, R. D. (1969). *Self and others.* Harmondsworth, England: Penguin.

Masterson, J. R. (1985). *The real self.* New York: Brunner/Mazel.

Ofman, W. V. (1985). Existential psychotherapy. In H. I.

Kaplan & B. J. Sadock (Eds.), *Comprehensive textbook of psychiatry: Vol. 1.* Baltimore, MD: Williams & Wilkins.
Zetzel, E. (1970). *The capacity for emotional growth.* New York: International Universities Press.

Existential Psychotherapy

Keith Hoeller

Definition

Psychotherapy is one of several contemporary ways of asking the question of the ultimate meaning of life, in other words, "How should I live?" This question is intimately entwined with questions of meaning, ethics, and politics. This means that an existential psychotherapist is concerned with the client's own world view and is willing to share his or her own world view as well. Since humans are free, we are not so much determined by our past as we are able to create our own future. The purpose of psychotherapy is to show the client, sometimes by example, that there are other ways to be and other choices that can be made. Choosing involves risk, however, as the human condition always contains an element of the tragic, and this is what makes humans noble.

Qualification Statement

Existential psychotherapy owes much to the philosophical movement called existentialism, which in turn owes much to a strain of philosophy that has its roots in ancient Greece. Existential belief holds that we are free to choose our own destiny and that all genuine questioning begins with the basic questions of human existence. These are questions that have long been the province of philosophy and religion but from which existential therapists do not shrink. Perhaps more than any other type of therapist, existentialists do not shy away from philosophical questions. As such, you will not find much in the way of technique anywhere in the literature. Is there a technique to finding the meaning of life? No, but there are several tried and true paths, one of which is entering into a structured dialogue with another person, preferably one experienced in the questioning process. The goal of such therapy is really to enable clients to say, "I know I can live a better life." At this point therapy has succeeded in changing the clients' world views and freeing them for future choices, which they are likely to make now that they have learned that to not choose is also a choice.

Biography

Keith Hoeller received his Ph.D. degree from Pennsylvania State University and is adjunct professor of psychology at Antioch University in Seattle, Washington. He is editor of the *Review of Existential Psychology and Psychiatry* (founded in 1961) and its companion book series, *Studies in Existential Psychology and Psychiatry* (founded in 1986). He is the editor of several anthologies, *Heidegger and Psychology, Sartre and Psychology,* and most recently, a textbook of classic articles entitled *Readings in Existential Psychology and Psychiatry.* He is also the author of numerous articles in philosophical and theoretical psychology, including "Phenomenological Foundations for the Study of Suicide," and "Phenomenological Psychology, and Science, Parts I and II." He is currently working on a new book entitled *Psychology: An Unnatural Science.*

Narrative Psychotherapy

George S. Howard

Definition

My model of human nature sees humans as self-determining, storytelling, active agents. From this narrative or storytelling perspective, the traditional causes articulated in psychological research (biological influences, environmental factors, unconscious motivation, and so on) are seen instead as *conditions* that render an active agent more or less likely to achieve his or her self-determined goals. This paper presents a model of therapy as a life-story modification process. People don't go insane — their life stories become ineffective! Therapy ranges from a joint therapist-client effort to rewrite parts of a client's story (short-term, minor adjustment) through major rebiographing undertakings (long-term, intensive therapy). The ultimate value in this process is to develop a story for the client that enables the person to achieve a degree of self-determination in the target domain that is appropriate for someone at the client's stage and state in life.

Qualification Statement

The narrative approach to psychotherapy represents a philosophical position that is crucially tied to the ontological view of humans as storytelling, active agents. A person proceeds through life with the fundamental task of making sense of his or her existence. The person (or self) is envisioned as a commentator, an author, a storyteller, and a personal scientist. The self (through consciousness) strives to make sense of the blooming, buzzing confusion of life. Order is imposed upon life by fitting experience into meaningful patterns. This is accomplished by seeing one's life and actions as part of a coherent story. Thus, therapists often involve themselves in helping clients to revise their stories about their lives. By altering somewhat their interpretation of the meaningful relationships in their lives, clients actually become able to achieve greater self-determination. Numerous approaches to therapy (such as Ericksonian) show how therapists employ teaching techniques such as stories to aid their clients in reframing their experiences.

From this agentic perspective, the traditional causal influences studied in psychological research come to be seen as conditions that either increase or decrease the likelihood that clients will achieve their therapeutic goals. Therapists can choose to help clients to reconceptualize their life experiences, to exert volitional control over the conditions related to therapeutic success (for example, enhance their social support system, improve their diet), or to undertake both tracks simultaneously.

Critique Statement

There is precious little empirical evidence that unequivocally demonstrates that self-determination represents an important causal force in the genesis of human action. It now seems evident that this dearth of empirical evidence is due to shortcomings in our notion of science and the methodologies necessary to demonstrate such human capacities. However, the clinical literature is replete with evidence that self-initiated, self-directed change can, and frequently does, occur (for example, Schachter, 1982).

There is a sense in which therapists are hard-pressed to see human action as volitional and therapy as a process of reestablishing self-determination in their clients' lives. People tend to come to therapy when their own efforts at self-change are unsuccessful. Thus, therapists often need to intervene to alter their clients' lives and their support systems. The view of therapy offered here considers the therapist's use of stories in effecting clinical changes. The impact of stories on people rests upon the meaning of the tale for each client. The major critique of this perspective lies in the fact that science simply does not know how to deal with meaningfulness effectively. Until science surmounts this hurdle, any therapy that acts upon a person's meaning-structure will of necessity be poorly understood scientifically.

Biography

George S. Howard is professor and chair of the Department of Psychology at the University of Notre Dame, Indiana. He received his Ph.D. degree (1975) from Southern Illinois University, Carbondale. He is a fellow of three divisions of the American Psychological Association, and winner of several teaching excellence awards. Howard has written approximately 100 articles, book chapters, and reviews. He has authored four books and coedited one book.

Recommended Reading

Howard, G. S. (1986). *Dare we develop a human science?* Notre Dame, IN: Academic Publications.
Howard, G. S. (1988a). The hardening of a "soft" science. Invited address presented at the APA Convention, Atlanta.
Howard, G. S. (1988b). *A tale of two stories: Excursions into a narrative approach to psychology.* Notre Dame, IN: Academic Publications.
Howard, G. S., & Conway, C. G. (1986). Can there be an empirical science of volitional action? *American Psychologist, 41,* 1241–1251.

Reference

Schachter, S. (1982). Recidivism and self-cure in smoking and obesity. *American Psychologist, 37,* 436–444.

Section 3
Transcendent Approaches

Transpersonal Psychotherapy

Allan B. Chinen

Definition

Transpersonal psychotherapy focuses on resolving emotional difficulties that impede an individual's fullest development as a psychological and spiritual being. It affirms the role of emotional and interpersonal factors in psychopathology, while emphasizing the validity and healing potential of transcendent experiences. Espousing no particular religion, this approach draws on Eastern and Western spiritual disciplines and on modern research in altered states of consciousness, at the same time retaining the insights of psychodynamic and behavioral psychology.

Qualification Statement

The foundation of transpersonal therapy is twofold. First is its rapidly expanding theoretical literature, beginning with Jung, Assaglioli, and Maslow, and continuing today with Wilber, Walsh, Engler, and Washburn, among others. These theoreticians analyze the psychological structures of altered states of consciousness and the commonalities between overtly different Eastern and Western spiritual traditions.

The basic concept of transpersonal psychotherapy is that everyday consciousness and the ordinary concept of the self are only limited facets of a more complex psyche. Higher levels of awareness possess definite psychological structure and are accessed through a variety of techniques, such as meditation, yoga, or spontaneous peak experiences. These transcendent states interact with ordinary consciousness in clinically relevant ways: for instance, emotional distortions like narcissism impede spiritual maturation, while meditation may help resolve longstanding character pathology. Transpersonal psychotherapy examines both directions — how numinous experiences help heal emotional wounds, and how psychological conflicts distort spiritual development.

The second basis of transpersonal therapy lies in the therapist's own spiritual practice: In analogy with psychoanalysis, a personal familiarity with transpersonal experiences is a prerequisite for empathic and knowledgeable therapy.

Just as transpersonal theory transcends traditional notions of the self and ego, its clinical practice goes beyond traditional therapeutic goals, such as strengthening self-esteem or developing adequate ego functioning. The ultimate goal of transpersonal psychotherapy is the individual's fullest development as a psychological and spiritual being. Thus, symptom reduction may or may not be important. (Indeed, symptoms are often the means by which an individual breaks through ordinary consciousness; for example, the mid-life depression that forces an individual to look beyond career or family.) However, transpersonal therapy does not presume to delineate spiritual goals: Those are left to the individual, particularly if he or she is part of a spiritual community or tradition.

In addition to the usual technical armamentarium from psychodynamic and behavioral schools, transpersonal therapy uses meditation, trance work, and imagery. The range of techniques is limited only by the therapist's experience, flexibility, and, of course, clinical judgment. Extraordinary techniques, however, are often not needed, because most individuals have spontaneous peak experiences that can be incorporated into therapy. Technique is thus less important than the therapist's respect for the transformative power of transpersonal experiences.

Although it is not yet clear which technique works for which client with what problem, a growing body of clinical lore suggests that transpersonal approaches work effectively even where prolonged behavioral or psychodynamic therapy has failed. Ironically, though, caution must be exercised with individuals who explicitly seek out transpersonal therapy, because spiritual practices can be used to compensate for major psychopathology.

If any therapeutic approach can be summed up in one sentence, transpersonal psychotherapy can be described this way: It is an attempt to bridge the long-neglected and often difficult gap between emotional development on one hand and spiritual maturation on the other — the instinctual and the sublime, the personal and the transpersonal.

Critique Statement

There are three major problems, or potential traps, in transpersonal psychotherapy. The first is becoming a *pseudo-guru*, such that the therapist acts as a spiritual teacher rather than as a psychotherapist. Rarely blatant, there are many covert forms of this behavior, in which the therapist's unspoken convictions influence the client's. To be sure, this can occur with any approach to therapy, whether psychodynamic or transpersonal, but the distortion can be particularly subtle when dealing with beliefs as personal as spiritual faiths. Nevertheless, most traditional therapies ignore spirituality, or worse, interpret it away as a manifestation of childhood neuroses. This devaluation is as dogmatic as any particular religion a therapist may espouse. Transpersonal therapy strives to articulate all spiritual presuppositions, opening them up for discussion: If sex was once socially taboo, religion still is. There are some cases, to be sure, where therapy works best if therapist and client share the same religious outlook and do not question that faith, although this is not generally true.

A second problem for transpersonal therapy lies in *romanticizing spirituality,* especially in over-interpreting emotional problems as spiritual developments. In extreme cases, frank psychosis can be mistaken for religious revelation. Or narcissistic withdrawal from the world is applauded as meditative introspection. Sound clinical judgment and broad experience with psychopathology is required here, as well as a discriminating knowledge of transpersonal processes — particularly the difference between "prepersonal" and transpersonal phenomena, between regressed and transcendent states.

One form of romanticizing spirituality is the temptation to use extraordinary techniques, like imagery or trance work, wildly, without adequate reflection. Because they seem new and exciting, transpersonal techniques may appear to be benign and wholly positive. However, meditation can have well-documented negative effects, including the precipitation of psychotic states.

A final limitation or problem with transpersonal psychotherapy lies in its relative *social isolation*. Historically focused on higher states of consciousness and Eastern traditions, transpersonal psychology has emphasized the individual and thus neglected interpersonal and societal processes. Only recently has work begun on the transpersonal dimensions of marital therapy, for instance, or group interactions. As with other individual therapies, the transpersonal approach also has a tendency to ignore social, economic, occupational, and historical factors — the context in which individuals live.

Though serious, these limitations are being vigorously addressed as transpersonal psychotherapy moves out of its initial heady and enthusiastic period into a more mature, reflective, pragmatic — and effective — phase. In the process, it takes its place alongside older therapeutic approaches.

Biography

Allan B. Chinen is assistant clinical professor of psychiatry, University of California, San Francisco. He received his M.D. degree (1979) from Stanford University. He has authored numerous articles on the transpersonal dimensions of adult development and aging and their application to psychotherapy. His most recent work is *In the Ever After: Fairy Tales and the Psychology of Aging*, which discusses the transpersonal tasks of later life as revealed in traditional fairy tales.

Recommended Reading

Boorstein, S. (Ed.). (1980). *Transpersonal psychotherapy*. Palo Alto, CA: Science and Behavioral Books.

Chinen, A. (in press). Clinical symposium: Challenging cases of transpersonal psychotherapy. *Journal of Transpersonal Psychology.*

Chinen, A. (in press). *In the ever after: Fairy tales and the psychology of aging.* Chicago: Chiron.

Walsh, R. (1980). The consciousness disciplines and the behavior sciences: Questions of comparison and assessment. *American Journal of Psychiatry, 137,* 663–672.

Washburn, M. (1988). *The ego and the dynamic ground.* Albany: State University of New York Press.

Wilber, K. (1981). *No boundary.* Boston: Shambhala.

The Love of Wisdom

Ronald D. Laing

Definition

Psychotherapy is what the practitioners of the dozens of accredited schools of psychotherapy say it is. All definitions imply an intention of the psychotherapist to help the client to resolve difficulties in living. I attempt to give undivided attention to *what goes on* in and between us: how we affect one another through vision, how we look, and move (kinesics), and how we sound (paralinguistics: the pitch, timbre, volume, rhythm, and tempo of our voices), as well as the content of what we say.

Qualification Statement

This predominantly nonverbal activity needs words and careful attention to words. It is meta-rational, or para-rational, but not irrational. It entails alert, wakeful awareness to respect the vastness of what we are unaware of (unconscious). I might call it "existential" if this word had not become associated with a school of philosophy rather than with, literally, the "love of wisdom"—the wisdom of the heart, if one can still think of the heart as something more than a pump.

Therapy requires, on my part, the development of *rapport,* of reciprocal communication that moves toward *communion* and—in so far as it does not achieve this—toward an attempt to explore the factors that stand in the way: withdrawal, withholding, mistrust, spite, malice, envy, fear. My attempts to address myself with skillful means to the specifics of the other's difficulties calls on all the resources of my repertoire of learned and acquired techniques of effectiveness-through-harmlessness.

Thus I have no hesitation in drawing, for example, on psychoanalytic theory, existential insights, or paradoxical communication. I do not preclude spontaneity, intuition, and creativity. I am drawing on my unconscious in rapport with the client's unconscious filtered through my critical consciousness, which is committed to the intention of being useful to the other's aspiration to lead a fuller life.

I do not think my range of intuition, my type of presence, or my repertoire of techniques can help everyone who hopes they can. I think it is appropriate that there are so many theories and practices that it has become difficult to say in theory what they all have in common.

Critique Statement

I have not written, so far, about my practice of psychotherapy. It has kept changing over a period of forty years and is still doing so. Some risky generalizations: It seems to me that the mutative zone in the relationship, the domain whence positive change occurs, is in that territory that is not heavily mined by transference or countertransference; or, to change the metaphors around, where both client and I can sense the sun through our rain and clouds—where each can hear a silence we share through the noise that divides us—where we are in tune with, attuned to, at-one-with values, an end, a meaning; a field effect when separate people generate a we-field, wherein there is not a loss of identity but a sharpening, clarifying, vitalizing, and stabilization of fuzzy, confused, not-fully-dreaming and not-fully-wake-and-alive, unstable, wobbling, and vacillating personal functions and structure.

My language here is intentionally nonlinearly lucid, as unambiguously paradoxical as feasible to avoid being disastrously understandable. This sort of speaking drives some people sane, but is an exasperating waste of time and money for others. These few sentences are given as a case in point about how defeatingly difficult it is to write about my practice of psychotherapy in descriptive generalizations that are unable to enable the variety of what I seem to see to be seen by others through the printed page.

Biography

Ronald D. Laing graduated in medicine from Glasgow University in 1951. From 1951 to 1953 he was a psychiatrist in the British Army. He was trained as a psychoanalyst at the British Institute of Psychoanalysis (1957–1961). Subsequently he worked in the Royal Gartnaval Mental Hospital, the Department of Psychiatry at Glasgow University, and the Tavistock Clinic, London, and from 1959 to 1965 was a research fellow of the Foundations Fund for Research in Psychiatry attached to the Tavistock Institute of Human Relations, undertaking research into the families and networks of schizophrenics and "normal" families. From 1964 to 1982 he was chairman of the Philadelphia Association, London, which set up Kingsley Hall and other small-scale households to explore the possibilities of a wholesome human environment without medication as a contribution to ameliorating profoundly disturbed states of mind by minimizing gross disturbances in communication. From 1982 to his death in 1989 he was a freelance practitioner of nonmedical psychotherapy. He was author or coauthor of fourteen books, including *The Divided Self* (1961), *Sanity, Madness and the Family* (with A. Esterson, 1964), *The Politics of Experience* (1966), *Knots* (1970), *The Facts of Life* (1976), *The Voice of Experience* (1982), and *Wisdom, Madness and Folly* (1984), as well as numerous reviews and articles.

Personal Mythology: Analysis, Transformation, and Reintegration

David Feinstein

Definition

Psychotherapy, from the perspective of the individual's developing mythology, is a process that guides the person in (1) becoming more conversant with his or her unique inner construction of reality, referred to here as a personal mythology; (2) assessing the ways in which that mythology does and does not serve his or her psychosocial adjustment and development; (3) initiating change in areas of the mythology that have proven to be limiting; and (4) integrating this expanded mythology into daily life.

Qualification Statement

A personal myth is a constellation of images, affects, and concepts organized around a core theme and addressing one of the domains within which mythology traditionally functions. According to Joseph Campbell, these include: the urge to comprehend one's world in a meaningful way, the search for a marked pathway through the succeeding epochs of human life, the need to establish secure and fulfilling relationships within a community, and the longing to know one's part in the vast wonder and mystery of the cosmos. Personal myths explain the world, guide individual development, provide social direction, and address spiritual longings in a manner that is analogous to the way cultural myths carry out these functions for entire societies (Feinstein & Krippner, 1988).

Personal myths are the product of four interacting sources. The most obvious are *biology* (the capacities for symbolism and narrative are rooted in the structure of the brain; information and attitudes are neurochemically coded; temperament and hormones influence belief systems), *culture* (the individual's mythology is, to an extent, the culture's mythology in microcosm), and *personal history* (every emotionally significant event leaves a mark on one's developing mythology). A fourth source is rooted in *transcendent experiences* — those episodes, insights, and visions that have a numinous quality, expand a person's perspective, and inspire more enlightened behavior. Thus the framework is able to accommodate biological, psychodynamic, and cultural approaches, and to integrate them within a broader spiritual perspective.

The methods for working with the individual's mythology emerge from an understanding of the way that personal myths naturally develop. Interventions are formulated to pace, bring awareness to, and facilitate this natural process. Focus is kept on the dialectic tension between prevailing and emerging ways of constructing reality. A five-stage model has been derived for working with this process (Feinstein, 1979). The stages include:

  I.   Identifying guiding myths and recognizing those that are inadequate to current circumstances, needs, and level of development
 II.   Gaining an emotionally informed understanding of the sources of these dysfunctional myths and perceiving new directions in which the psyche is pushing for expression ("counter-myths")
III.   Facilitating a synthesis that blends the elements of the old myth and the counter-myth into a new mythic image that embodies the most constructive elements of each
 IV.   Moving from the hypothetical realm of this expanded and newly integrated mythic image into a commitment toward action
  V.   Anchoring this renewed mythology in daily life

Dreams, interestingly, tend to parallel these progressive stages of reconciling new experiences with the individual's evolving mythology. A given dream may serve to (1) sustain an existing mythic structure, (2) create or strengthen an emerging counter-myth, (3) catalyze a higher-order mythic image that resolves the conflict between the two, (4) anchor this new mythic image in one's being, or (5) suggest how to weave this new mythology into one's daily life (Feinstein, in press).

Historically, rites of passage provided relatively unambiguous direction for regulating people's lives. For a variety of reasons, including the diverse individuality that characterizes modern Western cultures, this is no longer possible. The need for such direction, however, is even more pressing than in earlier eras as the myths of contemporary culture, which might guide and comfort, are themselves in unprecedented flux. The five-stage model described here can be used at any point during adult development. It is comprised of a series of personal rituals that lead to a renewed guiding mythology that is based upon an informed synthesis of the individual's history and developmental impulses, along with cultural and archetypal images that are pushing for expression. Weaving this renewed mythology into one's life can lead to fresh meaning and purpose while serving the vital functions that cultural rites and rituals no longer address.

Critique Statement

Bringing a mythological perspective to psychotherapy takes clinical practice out of the medical model and places it within a metaphor that focuses on the cultural and spriritual context of human development (Feinstein, Krippner, & Granger, 1988). Understanding one's past, present, and future in terms of an unfolding personal mythology brings daily concerns into the dignifying perspective of humanity's eternal dilemmas. It connects the individual with forces that transcend personal identity, and it lends itself to an approach that illuminates the relationship between one's inner life and one's experiences in the world. Additionally, rather than offering another psychotherapeutic system, the model provides a framework within which many contemporary psychotherapeutic modalities may be placed.

For instance, in the early stages of working with an individual's mythology, Piaget's preoperational level of thought is a natural focus for interventions. The mythic plane is engaged in delving into preoperational material, often using guided fantasy and cathartic techniques (stages I and II of the model). Once mythic conflicts have been accessed, they are reworked, drawing upon a blend of psychodynamic, cognitive, and meditative processes (stages III and IV). Finally, resolution images are anchored back into the preoperational system of thought using methods that correspond to its mode of logic, including emotionally charged visualizations, physical posturing and rehearsals, pleasurable reinforcement, and repetition (stage V). Thus, at different stages of the work, techniques from different modalities—psychodynamic, cognitive, behavioral, and meditative—are the most appropriate.

An advantage of maintaining a mythological perspective is that mythology provides the closest existing analog to the invisible workings of the human psyche. Personal myths emerge in the natural language of the individual's inner world. Furthermore, mythic thought can engage the full spectrum of human nature, from primal impulses to aesthetic longings. According to Joseph Campbell (1968, p. 3), "It would not be too much to say that myth is the secret opening through which the inexhaustible energies of the cosmos pour into human cultural manifestations." As the need to renew our connection with our spiritual roots is gaining broader recognition within the culture, the symbols of mythology provide a time-honored vehicle for entering sacred territory.

A frequent criticism of personality theories in psychology is that they do not adequately account for the social and cultural context of the individual. Because of the reflexive relationship between personal and cultural myths, a sound understanding of the way the person and the society operate in concert is inherent to the framework. In fact, as the culture's myths have been crumbling under the enormous pressure of social change— the half-life of a valid guiding myth has never been briefer—a well-articulated, carefully examined personal mythology may be one of the most effective devices available for countering the disorienting grip of a world in mythic turmoil. In addition, because of the dynamic equilibrium between personal and cultural myths, a mythological understanding of one's personality development also provides insight into the underlying myths of one's culture — how to recognize them and their influence, how to draw on some and resist others, and how to creatively participate in changing them.

Biography

David Feinstein is director of Innersource in Ashland, Oregon. He received his Ph.D. degree (1973) from Union Institute in clinical and community psychology. Feinstein has taught at the Johns Hopkins University School of Medicine, Antioch College, and the California School of Professional Psychology. He is coauthor (with Stanley Krippner) of *Personal Mythology: The Psychology of Your Evolving Self* and (with Peg Elliott) of *Rituals for Living and Dying*. He has lectured and consulted widely on the application of a mythological perspective for bringing about personal, organizational, and societal change.

References

Campbell, J. (1968). *The hero with a thousand faces* (2nd ed.). Princeton, NJ: Princeton University Press.

Feinstein, D. (1979). Personal mythology as a paradigm for a holistic public psychology. *American Journal of Orthopsychiatry, 49,* 198–217.

Feinstein, D. (in press). Myth-making activity through the window of your dreams. In S. Krippner (Ed.), *Language of the night: A dream anthology.* Los Angeles: Jeremy P. Tarcher.

Feinstein, D., & Krippner, S. (1988). *Personal mythology: The psychology of your evolving self.* Los Angeles: Jeremy P. Tarcher.

Feinstein, D., Krippner, S., & Granger, D. (1988). Myth-making and human development. *Journal of Humanistic Psychology, 28*(3), 23–50.

7

Eclectic and
Integrative Psychotherapy

Eclecticism, according to *Webster's Collegiate Dictionary,* is "the method or practice of selecting what seems best from various systems." In his *Handbook of Eclectic Psychotherapy,* John Norcross (1986) suggests that the foregoing is probably the most accurate definition. He further differentiates between eclecticism, which he describes as trending "toward a comprehensive approach to clinical work *predicated on demonstrated [technical] efficacy"* (p. 6, our emphasis), and integrationism, which denotes a multitheoretical convergence "incorporating parts into a whole" (p. 6).

Both integrative and the more broadly based eclectic approaches have gained steadily in popularity in recent years. While integrative approaches continue to strive for convergence among two or more theoretical bases, eclectic approaches are evolving along a continuum that ranges from utilization of a few favored techniques to creation of a highly complex system for determining which techniques are employed in a given therapeutic circumstance. According to Goldfried and Newman (1986), one of the earliest attempts at integration occurred when T. M. French, delivering an address to the American Psychiatric Association in 1932, endeavored to relate repression to extinction and inhibition. This move toward rapprochement met with limited acceptance. Two years later, L. S. Kubie (Goldfried &

Newman, 1986) published a paper maintaining that conditioned reflex could account for the functioning of certain aspects of psychoanalytic technique. During the course of the next three decades notable efforts were made to attend to commonalities among different therapies (J. Dollard & N. Miller, J. D. Frank, S. L. Garfield) and to integrate disparate concepts in the treatment process (F. C. Thorne, D. D. Glad). In 1967, Arnold Lazarus introduced the concept of "technical eclecticism," which eschewed the importance of theoretical validity in favor of empirical validity; convergence and explanation yielded to efficacy in this approach.

The specific units-of-analysis vary, depending upon one's stance within the eclectic discipline (all integrationists are eclectic, but not all eclectics are integrationists). Integrationists are guided by the two or more theories to which they subscribe, attending to elements emphasized by those theories. Technical eclectics attend to the symptoms as assessed in specific procedures and to relevant research. Some eclectic approaches may do both.

The present chapter is divided into four parts, consisting of an overview followed by sections on assessment models, integrative models, and common factors. In the overview section, John Norcross provides a broad description of eclectic-integrative therapy and addresses necessary elements of any therapeutic approach.

The assessment models section describes approaches based on procedures for selecting interventions. Arnold Lazarus discusses multimodel therapy, which details the specific dimensions of client functioning to be assessed in choosing the appropriate intervention. Larry Beutler's extensive contribution elaborates on several variables relevant both to producing therapy beneficial to the patient and to advancing the empirical base of the eclectic approach.

In the integrative models section, Paul Wachtel describes an approach that synthesizes diverse theories in producing successful outcomes. The common factors section addresses aspects of either the therapeutic process or client functioning that are worthy of attention by the astute eclectic therapist. Sol Garfield suggests that the therapist-offered explanation is a variable of profound import in influencing therapy outcome. David Blustein makes a case for vocational functioning as a focus of therapy. Finally, Adam Blatner proposes attention to client life roles as both a therapeutic approach and a step toward meta-theoretical development.

References

Goldfried, M. R., & Newman, C. (1986). Psychotherapy integration: An historical perspective. In J. C. Norcross (Ed.), *Handbook of eclectic psychotherapy* (pp. 25–61). New York: Brunner/Mazel.

Norcross, J. C. (1986). Eclectic psychotherapy: An introduction and overview. In J. C. Norcross (Ed.), *Handbook of eclectic psychotherapy* (pp. 3–24). New York: Brunner/Mazel.

Section 1
Overview

Eclectic-Integrative Psychotherapy

John C. Norcross

Definition

Psychotherapy, from my eclectic perspective, is the informed and intentional application of clinical methods and interpersonal stances derived from established psychological principles for the purpose of assisting people to modify their behaviors, cognitions, emotions, and/or other personal characteristics in directions that the participants deem desirable.

Qualification Statement

The discipline of psychotherapy has been historically stymied by an endless proliferation of psychotherapies — each purportedly unique and each purportedly superior. In turn, each psychotherapeutic tradition has developed its own jargon that confounds dialogue across orientations and widens the theoretical rift. Isolated language systems and rival definitions encourage clinicians to wrap themselves in semantic cocoons from which they cannot escape and which others cannot penetrate. In fact, the editors' instructions to define psychotherapy for this volume explicitly stated, "Please stress elements that *differentiate* your orientation from other methods."

Eclecticism seeks, in a modest manner, to move us beyond this "dogma eat dogma" atmosphere and to provide a transtheoretical conception of psychotherapy (Norcross, 1986). From an integrative perspective, an acceptable definition of psychotherapy will possess several necessary features (Norcross, 1987)

218

beyond the obvious need for accuracy. First, the definition should be descriptive, operationalizing the clinical phenomena at hand. Second, it will be accessible, readily available to clinicians and researchers alike. Third, it will eventually be consensual, subject to agreement and verification by psychotherapists of diverse persuasions. And fourth, for want of a better phrase, our generic definition should be respectfully even-handed. That is, it should treat theories equitably without sacrificing the integrity of any particular approach.

In this respect, the eclectic definition of psychotherapy offered here is a reasonably balanced one adapted from Meltzoff and Kornreich (1970) and a relatively neutral one in terms of theory, method, and format. I have, for example, not specified the number or composition of the participants since different theoretical orientations and client needs call for different combinations. Similarly, the precise training and qualifications of the psychotherapist have not been delineated. Perhaps most importantly, eclecticism recognizes multiple processes of change and the multidimensional nature of change; no effort is made here to delimit the methods or content of therapeutic change. The requirement that the methods be "derived from established psychological principles" is sufficiently broad to permit clinical and/or research validation.

In closing, I want to make three qualifying remarks about this definition that probably say more about me as a psychotherapist than about eclecticism as an orientation. The definition stipulates that psychotherapy is "informed and intentional." Many life experiences are therapeutic; psychotherapy is a specified subset of such experiences that is planned, not serendipitous. The definition also describes "clinical methods and interpersonal stances." In some therapy systems, the active change mechanism has been construed as a technique, while in other systems the therapeutic relationship has been regarded as the primary focus and source of change. Here, the interpersonal stances and experiences of the therapist are placed on equal footing with methods and interventions. Finally, I firmly believe that any activity defined as psychotherapy should be conducted only for the "purpose of assisting people" toward mutually agreed upon goals. Otherwise—though it may be labeled psychotherapy—it becomes a subtle form of coercion or punishment.

Biography

John C. Norcross is currently professor and chair of psychology at the University of Scranton and a clinical psychologist in part-time independent practice in Scranton. He received his baccalaureate *summa cum laude* (1980) from Rutgers University and his M.A. degree (1981) and Ph.D. degree (1984) in clinical psychology from the University of Rhode Island. He completed his internship at the Brown University School of Medicine. Norcross has published over eighty scholarly articles and has authored or edited five books, the most recent being *Therapy Wars* and *The Handbook of Eclectic Psychotherapy*. He has served as a clinical and research consultant to a number of organizations, including the National Institute of Mental Health and "CBS This Morning." He resides in Mt. Cobb with his wife, two children, and Weimaraner.

References

Meltzoff, J., & Kornreich, M. (1970). *Research in psychotherapy.* New York: Brunner/Mazel.

Norcross, J. C. (Ed.). (1986). *Handbook of eclectic psychotherapy.* New York: Brunner/Mazel.

Norcross, J. C. (Ed.). (1987). Special section: Toward a common language for psychotherapy. *Journal of Integrative and Eclectic Psychotherapy, 6,* 165–204.

Section 2
Assessment Models

Multimodal Therapy

Arnold A. Lazarus

Definition

Multimodal psychotherapy is the application of principles and techniques based largely on data from social, cognitive, and experimental psychology, plus clinical wisdom, for the alleviation of human suffering and the enhancement of adaptive living. The aim is educational, and emphasis is on both intraindividual functioning and interpersonal transactions (social and family systems). Durable outcomes require the acquisition of a wide range of coping skills and perceived self-efficacy. Thorough assessment calls for scrutiny of a client's BASIC ID (**b**ehaviors, **a**ffective reactions, **s**ensations, **i**mages, **c**ognitions, **i**nterpersonal relationships, and **d**rugs or biological factors).

Qualification Statement

Since the primary emphasis is on a broad-based model emphasizing coping skills and education, little time is devoted to symbolic meanings or putative repressed complexes. Social learning theory, in its widest and most sophisticated form (Bandura, 1986), provides a theoretical framework that draws from several areas of psychological research. Preferred techniques are those that have received empirical support (for example, modeling and observational learning procedures, social skills training, flooding and exposure, response prevention, desensitization, self-regulatory methods, cognitive restructuring, relaxation training), but effective psychotherapy also requires a storehouse of clinical wisdom that transcends the foregoing.

221

Multimodal practitioners straddle the fence between art and science. Always on the lookout for data-based methods of change, and respecting clinical and empirical research findings, they also draw on personal experience, intuitive judgment, and idiosyncratic communication skills. This technically electic stance calls for a thorough assessment of a client's behavioral difficulties, affective distress, sensory discomforts, negative images, cognitive distortions, interpersonal problems, and biological disorders (Lazarus, 1981, 1985). Thus, the emphasis swings back and forth between the individual and his or her social network.

The techniques and goals of the therapy vary from case to case. In some instances, it is merely a matter of providing support and encouragement. In others the client, in addition to reassurance, requires attention to certain deficits (and so might need, for example, assertiveness training). A combination of hypnosis and biofeedback might be the treatment of choice in yet other instances. The point is that a thorough multimodal assessment endeavors to determine who or what will be best for each individual. Most of the actual techniques are drawn from cognitive-behavior therapy since outcome studies suggest that they are the most effective for many dysfunctions (Rachman & Wilson, 1980). But multimodal assessment and therapy draws freely from other disciplines (for example, gestalt therapy, psychodrama, reality therapy, Transactional Analysis) without necessarily subscribing to any of their theoretical conceptions. The ideal goal is to ensure that people have adequate coping responses, minimal affective distress, the capacity for sensory pleasure and joy, a positive self-image, rational beliefs, and loving and rewarding interpersonal relationships, and that they follow sound health habits (for example, good nutrition, exercise, and rest). A basic goal is to change self-doubt into perceived self-efficacy. Competent functioning requires more than the possession of skills — the individuals also must believe in their ability to use them effectively.

Critique Statement

There does not appear to be a well-documented knowledge base that can show practitioners how to determine when "more will be better" or when highly targeted unimodal or bimodal interventions are likely to prove superior to multimodal therapy. For instance, when is cognitive therapy necessary and sufficient? When does behavioral retraining suffice? How can one gauge whether a client is ready for certain procedures? Of course, these criticisms are not limited to the practice of multimodal therapy per se but address the entire psychotherapeutic arena.

Because multimodal therapy focuses on the fact that everyone is unique and that therapy has to be tailored to each individual, the multimodal therapist does not have the luxury of leaning on a general theory that guides the treatment. The Rogerian counselor knows exactly how every client will be received — large doses of warmth and empathy will be dispensed in a basically nondirective context. But the first task for the multimodalist is to devise a plan for meeting the client's goals. The multimodal therapist must adjust his or her style to fit the needs of different people.

A basic question to be addressed is how *directive* and how *supportive* one should be. As Howard, Nance, and Myers (1987) have shown, the four possible combinations (low direction/high support; low direction/low support; high direction/high support; high direction/low support) meet different clients' needs and address differing needs of a particular client over time. But this calls for thought, planning, and considerable judgment. The multimodal therapist has to decide when and how to confront, nurture, admire, reinforce, ignore, or punish a variety of specific responses.

Similarly, whereas there are those who only see couples or only work with families, the multimodal therapist has to decide whether a particular person will profit most from individual, dyadic, triadic, family, or group therapy, or some combination of these. Thus, there are those who are intimidated by this orientation and claim that it expects too much from the therapist. How can one person be an expert at everything? The answer, of course, is that one cannot. Nevertheless, within the antiperfectionistic philosophy that we espouse, one can strive for a broad-based clinical adequacy, and one can master a reasonably wide range of techniques and modalities. The multimodal rationale is that clients' interests are usually better served when seeing a therapist who is adequate to good in many areas versus one who is excellent only in one or two.

Dryden (1986), in his critique of multimodal therapy, said that we need the following: more explicit guidelines for the selection of appropriate therapeutic arenas and movement between arenas; more precise information about therapeutic strategies and how these may suggest therapeutic methods; and a more clear-cut and central role for the mechanisms of change across the BASIC ID. In essence, the multimodal approach takes very seriously an observation underscored by Milton Erickson: "Each person is a unique individual. Hence, psychotherapy should be formulated to meet the uniqueness of the individual's needs, rather than tailoring the person to fit the Procrustean bed of a hypothetical theory of human behavior" (Zeig, 1982).

Biography

Arnold A. Lazarus is a distinguished professor at the Graduate School of Applied and Professional Psychology, Rutgers, the State University of New Jersey. He received his Ph.D. degree (1960) from the University of the Witwatersrand (Johannesburg, South Africa) in clinical psychology. He is the recipient of several awards, including the Distinguished Service to the Profession of Psychology Award from the American Board of Professional Psychology, and the Meritorious Achievement Award from the Arizona State Psychological Association. He serves on the editorial board of or as a consulting editor for ten journals. Lazarus has authored approximately 150 articles and book chapters and has written, edited, or coedited eleven books.

References

Bandura, A. (1986). *Social foundations of thought and action: A social cognitive theory.* Englewood Cliffs, NJ: Prentice-Hall.

Dryden, W. (1986). Eclectic psychotherapies: A critique of leading approaches. In J. C. Norcross (Ed.), *Handbook of eclectic psychotherapy.* New York: Brunner/Mazel.

Howard, G. S., Nance, D. W., & Myers, P. (1987). *Adaptive counseling and therapy: A systematic approach to selecting effective treatments.* San Francisco: Jossey-Bass.

Lazarus, A. A. (1981). *The practice of multimodal therapy.* New York: McGraw-Guilford.

Lazarus, A. A. (Ed.). (1985). *Multimodal therapy.* In R. J. Corsini & D. Wedding (Eds.), *Current psychotherapies.* Itasca, IL: Peacock.

Rachman, S. J., & Wilson, G. T. (1980). *The effects of psychological therapy* (2nd ed.). New York: Pergamon Press.

Zeig, J. K. (Ed.). (1982). *Ericksonian approaches to hypnosis and psychotherapy.* New York: Brunner/Mazel.

Systematic Eclectic Psychotherapy

Larry E. Beutler

Definition

Psychotherapy is a process of interpersonal influence or, more specifically, persuasion. The consultant or healer assumes the role of encouraging and persuading the patient or client to change perceptions, feelings, beliefs, and behaviors. Since the therapists are bound in these efforts by their own viewpoints, beliefs, and value systems, these very beliefs and values are the substances that direct the persuasion. While clients and patients do not always converge on the therapist's point of view, it is this point of view that determines the therapist's goals of treatment. Yet, while psychotherapy is a process of persuasion, it is not a process of coercion. The therapist models, encourages, and establishes the criteria by which change is assessed and attempts to move the patient toward those criteria. The therapist also acknowledges, rewards, and accepts change. In fact, the interpersonal relationship, as well as the techniques of psychotherapy derived from this relationship, are all in the service of the persuasion process.

Qualification Statement

The therapist has two tasks in the therapeutic persuasion process. First, it is the therapist's task to maintain the patient's focus upon those outcome goals and mediating tasks (that is, the therapeutic focus) that are defined as important and desirable to change by collaborative contract. Second, the therapist maintains the patient's arousal within those limits that are considered to be conducive to maintaining motivation and direction. The therapist's theoretical philosophy helps define what the therapeutic focus will be, while the therapeutic procedures and techniques that are used are the means by which the focus and optimal arousal are maintained.

In its simplest form one can consider the therapist's task to be that of defining *what* a patient is attempting to avoid and *how* that avoidance is taking place. Therapeutic procedures, therefore, attempt to expose the patient to what is being avoided, at least partially by removing the method of avoidance. This process is designed to induce cognitive dissonance. Exposure of the patient to that which is avoided is undertaken at such a level and speed as to maintain sufficient arousal through cognitive dissonance as to motivate the patient but not to produce so much arousal that problem-solving efforts will be unproductive. This process is facilitated by addressing three domains of fit between the therapy and the patient.

The first domain of fit is that occurring between the patient and the therapist. There are two aspects to this match, of which the first reflects the compatibility between the patient's and the therapist's backgrounds and views of life. Research has suggested (Beutler, 1981, 1983) that demographic similarities between the patient and therapist establish a basis for a relationship, while certain differences of perspective facilitate the patient's awareness of the potential for change (for example, cognitive dissonance). A second aspect of fitting the patient and therapist is based upon the therapist's ability to enhance the relationship quality, given an imperfect fit between patient and therapist's backgrounds and experiences. Therapists can enhance the quality of the relationship by communication and listening procedures that increase their credibility and persuasive appeal.

The second domain of fit is between the therapeutic technique and the patient's problem complexity, coping style, and interpersonal sensitivity. There are several aspects of this process. For example, some techniques and procedures are conducive to resolving repetitive behavioral patterns fed by internal conflicts, while others are focused more narrowly upon the alleviation of symptoms. By defining the complexity of the patient's problems along with a dimension of *breadth,* one can select procedures that address the degree of problem complexity presented by a patient.

Therapeutic techniques also vary in the level of their intervention, ranging from unconscious experience through affect and automatic thoughts to overt behaviors. In turn, patients' coping styles vary, ranging from the isolation of affect, through repression of conflicts, to externalization and acting out in the face of stress. The systematic eclectic psychotherapist selects therapeutic procedures that address the level of experience that characteristically represents the coping style of the patient. Procedures addressing the emotional and sensory levels of experience may be applied to patients who isolate and deny emotions; procedures aimed at inducing awareness of unconscious conflicts may be applied to those who repress and deny conflict; procedures aimed at the cognitive level of experience may fit those who lack cognitive controls; and procedures aimed at the behavioral levels of experience may be helpful for those whose external coping styles are manifest in behavior that is disruptive.

Another aspect of fitting the technique to the patient addresses the mediating tasks the therapist constructs en route to the final conflictual or symptomatic change goals. Some mediating tasks are focused on creating awareness of behaviors, cognitions, emotions, or conflicts. Other tasks are focused upon personal or interpersonal change or upon maintaining gains once made. The stage of the patient's problem-solving efforts corresponds with and dictates the nature of these mediating targets.

Still another aspect of matching the technique to the patient's needs revolves around the patient's sensitivity to external controls and directions. Patients who are highly sensitive or counterreactant to external controls may find it difficult to adapt to a therapist who directs and structures change efforts. Alternatively, those who are compliant and nonreactive to external demands may do well with a therapist who provides some direction and structure. Hence, the patient's reactance level may determine for the therapist the degree to which directive as opposed to evocative interventions are utilized.

The third domain of fitting the therapy to the patient addresses the changes that take place across time. Two aspects of change are important to consider in this domain. The first is indexed by changes in the patient's problem-solving phase, and this phase can be used to shift mediating tasks of treatment. The second has to do with changes across sessions, wherein the therapist observes moment-to-moment changes in patient reactance level and coping style, adjusting the level and the directiveness of the intervention accordingly.

To summarize, effective eclectic psychotherapy is implemented by blending the processes of matching the patient and the therapist to facilitate the development of optimal treatment relationships, enhancing the nature of those relationships by modifying the structure of therapy, attending to the match between therapeutic goals and the complexity of the patient's problem, adjusting the level of the intervention to the coping style presented by the patient, adjusting the level of directiveness to the patient's level of resistance, and then modifying all of this both within and across sessions to fit the tasks of treatment and the peculiarity of the patient's response. The complexity of this task matches the complexity of human behavior itself.

Critique Statement

There are three domains of criticism that serve as measuring sticks for assessing the practical truth and usefulness of any treatment approach. These domains serve as the foundation blocks for clinical applications and separate credible from incredible treatment philosophies. Specifically, to emerge from the ranks of interesting pseudoscience to assume a place in the ranks of legitimate professional practice, a treatment must pass the tests of theory, empiricism, and practicality.

The *theoretical validity* of any treatment approach can be determined by asking whether this approach helps us understand and predict behavior. Yet systematic eclectic psychotherapy offers no new theoretical insights into the development of psychopathology. Indeed, it disclaims such theoretical intentions and confines its theoretical contributions to the level of describing and prescribing interventions.

Some would argue that without a formal theory of disordered behavior, growth in the field will be hampered — science relies on inferential, not descriptive, theories for the development of new techniques. This would suggest that without theories of how disordered behavior occurs, no new procedures will evolve and no new understanding will occur.

To this criticism, the systematic eclectic therapist responds with two observations. First, while the systematic eclectic approach does not offer a new and better theory of psychopathology, it does not eschew theory. In fact, it argues that there already are entirely too many contradictory theories of psychopathology in existence to warrant another speculation. Yet it holds that the work of psychotherapy is teaching the patient a new view of past, present, and future experiences. From this perspective, the aspects of theory that serve clinicians best are amalgamations of a preferred formal theory and their personal philosophy of living. In the trenches, there are no theoretical purists — all theoretical views are modulated and tempered by personal experiences and beliefs. These are what the patient learns in effective treatment, and these are what guide the goals and subgoals of treatment.

Systematic eclectic psychotherapy maintains that since psychotherapy is a process of persuasion, either implicitly or explicitly, we will teach most effectively what we believe. It is impractical to insist that all therapists share the same world views and philosophies of living in order to practice systematic eclectic psychotherapy. Hence, theoretical divergence is encouraged, and from this divergence there is an opportunity for new techniques to arise.

Second, systematic eclectic psychotherapy would point out that one need not have a theory of psychopathology to predict and control behavior. One need not know what caused a depres-

sion to know that depressed people with x, y, and z qualities
will respond well to cognitive interventions, while those with
a, b, and c qualities will not but may respond to interpersonal
interventions or to antidepressant medications. Systematic eclectic psychotherapy emphasizes the importance of obtaining valid
descriptions of the relationships among patients, circumstances,
treatments, therapists, and outcomes.

The foregoing leads naturally to a consideration of the second domain to which criticism might be addressed. Concerns
with the *empirical veracity* of systematic eclecticism can be reduced
to the question of whether this model fits what we know about
relationships among patient characteristics, therapist characteristics, interventions, and outcomes. The realistic answer to critics
who suggest that the model of treatment selection posed here
does not correspond to empirical conclusions is to suggest that
it does and it doesn't. On the positive side, this model is specifically built around research findings. Unlike more doctrinaire
approaches that begin with theory and then attempt to gather
facts, systematic eclectic psychotherapy begins with what have
become reasonably consensual views of how psychotherapy
works. Specifically, it acknowledges that most psychotherapists
yield similar outcomes and that the largest contributions to treatment outcomes come from the patient and from the bonding
relationship between the patient and the therapist.

Yet beyond this level of greatest consensus — the domain of
those "common-factors eclectics" who suggest that all treatment
benefits are attributable to common principles — the systematic
eclectic model proposes two other less certain empirical principles. Like all technically eclectic models, this one proposes that
despite the benefit to be gained from a caring therapist, there
will still be differences in outcomes between two equally well-
intentioned patients, and that these differences indicate that
cross-matching patient characteristics and therapy characteristics may enhance quality of care. Those who share with me a
belief in technical eclecticism would agree with this interpretation of available research literature, but we might disagree about
what this literature suggests should be the objects of our cross-
matching procedure.

At each new level of specificity—beginning with common-factors interpretations and passing through technical eclecticism to systematic eclectic analyses—there is less foundation research available and less consensus of interpretation. There are dozens of different eclectic models and hundreds of purist theories of psychotherapy. In our heart of hearts, we each believe that our view of what makes a difference in psychotherapy is the most accurate interpretation of current literature. The empirical test has yet to be passed by any of these approaches.

To pass the test of empirical veracity, it is not enough to build a model of treatment on past research. We must also construct prospective studies that will specifically test our assumptions. This work is just beginning, with many theorists beginning to test their own methods and others hoping to win by default and force of persuasion. As new findings evolve, all will be forced to incorporate them into their own viewpoints. In this process, it is inevitable that we eventually will move closer to one another. Indeed, this process of convergence is already beginning. For example, I am currently collaborating with John Clarkin, a proponent of differential therapeutics, to compose a second-generation model of technical eclecticism that seeks common ground among our two eclectic approaches and aspects of several others as well (Beutler & Clarkin, 1990). We are basing the second-generational eclectic analysis on empirical data, with special attention to that accumulating specifically on predictors of differential treatment outcomes.

The third foundation block that must stand the test of critique is that of *practical utility*. Criticisms in this domain can be reduced to questions of whether this approach to treatment assignment can be learned and reliably implemented. It is in this domain that we have the least knowledge.

To pass the test of practical utility, one must demonstrate that psychotherapists can and will learn the principles of treatment selection, can and will extend their own armamentarium of procedures to accommodate the eclectic model, can and will practice the principles, and can do all of these things at an acceptable cost in time and resources.

Until recently, we have not known if therapists could learn

procedures from very discrepant psychotherapy models (for example, psychoanalysis and behavior therapy) and apply them
both at an equivalent level of competence. Moreover, we have
not known if therapists would have any interest in doing so.
Now, however, it is becoming apparent that there is tremendous interest in both this and other eclectic models. Within the
past decade, there have emerged the Society for the Exploration of Psychotherapy Integration, the International Fellowship
of Eclectic Psychotherapy, and a professional journal devoted
to eclecticism (*Journal of Integrative and Eclectic Psychotherapy*), all
of which suggest the presence of interest in this area.

Likewise, in the past decade therapists have increasingly identified themselves as eclectic, there has been a healthy accumu-
lation of research specifically on eclectic psychotherapy, and there
has been at least a modest amount of prospective research on
the model of systematic eclectic psychotherapy described here.
There even has been research to suggest that therapists can effectively combine procedures from different approaches without
sacrificing skill (Beutler & Clarkin, 1990, presents a review of
research in these areas).

In spite of progress in all of these areas, it remains true that
much needs to be done before systematic eclectic psychotherapy can pass the trifold test of validity. The strongest case for
validity can be derived for those who criticize the model's theoretical rationale. The next strongest case for validity rests on
the correspondence between empirical findings and the basic
principles of differential effectiveness of psychotherapy, although
the strength of this latter test of validity declines both as the
dimensions of this model become more exclusive and as accompanying research is less available. Finally, the practical test of
validity remains to be demonstrated, although research accumulating here gives us cause for optimism.

Biography

Larry E. Beutler is director of the Counseling Psychology Program at the Graduate School of Education, University of California, Santa Barbara. He received his Ph.D. degree (1970) from

the University of Nebraska in clinical psychology. Beutler is also associate editor of the *Journal of Consulting and Clinical Psychology,* a diplomate in professional psychology (clinical), past president of the Society for Psychotherapy Research, and past secretary of the Arizona Board of Psychologist Examiners. He is the author of *Eclectic Psychotherapy: A Systematic Approach,* coauthor (with John Clarkin) of *Systematic Treatment Selection: Toward Integrated Therapeutic Interventions,* and coeditor of the *Comprehensive Handbook of Cognitive Therapy,* as well as coauthor or coeditor of three other volumes and over 150 published papers on psychotherapy, research, and mental health.

References

Beutler, L. E. (1981). Convergence in counseling and psychotherapy: A current look. *Clinical Psychology Review, 1,* 79–101.

Beutler, L. E. (1983). *Eclectic psychotherapy: A systematic approach.* New York: Pergamon Press.

Beutler, L. E., & Clarkin, J. (1990). *Systematic Treatment Selection: Toward Targeted Therapeutic Interventions.* New York: Brunner/Mazel.

Section 3
Integrative Models

Psychotherapy from an Integrative Psychodynamic Perspective

Paul L. Wachtel

Definition

Psychotherapy is a human relationship in which the primary goal is to bring about changes desired by one of the participants, who is usually described as the patient or client. In helping the patient to change, the therapist draws on influences and processes common to all significant human relationships, but in addition, he or she is usually guided by an explicit theory of human behavior and psychological distress.

From an integrative psychodynamic perspective, the therapist's efforts are guided in particular by an understanding both of the role of unconscious motivations and conflicts and of the crucial role of active intervention to interrupt vicious circles in the patient's daily life.

Qualification Statement

The theory guiding the integrative psychodynamic approach to therapy, *cyclical psychodynamics,* is an amalgam of concepts from psychodynamic, behavioral, and systems theories, reworked and put together in such a way as to enable a theoretically coherent model to evolve. It is but one of numerous efforts currently ongoing to transcend the limits of the school-oriented approaches that have tended to dominate our thinking about psychotherapy until quite recently. It shares this aim with approaches labeled "eclectic" but is more committed to achieving a thoroughgoing

234

integration: It aims, first, for a theoretical model that is internally consistent and attuned to the full range of observations on which the various schools base their thinking and, second, for a melding and reworking of their concepts and methods so that what results is not merely a mix of simple elements from different sources but rather a true synthesis of those elements that mark the evolution of new concepts and methods.

A key assumption is that most of the present schools have remained viable because they are each based on significant observations—observations that in turn are ignored or minimized by proponents of other schools. Therefore an integrative approach takes as its aim to attend seriously to what has been observed by proponents of *all* of the major schools and to incorporate those observations and the methods they have spawned into a framework that is comprehensive, coherent, and continually evolving. In the process, the concepts and methods drawn from the currently existing schools are likely to change (Wachtel, 1985). A truly integrative approach is thus neither a grab bag of methods nor a simple sum of prior separate approaches but rather a unified and continually developing framework.

Central to the approach to integration guided by the theory of cyclical psychodynamics is an emphasis on the vicious circles that characterize psychological difficulties and on the more benign circular processes that maintain healthy functioning and/or break the cycle of psychopathology. From the point of view of cyclical psychodynamics, psychological difficulties are never strictly an individual matter; every neurosis requires accomplices (Wachtel, 1987). An emphasis on circular processes, both intrapsychic and interpersonal, provides a key to bringing together the perspectives of individual psychodynamic and family systems approaches (Wachtel & Wachtel, 1986) and to understanding how the characterological emphasis of psychoanalytically based approaches and the situational emphasis of behavioral approaches can be reconciled (Wachtel, 1977).

Critique Statement

There is always the danger of fashioning a theoretically organized approach to integration that it will eventually become

just one more competing theory, one more school. That would
be ironic and self-defeating. What helps to minimize that danger
is that basic to the approach addressed here is a commitment
continuously to examine and incorporate contributions from
other approaches—including other integrative approaches.

The approach referred to here, while incorporating in significant ways ideas and methods from a variety of perspectives,
is nonetheless still characterizable as rooted in the broad psychodynamic point of view. A central assumption is that individuals frequently engage in defensive operations that, in the
service of warding off distressing anxiety, render them unclear
about their motives, affects, and thoughts. Conflict is seen as
a pervasive feature of psychic life and the resolution of conflict
and clarification of experience a central concern of the therapeutic effort. People are seen, on close examination, to be guided
by assumptions (unconscious fantasies) and to be striving for
goals (unconscious motives) that can be quite at odds with the
consensual reality that is treated as normative in our society.
To miss these nonnormative thoughts and strivings is to subscribe to a limited and superficial view of human psychology.

Unconscious motives and thoughts, however, are not viewed
from the perspective of cyclical psychodynamics as the preserved
remnants of childhood, locked away by processes of fixation or
arrest and therefore impervious to the impact of ongoing life
events. Quite the contrary, these unconscious processes, so important in influencing how we construe and experience events
and how we behave in response to them, are in turn understandable as also a response *to* those same events. Close inspection
reveals that, far from persisting in spite of any input from everyday reality, and far from being simply unrealistic and infan-
tile, these unconscious processes can be seen as being maintained
by the very circumstances they bring about. The distorting lenses
of our defenses and conflicts are not autonomous prime causes
in the psyche. When they lead us astray in our dealings with
others they produce correspondingly distorted feedback from
others, and that feedback in turn is what maintains the psychic
structures that more classical analysts treat as locked-in remnants of the past. The question "From when do this patient's

difficulties date?" is not answered from a cyclical psychodynamic perspective in terms of a particular phase of childhood but rather in terms of what happened perhaps just a few minutes ago that kept the neurotic pattern going once again.

As a consequence of this perspective on unconscious processes and the influences that maintain them, the approach described here points to supplementing psychodynamic understanding both with an understanding of the ongoing systems or sequences of interaction that characterize the person's life and with the use of a variety of active intervention methods to interrupt the vicious circles. Those methods include those borrowed from behavioral, family systems, and other orientations, but include as well evolving interventions that either originate from the present perspective or reflect the ways in which the methods derived from other approaches gradually change as they are assimilated into a different framework (Wachtel, 1987).

Biography

Paul L. Wachtel is Distinguished Professor of Psychology at City College and the Graduate Center of the City University of New York. He received his Ph.D. degree (1965) from Yale University in clinical psychology. He is an internationally known expert on integrative approaches to psychotherapy and has been invited to lecture and give workshops on four continents. His book *Psychoanalysis and Behavior Therapy* is widely regarded as a classic. He has also written *The Poverty of Affluence: A Psychological Portrait of the American Way of Life, Action and Insight,* and (with Ellen F. Wachtel) *Family Dynamics in Individual Psychotherapy* and is the editor of *Resistance: Psychodynamic and Behavioral Approaches.* Wachtel is on the editorial board of numerous journals and is one of the founders of the Society for the Exploration of Psychotherapy Integration.

References

Wachtel, E. F., & Wachtel, P. L. (1986). *Family dynamics in individual psychotherapy.* New York: Guilford.

Wachtel, P. L. (1977). *Psychoanalysis and behavior therapy: Toward an integration.* New York: Basic Books.

Wachtel, P. L. (1985). Integrative psychodynamic therapy. In S. Lynn & J. Garske (Eds.), *Contemporary psychotherapies* (pp. 287–329). Columbus, OH: Merrill.

Wachtel, P. L. (1987). *Action and insight.* New York: Guilford.

Section 4
Common Factors

Multivariant Eclectic Psychotherapy

Sol L. Garfield

Definition

Psychotherapy is a planned interpersonal process in which the less disturbed person, the therapist, attempts to help the more disturbed person, the patient, overcome his or her problems. The interaction between the two participants is mediated primarily by verbal means, although bodily gestures, movements, and outward displays of affects also enter in. Currently, there is no unanimity concerning the variables that influence outcome. However, such common factors as the generation of hope, emotional release, and the explanations, support, and interest of the therapist appear potentially important in helping the patient to change faulty perceptions, emotions, and behaviors.

Qualification Statement

Individuals usually seek out psychotherapeutic help when they are experiencing discomfort or pain. Although the primary complaint may vary, feelings of low self-esteem, hopelessness, demoralization, and anxiety, as well as interpersonal difficulties, are quite common. Not everyone with such symptoms seeks psychotherapy. However, the feelings described do characterize most of those who come to the psychotherapist's office seeking help. The amelioration of the patient's problems is the obvious goal of therapy.

Although there are several hundred different forms or approaches to psychotherapy, the positive results claimed for all of them — and documented for some — suggest the likely possibility of factors or variables common to most of them (Frank, 1971; Garfield, 1980, 1989). Although this possibility has been mentioned for over fifty years, it is only in the last decade or so that this view is receiving recognition. Obviously, it is difficult for individuals who have invested considerable effort in trying to master one particular therapeutic approach to acknowledge the importance of common factors in psychotherapy.

Space limitations allow for only a brief reference to a few of the possible common factors that appear to be important in facilitating positive change in psychotherapy. One obvious factor is the therapeutic relationship, which is acknowledged to be important by adherents of practically all approaches to psychotherapy. If the therapist is perceived by the patient as an interested, competent, and nonjudgmental person, the likelihood of a positive outcome is increased. Another common variable emphasized by adherents to many different therapeutic orientations is the client's motivation and desire to collaborate in the therapeutic undertaking. The expectations of the client about therapy is still another common variable that has been recognized as important by therapists of different schools.

These common factors are quite obvious and are really noncontroversial. However, other potential common variables are less well accepted. One such variable can be categorized as therapist-offered explanations, interpretations, or rationales. It is a potential variable that probably has influenced me the most in perceiving and conceptualizing common factors in psychotherapy. Clearly, diverse types of explanations are offered by therapists of different orientations to aid patients in obtaining insight or understanding into their problems. Even among psychodynamic therapists, a variety of different interpretations are apparently possible. What this strongly suggests is that the *specific* interpretation or explanation provided by the therapist is not the really important factor. What is important is whether the interpretation or explanation is meaningful to the patient *and* is accepted by the patient. Essentially, there is *no one correct* interpretation. Cognitions, however, do appear to be of some significance to the patient. They provide a basis for understanding and acceptance by the patient. As long as they appear to be meaningful, they have positive explanatory value, for they can reduce uncertainty and may increase the hope and expectation for improvement.

There are a number of other common variables that only can be mentioned here. Such variables as suggestion and encouragement receive little emphasis in most of the treatises on specific forms of psychotherapy, yet they are used by many therapists of different theoretical persuasions. The opportunity to discuss troublesome topics and the opportunity to secure emotional release are additional common factors. Providing information and giving reassurance are other common therapist activities that appear to have positive impacts when used judiciously.

Critique Statement

Eclecticism currently is a popular orientation among those who practice psychotherapy (Garfield & Kurtz, 1976; Prochaska & Norcross, 1983; Smith, 1982). Furthermore, its popularity appears to be increasing. In a recent national survey of clinical psychologists, psychiatrists, marriage and family therapists, and clinical social workers, 68 percent of the sample indicated such an orientation (Jensen & Bergin, 1988). With so many theoretical orientations available today, it is extremely interesting that such a large number of psychotherapists have identified themselves as eclectics. It is worthwhile, therefore, to speculate about the possible reasons for this phenomenon.

It is my feeling that most eclectic psychotherapists, who represent either the most thoughtful or the most disorganized therapists, depending on your point of view, choose an eclectic way of life for one of two reasons: Either they have become dissatisfied with following a particular approach or they feel it is the best way to adapt therapeutic procedures for the individual client. In my own case, both reasons played a role, but I also was impressed by the possibility that there were common factors among the different forms of psychotherapy.

Another aspect that impressed me early in my career was the apparent difference between what an individual therapist said he or she did in therapy and what actually took place. A related observation was that a therapist bound by one specific theoretical orientation tended to view events from that perspective and to credit as therapeutic variables those designated by the theory. This process could distort what actually occurred, and other explanations could be of equal or greater validity. For example in some instances, the opportunity to unburden oneself to a noncritical and empathic healer might be the variable of significance and not the transference relationship per se or a particular interpretation.

Thus, in my own case, I utilized emphases and procedures from several different orientations; for example, the importance of a good relationship, empathic listening, cognitive restructuring, desensitization, and homework assignments, to name a few. I also perceived common factors as being important therapeutic variables and tried to utilize them in my therapeutic work. This was my own version of being an eclectic therapist.

At the same time, I am clearly aware that eclecticism as practiced varies considerably among eclectic therapists (Garfield & Kurtz, 1977). Although eclecticism is unambiguously defined as "choosing what appears to be best from diverse sources, systems, or styles" (*American Heritage Dictionary,* 1971), what individual therapists choose as the "best," and how they use it in practice, undoubtedly varies greatly. The only thing they have in common is the desire to select whatever procedures seem best for the individual patient and not to be limited to following slavishly one single therapeutic orientation.

In the long run, however, we have to try to identify, objectify, and evaluate the variables that are truly therapeutic. On the basis of both patient reports and the research results on outcome, I expect that many of them will be factors common to most forms of psychotherapy (Garfield, 1980, 1982).

Biography

Sol L. Garfield is professor emeritus of psychology at Washington University, St. Louis, Missouri. He received his Ph.D. degree (1942) from Northwestern University. He has received several awards from the American Psychological Association, including the Distinguished Professional Contribution to Knowledge Award in 1979. He is an ABPP diplomate in clinical psychology and a fellow of the APA. Garfield is also a former president of APA's Division of Clinical Psychology and of the Society for Psychotherapy Research. A former editor of the *Journal of Consulting and Clinical Psychology*, he is also the author of *Clinical Psychology: The Study of Personality and Behavior, Psychotherapy: An Eclectic Approach*, and *The Practice of Brief Psychotherapy* (1989). With Allen E. Bergin, he coedited the *Handbook of Psychotherapy and Behavior Change*.

References

American Heritage Dictionary of the English Language. (1971). New York: American Heritage.

Frank, J. D. (1971). Therapeutic factors in psychotherapy. *American Journal of Psychotherapy, 25,* 350–361.

Garfield, S. L. (1980). *Psychotherapy: An eclectic approach*. New York: Wiley.

Garfield, S. L. (1982). Eclecticism and integration in psychotherapy. *Behavior Therapy, 13,* 610–623.

Garfield, S. L. (1989). *The practice of brief psychotherapy*. New York: Pergamon Press.

Garfield, S. L., & Kurtz, R. (1976). Clinical psychologists in the 1970's. *American Psychologist, 31,* 1–9.

Garfield, S. L., & Kurtz, R. (1977). A study of eclectic views. *Journal of Consulting and Clinical Psychology, 45,* 78–83.

Jensen, J. P., & Bergin, A. E. (1988). Mental health values of professional therapists: A national interdisciplinary survey. *Professional Psychology: Research and Practice, 19,* 290–297.

Prochaska, J. O., & Norcross, J. E. (1983). Contemporary psychotherapists: A national survey of characteristics, practices, orientations, and attitudes. *Psychotherapy: Theory, Research and Practice, 20,* 161–173.

Smith, D. (1982). Trends in counseling and psychotherapy. *American Psychologist, 37,* 802–809.

An Eclectic Definition of Psychotherapy: A Developmental Contextual View

David L. Blustein

Definition

Psychotherapy is a systematic helping process that fosters change and development in intrapsychic functioning, interpersonal relationships, and one's capacity to negotiate important life tasks. Using information that is gathered from theoretically derived observations of the client's relationships with the therapist, others, and salient environmental contexts (for example, work), psychotherapy focuses on adapting one's intrapsychic structures, cognitive processes, and behavioral repertoires in a manner that is consistent with one's needs and capacities.

Qualification Statement

This definition, while eclectic in its theoretical allegiance, is based on a number of assumptions that are derived from a developmental and contextual view of human behavior. One of the underlying assumptions is that psychotherapy facilitates development, which is broadly conceived to encompass a wide array of intrapsychic structures and environmental contexts. The notion that psychotherapy fosters development is clearly not new. For example, various psychoanalytic theories each posit developmental sequences that can be enhanced and remediated by psychological treatment. Further, recent theoretical positions have adopted an explicit developmental focus based on life-span developmental theories (for example, Ivey, 1986). Thus, the focus on development provides a meta-theoretical framework for the design and delivery of psychotherapeutic interventions.

Another salient feature of this definition is the explicit acknowledgment that psychotherapy would encompass a broad array of domains, including intrapsychic functioning, cognitive processes, and various environmental contexts. The assumption here is that behavior is determined and influenced by a multitude of forces, both external and internal to the client. The notion that behavior is determined and sustained by a diverse range of factors therefore allows for the synthesis of relevant principles and propositions emerging from learning theories and systems theories, as well as psychoanalytic and existential theories. As many recent scholars have noted, these seemingly diverse views of human behavior are not mutually exclusive, particularly if they are integrated by a meta-theoretical or systematic framework (for example, Beitman, 1987; Wachtel, 1977). Finally, in keeping with the broad-based view that is implied in this definition, the term *client* encompasses individuals, couples, families, and groups.

By incorporating the notion of the context, this definition suggests that a client's behavior can be evoked, sustained, and manifested in many domains. One of the most pervasive contexts in which clients interact is work, and this definition assumes that psychotherapy can address issues that arise from a vocational context in an integrative fashion, along with the other contexts that form the traditional focus of psychotherapeutic interventions.

A fundamental assumption of this definition is that observations about clients and corresponding treatment strategies should be governed by coherent bodies of theory. Theory, which ideally would address both personality development and behavior change, allows the therapist to place observations about a client into a framework that leads to the development of hypotheses and inferences about the nature of a client's problems and personality structure. Thus, each decision to invoke a selected treatment approach would be logically tied to theoretically derived formulations about a client's personality structure and presenting concerns. The emphasis on theory thus places psychotherapy directly into the growing knowledge base that is generated in scholarly thought and empirical research in psychology and related disciplines.

Critique Statement

In order to address some of the criticisms of eclectic orientations, which have highlighted the atheoretical or conceptually ambiguous nature of such approaches, this definition makes explicit assumptions about human behavior. Specifically, psychotherapy is viewed as a means of facilitating development in such domains as intrapsychic structures (for example, the self), interpersonal functioning (for example, developing the capacity for intimacy), and various environmental contexts (for example, vocational behavior). Further, by adopting a developmental perspective, this position does not necessarily suggest that psychotherapy exists solely to reduce psychopathology; it is conceived of as a means of helping relatively well-adjusted individuals cope with various developmental tasks.

Psychotherapy, as it is defined here, is characterized by the search for meaningful patterns of personality functioning and behaviors, which are inferred from the client's interactions with significant others and the therapist. However, in addition to the traditional focus on relationship issues and other psychological symptoms, this definition also views as potentially relevant to diagnosis and treatment material pertaining to the client's characteristic approaches to important life tasks. One of the unique advantages of this approach is its explicit acknowledgment that therapy can and should address those problems and unresolved developmental issues that stem from one's contact with various environmental contexts. The most obvious example of this is the focus on work as a relevant domain for consideration in psychotherapy. With few exceptions, vocational issues have been treated separately from nonvocational issues in most forms of psychotherapy. Yet compelling arguments have been invoked to suggest that clients select and adjust to careers in a manner that is analogous to the coping strategies manifested in other major life issues (Blustein, 1987; Brown & Brooks, 1985). Moreover, many clinicians have found that the occupational context can evoke a host of client problems that may be as salient and disabling as intrapsychic, interpersonal, and family concerns (Manuso, 1983). Thus, this definition implies that the therapist can view the vocational realm as a potentially rich source of diagnostic material and as a means of helping a client manifest behavior change.

Despite the relative advantages that have been cited thus far, this definition has some possible disadvantages as well. For example, the conceptualizations of both context and development represent a potentially problematic issue. One might suggest that the use of such broad and overarching terms as *context* and *development* introduces ambiguity into the clinical assessment process. However, this problem is mitigated to some extent by the focus on explicating the precise pattern of relationships between the developmental status of the client and the various external contexts in which the client functions. As occurs in the practice of other modalities, continued experience in assessing and facilitating development and contextual functioning produces an increased competence or "feel" within the therapist. Moreover, by focusing on the context, the therapist can include domains of activity that have been relatively neglected in the past.

Finally, this approach is limited to some degree by the skills, experiences, and sensitivity of the psychotherapist. The type of psychotherapy implied in this definition does not simply involve the development of specific skills and techniques; rather, it assumes that the therapist will have the capacity to be empathic and insightful in a way that encompasses the complex network of feelings, thoughts, and motivations of a given client.

Biography

David L. Blustein is an assistant professor in the Department of Counseling Psychology at the University of Albany, State University of New York. He received his Ph.D. degree (1985) from Columbia University. Prior to joining the faculty at the University of Albany, he was a college counselor, providing psychotherapeutic and vocational counseling services to students at three diverse institutions. He has published twenty articles in various national journals, including *Psychotherapy, Journal of Vocational Behavior,* and *Journal of Counseling Psychology.* In addition, he serves on the editorial board of the *Journal of Vocational Behavior.*

Blustein's present research program focuses on three inter-related areas. One line of work is devoted to the examination of the nature of vocational themes in psychotherapy, in an attempt to develop a clearer understanding of how work-related issues impact upon one's treatment. He is also investigating the process of career exploration and commitment to a career choice; the intention of this research is to identify how individuals develop and implement career plans. Finally, he is developing a line of empirical research that will attempt to bridge various conceptual and empirical views of the self and identity.

References

Beitman, B. D. (1987). *The structure of individual psychotherapy.* New York: Guilford.

Blustein, D. L. (1987). Integrating career counseling and psychotherapy: A comprehensive treatment strategy. *Psychotherapy, 24,* 794–799.

Brown, D., & Brooks, L. (1985). Career counseling as a mental health intervention. *Professional Psychology, 16,* 860–867.

Ivey, A. E. (1986). *Developmental therapy: Theory into practice.* San Francisco: Jossey-Bass.

Manuso, J. S. J. (Ed.). (1983). *Occupational clinical psychology.* New York: Praeger.

Wachtel, P. L. (1977). *Psychoanalysis and behavior therapy: Toward an integration.* New York: Basic Books.

Role Dynamics

Adam Blatner

Definition

A comprehensive approach to psychotherapy requires an eclectic orientation. The many aspects and levels of complexity of human experience imply a variety of etiological factors that in turn can only be addressed by a correspondingly broad range of treatments. A theoretical framework based on the concept of *role* can integrate the best insights of the different therapies and therefore serves as a foundation for eclecticism.

Qualification Statement

No single theory can address all psychosocial phenomena, but it is possible to have a meta-theoretical system that can serve as an intellectual foundation for eclecticism. An analogy may be drawn to the present situation in medicine, in which there are numerous etiological factors operating on different levels of organismic complexity, ranging from the atomic through molecular, cellular, tissue, organ, systemic, gross physical, and/or psychosomatic levels.

A general meta-theoretical term, *physiology,* may be used to describe the overall quasi-mechanistic model. The mind involves many interpenetrating and nonhierarchically organized activities that cannot be described in mechanistic terms, and thus another model is needed. Role dynamics is based on a dramaturgical paradigm of human experience and is unique because the concept of role can deal with several levels of functioning: Biological, intrapsychic, interpersonal, family, group, and cultural.

Role dynamics is a kind of language as much as it is a meta-theory, and it describes psychosocial phenomena in terms of the roles people play, how they are defined, how they interact, and how they can be changed. The concept of role is a rich metaphor with many associations. The idea of playing a role, for instance, suggests that the actor is not the performance; speaking in these terms results in a sense of "role distance" that helps patients to be more reflective. Since the terminology of role dynamics is such that patients, family members, and professionals can easily understand it, this approach serves as a user-friendly language that allows patients to be actively involved in the therapeutic process.

Another advantage of role dynamics is its comprehensiveness. The dramaturgical metaphor promotes a view of life as consisting of innumerable roles to play and an equivalent variety of ways that they can be enacted. The range of roles includes a number of dimensions that tend to be neglected by other theories, such as our spirituality, playfulness, artistic self-expression, and those generally disowned qualities that must find some socially acceptable channel if they are not to emerge in distorted and otherwise pathological forms. Working with patients' alternatives leads to a development of their sense of the "choosing self," a more easily understood way of thinking about the ideas of responsibility or locus of control.

Role dynamics can be useful in diagnosing and dealing with specific problems, and it is also a systems theory in that it may function as a guide to helping individuals, families, or groups to develop their strengths. Roles can be learned and refined, and so this theory is in part educational, supporting the development of skills such as meta-cognition — thinking about how one detects and corrects problems. This helps patients to go beyond dealing with the problem at hand and become capable of coping with future difficulties. There are numerous advantages to role dynamics, and I find it a highly workable framework and the basis of an eclectic approach to psychotherapy.

Critique Statement

Role dynamics is a theory oriented to clinical practice, and its strengths lie in its relevance to the psychotherapist rather than the academician doing research. Because the concept of role is elusive and lacks precision, it is relatively resistant to traditional kinds of investigation. This theory is derived from the ideas of J. L. Moreno, the originator of psychodrama and a major pioneer of group psychotherapy. His intention was to help people by giving them tools they can use to understand themselves. Practical applicability is thus a major criterion.

There is both a disadvantage and an advantage to the idea of eclecticism. This idea has been criticized because it has served as a rationalization for a relatively atheoretical empiricism. It was feared that professionals would fail to develop their skills in really understanding their patients. Yet eclecticism is also the only orientation that addresses the whole range of useful treatment approaches. Role dynamics resolves this problem by providing a theory whereby clinicians can more readily generate multidimensional formulations. It is a theory that, in spite of its seemingly simple essential structure, nevertheless demands more from the professional than perhaps any other approach. Therapists are enjoined to develop their own broad role repertoires, and this is a process of lifelong learning. Like medicine, there are always new areas to learn about, and role dynamics is the kind of general framework that invites the exploration of frontiers.

Another disadvantage of role dynamics is that it can't include the details of some other therapies. It's a meta-theory, an overarching system that allows for integration, and in practice this is quite possible. Thus, it is necessary for the psychotherapist to become acquainted with the most productive ideas and methods of a number of different approaches and to continue to supplement this learning. This is, I think, the way it should be. Those who seek a more limited approach are denying the complexity of the subject matter.

One of the benefits of this theory is that it is associated with a group of methods such as role playing, psychodrama, and other action techniques; the key principle here is that flexibility of mind is enhanced through the exercise of dealing with a situation from several points of view. Another benefit is a corollary of a commitment to eclecticism. Therapists can utilize the fact that there are many kinds of help that facilitate patients' learning the skills of mutuality: The technique consists of teaching the patient to negotiate for the type of help desired as one of the ways to learn empowerment in relationships.

In summary, role dynamics as a meta-theory offers the potential for integrating various other psychotherapeutic methods. Eclecticism is a necessary and attainable goal, and role dynamics can function as its intellectual foundation.

Biography

Adam Blatner is director of Pediatric Consultation-Liaison Services at the Bingham Child Guidance Clinic and an assistant professor of child psychiatry at the University of Louisville School of Medicine in Louisville, Kentucky. A board-certified trainer of psychodrama, he received his B.A. degree (1959) from the University of California at Berkeley and his M.D. degree (1963) from the California Medical Center in San Francisco. His specialty training included adult and child psychiatric residencies at Stanford University Medical Center in Palo Alto and Cedars-Sinai Medical Center in Los Angeles. He was in the U.S. Air Force at its regional hospital in England as medical director of the child psychiatry service. On returning to California in 1972, he began private practice in the San Francisco Bay Area. Prior to his present position, he was on the staff of the Menninger Foundation in Topeka, Kansas. He is the author of several books and articles on psychodrama and its applications.

Recommended Reading

Blatner, A. (1988). Role dynamics. In *Foundations of psychodrama: History, theory, and practice.* New York: Springer.

Blatner, A. (1989). *Acting-in: Practical applications of psychodramatic methods* (2nd ed.). New York: Springer.

Blatner, A., & Blatner, A. (1988). *The art of play: An adult's guide to reclaiming imagination and spontaneity.* New York: Human Sciences Press.

8

Family and Systemic Psychotherapy

The theory that defines membership in the family therapy "genus" holds that change in family dynamics is essential to problem resolution. This is as opposed to theories that focus only on intrapersonal dynamics and imply that family and social contexts are relatively static environments to which the individual, perhaps through therapy, must adapt. Ongoing family functioning is a factor in both problem maintenance and resolution, and as such is the focus of analysis and intervention. Therapist and patient examine the interpersonal function of problems within the family structure in order to make change possible.

The primary unit-of-analysis is relationship. Concomitant lenses focus the therapist on broad categories, such as communication patterns, power distribution, reality construction, and family development. Each aspect may be examined in combination with one or several others, yielding a plethora of permutations. This variety reflects the development of the family therapy movement, which was decentralized compared to psychoanalysis.

Although some observers endeavor to trace the origins of family therapy to Freud (Foley, 1974), when he consulted the father in the treatment of young "Hans" in 1909, it is generally accepted that until the early 1950s involvement of the family in an individual's treatment was regarded as antithetical to the process. Family therapy emerged almost simultaneously on the eastern and western seaboards of the United States (Kolevzon and Green, 1985). Research contributed greatly to this emergence: In the West, Gregory Bateson, Jay Haley, Donald Jackson, and John Weakland collaborated on the double-bind theory, a communications-based theory of family contributions to schizophrenia that influenced many approaches, including the contributions of Virginia Satir. In the East, John Bell began meeting regularly with whole families and observing a relationship between family interaction and problem behaviors. Psychoanalytically schooled Nathan Ackerman and Murray Bowen also began systematic observations of family interaction. Haley joined Salvador Minuchin in Philadelphia, and Minuchin developed his structural model of family therapy in the mid-1960s.

From these beginnings, the development of family-based treatment was rapid. Current approaches vary along multiple dimensions, including duration of treatment, number of generations involved, importance of insight, degree and type of therapist involvement (that is, observer versus participant), and technical applications (for example, strategic prescription, communication skills enhancement, and so on).

The present chapter is divided into sections on general family therapy, strategic and structural approaches, couples therapy, and technique- and problem-oriented approaches. The general family therapy section begins with a brief definition and statement by Carl Whitaker, who utilizes foster parenting as a metaphor to describe the therapeutic process. James Framo discusses his intergenerational approach, characterized as an amalgam of dynamic and systems concepts. Gerald Weeks addresses the paradoxical nature of all psychotherapy.

In the strategic and structural approaches section, Paul Watzlawick discusses reality and constructivism as related to strategic intervention. A brief, strategic orientation is the backbone of Richard Fisch's problem-solving approach. Family development, utilizing multiple generations when possible, is central to Maurizio Andolfi's current work. Steve de Shazer and Eve Lipchik each discuss solution-oriented brief therapies. Three authors address the issue of moving families beyond developmental blockages; Michaelin Reamy-Stephenson (from a constructivist perspective), Joel Bergman (as a life transition issue), and Charles Fishman (in light of catastrophe theory).

In the couples therapy section, Ellyn Bader and Peter Pearson describe developmental theory and stages in a marriage. In the technique- and problem-oriented section, the posttraumatic-stress-disordered patient as a special problem population is discussed by Charles Figley. Ruth McClendon and Leslie B. Kadis collaborate in explaining redecision therapy, an amalgam of individual and family work based in Transactional Analysis and gestalt practice. Florence Kaslow describes an integrative approach to family therapy. Finally, a seven-step procedure for dealing with families in crisis is detailed by Frank Pittman.

References

Foley, V. D. (1974). *An introduction to family therapy.* New York: Grune & Stratton.

Kolevzon, M. S., & Green, R. G. (1985). *Family therapy models.* New York: Springer.

Section 1
General Family Therapy

Symbolic Experiential Therapy

Carl A. Whitaker

Definition

Psychotherapy is professional foster parenting with the deliberate function of facilitating the patient's effort to be more himself or herself.

Qualification Statement

Psychotherapy is a symbolic experience if it is effective. Education is not psychotherapy. The therapist takes a parental role to force patient regression. The therapist then forces the patient both to take back responsibility for his or her own life and to separate from this foster parent.

The process with the family is to reempower its members to be therapeutic to subgroups and individuals. The symbolic experience is necessary to break up the programmed fix of each family member's past life.

Biography

Carl A. Whitaker has practiced psychotherapy for more than forty years and is currently in private practice in Milwaukee, Wisconsin. He received his M.D. degree (1936) from Syracuse University. For nine years, he was professor and chairman of the Department of Psychiatry at Emory University College of Medicine. For almost twenty years, he was professor of psychiatry at the University of Wisconsin Medical School. Whitaker is one of the founding fathers of family therapy. He received the Distinguished Family Therapy Award from the American Association for Marriage and Family Therapy. His approach has been named the "experiential school." Whitaker has coauthored two books, edited one, and there is an edited volume about his approach. He has almost sixty contributions to books, including introductions, chapters, and forewords. Additionally, he has published more than seventy papers. Whitaker is former president of the American Academy of Psychotherapy.

Recommended Reading

Napier, A. Y., & Whitaker, C. A. (1978). *The family crucible.* New York: Harper & Row.

Intergenerational Family Therapy

James L. Framo

Definition

In my approach to psychotherapy, current intrapsychic, marital, and parenting difficulties are viewed as reparative efforts to master, correct, or live through old, conflictual relationships in the family of origin. Most therapists believe that these problems can best be worked out via the relationship with the therapist. This present intergenerational approach takes the problems back to where they began by preparing clients in individual or marital therapy to have face-to-face sessions with parents and siblings. The family of origin then deals with the difficult issues of the past and present, and these sessions can have more powerful effects than the entire course of a psychotherapy.

Qualification Statement

Intergenerational family therapy has an object-relations theoretical foundation in its approach to psychotherapy (individual, marital, and family therapy), focusing on the relationship between the intrapsychic and the transactional. This work attempts to provide an amalgam of dynamic and systems concepts, thereby providing a bridge between the personal and the social. It stresses the interlocking, multiperson motivational systems of intimate relationships, and suggests that people in close relationships collusively carry out psychic functions for each other (for example, the unconscious deal: "I will express your forbidden wishes if you will never leave me").

The most powerful obstacle to change in psychotherapy is people's attachments to their parental introjects. When people marry, they act out and live through the internal objects with their spouses and children. Children and spouses, then, are caught in transference fixes: The mate or child must be perceived in a certain kind of way (as malevolent, spoiled, nurturant, demanding, incompetent, or what have you), and nothing that person can do can make a difference. Consequently, present-day marital or family difficulties are looked upon as elaborations of relationship patterns that evolved from the family of origin.

Current marital problems are viewed as derived from experiences with family-of-origin members. The partners attempt an interpersonal resolution of intrapsychic conflicts by transferring these conflicts to marital blame. Such relationship problems as distrust, driving each other crazy, who's going to take care of whom, endless bickering, pursuing-distancing, unfaithfulness, struggle for control, sexual difficulties, under-and-over-functioning, marital emptiness, and fusion versus differentiation are explainable on the basis of the different meanings attached to concepts of intimacy, love, aggression, separateness, privacy, and so on, that the partners learned in their original families.

I have developed a method of preparing adults who are in individual, conjoint marital, or family therapy to bring in their parents and brothers and sisters for family-of-origin consultation, bringing present-day difficulties back to their etiological source. Special procedures have been developed for dealing with difficulties, including resistance of clients to bringing in the family of origin; preparing for the consultations; conducting the sessions; and helping the family members to deal with past and present issues they have had with each other. During these sessions the cotherapists manage family myths, hurt feelings, and old misunderstandings as adult children and parents try to come to terms with each other. Following these sessions, relationship problems in the family of origin usually abate (for example, family cutoffs and alienations are healed), and there are usually positive changes in clients' internal problems, their marital relationship, and their capacity to relate to their children as persons in their own right.

Critique Statement

Utilizing the conceptual formulation that hidden transgenerational forces exercise critical influence on present-day relationships with the self and one's intimate others, I have developed a method of directly involving the family of origin when treating individuals, couples, and families, taking the problems back to where they began.

Family-of-origin therapy is the major surgery of psychotherapy, and like major surgery there can be side effects and difficulties. Sessions with adult children (including siblings of the client) and their parents are powerful, disturbing, and intense as the members deal with secrets, hurt or anger over perceived rejections or neglect, thwarted yearnings and misunderstandings, and finally, the forgiveness of each other when positive feelings are expressed. There are risks involved in having these sessions in that the family members do get upset when confronted with truths long suppressed, and the fear exists that the family will be torn asunder. Considering these fears, why should anyone have family-of-origin sessions? The answer: because the great majority of anticipated fearful events never happen, and also because the rewards make the experience worthwhile. The parents get to see their children more as adults, and the adult children get to know their parents as real people rather than as roles. The adult children come to recognize that the parents did the best they could with what they had to work with.

Old family conflicts and feuds are brought up for discussion and disposal. Past losses and traumas can be discussed openly for the first time, and delayed mourning dealt with effectively. After these sessions, family members often report feeling more whole and congruent; psychological symptoms are often abated. There are usually spreading effects to improved relationships with extended family; cutoffs in the family get repaired; sibling relationships often improve; disengaged families get closer; and fused families become more differentiated. Settling important matters with parents and siblings releases psychic energy for investment in one's self, one's partner, and one's children, resulting in less pathological use of projective identification.

The family-of-origin intervention is not a routine procedure, a complete form of therapy, or an all-purpose method to be used in all or even most clinical situations. It is a highly specialized procedure that can, nonetheless, have powerful effects when integrated with other forms of psychotherapy. One can speculate as to whether the length of all psychotherapies can be reduced by appropriately timed family-of-origin sessions.

This procedure is particularly useful in the following situations: People who are unable to commit to a relationship until issues are worked out with a parent or sibling; parents who were abused as children and are fearful of repeating this pattern with their own children; the long-term negative effects of divorce of one's parents in years past; alienated families with a history of cutoffs; adult children who want to come to terms with their parents before they die; adults who are unable to form a satisfactory intimate relationship; families with intrusive mothers and distant fathers, and so on. Many of our relationship problems are rooted in our bonds and hidden loyalties to those people who shaped our lives. It is necessary to allow forgiveness of old pains and sorrows to occur and to know and be known by these people who, in a way, will always live within us.

Biography

James L. Framo is Distinguished Professor of Marital and Family Therapy at U.S. International University in San Diego, California. He received his Ph.D. degree (1953) from the University of Texas in clinical psychology. He is an internationally renowned pioneer in family therapy who has over fifty publications in his field. A founding member and past president of the American Family Therapy Association, he was presented with the Distinguished Achievement in Family Therapy Award by AFTA. He has given over 300 workshops in the United States and nine foreign countries. Framo's major clinical innovation is his practice of bringing in the family of origin of clients who are in individual or marital therapy. Books in progress include *An Intergenerational Approach to Marital and Family Therapy: Marriage, Divorce, and Family of Origin,* and *Coming Home Again* (with Timothy Weber and Felise B. Levine).

Recommended Reading

Framo, J. L. (1972). Symptoms from a family transactional viewpoint. In N. Ackerman et al. (Eds.). *Family therapy in transition.* Boston: Little, Brown.

Framo, J. L. (1976). Family of origin as a therapeutic resource for adults in marital and family therapy: You can and should go home again. *Family Process, 15,* 193–210.

Framo, J. L. (1982). *Explorations in marital and family therapy: Selected papers of James L. Framo.* New York: Springer.

Framo, J. L. (in press). *Family of origin consultations: An intergenerational approach* (Vol. 1). New York: Brunner/Mazel.

Paradox

Gerald R. Weeks

Definition

Psychotherapy is a complex human relationship that defies simple definition and description. The purpose of psychotherapy is to change what an individual presents as symptomatic behavior. A symptom is a behavior that is characterized by some combination of being spontaneous, uncontrollable, and/or involuntary. To change this behavior the therapist must generate a paradox. The paradox is to create conditions under which spontaneous compliance will occur. An individual cannot be forced to change. Change must develop out of a special relationship that allows the individual to change in a way that appears spontaneous. This phenomenon enhances the person's sense of freedom, empowerment, and motivation and prevents relapse. The individual learns to control what was experienced as symptomatic behavior.

Qualification Statement

Several groups of therapists and researchers have concluded that paradox is a universal element in psychotherapy (Weeks, 1977, 1985, and 1989; Weeks & L'Abate, 1982; Strong & Claiborn, 1982; and Seltzer, 1986). These therapists have examined a variety of therapeutic approaches and found they all contain paradoxical strategies. All therapies have as their goal making behavior that is involuntary, voluntary; behavior that is spontaneous, planned; and behavior that is uncontrollable, controllable.

The way to achieve these goals is complex but reducible to

several basic concepts and principles — all paradoxical in nature. First, the therapist must somehow manage to take control without appearing to take control. Second, the therapist must maintain a positive view of the symptom. The symptom is not the enemy of either the client or the therapist. It has served a purpose and must be understood and used as a point of departure. Third, not just the symptom but the person also must be viewed positively and accepted, no matter how much the client may be self-rejecting and expect the same rejection from the therapist. These points refer to the relationship between the therapist and the client. They are paradoxical in that they are counter to what the client expects.

The change process emerges from this relationship and builds on it. The client's experience of change must be that he or she *is* different, rather than *doing* something different. The client must be able to say, "I'm different." This statement reflects a change in attribution. An individual who is forced to make a change will experience *doing* things differently without *being* different. In order to change the meaning of the behavior (symptom), the client must attribute the change to himself or herself — not to the therapist. Creating this self-attributional process is psychotherapy at its best.

Using paradoxical methods is one way of creating spontaneous compliance and self-attribution (Weeks, 1989). The client is told explicitly to maintain the symptomatic behavior while being told implicitly to change it. The therapist may use methods such as symptom prescription, restraining, prediction, and negative consequences of change. The paradox being prescribed gives the client an opportunity to experience control over the symptom, thereby changing its definition or meaning from symptom to nonsymptom. Most therapists are straightforward or at least appear so. These therapists rely less on the change process just described and more on the inherently paradoxical nature of therapy. In each case, the client is empowered and taught self-control, and the therapist attributes change to the client. The therapist uses techniques that simultaneously increase compliance while promoting self-attribution of change.

Critique Statement

The approach to psychotherapy I am currently advocating is relatively new and evolving. The entire system began ten years ago with explicit paradoxical work. The first theoretical presentation of this system occurred in 1989. Thus, these ideas have not been exposed long enough to bring in criticisms.

Based on my previous work, I could imagine two criticisms. First is a total rejection by some groups of therapists of the idea that their work is in fact paradoxical. For example, gestalt therapists have generally rejected this description. Yet gestalt therapists use "symptom exaggeration" in session, and one prominent gestalt author claimed that a paradoxical theory of change was at the heart of gestalt therapy. Second, because this way of conceptualizing therapy is abstract, complex, and philosophical, a therapist who is still at the technician level will have difficulty using this system. It requires theoretical and philosophical sophistication, mastery of many therapeutic modalities and techniques, and a high level of experience in the use of self.

The major advantage of this system is that it is based on foundational thinking. Systems of therapy have multiplied without any sense of how they are connected or what they share in common. The goal of this system is to create a general theory or meta-theory of psychotherapy. Meta-theoretical understanding will free us to transcend the differential therapies to which we sometimes try to fit our clients.

Biography

Gerald R. Weeks is the director of training and clinical associate professor of psychology in psychiatry with the Marriage Council of Philadelphia and the Division of Family Studies, Department of Psychiatry, University of Pennsylvania School of Medicine. Weeks has published numerous scientific articles, served on various editorial boards, and has authored or edited five books. He is a diplomate in marital and family therapy and has served two terms as president of the American Board of Family Therapy.

References

Seltzer, L. (1986). *Paradoxical strategies in psychotherapy: A comprehensive overview and guidebook.* New York: Wiley.

Strong, S., & Claiborn, C. (1982). *Change through interaction: Social psychological processes of counseling and psychotherapy.* New York: Wiley.

Weeks, G. (1977). Toward a dialectical approach to intervention. *Human Development, 20,* 277–292.

Weeks, G. (1985). *Promoting change through paradoxical therapy.* Homewood, IL: Dorsey Press.

Weeks, G. (1989). An intersystem approach to treatment. In G. Weeks (Ed.), *Treating couples: The intersystem model of the Marriage Council of Philadelphia* (pp. 317–340). New York: Brunner/Mazel.

Weeks, G., & L'Abate, L. (1982). *Paradoxical psychotherapy: Theory and practice with individuals, couples, and families.* New York: Brunner/Mazel.

Section 2
Strategic and Structural Approaches

Psychotherapy of "As If"

Paul Watzlawick

Definition

Psychotherapy endeavors to change people's assumptions about the nature of reality — assumptions they consider to be true, objective, platonic aspects of the "real" world. The systemic-constructivist approach considers these assumptions to be the outcome of human communication, and its goal is to replace pain-producing reality constructions by less painful ones through the introduction of different interactional patterns into the human relationship system concerned.

Qualification Statement

The internationally accepted criterion of mental health or illness is the degree of a person's reality adaptation. This concept tacitly and unquestioningly presupposes that there is such a thing as an objective reality, of which sane people are more aware than disturbed ones.

Modern constructivism, on the other hand, postulates that reality is not discovered, but is merely a more or less expedient fiction (compare Vaihinger, 1924) where *expedient* means that it permits a more or less pain- and problem-free life. It is at the same time an "as if" *fiction* because it is a complex web of assumptions, belief systems, and, above all, the *emergent qualities* of complicated interactions on personal, familial, societal, cultural, and other levels.

In view of this complexity and the impossibility of reducing it to single components, systemic therapy does not even try to analyze the origin and development of pain-producing, ill-adapted assumptions about the supposedly objective nature of reality and to bring about insight; rather, it attempts change in the here and now.

The therapist first obtains a description (not an explanation!) of the present problem. To achieve this, he or she cannot rely just on the information given by one person. The therapist must also observe the function of the particular problem within the context of the particular system of human relations. In other words, the therapist does not ask *why?* but *what for?*

The therapist then explores the solutions that the members of the system have so far attempted. This information enables him or her to block and replace that problem-perpetuating pseudo-solution by means of *active* interventions into the functioning of the system; for example, by requests to behave differently. These different behaviors — preferably small and seemingly insignificant — were not resorted to by the clients themselves because they made no sense in the frame of their reality construction.

The compliance with these behavior prescriptions thus changes the clients' reality. This may, but need not, be followed by insight, but it would be insight *after* action, rather than insight as precondition and precursor of change, as postulated by the classical schools of psychotherapy. Or, to quote the famous bio-cybernetician Heinz von Foerster on this subject: "If you desire to see, learn how to act" (1984, p. 61).

Critique Statement

The advantage of this approach lies in the fact that, in Vaihinger's sense, it is an *expedient* fiction, greatly reducing the length and the complexity of treatment. Furthermore, since the interventions are minor and peripheral, it follows that where they do not help, at least they do not harm.

This alone is the object of frequent criticism, based on the seemingly superficial or cosmetic nature of the interventions and their disregard for the assumed deep, underlying problem of which the symptom is only the surface manifestation. The proponents of this view seem unaware that the assumption of a deep, unconscious conflict is merely another fiction — albeit a less expedient one.

Another frequent rejection of this approach is its allegedly manipulative nature. The proponents of this view have yet to define an act of help that is not manipulative in a positive sense. After all, people come to therapy in order to be helped, that is, to be influenced and changed; and even the most nondirective therapists could be accused of manipulation, precisely because they define their techniques as nonmanipulative.

Perhaps the most frequent reason for the failure of this technique lies in the therapist's inability to motivate clients to engage in behaviors that seem un-understandable, unrelated to the problem, and therefore senseless. In this connection, a knowledge of Ericksonian techniques (for example, learning and speaking the client's language, reframing, and so on) proves extremely valuable.

Another cause of failure is not limited to this approach, but was already described by Alfred Adler: the inability of certain clients to agree on a *goal*. Obviously, a goal-less treatment will be long and vague, especially if the therapist is convinced that, in any case, he or she knows better than the client what the latter really needs.

Biography

Paul Watzlawick has been a research associate at the Mental Research Institute in Palo Alto since 1961 and is currently a clinical professor, Department of Psychiatry and Behavioral Sciences, Stanford University. Born in Austria in 1921, he obtained his Ph.D. degree (1949) in philosophy and modern languages from the University of Venice. From 1950 to 1954, he studied at the C. G. Jung Institute in Zurich, obtaining a diploma in analytical psychology. From 1957 to 1959 (three academic years) he was professor of psychotherapy at the Medical School and the Department of Psychology at the University of El Salvador. In 1960, he worked as research associate at the

Institute for Study of Psychotherapy, Department of Psychiatry, Temple University Medical Center, Philadelphia. He is the author of eleven books (available in over fifty foreign translations) and of eighty-five book chapters and articles in professional journals. Being fluent in five languages, he has lectured widely at universities and psychiatric training institutes in North and South America as well as Europe. For the last ten years he has also worked as consultant to large international corporations.

Recommended Reading

Watzlawick, P. (1978). *The language of change: Elements of therapeutic communication.* New York: Basic Books.

Watzlawick, P., Weakland, J. H., & Fisch, R. (1974). *Change: Principles of problem formation and problem resolution.* New York: Norton.

References

Vaihinger, H. (1924). *The philosophy of "as if."* London: Kegan Paul, Trench, Trubner & Co.

von Foerster, H. (1984). On controlling a reality. In P. Watzlawick (Ed.), *The invented reality,* pp. 41–61. New York: Norton.

Problem-Solving Psychotherapy

Richard Fisch

Definition

Since I do not think in terms of "psyche" or "treatment," I must define psychotherapy in much broader and nontraditional terms. I view it as a formal or informal arrangement between two or more people, primarily one of verbal interchange, in which one person utilizes expertise to influence the other(s) to get unstuck from personal or interpersonal problems experienced as painful. Implicit in this definition is that no distinction is made between clinical problems and problems in general, nor are formal credentials required by the expert. Getting unstuck also implies that relief from the problem may come about through either changes in the problem situation *or* a redefinition of the situation as problematic.

Qualification Statement

That people have experienced persistent and therefore painful personal or interpersonal situations has been known since the dawn of humankind. When these painful situations have not responded to common solutions, they have usually been regarded as exceptional and classified as stemming from some special cause. The faultiness of the common solution is rarely questioned. The special cause in more recent times is attributed to factors that are unobvious either within the individual (intrapsychic) or within the social matrix in which the problem occurs (interactional). Thus, whether complex or simple, the problem is assumed to be created and/or supported by an infrastructure not reportable by the troubled individual(s); for example, by the unconscious or by implicit "family rules." In addition, the infrastructure is regarded as an undesirable factor; that is, it is regarded as pathological, and phrases such as the following are applied to it: "abreaction," "displacement," "learning deficit," "dysfunctional family homeostasis," "metabolic disorder," "restrictive family rules," and so on.

All of these factors are regarded as truer and more enlightened than traditional explanations such as possession, influence of the stars, evil spirits, or the influence of the gods but do share in common with them an unobvious, exceptional play of forces that sets the troubled person apart from those whose problems succumb to common solutions.

During the past twenty-two years, the members of the Brief Therapy Center at the Mental Research Institute in Palo Alto, California, have evolved a model for dealing with problems that departs from this pathological and "exceptional" tradition, a model that encompasses the full range of human personal and interpersonal problems from the mundane ("my son won't study") to the catastrophic (suicide, self-starvation, schizophrenia). In its essence it explains the persistence of problems as requiring continued effort by the complainant(s) to maintain the problems. The origin of the problem is not considered relevant. The strategic problem-maintaining effort is actually fueled by the desire to resolve the problem, and most often these efforts (attempted solutions) are common-sensical. Therefore, pathology is unnecessary to explain persisting problems: People need to stop doing something that isn't working, logical or as common-sensical as it may seem.

Thus, the principal job of the expert in psychotherapy is to assess where the clients are stuck, what mainly they are doing to get unstuck, and how to influence them to stop doing what they regard as logical or necessary. These tasks require verbal exchange (oral or written) but do not require a formal contract; that is, one can do psychotherapy in informal contact with friends, relatives, or, for that matter, strangers. Nor does it require that psychotherapy be limited to clinical problems. In fact, that distinction is more counterproductive than useful. While the form of painful events can differ widely depending on context, the individuals involved, and other factors, the common element in personal and interpersonal problems, in our model, is that people who are stuck keep at a solution that is not working.

Critique Statement

There are two major areas of criticism. The more frequent is that because our approach is avowedly manipulative, our work is unethical, primarily because we may say things to clients we do not believe. Those criticisms, we believe, overlook the inherent nature of psychotherapy as a manipulative medium and also do not allow for a *different* ethical base depending on how the therapist sees his or her moral obligation to a client. In our view, the obligation is to resolve the problem expeditiously (as opposed to being "honest") and to take responsibility for one's manipulations.

A second criticism comes from trainees as well as ourselves. Since the model is deceptively simple but its implementation is difficult, we have felt frustrated by the limitations of our teaching skills to ease the transition from familiar models to our own. Trainees' criticisms have dealt both with the requirement that language be used more precisely and persuasively in our approach and with the need to think in terms of getting people to *do* things rather than *understand* things. In sum, the approach has been criticized as requiring a special gift or talent and therefore not easily transmittable to most therapists. While we acknowledge the difficulties in shifting to a different frame of reference, we believe that obstacles to learning lie not in the trainee but in the limitations of training and teaching expertise on the part of the trainers.

The advantages of our approach are quite apparent. Primarily it allows for a significant shortening of therapy. There is simply less work seen as necessary. Time is not needed in reworking the past, in getting people to gain insight, in nonproductive struggle with a nonmotivated client, in reworking the "family homeostasis." The work and tasks are limited to gathering clear information about where the client is stuck and how he or she keeps himself or herself stuck and assessing the optimum framing for persuading the client to do something different. While these tasks are not easy, the work is quite delimited in its scope. As a problem-solving approach, there is also less risk of burnout. Each client is a new and different chess game, and the approach makes the work challenging, with little if any element of grimness about it. When people are seen as having trouble because of persisting with a nonworking solution, the therapist is not likely to see them as fragile and requiring careful handling. It can add a new dimension to everyday life and problems, especially if one enjoys being a problem solver.

The main disadvantage is that it is hard work. It takes persistence and concentration to get people to be clear about events; it requires extra time in presession planning as well as difficult thinking about strategies and framing of assignments to clients.

One also has to find different things to discuss with one's old psychoanalytic buddies than cases.

Biography

Richard Fisch is a psychiatrist in private practice in Palo Alto, California. He organized the Brief Therapy Center of the Mental Research Institute in Palo Alto in 1966 and is its director and principal investigator. He is a consultant to the Juvenile Probation Department of San Mateo County and is a clinical associate professor of psychiatry at Stanford University's Department of Psychiatry and Behavioral Medicine. He received his M.D. degree (1954) from New York Medical College and took his psychiatric training at the Sheppard and Enoch Pratt Hospital, Towson, Maryland.

Fisch is coauthor (with P. Watzlawick and J. Weakland) of *Change: Principles of Problem Formation and Problem Resolution* and (with J. Weakland and L. Segal) of *The Tactics of Change: Doing Therapy Briefly*. He is also author of numerous articles and chapters on brief psychotherapy and family therapy. He was a recipient of the 1981 Family Therapy Association Award for Distinguished Achievement in New Directions of Family Therapy.

Recommended Reading

Fisch, R., Weakland, J. H., & Segal, L. (1982). *The tactics of change: Doing therapy briefly*. San Francisco: Jossey-Bass.
Watzlawick, P., Weakland, J., & Fisch, R. (1974). *Change: Principles of problem formation and problem resolution*. New York: Norton.

Systemic Family Psychotherapy

Maurizio Andolfi

Definition

Psychotherapy is an opportunity for bilateral growth for clients and the therapist. Mutual growth can only occur when there is sufficient pain and impotence, along with the opportunity to freely choose to engage in the therapeutic process. Symptoms are the synthesis of the family fears and destructiveness and provide the metaphor in which alternatives and solutions can be found. Often, however, positive resources also are embedded in the destructiveness and need to be elicited from the family rather than being invented or injected from the outside.

Qualification Statement

The emergence of pathology is seen as a critical moment in the evolution of a family that seems incapable of using its own resources at a particular stage of its development. This incapacity can make excessive and disorderly demands on these resources, and it can produce an actual developmental block. Seeing mental illness in a developmental framework is the aspect of my work that has most stimulated the growth of my ideas in the past few years.

Another constant that has guided my clinical work and teaching is the position of the therapist in the construction of the therapeutic story. The therapist is called upon to use himself or herself fully by entering the family story and by taking the same risks that he or she expects of the family. For example, if the therapist wants the family to move and overcome its own resistance in order to regain greater authenticity, he or she cannot stay still and watch without revealing herself or himself personally.

When we are unable to understand the families' experience in developmental terms, we should ask ourselves if there is more pathology in the actions of the clients or in our heads. The therapeutic struggle consists of learning how to normalize the hypotheses that we formulate in therapy. Experience has convinced me that when we succeed in doing this, the family accepts us as insiders and moves toward change with less difficulty and in less time.

In recent years I have added another dimension to my previous formulations of family therapy. Moving from a model of the nuclear family to include the generation of the grandparents in my conceptual schema has not only allowed me to add more people to the session, but has also been a way to better understand the individual. Through specific ways of interacting with the trigenerational family, the individual appears as a complex entity, full of contradictions and conflicts. For the skilled observer, however, these interactions become tools for understanding the individual's internal world when trying to grasp the links between current behaviors and experiences and the unmet needs of the past.

The study of myths has been extremely useful in my attempt to grasp the historical, developmental aspect of the family. I wonder if the degree to which each person can change over time is closely dependent on the degree of freedom that he or she is allowed by the family myth and, consequently, on the greater or lesser rigidity of the role and functions that he or she fulfills at home.

I consider myths as mobile structures that are constructed and modified over time. Through their elaboration in therapy we help the individual members of the family distance themselves from what is represented in myth in prescriptive terms, but at the same time to accept the parts of the myth that do not conflict with their search for a personal identity.

I have used time as a fundamental parameter to evaluate change in the developmental progression of the family, especially when it has created a block for itself. And I use time to scan the phases of therapy, as an alternation of joining and separation between therapist and family.

Critique Statement

I have become less interested in theoretical formulations and strategies of paradoxical interventions, which reduce the field of observation. In particular, I refrain from formulating hypotheses about family functioning that exclude the therapeutic context as the proper place for elaborating and verifying these hypotheses. It was exactly this attention to the subject, to the individual therapist's cognitive and emotional states, that moved me away from concepts that were rigidly opposed to individual considerations to study the therapeutic context as a meeting ground and a place for forming new choices and experiences. In this dimension, either the acceptance or the rejection by the therapist of attributions that the family makes about him becomes part of the construction of a new system — the therapeutic system (leaving aside whatever intentions the family has in making its attributions).

Therefore, the therapist is required to have his or her own internal coherence, in order to set up a useful atmosphere of rapport, a touching quality of contact. The therapist essentially engages in a process of moving in and out. This balancing of both the sick and helpful emotional forces requires a flexible, open, and undefensive use of the self by the therapist, often in a playful manner.

When the therapist makes use of play in therapy it becomes a technique. However, it is also necessary to recognize that the therapist needs to learn how to play. Therapists who are able to rediscover the value of play will learn not to take themselves too seriously and will be able to consider their own and others' constructions of reality as temporary and changeable because of the flexibility of their own cognitive operations.

Play also can include a provocative element in therapy. However, it is essential that therapeutic provocation must be accompanied by a joining attitude. That is, it must succeed in communicating that the therapist is standing by the system and connected with the pain while provoking and activating a crisis. Provocation often involves the use of metaphors and metaphorical objects such as toys, as well as a playful use of the self and the system.

Biography

Maurizio Andolfi, M.D., is associate professor of psychology at the University of Rome. He is scientific director of the Family Therapy Institute in Rome, president of the Italian Society of Family Therapy, and editor of the Italian journal *Terapia Familiare,* and he is on the editorial board of *Family Process* and the *Journal of Marital and Family Therapy.* His training in family therapy was at the Ackerman Institute for Family Therapy and Philadelphia Child Guidance Clinic. He also received training in psychoanalysis at the Karen Horney Clinic in New York and was a fellow in Social and Community Psychiatry at the Albert Einstein College of Medicine in New York. He has written ten numerous journal articles as well as several books.

Recommended Reading

Andolfi, M. (1979). *Family therapy: An interactional approach.* New York: Plenum.

Andolfi, M., Angelo, C., & DeNichilo, M. (1989). *The myth of Atlas — Families and the therapeutic story.* New York: Brunner/Mazel.

Andolfi, M., Angelo, C., Menghi, P., & Nicolo-Corigliano, A. (1983). *Behind the family mask.* New York: Brunner/Mazel.

Andolfi, M., & Zwerling, I. (1980). *Dimensions of family therapy.* New York: Guilford.

Brief Therapy

Steve de Shazer

Definition

Psychotherapy deals with the not-so-useful ways people depict their construction of reality. It is a conversation between two people (at least), one of whom (labeled therapist) serves as an editor of the other's descriptions. As an editor, the therapist points out other directions the story might take. When the therapy is successful, the clients subsequently describe their reality in a different way.

Whereas most therapy is based on a "power resistance" metaphor, my model is instead based on a cooperative metaphor (de Shazer, 1980, 1982, 1985, 1988).

Qualification Statement

It should be noted that *psychotherapy* is a misnomer. The term *therapy* implies that there is an illness to cure, while the term *psyche* implies that the illness is one involving the psyche, that is, something psychological. It is important to remember that psyche is a metaphor and therefore the illness is metaphorical. Thus, therapists attempt to cure sick metaphors.

The goal of therapy is to meet the client's goal; that is, if the client says he wants to stop being depressed, then the success of therapy can only be measured by the client no longer saying to the therapist that he is depressed. For this change to be possible, one does not even need to know what the problem is; perhaps it cannot be known, and therefore client and therapist together need only to begin a solution (de Shazer, 1985, 1988).

My own particular version of therapy springs from the premise that the therapist and client work together cooperatively (de

Shazer, 1980, 1982) to construct a therapeutic reality. The bricks for this project are the words they use, and whatever these words depict is the mortar that holds the bricks together. My particular view has been influenced by Ludwig Wittgenstein (1958, 1968), who argued that we can only know the meaning of a word through how that word is used within what he called a "language game" or a specific social context — for example, therapy.

As client and therapist talk together, the client is using words to depict her reality. These words carry with them all previous uses of the words that both client and therapist have experienced. Whatever these words depict is always undecidable. (It is important to understand that this is not a problem to be solved, just a fact to be lived with.) Therefore, client and therapist need to negotiate what these words are going to mean within the context of this particular therapy.

When therapy begins the client uses words (a map) to depict a problematic reality (a territory); for example, the children who are sitting quietly in the office are described as always misbehaving. The therapist has to make a choice about how to misunderstand this depiction.

Frequently this process can be initiated by the therapist's helping the client to find and describe exceptions to the problem statement (de Shazer, 1988); that is, times when he is *not* depressed, or when he feels *least* depressed, or when he thinks others think he is *not* depressed, or when he imagines what it *will* be like to no longer be depressed (de Shazer, 1985).

In a very real sense, talk is the data of therapy. As therapists, my colleagues and I are interested in words that depict change. As therapists, we consider talking about change during therapy as a description of a map of the client's reality and thus as a representation of change in the territory of real life.

Since therapy deals with the present and the future, we are interested in "solution talk" rather than "problem talk." Talking about exceptions or unseen areas of the clients' problem map allows us to begin constructing a solution, helping clients to change their map and thus, recursively, to change the problematic territory — changes that, in turn, will subsequently be revealed through "change talk" and "solution talk."

Critique Statement

My model is most frequently charged with being "too simple" or even "simple-minded." From my frankly minimalist perspective, they are exactly correct. However, what they see as
my vice, I see as my virtue.

Most forms of therapy are based on what seems to be a common-sense point of view about problem solving: Before a problem can be solved or an illness cured, it is necessary to find out
what is wrong. Most forms of therapy share the assumption that
a rigorous analysis of the problem leads to understanding it and
its underlying causation. That is, the presenting complaint is
ordinarily seen as a symptom.

This supposition leads to the idea that symptoms are the result
of some other problems. These "causal problems" include, but
are not limited to, "incongruent hierarchies," "covert parental
conflicts," "low self-esteem," "lack of individuation," various
"traumas," "deviant communication," "repressed feelings," "dirty
games," and so on. Frequently, symptoms are seen to have beneficial effects, such as preventing something worse from happening; that is, anorexia is seen as preventing destruction of the
family unit. This benevolent assumption leads to the idea that
there must be a family problem underlying or creating a situation in which anorexia develops. It is generally assumed that
therapy focuses on getting rid of these causes in order to solve
the problem (or cure the illness); thus, the therapeutic
objective encompasses breaking up the problem-maintenance
mechanisms.

But these assumptions are not the only ones possible. That
is, they are not necessary, although they are frequently useful.
When taken together as a group, the various models of therapy
have explained both how problems develop and how problems
are maintained. When these constructions are superimposed they
tell a complete story: Families can be seen as complex systems
involving sociological, psychological, ideological, biological, and
biochemical aspects. It is not that the various models are just
different levels of description: Rather, they are different pieces
of the same puzzle.

This view leads to a complex, complicated, and perhaps contradictory model that is beyond our ability to comprehend, a situation computer scientists refer to as a "combinational nightmare." This excess of descriptive metaphors calls for Ockham's razor: *What can be done with fewer means is done in vain with many.* The only way to escape from the intolerable contradictions involved in such a project is to turn around the whole perspective from which we look at things.

Perhaps we need not be concerned with constructions involving problems and problem maintenance; what we want instead is to command a clear view. Wittgenstein (1968, p. 129) puts it best: "The aspects of things that are most important for us are hidden because of their simplicity and familiarity. (One is unable to notice something — because it is always before one's eyes.)" This line of thought leads to an altogether "too simple" view of therapeutic change.

In all models, success is measured, at least in part, by described, observed, and/or measured changes in behavior; for whatever reason, someone is reporting doing something different or is reported as doing something different or is actually doing something differently. Following the systemic metaphor, any change stands a chance of being a difference that makes a difference. Any change stands a chance of having an impact on the sociological, psychological, ideological, biological, and/or biochemical aspects of the system.

My view is, however, seen as "too simple" and as disregarding too much of the common therapeutic point of view. Given the general therapeutic metaphor, my critics feel it should not be enough to begin therapy by constructing solutions rather than by finding out what the problem "really is."

Biography

Steve de Shazer is the cofounder and codirector of the Brief Family Therapy Center in Milwaukee, Wisconsin. He is the author of three books, *Patterns of Brief Family Therapy* (1982), *Keys to Solution in Brief Therapy* (1985), and *Clues: Investigating Solutions in Brief Therapy* (1988), as well as numerous professional articles. De Shazer is on several editorial boards and is a member of the faculty at various research and training institutes in the United States and Europe. He has conducted workshops and trainings in the United States, Europe, and Asia. He and his colleagues are currently working on the continued development of an "expert system," called BRIEFER, which is designed to advise brief therapists on intervention design.

References

de Shazer, S. (1980). Brief family therapy: A metaphorical task. *Journal of Marital and Family Therapy, 6*(4), 471–476.
de Shazer, S. (1982). *Patterns of brief family therapy.* New York: Guilford.
de Shazer, S. (1985). *Keys to solution in brief therapy.* New York: Norton.
de Shazer, S. (1988). *Clues: Investigating solutions in brief therapy.* New York: Norton.
Wittgenstein, L. (1958). *The blue and brown books.* New York: Harper.
Wittgenstein, L. (1968). *Philosophical investigations* (rev. 3rd ed.). New York: Macmillan.

Brief Solution-Focused Psychotherapy

Eve Lipchik

Definition

Psychotherapy is an interactional process between a person trained in solution construction and a person or persons experiencing emotional pain or behavioral difficulties, or perceived by others to be doing so. This interaction, guided by the therapist's focus on the present, the future, and existing strengths, leads to a difference in the client's reality with respect to the problematic situation; and this in turn promotes the necessary motivation and confidence in the client to explore other options for solution.

Qualification Statement

My definition emphasizes the interactional aspect of psychotherapy because brief solution-focused therapy has a systemic foundation. Theoretically, solution construction is the outcome of the differences generated by the interactional process of a therapeutic supra-system (therapist and/or team and one or more clients) formed for the duration of treatment. The therapist's interview and interventions, which are guided by basic assumptions about inherent strengths and the existence of exceptions to every problem, challenge the client's belief about the present lack of solution to complaints, thereby opening the way for alternative thoughts, behaviors, and feelings that may make the necessary difference.

This model is also theoretically rooted in Ericksonian hypnotherapy in terms of indirect suggestion and the absence of the concept of resistance. The therapist's respectful acceptance of the clients' present reality and patient effort to help clients define goals that have specific fit creates a nondefensive climate in which inner resources can be accessed more easily. A break toward the end of each session, after which the therapist reads a message complimenting the clients for what they are already doing well, establishes a "yes set" (Erickson, Rossi, & Rossi, 1976; Erickson & Rossi, 1979; de Shazer, 1982) that makes the client more receptive to task assignments. When tasks are accomplished outside the session, it promotes independence from therapy.

Although the focus of psychotherapeutic treatment has been broadened from the intrapsychic to the interpersonal in the past few decades, it still rests largely on the presenting problem, which is either seen as a repetition of intergenerational patterns (Bowen, 1978), as a structural fault (Minuchin, 1974); as functional for the system (Selvini-Palazzoli, Boscolo, Cecchin, & Prata, 1978);

or as being a faulty attempt at solution (Weakland, Fisch, Watzlawick, & Bodin, 1974).

The brief solution-focused model developed in Milwaukee over the past ten years (de Shazer, 1982, 1985, 1988) focuses on what is going well in the present and the future because theoretically it does not consider a causal relationship between the past and the present or between problem and solution. The assumption is that change is inevitable but variable, depending on specific context.

Research at the Brief Family Therapy Center in Milwaukee has indicated that solutions may have little relationship to the problems described by clients or therapists (de Shazer, 1985). This further confirmed that time spent on trying to understand the problem may not be useful and that in spite of their knowledge and expertise therapists cannot presume to know which solution will be the right one for a particular client (except in terms of socially acceptable and ethical boundaries). Thus the therapist's role must essentially be thought of as cofacilitator for the client's construction of a uniquely fitting solution.

Clients usually come to therapy totally blinded to positive possibilities by the negative emotions evoked by their problems. But eliciting negative information and details about the complaint is only useful to distinguish clients' future expectations and to allow clients to feel heard and understood. The building blocks for solution construction are a focus on clearly defined goals, recognizable steps toward their achievement, and the bits of positive information elicited during the interview. Various direct and indirect techniques are selected by the therapist to maintain a cooperative climate, including compliments for existing efforts and strengths, task assignments, reframing, symptom prescription, and restraining. Brevity is not a goal but a natural byproduct of the guiding principles about cooperation versus resistance, the systemic ripple effect (whereby one change has a snowballing effect), and an inductive methodology.

Critique Statement

The most frequent criticism of the brief solution-focused model is its dramatic departure from traditional methods of psychotherapy in terms of its nonpathological concept. In an era that places increasing value on hard outcome data, a model that defies the use of diagnostic categories as guidelines for treatment planning and evaluation by assessing and treating each case according to specifically set goals determined by the client is seen as too drastic a departure from the norm. Yet there are outcome studies on brief nonmedical models that point to a high rate of lasting satisfaction (Weakland et al, 1974; de Shazer et al, 1986), as well as clinically significant research focused specifically on how the therapy is conducted (Matsui, 1988; Gingerich, de Shazer, and Weiner-Davis, 1988).

Another frequent criticism is the fact that brief solution-focused therapy is a band-aid approach that results in symptom substitution because it focuses on symptoms as defined by clients rather than on developing insight about their underlying causes as defined by the therapist. There does not seem to be any statistical evidence that this criticism is any more valid than the belief that insight leads to lasting change. However, a seasoned solution-focused therapist will attest to the fact that insight usually develops as a natural byproduct of solution construction in spite of the fact that it is not a goal.

One of the greatest advantages of doing psychotherapy this way is its benefit for clients. When client assessment is made without the constraints of preconceived diagnostic categories and with attention to strengths and positive behaviors, as opposed to pathology, there are many more options for solution. An interview directed at the problem for the purpose of establishing a diagnostic classification will be guided by the therapist's knowledge about the symptomatology of the various classifications and is more likely to find the "right" symptoms than an interview conducted on the basis of trying to understand the nature of the client's complaint, his or her ideas of solution, and whether or not there are existing possibilities for solution. In most cases, it is an advantage for a client to be treated with the latter approach rather than the former because it is less painful and quicker and avoids the danger of a less individualized diagnosis that may misguide treatment.

The answer to the question of whether the therapist is not apt to miss important treatment issues by not searching for specific problem information is that a good assessment, including one done in the brief model, must include some understanding of the specifics of the complaint. However, clients are acculturated to providing therapists with negative information, and are more likely than not to divulge it directly or indirectly anyway, while they are generally not aware of the positives and very unlikely to report them without the therapist's careful probing. An information-gathering process that focuses only on negatives has the potential of making the existing reality appear even worse. Therefore, in theory, solution-focused therapy tries to divert the client from such an approach. Finally, since the goal of psychotherapy, regardless of theoretical orientation, is for clients to function well outside of therapy, a treatment method that is positive and builds self-confidence from the start is desirable.

The advantages for the therapist practicing brief solution-focused therapy are twofold. First, it is much less stressful to work in a climate of cooperation with the client than to be confrontive, trying to break down resistance. Second, the ultimate responsibility for change rests on the client. Too many therapists struggle for years with clients who will not change according to the therapeutic treatment goals they have set. In solution-focused work, the therapist must use every strategy possible to help the client help himself. If, in spite of that, the clients refuse to change—either because they do not wish to or because they expect someone to do it for them—then the therapist admits defeat for the time being and offers a referral. More likely than not clients will then begin to take some responsibility for their own solution or leave and return at a later date when they are more ready to do so.

The unorthodoxy of this model sometimes makes it difficult to practice with credibility among people who are unfamiliar with or unaccepting of it. It is rumored, however, that with patience this positive approach can be used to construct solutions for problems with colleagues as well.

Biography

Eve Lipchik, ACSW, is presently in private practice in Milwaukee and working as a free-lance trainer and consultant. She received her M.S.W. degree (1978) from the University of Wisconsin, Milwaukee. Lipchik was a full-time member of the Brief Family Therapy Center in that city for nine years and participated in the development of the brief solution-focused model this group is known for. Her particular contribution lies in the area of interviewing, about which she has lectured and written extensively. She has edited a special volume on interviewing for the *Journal of Strategic and Systemic Therapies* and a book on the same subject for Aspen.

References

Bowen, M. (1978). *Family therapy in clinical practice.* New York: Jason Aronson.

de Shazer, S. (1982). *Patterns of brief family therapy.* New York: Guilford.

de Shazer, S. (1985). *Keys to solution in brief therapy.* New York: Norton.

de Shazer, S. (1988). *Clues: Investigating solutions in brief therapy.* New York: Norton.

de Shazer, S., Berg, I. K., Lipchik, E., Nunnally, E., Molnar, E., Gingerich, W., & Weiner-Davis, M. (1986). Brief therapy: Focused solution development. *Family Process, 25,* 207–222.

Erickson, M. H., & Rossi, E. (1979). *Hypnotherapy: An exploratory casebook.* New York: Irvington.

Erickson, M. H., Rossi, E., & Rossi, S. (1976). *Hypnotic realities.* New York: Irvington.

Gingerich, W., de Shazer, S., & Weiner-Davis, M. (1988). Constructing change: A research view of interviewing. In E. Lipchik (Ed.), *Interviewing.* Rockville, MD: Aspen.

Matsui, W. T. (1988). The process of structural family therapy: Level of experience makes a difference. In E. Lipchik (Ed.), *Interviewing.* Rockville, MD: Aspen.

Minuchin, S. (1974). *Families and family therapy.* Cambridge, MA: Harvard University Press.

Selvini-Palazzoli, M., Boscolo, L., Cecchin, G. F., & Prata, G. (1978). *Paradox and counterparadox.* New York: Jason Aronson.

Weakland, J., Fisch, R., Watzlawick, P., & Bodin, A. (1974).

Brief therapy: focused problem resolution. *Family Process, 13,* 141–168.

Strategic-Systemic Family Therapy

Michaelin Reamy-Stephenson

Definition

Psychotherapy focuses on accessing personal resources, not defining pathology. It is the directive, goal-oriented process of providing clients with new experiences that change outdated internal maps and rigid interactive patterns supporting symptomatic behavior. Resistance is avoided through a nonjudgmental stance normalizing individual perceptions, feelings, and attempts at solution. Within a trusting relationship—through the language of change—a new beginning is created. As therapist, I negate blame yet elicit the reality of choice, the owning of responsibility for behavior and acceptance of natural consequences. As therapist, I am each and all: a manipulator of the ecology, a shaman, a problem solver, a healer.

Qualification Statement

Theoretical assumptions directing my work have been gathered from the basic radical assumptions underlying strategic therapy and from the biological sciences; most specifically, ethology. I assume that humans are essentially a life form, part *of,* part *in* the broader ecology. An important clarification: When I speak of theoretical assumptions, I am not speaking about "the truth." I agree with Haley (1979) that the value of theory for clinical practice is determined by whether it works. I don't believe that people like being miserable. I assume my first task to be that of instilling hope (Rabkin, 1977). I assume that what the client(s) and I believe determines what is possible; and I assume that one can only change if one experiences something new—that insight alone does not lead to change.

The assumption of nonobjective reality is central to my work—the assumption that reality, like beauty, is in the eyes of the beholder—that what you look for determines what you find. This assumption, organized around the concept of internal maps, becomes the basis for *avoiding blame and avoiding judgment.* The human species, with its highly developed brain, relies more on learning, less on instinctual maps than other life forms. Bateson (1979) pointed out that people learn in stories, in patterns; Korzybski, that people operate out of internal maps rather than out of sensory experience (Lankton, 1980). It seems to work for me to think of clients behaving out of internal maps that historically fit with survival, with early experiences, with familial and cultural context; maps that give life order, predictability. These survival maps, *often outdated,* are more apt to be heavily relied upon when demands for change in the ecology raise levels of stress—for example, in life-stage transitions. In a corresponding way, attempted solutions emerging from these maps are seen as predictable, as are the rigid interactive patterns (built out of each person's attempted solution) that fit with symptomatology. *There are no bolts from the blue* (Reamy-Stephenson, 1986).

Consistent with the Mental Research Institute approach, my assumptions about problem resolution fit with my assumptions about problem formation (Watzlawick, Weakland, & Fisch, 1974). Thus, my tasks become seeking out and acknowledging each person's perception of the problem, accessing and normalizing internal maps and related attempted solutions, and declaring a new beginning. Genograms and cultural observations are invaluable in this process. Belief systems are challenged. New, more adaptive solutions are suggested and structured through homework tasks, providing new experiences that access personal resources leading to change. The establishment of measurable goals, while providing a framework for documenting change, helps avoid drifting. Rituals are used to punctuate this new beginning. Assumptions are clarified, life tasks negotiated, commitment defined.

A word about the relationship of therapist and client(s). The person of the therapist is inherently part *of,* part *in* the client's ecology. My assumptions, values, way of being in the world influence and are influenced implicitly, much as a change in the river reflects a change in the forest. My clients are not perceived as ill—not patients—but as humans, stuck in a predictable logjam. As a person who relates comfortably on a rather intimate level in life beyond therapy, so I relate to my clients. Self-disclosure works to normalize the human dilemma. As I encourage the reality of choice and responsibility for behavior, so must I acknowledge my own choices and responsibility for my own behavior. As I encourage self-forgiveness, so must I forgive myself again and again.

Critique Statement

Psychotherapy is a relatively fitting frame for what I do for a living. There is no school where I find a perfect fit. I usually meet with couples and families. More important is the way I think. I consider myself an ecosystemic therapist, the family being a critical part of the ecology. I passionately resist the arrogance that separates the human species from the broader ecology. A psychotherapy that emphasizes "fit" rather than lineal causality has the advantage of helping me to avoid cognitive dissonance. Homeostasis can be readily normalized around protection and survival of the species. Fear of the unknown does not appear to be uniquely human.

Focus is on pattern, not damaging event. The map is not confused with the territory. Events cannot be erased, but the emerging maps can be changed. It is a hope-filled therapy. In utilizing the resources of family members—dealing with the real players—behavioral cues fit more precisely and hence dysfunctional patterns are more efficiently changed. As a species we have been catapulted into cataclysmic change, brought about by our own collective brain. It makes sense that logjams would readily develop as maps quickly become increasingly homogenized, while valuable rituals facilitating transitions have been lost. Rituals give structure, reduce anxiety. Spirituality is inherent in the ritual of forgiveness. There is an implicit message: "You are just where you need to be to get where you are going." Perhaps a new beginning taps into the universal—the renewal of springtime.

When resentments are clearly heard, yet blame negated, insight can be used without resistance. As maps are raised to consciousness and choices become clarified, responsibility for behavior is underlined. A victim stance is no longer tenable. With self-forgiveness comes forgiveness of others—spouse, parents—who themselves had their own set of outdated maps. This psychotherapy avoids emotional cutoffs, promotes gifts to future generations. Through self-disclosure, I share in vulnerability, avoiding overexposure of client(s) and barriers to intimacy that fit with such imbalances. With the building of trust and mutual respect, directives are more apt to be followed.

Every asset incorporates liability. Any psychotherapy involves meddling in other people's lives. If one person changes, the ecology changes. People are affected who haven't necessarily contracted for therapy. Certainly, a directive approach involves significant meddling. My justification is found in the belief that people have a right to ask for help and advocate for improvements in the quality of their lives. I find ways to put limits on meddling. I acknowledge my own biases. I'm careful to offer choice. I avoid techniques—things that have a quality of doing to a client. My way of working flows naturally out of my belief system. Reframing and paradox are not perceived as techniques. Reframing is simply rearranging data to fit a different pattern, a different reality; paradox, the universal tension between change and restraint from change (Hoffman, 1981).

I have learned to amplify my natural tendencies to give them more power (Zeig, 1980). Somewhere I read that Socrates claimed that the cure of souls is accomplished by the use of certain charms, and these charms are fair words. I attend to language, make use of naturalistic trance (Zeig, 1980; Carter & Gilligan, personal communication, February 4–6, 1983). I tell a lot of stories. As I have increasingly avoided techniques, it makes my job as trainer more difficult. There seems to be a demand for techniques. In recent years, my focus has been on helping train-

ees experience other realities, access and amplify personal resources — find a niche that fits their own integrity (Carter, 1982).
There is nothing flashy about my work. This is, perhaps, a liability. Perceiving resistance as existing between people, not in
the client, means accountability. With self-disclosure comes vulnerability. I must stand behind my words, carefully tend my
own hearth. Boundaries must be carefully monitored. Finally,
I run the risk of believing too much in my own client(s). However, when psychotherapy works, new stories develop, new tales,
and my clients and I have better tools to get ourselves out of
future logjams.

Biography

Michaelin Reamy-Stephenson, along with her husband, Rick
Stephenson, maintains a private practice in marriage and family therapy, called Perspective, in Atlanta, Georgia. She received
her M.S.W. degree (1979) from the University of Georgia.
Former positions include director of social services at Brawner
Psychiatric Institute, where her work focused on breaking the
cycle of rehospitalization through the integration of individual,
group, and family therapy. As director of training (extramural)
at the Atlanta Institute for Family Studies (1983–1986) she
headed the development of a comprehensive postgraduate training program focused on teaching therapists to think systemically at multiple levels. Her interest in training has continued
through participation on the American Association for Marriage
and Family Therapy's Commission on Supervision (1986–1988),
as an AAMFT-approved supervisor, and as an adjunct clinical
assistant professor at Georgia State University. In addition to
developing training films, Reamy-Stephenson has made significant contribution to the training literature in strategic and
systemic therapy. She serves on the editorial advisory board of
the *Journal of Strategic and Systemic Therapies* and is a board-certified
diplomate in clinical social work. Her interest and contributions
have expanded to the application of systemic thinking to family-
owned businesses.

Recommended Reading

Alcock, J. (1975). *Animal behavior: An evolutionary approach*. Sunderland, MA: Simaur Associates.

Cousteau, J. Y. (1953). *The silent world*. New York: Harper.

Dell, P. (1982). Beyond homeostasis: Toward a concept of coherence. *Family Process, 21,* 21–41.

Haley, J. (1976). *Problem-solving therapy*. San Francisco: Jossey-Bass.

Reamy-Stephenson, M. (1983). The assumption of non-objective reality: A missing link in the training of strategic therapists. *Journal of Strategic and Systemic Therapies, 2*(2), 51–68.

Reamy-Stephenson, M. (1984). Psychiatric inpatient units. In M. Berger, G. L. Jurkovic, and Associates (Eds.), *Practicing family therapy in diverse settings*. San Francisco: Jossey-Bass.

Ward, B., & Dubos, R. (1972). *Only one earth*. New York: Norton.

Weakland, J., Fisch, R., Watzlawick, P., & Bodin, A. (1974). Brief therapy: Focused problem resolution. *Family Process, 13*(2), 141–169.

References

Bateson, G. (1979). *Mind and nature: A necessary unity*. New York: Dalton.

Carter, P. (1982). Rapport and integrity for Ericksonian practitioners. In J. Zeig (Ed.), *Ericksonian approaches to hypnosis and psychotherapy*. New York: Brunner/Mazel.

Haley, J. (1979, April). Workshop on strategic therapy. Washington, DC.

Hoffman, L. (1981, April). Workshop: Dialogues in family therapy; a little humor, a little madness. Atlanta Institute for Family Studies.

Lankton, S. (1980). Workshop: Psychological level communication. International Congress on Ericksonian Approaches to Hypnosis and Psychotherapy, Phoenix, AZ.

Rabkin, R. (1977). *Strategic psychotherapy*. New York: Basic Books.

Reamy-Stephenson, M. (1986). No bolts from the blue. In D. Efron (Ed.), *Journeys: Expansions of the strategic-systemic therapies.* New York: Brunner/Mazel.

Watzlawick, P., Weakland, J., & Fisch, R. (1974). *Change: Principles of problem formation and problem resolution.* New York: Norton.

Zeig, J. (1980). *A teaching seminar with Milton Erickson, M.D.* New York: Brunner/Mazel.

Brief Systemic Psychotherapy

Joel S. Bergman

Definition

Brief systemic psychotherapy is an attempt to quickly focus in on and eliminate a presenting problem in as few treatment sessions as possible. I try to understand both how the problem is related to some transition in the family life cycle and how it is currently sustained by the family system in which the symptom occurs. Once this information is obtained and a hypothesis is formed about the function that a symptom serves in a family system, a prescription, task, or ritual is prescribed in a way that, if acted upon, will lead to critical changes in interpersonal behaviors of the patient. These changes will subsequently change the stabilizing function any symptom serves in the family system.

Qualification Statement

Psychological symptoms result from transitional crises related to the family life cycle. Emotional problems occur when people get stuck in their life, particularly when they are trying to leave someone else and emotionally grow up. Symptoms occur around these transitional times when, for example, the only or last child tries to leave home; when a spouse wants to leave a partner; or when someone is trying to get married and must emotionally separate from their parents in order for the marriage to work. (For the theory behind these assumptions, see Bowen, 1978.)

Besides explaining why a symptom takes place, a workable clinical hypothesis also must require knowing how a symptom is maintained, sustained, or amplified in the current social system in which it occurs. All symptoms take place in interpersonal (social) contexts, and one must understand how such contexts operate in order to alter the interpersonal context that sustains the symptom (Watzlawick, Weakland, & Fisch, 1974).

Once a clinical hypothesis is developed, a ritual or prescription is devised that, when acted upon, will change the ongoing interpersonal behaviors between the symptom bearer and his or her social context. If the clinical hypothesis is correct, these prescribed changes will reduce symptomatic behavior and produce a transitional crisis in the family system. This transitional crisis is necessary for the family to evolve to the next stage in the family life cycle. Once the transitional crisis develops the family system may reorganize with a nonsymptomatic solution with or without therapeutic help from a therapist.

The techniques I frequently use to gather information and devise prescriptions come from the work of Bowen (1978), the Milan Group (Selvini-Palazzoli, Boscolo, Cecchin, & Prata, 1978), and Milton Erickson (Haley, 1967). This would include using reversals, positive connotation, and reframing; prescribing the symptom, system, or resistance; prescribing rituals and tasks aimed at eliciting new behaviors and shifting entrenched coalitions; and using metaphors or storytelling with embedded messages.

Since brief systemic therapy views all symptoms as separation issues between two generations, treatment often includes inviting two or three generations to the session. Difficult or resistant symptoms such as psychosis, eating disorders, or chronic depression are seen as the child protecting the parent(s) from the unresolved separation issues between the parent(s) and the grandparent(s). When this is the case, inviting the three generations to the session provides the opportunity to deal with the two sets of separation issues among the three generations. With all members of the family available, the treatment becomes more powerful and requires less time (Bergman, 1985).

Critique Statement

One of the often-cited criticisms of brief systemic therapy is that it is superficial and does not deal with the real problem or the deep-seated causes responsible for the occurrence of symptoms. This is a moot point as I know of no research that substantiates this criticism.

Another criticism sometimes offered is that this kind of treatment is manipulative. For me, the word "manipulative" means to be deceptive in some way that will benefit someone at some cost to others. Since brief therapy is based upon mutual and overt agreement between the therapist and patient to change a particular behavior, I see little manipulation here.

Advantages

This method appears to be more efficient than some of the traditional longer-term treatments. As a consequence, more patients and families can be seen in clinics, which are overwhelmed with too many cases.

Families and patients from lower socioeconomic classes can be offered this therapy rather than being given the usual treatment of psychoactive drugs. Since this approach is more action-oriented than the "talking therapies," brief systemic therapy may appeal more to these generally less verbal and financially able families.

This approach could be viewed as a more respectful treatment in the sense that the therapy stays focused on the presenting problem, remains so until the problem is resolved, and does not get into other problems unless that is requested by the patient. It may also be more respectful in the sense that systems thinking involves considerable depathologizing and positive connotation, and most people prefer to see their difficult situations as a result of being "stuck" rather than "sick."

Brief systemic therapy seems more appealing to the American public in that it is pragmatic, direct, and short. The public is suspicious (sometimes correctly) of therapists keeping patients in treatment longer than necessary.

Finally, another advantage of this therapy is that since more clinical cases are seen less often, this treatment maximizes the therapist's curiosity and excitement over problem solving and is more intellectually challenging. In addition, brief systemic therapy is more rewarding since change takes place quickly, providing more frequent satisfaction and reinforcement to the agent of change.

Disadvantages

This treatment may exclude certain families from treatment who are not willing to participate when crucial family members refuse treatment. If the anorectic, alcoholic, psychotic, or schizophrenic patient refuses to be in treatment, the therapist may postpone family therapy. If the therapist agrees to see family members without these crucial others (like the identified patient), then the therapist may treat those who do come to treatment, but might abandon a brief therapy model.

The role of brief systemic therapist is probably more suited to experienced rather than beginning therapists. Time is needed for a beginning therapist to develop the necessary training, supervision, and growth and acceptance of self; and beyond that it takes years of experience to develop one's own style and clinical norms and learn to adopt what works and drop what doesn't. Beginning therapists can practice doing brief systemic therapy, but I suspect the average course of treatment for these therapists will be a bit longer than for seasoned therapists.

Finally, another disadvantage for the brief systemic therapist in private practice is that this form of treatment requires a larger volume of patients for the practitioner to make a living. Working this way is probably easier in a large urban setting where there is a larger flow of potential referrals.

Biography

Joel S. Bergman is a senior supervisor, faculty member, and
founding member of the Brief Therapy Project at the Ackerman Institute for Family Therapy in New York City, where
he also conducts his private practice. He is a supervisor of psychotherapy at the Ferkauf Graduate School of Yeshiva University. He received his Ph.D. degree (1970) from Bowling Green
University in clinical psychology. He also does management consultations for corporations and family-owned businesses. Bergman is an adjunct editor of *Family Process* and is an approved
supervisor and fellow of the American Association for Marriage
and Family Therapy. He has written extensively and exclusively
on brief therapy, his most recent book being *Fishing for Barracuda:
Pragmatics of Brief Systemic Therapy.*

References

Bergman, J. S. (1985). *Fishing for barracuda: Pragmatics of brief
systemic therapy.* New York: Norton.
Bowen, M. (1978). *Family therapy in clinical practice.* New York:
Jason Aronson.
Haley, J. (Ed.). (1967). *Advanced techniques of hypnosis and ther-
apy: Selected papers of Milton H. Erickson.* New York: Grune &
Stratton.
Selvini-Palazzoli, M., Boscolo, L., Cecchin, G., & Prata, G.
(1978). *Paradox and counterparadox.* New York: Jason Aronson.
Watzlawick, P., Weakland, J., & Fisch, R. (1974). *Change: Prin-
ciples of problem formation and problem resolution.* New York:
Norton.

Structural Family Therapy

H. Charles Fishman

Definition

Structural family therapy works with the *contemporary* social forces that are maintaining the individual's problem. The therapist observes dysfunctional behaviors in the client's system (family, extended family, and other significant social forces), and through the use of self seeks to transform these dysfunctional patterns. The systems are assessed on the basis of structure (proximity and distance between family members and between other members of the system) as well as gauged against a backdrop of what is appropriate developmentally. The therapist then follows the progression of therapy, seeking both to transform the dysfunctional system and to work with the system toward the stabilization of new structures.

Qualification Statement

Structural family therapy was pieced together by Salvador Minuchin with considerable input from, according to Minuchin, "many voices." It is a systems therapy in which treatment is directed to the individual and the context in which he or she is imbedded. In systems therapies, causality is seen as circular, with each part affecting every other part: The individual is seen as both organizing and being organized by others.

Central to systems theory is the idea of organization. Structural family therapy differs from other therapies in the *explicit* elucidation of the structure of the individual's context. The concept of structure, albeit ancient, has been reborn in the twentieth century as structuralism. Indeed, in our century, structuralism has touched every area of our lives: Levi-Strauss in anthropology; Barth and Chomsky in linguistics; Piaget (1970) and Bruner in developmental psychology; von Bertalanffy (Davidson, 1983) in biology and systems research; Foucault in psychoanalysis. According to structuralism, truth lies in relationships, and the relationship patterns can be charted.

Applying structuralism to clinical work involves examining relationships between the social ecology, the immediate family, and the extended family, and between the family system and the other social institutions—the school, courts, larger community, and helping professionals such as doctors and therapists. Important in the clinical work is not only the context of the family but the clinician's context. Is the clinician's context affecting the work with the family and vice versa?

As the therapist assesses the system, what emerges is a schema that compels active intervention. Here is a tiny universe of troubled relationships—all contemporary—that command the attention of the therapist. The structural map also spells out the path and goal of therapy—to work with the system so that these troubled relationships are ameliorated.

To the clinician working with a broad system and struggling to produce the fastest change possible, there is always the problem of where to intervene. As I apply the structural family therapy model, I use the concept of the "homeostatic maintainer" to lead the way.

Homeostasis is a static descriptive concept that has been used in the family field since its inception. Don Jackson and Virginia Satir described the beautifully choreographed family dance of interdependent members. It is more informative to the therapist, however, to assess the system when it is disturbed. Essentially important information emerges when the therapist, after perturbing the system, ascertains *who activates in such a way that the system returns to its status quo.* Then therapy can be addressed to rendering ineffective the family's stereotyped, stable ways of responding.

Another influence in this work is catastrophe theory. Rene Thom and other mathematicians talk about the fact that in nature there is more than one kind of change (Hampden-Turner, 1982). Newtonian and Leibnizian calculus described gradual change. During an earthquake, however, there is a sudden re-organization of a system. In structural family therapy, the therapist strives for a sudden reorganization of the system in the therapy room. Since the important individuals in the client's life are present, there is considerable likelihood that these new patterns will generalize to the outside.

This brings in another significant influence in this work: gestalt therapy and the work of Fritz Perls, as well as the psychodramatists J. L. and Zerka Moreno. Enactment, a central technique in this model, is based on the notion that systems transform when the customary interactional patterns change. The therapist strives to get the family members to enact their usual interactions in the treatment room. And then, with the aid of a decentralized therapist, the family enacts more functional interactional patterns. In some ways, structural family therapy is a kind of gestaltian psychodrama: The family members indeed have a new experience in the room. What is different about this therapy, compared to gestalt and psychodrama, is the fact that the significant people in the person's life are involved, so that influential individuals are rendered changed by the experience. Thus, there is a greater likelihood that the changes carry over to home.

Enactment is essential, not merely for conflict resolution per se, but for enacting the resolution of pivotal conflicts — those conflicts that are central to the family's difficulty. For example, with anorectics, having the parents get the youngster to eat tends to force a transformation of the undermining patterns that maintain the anorexia. Indeed, it is through the utilization of significant conflictual issues in the treatment room that the therapist is able to restructure the system.

Another important influence in this work is the articulation of developmental thinking over the last ten years. Children used to be described as if they were growing up alone in the woods or in petri dishes. There is, however, increasing literature supporting the notion that the people surrounding the child are also going through regular developmental changes. Indeed, according to Daniel Levinson (1978) and others, adults develop and follow regular developmental milestones with the same regularity as children. Furthermore, families, as social organisms, go through regular, predictable stages.

Developmental ideas are critically important when structure is utilized as a clinical concept. In order to ascertain the structure of a system, the therapist must gauge the proximity and distance between family members against the backdrop of what is developmentally appropriate. Furthermore, concepts of development profoundly affect the goals of therapy. The jurisdiction of the therapist includes working with the system — not only to the point of amelioration of the symptom, but to the point where the system is stabilized at a new level of complexity appropriate to the developmental stages of the individuals.

In conclusion, I would like to end with a quote of Charcot's that, according to Richard Gay (1988, p. 51), fascinated Sigmund Freud: "La théorie, c'est bon, mais ça n'empêche pas d'exister." (Theory is all very well, but it does not prevent facts from existing.) I believe structural family therapy, albeit a theory, gets closer to the facts because of its attempt to observe seminaturalistic interactional patterns as they emerge in the room.

Critique Statement

At times, when I have been teaching structural family therapy, I have been reminded of how William James described the philosophy he called pragmatism: If it works, it's true. Originally created to treat the disadvantaged families of Harlem (Minuchin, Montalvo, Guerney, Rosman, & Schumer, 1967), structural family therapy is pragmatic and based on common sense. The therapist seeks to involve in therapy *all* of the significant individuals and agencies who are maintaining the problem. By working at these *contemporary* forces, fast change can occur. And, as importantly, since we are working with interactional patterns in the here-and-now, the therapist can *see* changes in these patterns in the therapy room.

The "show me" challenge provides some objectivity to the assessment of the system and to the course of the therapy. I remember as a young trainee, a refugee from the subjectivity of philosophy and psychoanalytic theory, how elated I was to find this model of psychotherapy. The clinician can actually see interactional patterns and follow these patterns as they change during the course of therapy.

I remember a case in the psychosomatic research project at the Philadelphia Child Guidance Clinic in the early 1970s. A family was referred by Children's Hospital because the doctors believed that the fourteen-year-old girl's weight loss was due to anorexia. Part of the research design had the family evaluated by means of a videotaped interactional task, which was then scored by neutral raters to ascertain whether the family was a psychosomatic family—that is, a family that exhibited characteristic interactional patterns such as enmeshment, conflict avoidance, rigidity, and triangulation.

The family was administered the family task. The results were surprising. The family did not exhibit the characteristic patterns of a psychosomatic family. Informed of this, the doctors did more testing and found that the girl had a pituitary tumor. This sounds almost like science!

In criticizing this model, it is useful to break down the various components of the model. The notion of working with all of the contemporary social forces that are maintaining the homeostasis is essential to all clinical situations. Mapping the family system is a useful tool for conceptualizing the system and for goal setting. The use of enactment of the family's dysfunctional problems is essential for assessment of the problem.

What I have described as the structural family therapy model implies that the therapist works in proximity to the family. Over the years I have found this model to be extremely effective with psychosomatic families, a majority of delinquent families (those that tend toward enmeshment), and the generic kind of families that have severe boundary dysfunction. Families like these can evidence a myriad of presenting problems.

There are, however, certain systems in which proximity of the therapist can render the therapist rapidly part of the stalemated system. In certain chronic systems and disengaged families, proximity of the therapist is not the answer. What is necessary for these families is a range of interventions, such as paradoxes and tasks. As therapy proceeds, however, it is essential for the therapist to use as markers of progress not only the symptom but also the interactional pattern between the members of the system.

As I have worked with this model over the years, I have been impressed with the fact that the therapist must be exquisitely sensitive to the extrafamilial context to support change. For example, with adolescent delinquents it is important to make every attempt to connect the adolescent to a nondelinquent context that will support and confirm the youngster's nondelinquent self. Another manifestation of my waning hubris (I once believed that family therapy was the only context necessary for change) is my use of self-help groups, when available, to support change.

In my opinion, the structural family therapy model is fairly well elaborated in terms of therapeutic techniques and paradigms for supervision. There is, however, insufficient elaboration of the theory for working with the external systems and the theory of how systems converge. To date, structural family therapy is only a model of the interior of the family. There are not well-articulated interventions beyond that to aid the practitioner.

Finally, like so many other psychotherapy models, structural family therapy is insufficiently tested in terms of follow-up. Furthermore, there needs to be a greater specificity regarding specific interventions for specific kinds of systems and problems.

Biography

H. Charles Fishman is the executive director of the Institute for the Family, Princeton, New Jersey. He received his M.D. degree from the Medical College of Wisconsin and trained in child psychiatry at the University of Pennsylvania and later at the Philadelphia Child Guidance Clinic. While there, he had the opportunity to work closely with Jay Haley, Carl Whitaker, and Salvador Minuchin. Fishman is coauthor of *Family Therapy Techniques* (with Salvador Minuchin) and *Evolving Models of Family Change* (with Bernice Rosman) and author of *Treating Troubled Adolescents: A Family Therapy Approach.* Fishman has lectured widely and is recognized as one of the foremost authorities on structural family therapy and its application to the treatment of child and adolescent problems.

Recommended Reading

Haley, J. (1973). *Uncommon therapy.* New York: Norton.
Levenson, E. A. (1972). *The fallacy of understanding.* New York: Basic Books.
Moreno, J. L. (1983). *The theatre of spontaneity.* New York: Beacon House.
Sheridan, A. (1980). *Michel Foucault: The will to truth.* London: Tavistock Publications.

References

Davidson, M. (1983). *Uncommon sense: The life and thought of Ludwig von Bertalanffy, father of general systems theory.* Boston: Houghton Mifflin.
Gay, P. (1988). *Freud: A life for our time.* New York: Norton.
Hampden-Turner, C. (1982). *Maps of the mind.* New York: Macmillan.
Levinson, D. J. (1978). *The seasons of a man's life.* New York: Knopf.
Minuchin, S., Montalvo, B., Guerney, B. G., Jr., Rosman, B. L., & Schumer, F. (1967). *Families of the slums.* New York: Basic Books.
Piaget, J. (1970). *Structuralism.* New York: Basic Books.

Section 3
Couples Therapy

A Developmental Approach

Ellyn Bader
Peter Pearson

Definition

Psychotherapy is the art of creating environments (mentally, metaphorically, and actually) that facilitate change. Psychotherapy with couples is the process of helping the couple create an environment within their relationship that supports growth and ongoing self-differentiation for each partner while allowing the relationship to unfold and mature. This is opposed to the perspective of most clients entering couples therapy, who view this as "an opportunity to change my partner."

Qualification Statement

Our theoretical underpinnings are based in a developmental model. Specifically, we look at the parallel between Margaret Mahler's developmental stages of childhood — symbiosis, differentiation, practicing, and rapprochement — and the stages that emerge in a couples relationship. We believe that an adult couples relationship will evolve through a series of similar stages on its journey to more committed intimacy.

What are the adult correlates of these early stages? In the Western world, many relationships begin with "falling madly in love," a symbiotic state characterized by merged boundaries and intense bonding. A major purpose of this stage is attachment. To allow for the bonding, similarities are magnified and differences are overlooked. Over time, evolution occurs and one partner begins recognizing differences and taking the lover down from the pedestal.

Focus shifts from giving attention to the other to refocusing on the self. This differentiation stage is the time for identifying and expressing individual thoughts, feelings, and desires. From this evolves negotiation on behalf of one's self that addresses the complex process of being a couple and maintaining individual boundaries. This stage, while it may be characterized by grief and loss or guilt and anger, also is an opportunity for profound individual growth that was not possible during the symbiotic stage.

Successfully addressing the issues of the differentiation stage enables the individuals to evolve into a practicing stage where energy is refocused toward the external world. Here, autonomy and individuation are primary; at this point the partners are rediscovering themselves as individuals away from the relationship. Issues of self-esteem, individual power, and competency become central.

Rapprochement arrives and vulnerability reemerges once each partner has established a more clearly defined, competent identity. Partners once again seek comfort and support from each other. They alternate (sometimes easily and sometimes rockily) between periods of increased intimacy and efforts to reestablish independence.

As this alternation becomes smoother and both partners are strengthened by an acquired foundation of skills and the knowledge that each is loved by the other, the couple may enter a phase of mutual interdependence. Now, the perfect is reconciled with the real, and the couple has built a relationship based on a foundation of growth, rather than one of need.

Unfortunately, all relationships do not evolve smoothly or at the same speed. The relationship may become stuck before movement ever begins, and an enmeshed or hostile-dependent pattern will solidify. Or, an impasse may occur because one individual changes and the other wants to maintain the status quo, thus unbalancing the relationship and creating polarized interaction.

When the relationship reaches an impasse, the effects frequently become debilitating for one or both partners. We view couples therapy as the process of intervening at the nodal developmental impasse to enable the relationship to unfold again on its own.

Our goals include diagnosing the impasse and then intervening with the couples to help them create an environment within their relationship that is conducive to the change requested. We do this by focusing the treatment contract in the future; that is, we ask, "If our work together is successful, what will the two of you create together?" Once the contract is established, we focus both on autonomous change for each individual (which includes re-owning projections and using self rather than other as a target for change) and on working through developmental deficits such as separation anxiety, boundary confusion, object constancy, and capacity for self-other differentiation. We also work to resolve "early decisions" (Goulding & Goulding, 1979) that are being reenacted in the relationship and are inhibiting the relationship from evolving to the next stage.

Critique Statement

Critiquing one's own theory involves a high level of differentiation, both to expose the weaknesses and to praise the strengths. With humility, we undertake this task.

Disadvantages

Since our developmental model focuses primarily on intrapsychic factors being activated in the here-and-now relationship, we do not adequately address other significant forces (economic, cultural, social, genetic) that have a major impact on marital hopes and expectations. This means that while many couples' issues readily may be understood in our developmental model, not all problems will be succinctly identified by our framework.

Also, our approach is not simple to learn. It requires a variety of complex skills and a comprehensive knowledge base. Since we work to change a system from an individual perspective, therapists who use our model must be well versed in individual psychodynamics, couples dynamics, and object relations theory, as well as having a variety of techniques available for resolving intrapsychic impasses. Even when a therapist possesses all these skills, there often remains the problem of unequal motivation for change between the two partners. Thus far, our model is incomplete in addressing this complex issue of differing desires for relationship change or individual growth.

Although we occasionally see couples for fewer than twelve sessions, we are not brief therapists. Our thrust is to help couples develop an environment within their relationship that effectively supports each partner. To do this, we work with most couples for six months to one and a half years. Hence we are not compatible with the mental health insurance industry, which progressively demands fewer sessions and more rapid results.

Advantages

Since we are relationship focused but use the individual as the focal point for autonomous change, we simultaneously facilitate growth in three units (each partner and the relationship). We believe this means that in some cases our method will be faster than individual therapy; at a minimum, it provides a powerful adjunct to shorten individual therapy.

Our approach is targeted and provides a road map for the couple and the therapist. Our developmental structure enables both the couple and the therapist to set a definite contract with identifiable goals. This model leads to more focused interaction in each session and helps avoid those tendencies to wander from session to session. This focus assists in our training with therapists from many divergent backgrounds. They have reported refinement of their skills as well as increased clarity about when to apply specific techniques from their prior training.

Additionally, our approach demystifies couples therapy. When couples are given a brief overview of the development stages, they are able to normalize their struggles and reduce blame. In fact, they find their dramas much more understandable when they are placed in the context of each partner's journey toward psychological identity.

A final note that is both an advantage and a disadvantage—ours is a relatively new model. Our thinking and our intervention strategies are continually being refined. Consequently, we are an incomplete and evolving model for facilitating couples' growth.

Biographies

Ellyn Bader, Ph.D., and Peter Pearson, Ph.D. are founders and directors of the Couples Institute in Menlo Park, California. Bader received her Ph.D. degree (1976) from the California School of Professional Psychology in clinical psychology. Pearson earned his Ph.D. degree (1973) at the University of Southern Mississippi in counseling psychology. Bader is also clinical director, Department of Psychiatry, Stanford University School of Medicine, and is past president of the International Transactional Analysis Association. Bader and Pearson conduct training programs in couples therapy both nationally and internationally and have authored a book on their approach to couples therapy.

Recommended Reading

Bader, E., & Pearson, P. (1988). *In quest of the mythical mate.* New York: Brunner/Mazel.
Mahler, M., Pine, F., & Bergman, A. (1975). *The psychological birth of the human infant: Symbiosis and individuation.* New York: Basic Books.

Reference

Goulding, M. M., & Goulding, R. L. (1979). *Changing lives through redecision therapy.* New York: Brunner/Mazel.

Section 4
Technique- and Problem-Oriented Approaches

Family Therapy with the Posttraumatic-Stress-Disordered Client

Charles R. Figley

Definition

Psychotherapy is a concept that describes the clinical treatment activities of psychologists, clinical social workers, family therapists, psychiatrists, and others. The activities involve attempting to initiate change in the client that will prevent or ameliorate unwanted symptoms, behavior patterns, or perceptions and result in a sense of well-being and life satisfaction. I generally tend to be an optimist and believe that any human being or system is able to overcome adversities of all kinds. The role of the psychotherapist is to serve as facilitator to clients empowering them with information and training (for example, improving the effectiveness of their decision-making, problem-solving, and communication skills). As a result, they will be able not only to solve current problems but to deal more effectively with future problems, perhaps even avoiding them altogether.

Qualification Statement

Much of my work has focused on helping people and groups of people to recover emotionally and behaviorally from highly stressful experiences. Thus my work is rooted in human stress, particularly traumatic stress adaptation theories (Figley, 1983, 1985, 1988, 1989a, 1989b).

With respect to clients who seek relief from the symptoms of posttraumatic stress disorder (PTSD), I attempt to reach eight separate treatment objectives. In the process I work with and utilize various measurement instruments to evaluate my impact. These objectives are (1) building rapport and trust between the therapist and the client family, (2) clarifying the therapist's role, (3) eliminating unwanted consequences, (4) building family social supportiveness, (5) developing new rules and skills of family communication, (6) promoting self-disclosure, (7) recapitulating the traumatic events, and (8) building a family healing theory.

Generally, this traumatic stress therapy follows five phases. In phase one (building commitment to the therapeutic objectives), I attempt to establish the presenting problems and goals from the client's perspective and help the client develop and build commitment from all members of the traumatized family to work with me to reach agreed-upon objectives. These objectives, of course, include but are not limited to those set forth in the previous paragraph. Without a minimal degree of commitment from the family, it is unwise to proceed to phase two (or any of the later phases). But once the foundation of commitment has been laid, one can proceed to framing the current presenting problem perceived by the family.

Phase two (framing the problem) involves encouraging the client or client family to tell the story of the traumatic event that brought them to my office. I am especially interested in the things in the client's life that are unpleasant and require changing. These things most often include a wide variety of hardships and symptoms associated with a family member's PTSD and the breakdown and dysfunction of the family system associated with PTSD.

Once the problems are identified to the satisfaction of all family members who wish to be considered clients, the third phase begins. Phase three (reframing the problem) involves helping the clients discover or be introduced to ways of thinking about the predicament that are more tolerable and adaptable for family functioning. These new insights or perceptions usually include the basic ingredients for a family healing theory.

Phase four (developing a healing theory) consists of generating a set of propositions about a particular situation that is useful both in explaining the current predicament and need for assistance *and* in predicting future outcomes. Through a continuing discussion among family members, such a theory emerges. Though less elegant than most scientific theories, a family's healing theory provides a semantic antidote or medicine for treating and "curing" the trauma "infecting" the family system.

Finally, phase five (closure and preparedness) involves bringing the intervention to a successful closure by ensuring that the family clients have not only reached their treatment objectives but are well prepared for future adversities. This phase is either the hardest or the easiest. What is important, however, is getting client families to appreciate their accomplishment in successfully coping with an extraordinary traumatic stressor and to acknowledge that they are sufficiently equipped with the resources (both skills and attitudes) necessary for coping with potential future traumas.

Critique Statement

The therapists with whom I have trained, supervised, or consulted seem to be genuinely interested in helping traumatized clients. Yet most find it difficult to believe that a single traumatizing event — or even an extended series of events — could be the primary reason why clients are so troubled so long afterwards (Figley, 1985).

Few psychotherapists enjoy working with victims, people who suffer from PTSD. Conversely, an extraordinary number of victims report dissatisfaction with past experiences in psychotherapy (Figley, 1988). This is the fault of neither the client nor the therapist. Most psychotherapy practice is based on the assumption that presenting problems are a function of long-term dysfunction. Clients who complain of depression, general anxiety, sleep disorders, intrusive imagery, startle responses connected with PTSD, or unproductive methods of coping with these symptoms (for example, social isolation, substance abuse, or physical or verbal violence against self or others) often are misdiagnosed. This may be due to a failure on the part of either therapist or client to make connection between the symptoms and the traumatizing event. It may also be due to being unfamiliar with the symptoms of PTSD or to discomfort over talking and thinking about traumatic experiences (Figley, 1986).

My approach is extremely focused and time-limited (Figley, in press), as noted before. Its limitation is that it serves a narrowly defined treatment population; it is designed to help families who are dysfunctional primarily because of traumatic stress. The advantage is that the intrapsychic and interpersonal conflicts associated with traumatic stress and PTSD can be resolved rather quickly, usually within three months.

Biography

Charles R. Figley is professor of family therapy and social work and director of the Interdivisional Program in Marriage and Family at Florida State University, Tallahassee, Florida. He is also founding president of the International Society for Traumatic Stress Studies, current editor of the society's *Journal of Traumatic Stress,* a fellow of numerous national associations, and author of more than 100 scholarly articles and ten books. He received his Ph.D. degree (1974) from Pennsylvania State University.

Recommended Reading

Figley, C. R. (Ed.). (1978). *Stress disorders among Vietnam veterans: Theory, research, and treatment.* New York: Brunner/Mazel.
McCubbin, H. I., & Figley, C. R. (Eds.). (1983). *Stress and the family: Vol. 1. Coping with normative transactions.* New York: Brunner/Mazel.

References

Figley, C. R. (1983). Catastrophes: An overview of family reactions. In C. R. Figley & H. I. McCubbin (Eds.), *Stress and the family: Vol. 2. Coping with catastrophe* (pp. 3–20). New York: Brunner/Mazel.

Figley, C. R. (1985). From victim to survivor: Social responsibility in the wake of catastrophe. In C. R. Figley (Ed.), *Trauma and its wake: The study and treatment of post-traumatic stress disorder* (pp. 398–416). New York: Brunner/Mazel.

Figley, C. R. (1986). Traumatic stress: The role of the family and social support system. In C. R. Figley (Ed.), *Trauma and its wake: Vol. 2. Traumatic stress theory, research and intervention* (pp. 398–416). New York: Brunner/Mazel.

Figley, C. R. (1988). Victimization, trauma, and traumatic stress. *Counseling Psychologist, 16*(4), 635–641.

Figley, C. R. (1989a). *Helping traumatized families.* San Francisco: Jossey-Bass.

Figley, C. R. (Ed.). (1989b). *Treating stress in families.* New York: Brunner/Mazel.

Redecision Therapy

Ruth McClendon
Leslie B. Kadis

Definition

Psychotherapy is an interactive process grounded by a contractual agreement between client and therapist. Psychotherapy uses the natural environment of the family setting to establish the context for individual transformation. Interpersonal and intrapsychic change is accomplished by altering the pattern of interactions in the current family context while helping individual clients to modify the early decisions and internal belief systems that have led to their current misperceptions and dysfunctional behaviors.

Qualification Statement

Redecision family therapy, our framework for psychotherapy, combines both systemic and individual approaches within
a three-stage model. In stage one, the systemic stage, we work
toward symptom or problem resolution. In stage two, the redecision stage, we focus on the transformation of personal structure. In stage three, reintegration, we teach clients how to prevent future individual and systemic disablement.

Redecision family therapy holds that individuals change the
way they interact with other people or systems when they are
able to change their underlying beliefs about themselves and
others. We refer to these beliefs as "early decisions." Early decisions are active and healthy processes by which the young child
adapts to the individuals in the family and the family environment as a whole. Early decisions form a basis for all future beliefs about self and others and the basis for all future behavior.
Changing early decisions requires an emotional experience that
accesses early feelings. When these early feelings are connected
to the beliefs they represent, comparison with current circumstances can be accomplished and the early decision becomes subject to change.

The goals of redecision family therapy are (1) to help individuals and families resolve the particular presenting problems that
they bring to the psychotherapeutic environment and (2) to initiate change within individuals so that their internal conversations and external behaviors change in the directions they desire.
Underlying redecision family therapy are the following beliefs:

1. Psychotherapy is based on a model of health that utilizes
    the natural strengths of all participants.
2. Clients must conserve as well as change themselves.
3. Therapists do not change people. They design an environ-
    ment in which people respond and change themselves.
4. The client, not the therapist, always controls the process.
5. The therapist's office is simply one step in the individual's
    or family's change process.
6. The psychotherapy process sets clear boundaries, establishes
    concrete expectations, and formulates clear contracts.

7.   Psychotherapy is an active process.
8.   Psychotherapy is most effective when an affective experi-
     ence is grounded in current reality and achieves cognitive
     resolution.

Critique Statement

Redecision family therapy is an integrative approach to psychotherapy. It is an active model that begins with the family
system, proceeds to the individual as the creator of the system,
and finishes with the system as a healthy and supportive entity.
The advantages of redecision family therapy are:

1.   It gives meaning to change within both the internal and
     external environments of the client by focusing on the in-
     dividual within his or her contextual reality.
2.   It continually validates personal worth by focusing on health
     and the conservation of personal resources.
3.   It empowers clients to take charge of their own lives and
     supports their abilities to do so.
4.   Powerful affect is evoked that facilitates the uncovering of
     archaic material, allows for the detoxification of past in-
     fluences on the present, and has a distinct demystifying or
     humanizing effect; this humanizing effect in turn promotes
     reassessment of the archaic beliefs.
5.   It solidifies individual and systemic change by providing
     the tools for continued problem solving during the normal
     cycles of development for both family and individual.
6.   It starts from the present, moves to the past, and recon-
     nects with the present, a method that allows many of the
     various psychotherapeutic principles and techniques to be
     included within the model.

The disadvantages of redecision family therapy are:

1.   The affective experience is powerful but imposes constraints
     on the material that an individual can and will bring up.
     Some of the constraint comes from having other family
     members present (whether or not actually in the room), and

some comes from the fact that the material may be frightening to the children.
2. The active directed approach can miss important personality issues that underlie early decisions, creating a possible danger that changes will be superficial rather than integrated.

Biography

Ruth McClendon is cofounder and codirector of the Institute for Family Business, an organization offering services to family firms across the United States, and a founding board member of the Family Firm Institute, a national forum for family busines practitioners. She also has a private practice in Aptos and San Francisco, California. She received her M.S.W. degree (1967) from the University of Michigan. During the last fifteen years, she has been training and teaching professionals throughout the United States, Europe, and South America. McClendon is an assistant clinical professor of psychiatry at Langley Porter Neuropsychiatric Institute, University of California Medical School, San Francisco, and on the staff of the Fielding Institute, Santa Barbara, California. She is a clinical teaching member and past president of the International Transactional Analysis Association; a clinical supervisor of the American Association for Marriage and Family Therapy; and a charter member of the American Family Therapy Association. She is coeditor of the international division of the *American Journal of Family Therapy*.

Leslie B. Kadis is assistant clinical professor of psychiatry at Langley Porter Neuropsychiatric Institute, University of California Medical School, San Francisco. He is also codirector of the Institute for Family Business and maintains a private practice in Santa Cruz and San Francisco, California. He received his M.D. degree (1961) from Albert Einstein University. Kadis has had considerable experience teaching family therapy to private and university groups throughout the United States, Europe, Canada, and Mexico. He is the coauthor (with Ruth McClendon) of a book on family therapy, *Chocolate Pudding and Other*

Approaches to Intensive Family Therapy, and editor of a book on psychotherapy, *Redecision Therapy: Expanded Perspectives.* He has authored and coauthored numerous professional papers. Currently, Kadis is the coeditor of the international division of the *American Journal of Family Therapy* and on the editorial board of the *Family Business Review.* He has been honored as a fellow by the American Psychiatric Association for his professional and community work. He is a charter member of the American Family Therapy Association and a clinical member of the International Transactional Analysis Association.

Recommended Reading

Goulding, R., & Goulding, M. (1979). *Changing lives through redecision therapy.* New York: Brunner/Mazel.

Kadis, L. B., & McClendon, R. (1984). Integrating redecision and family therapy. In A. Gurman (Ed.), *Family therapy* (pp. 147–154). New York: Brunner/Mazel.

McClendon, R., & Kadis, L. B. (1983). *Chocolate pudding and other approaches to intensive family therapy.* Palo Alto, CA: Science and Behavior Books.

"Diaclectic" Psychotherapy

Florence W. Kaslow

Definition

My teaching and practice is predicated on the belief that psychotherapy is a healing process. This process occurs when the therapist and patient establish a solid therapeutic alliance within the context of a safe sanctuary. Here patients can explore their attitudes, values, behaviors, demons, fantasies, and goals—any aspect of their intrapsychic and interpersonal lives that is troubling to them.

My "diaclectic," integrative model enables me to select the treatment modality and therapeutic persona that I believe will be most advantageous in helping the patient confront, unravel, and resolve internal and relational losses, fears, and other dilemmas.

Qualification Statement

The diaclectic model posits that no one model, theory, or intervention strategy constitutes a therapeutic panacea for all patients, problems, or syndromes. Human interactive behavior, particularly in its dysfunctional or pathological forms, is multi-determined and complex and is rarely likely to respond to simplistic assessments and prescriptive interventions alone. Our patients are not robots on an assembly line to whom we can administer predetermined formulas that will rapidly "fix" them.

Rather, individuals uniquely bring to treatment their universal and idiosyncratic traits, characteristics, feelings, strivings, transactional patterns, and individual actions. To help them most effectively we need to know something about their perception of self and of the family system (and its other members) of which they form a part. The treatment should be individually tailored for patients based on such factors as the amount of time and effort they are willing to invest in treatment, the acuteness or chronicity of symptomatology, the patient's goals, the severity and nature of problems, and the resources available; that is, what will help this patient most efficaciously at this point in time.

Theoretical orthodoxy that asserts that any one school of thought and treatment approach is right and best leads to counterproductive rigidity. Therefore, I try to be conversant with and avail myself of numerous theories of psychotherapy and family therapy and their accompanying techniques. I continually cull judiciously from the wonderfully rich, vast array of extant approaches — or create new ones when the need arises. This is not an atheoretical or nontheoretical paradigm. Rather, it purports to expand the parameters — seeking ever new synthesis between different theoretical systems in the quest for greater illumination of the patient's quandary and greater therapeutic lever-age (Kaslow, 1981).

The term *diaclectic* was coined "to convey that this nonmodel model draws selectively and eclectically from numerous sources and seeks a new, more compelling dialectic approach to analyz-ing a family's difficulties and facilitating the resolution of the troubles and dysfunctions. Clinically, it makes treatment a con-tinuing challenge in which therapist and patient(s) explore to-gether—tuning into each other's conscious and unconscious pro-cesses, and verbal and nonverbal communications" (Kaslow, 1981, p. 348). Thus, depending on my mapping or assessment of the disorder or dysfunction, I may use circular questioning, reframing, symptom prescription or another paradoxical strat-egy, a behavioral prescription or reinforcement, clarification or interpretation, an enactment or sculpting, or a combination of interventions drawn from the myriad available. Such a com-prehensive view of the world of therapy appears to enhance the amalgamation of the finest of the science and art of psychother-apy (Kaslow & Schwartz, 1987).

Critique Statement

Eclecticism is usually decried as nonscientific and not suffi-ciently rigorous. Many view it as a hodgepodge utilized when one is not solidly grounded in theory, technique, and research methodology and findings. Purists see departures from the clas-sical tradition of their school of thought as heresy, as a kind of rebellious disloyalty to the theory's progenitors. Continuous, dy-namic change that permits refining, discarding, and expansion of theory—sometimes even incorporating seemingly oppositional ideas from a previously disparaged or rival school of thought as a new synthesis is achieved—is certainly disconcerting to true believers. It is also harder to teach a dynamic theory that is con-tinually evolving than one that is static and taught as if fully evolved and definitive.

Another disconcerting issue is that an approach that heralds uniqueness and individualized treatment planning and inter-vention leaves a great deal to the discretion of the practitioner, and he or she may do the wrong thing. The problem with this criticism is that it assumes that if one follows a particular yellow brick road, it will always lead to the land of Oz and the magical cure.

Related criticism is that eclecticism allows for too much flexibility and may contribute to further chaos for patients and therapists alike. Yet the person of the therapist and the quality of the therapeutic alliance are critical ingredients in the success or failure of the therapeutic endeavor, and to nullify therapist style is to minimize the power necessary to harness patients' energy to bring about desired transformations. Somewhere between rigid adherence to "This is how it must be done" and the chaos-producing dictum of "Do your own thing" lies the golden mean. The diaclectic approach seeks this holy grail.

Biography

Florence W. Kaslow is currently director of the Florida Couples and Family Institute, West Palm Beach, Florida, as well as a visiting professor of medical psychology in psychiatry at Duke University and a visiting professor of psychology at Florida Institute of Technology in Melbourne. She received her Ph.D. degree (1969) from Bryn Mawr College. She is the recipient of numerous awards, including the Family Psychologist of the Year Award from the Division of Family Psychology of the American Psychological Association in 1986. Kaslow was elected to the National Academies of Practice as a distinguished psychologist in 1987. She is serving as first president of the International Family Therapy Association.

Kaslow has authored or edited twelve books and over 100 articles and chapters for others' books. She is a former editor of *Journal of Marital and Family Therapy* and serves as consulting editor or an editorial board member of sixteen American and foreign journals.

References

Kaslow, F. W. (1981). A "diaclectic" approach to family therapy and practice: Selectivity and synthesis. *Journal of Marital and Family Therapy, 7*(3), 345–351.

Kaslow, F. W., & Schwartz, L. L. (1987). *Dynamics of divorce: A life cycle perspective.* New York: Brunner/Mazel.

Family Crisis Therapy

Frank S. Pittman III

Definition

Psychotherapy is an educational and experiential process of psychic healing through which one or more people engage in problem definition, problem resolution, and behavioral change in specific, emotionally charged areas. After change, there follows insight, through which people may change their relationship to one another, to their past and future, to their sense of the world, and especially to their sense of themselves. The efficacy and effectiveness of psychotherapy are enhanced by emotional urgency, specificity of focus, and family context.

Qualification Statement

While my theoretical underpinnings remain grounded in the treatment of families in crisis, I also do psychotherapy with individuals in various transitions and dilemmas. The process is philosophically the same. I prefer to begin therapy with a clear definition of a specific problem, not because I expect the process to be bound by that problem, but because I want it to remain centered on the pain or dilemma that led the patient to take the extraordinary step of engaging a therapist. Whatever else takes place develops from that structuring center.

As I conceive of family crisis therapy, it has seven overlapping steps. The first of these is an emergency response. I try to begin the therapy by responding to the patient's sense of emergency by offering only to help and not getting entrapped by the patient's desperation into taking some action (hospitalizing someone, following some preconceived therapeutic format, keeping something secret) that could interfere later with change. As the second step, I then arrange whatever family involvement seems appropriate. I don't insist that all the family be present, merely that they be invited and thus involved. I may begin therapy with one person, but without conspiring to keep things confidential from the family.

Third, I try to define the problem, seeking to answer the question "Why now?" to elicit the current stress that is throwing the system into crisis. I cannot begin to prescribe change until I know what has thrown this system outside its comfortable repertoire. Once we have defined the crisis, I can go on to a fourth step, biological prescription for relief of symptoms and pain. Biological prescriptions may involve psychotropic medication, stress reduction suggestions, or merely the therapist's sense of comfort with the situation. The next crucial step is the specific prescription, which entails pointing out to the patients what sensible steps other people might take to solve their particular problem. For instance, if the problem involved alcohol, I might suggest that the patient drop drinking. If the symptom was anxiety, I might recommend entering the phobic situation. If a child was out of control, I might tell the parents to control the child. Symbolic or practical tasks would be assigned.

The sixth step would be to negotiate resistance to change, and while the first five steps might take a few minutes, this one might take weeks or years. The task here is to understand why people don't do sensible problem-solving things, what they fear, where they learned to do what they do, and what, above all, they are determined not to change. The snag points that make the family inflexible are uncovered and smoothed down. While the territory covered in these negotiations may extend as far as any psychotherapy extends, the process remains centered on the pain of the original stress.

Finally, as the seventh step, I prefer a soft termination, since life is inherently stressful and presents many turning points at which new crises may reveal further snag points of inflexibility that will make smooth transitions difficult. People may have to practice a few repetitions of the crisis and its resolution before incorporating the new behavior and the new way of looking at things. It may take coaching and training.

There are specific solutions to specific problems, ranging from biological conditions with psychological and behavioral manifestations (for example, manic-depression or schizophrenia) to the purely structural situations like violence or infidelity. However, the process is much the same. The psychotherapy centers on adaptation to reality, emotional learning, and the experience of change. This is easier and seems to stick better if it is reinforced by the family format. The family is not necessarily the unit of pathology, but it is the unit of change.

Critique Statement

Family crisis therapy is most dramatically and demonstrably effective as an alternative to psychiatric hospitalization. It can render essentially any psychiatric hospitalization unnecessary, but it can also be adapted to situations in which one or more family members are hospitalized. Most of the time families in crisis can fit neatly into the therapist's schedule, but at times such cases are a strain and a bother, and hospitalizing one or all might reduce the stress on the therapist — especially if the therapist is already treating people in the hospital. It may be difficult to justify keeping a full-blown manic or a roaring drunk at home, but the bother is of short duration, and it does seem to be effective in teaching the family how to drive one another sane.

Follow-up results for family crisis therapy are encouraging. Research conducted in Denver and subsequent experience in Atlanta's public mental health services demonstrated no increase in suicides, homicides, or family disruption and an actual decrease in subsequent psychiatric hospitalization. The approach sits well with private practice. It is applicable to family disasters, but also to families that cannot seem to make orderly transitions through the stages of the life cycle. It works well with families that are structurally inflexible and go through regular crises of exacerbation. It combines well with psychopharmacology and psychoeducation for psychiatric disorders of brain chemistry.

Psychotherapy that begins with family crisis therapy can go on to any combination of individual, couples, family, or group approaches, as the situation warrants. The family involvement offers flexibility in subsequent format as the crisis cools and the focus gradually shifts to the family, or to individual inflexibilities, or just to the mysteries of living.

Psychotherapy might be understood as the transfer of sanity from the therapist to the patients. Sanity is transferred by way of the therapist's accurate comfort with the emotions of the situation and accurate discomfort with proposed actions. The therapist must understand and tolerate the range of human dilemmas and their accompanying emotions but must also have clear reality testing to help patients choose actions that lead to mastery, comfort, self-confidence, and whatever constitutes mental health. Regardless of whether the therapist attempts neutrality or is willing to be openly directive, the therapist nonetheless influences the course of events. The therapist's own value system has enormous direct and indirect influence. Neutrality is impossible to achieve and would not be desirable even if it were possible. The therapist is called upon to offer an alternative view of reality and its possibilities, and that alternative view is likely to be more objective and less desperate than the patient's sense of possibilities. The therapist is supposed to be an expert, not just on mental illness, but also on mental health and on healthy problem solving.

Family therapy has been seen as blaming the family for causing the problems, even for causing schizophrenia. Family therapy sessions have been thought of as orgies of emotional expressiveness. Blaming the family for the pathology and bringing about family confrontation need not be a part of family therapy. The family can learn how to deal with things in a way that decreases rather than enhances pathology. The family can be cotherapists as well as copatients.

Family crisis therapy is directive, often firmly so, and the therapist is a kind of coach. Directive therapists can be destructive if they are not wise and sensitive. But unwise, insensitive, nondirective therapists can be just as destructive and even more confounding. Family crisis therapy is structuring, not confounding.

Biography

Frank S. Pittman III is a psychiatrist and family therapist in private practice in Atlanta, Georgia. He is on the visiting faculty of Emory and Georgia State Universities and teaches extensively nationally and abroad. He received his M.D. degree (1960) from Emory University and has been at the center of family therapy since the mid 1960s. Pittman has served as advisory editor to *Family Process* and the *Journal of Marriage and Family Therapy* and on the board of directors of the American Family Therapy Association. In 1981, he received the association's first annual Award for Distinguished Achievement in Family Therapy Research. He was cited for work done in Denver from 1964 to 1968 that demonstrated family therapy as an effective alternative to psychiatric hospitalization.

Pittman has written over 100 articles, reviews, and essays—many on the subject of family crisis therapy, most notably "Wet Cocker Spaniel Therapy: An Essay on Technique in Family Therapy." Though he had contributed sections and chapters to various books (for example, *The Treatment of Families in Crisis,* by Langsley et al., in 1968; *Techniques of Family Therapy,* by Haley and Hoffman, in 1967) his first solo effort appeared in 1987. This was *Turning Points: Treating Families in Transition and Crisis,* an effort to delineate the syndromes of family crisis. In 1989, he studied the variations on a specific crisis in *Private Lies: Infidelity and the Betrayal of Intimacy.*

Recommended Reading

Langsley, D. G., Kaplan, D. M., Pittman, F. S., Machotka, P., Flomenhaft, K., & DeYoung, C. D. (1968). *The treatment of families in crisis.* New York: Grune & Stratton.

Pittman, F. S. (1984). Wet cocker spaniel therapy: An essay on technique in family therapy. *Family Process, 23*(1), 1–9.

Pittman, F. S. (1987). *Turning points: Treating families in transition and crisis.* New York: Norton.

9
══
Group Psychotherapy

<hr>
<hr>

The theory and history of group intervention are intermeshed for the simple reason that, historically, group therapy does not evolve from a theory of personality; rather, explanations of group process derive from observations of actual practice. In 1907, Joseph Pratt used a group setting to confront the problems of tuberculosis patients (Anthony, 1971). That technique was first employed with psychotic patients in 1921 by E. W. Lazell, and later (in 1931) by L. Cody Marsh. From those sporadic beginnings, W. R. Bion, S. H. Foulkes, Paul Schilder, S. R. Slavson, J. L. Moreno, and George Bach all made significant contributions to the early development of group psychotherapy. Since the early 1950s, there has been a proliferation of groups of several types, including self-help groups (Alcoholics Anonymous, Synanon), growth-oriented groups (encounter groups, sensitivity training), and technique-oriented groups (psychodramatic groups, cognitive groups, Transactional Analysis).

The general premise that unifies these approaches is the notion that groups are potentially less threatening than individual therapy. More importantly, it is felt that the social context provides for a type of social (peer) feedback and validation that is unavailable in the individual therapy context. All groups are assumed to progress through processes revolving around conflict, developmental stages, alliances, new members, cohesion, and group dynamics. The group therapy format is compatible with most theoretical formulations, thus allowing for variants such as psychodynamic group therapy, client-centered group therapy, and even groups of families. The lens, then, is dictated by either a particular theoretical base or the specified content and format (as in a self-esteem enhancement group) in tandem with group process variables. The primary unit-of-analysis is relationship. Humans are social animals and are strongly influenced by social forces. Interaction in the family is only one type of relationship. By interacting with people within less natural groups, convertible interactional patterns emerge.

The present chapter examines the group process in the overview section and some specific approaches in the modalities section. Saul Scheidlinger articulately addresses the convergence of group process and theoretically based technique, as well as elaborating on types of groups. Psychotherapy in general, and in the context of the therapy group, is discussed by John Gladfelter.

The philosophical foundation of psychodrama is elucidated by Zerka Moreno in the first part of the modalities section. The psychodramatic method is the functional base of clinical role playing, which David Kipper describes as a valid technique that stands independent of any specific theoretical affiliation. David Roth details the advantages of the group as a context for cognitive intervention.

The small number of contributions to this section probably reflects the fact that group therapy has been integrated into the general practice of therapy. Many practitioners use group as an adjunct and do not identify themselves primarily as group therapists.

Reference

Anthony, E. J. (1971). The history of group psychotherapy. In H. I. Kaplan & B. J. Sadock (Eds.), *Comprehensive group psychotherapy* (pp. 4–31). Baltimore: Williams & Wilkins.

Section 1
Overview

Psychodynamic Group Psychotherapy

Saul Scheidlinger

Definition

Group therapy is a specific method of clinical practice within the broader field of the psychotherapies. It entails a psychosocial process wherein a specially trained mental health practitioner (usually psychiatrist, psychologist, social worker, or nurse-clinician) utilizes the emotional interaction in small, carefully planned groups to effect amelioration of personality dysfunctions in individuals specifically selected for this purpose. Each group member has undergone a prior diagnostic assessment of his or her personality problems and strengths and has accepted the group approach alone or in combination with other modalities as a means to modify a pathological mode of functioning.

Qualification Statement

Before placing patients in a group, it is desirable to see them individually for at least a few times to ascertain whether or not they are likely to benefit from group treatment alone or in combination with other interventions. In addition, there is the need to form a balanced group with respect to such criteria as sex; age; ethnic, socioeconomic, and educational background; and especially the specific nature of the pathology.

Combined individual and group sessions, each held weekly, are especially useful in cases of deep-seated pathology where character reconstruction is sought. The one-to-one sessions then serve to complement the input from the group setting, allow-

331

ing for the repetitive and slower process of mastering the group-derived ideations and insights to occur ("working through").

All theorizing in group therapy must include some kind of integration of two disparate yet related conceptual systems, each complex in its own right: (1) the *group process system,* which involves asking the question "What makes groups tick?" (applicable to all groups); and (2) the *group psychotherapy system,* a clinical intervention modality with assumed therapeutic elements and specific techniques aimed at inducing behavioral change in each group member. In every group there is a continuous interplay between individual personality and group process manifestations on both conscious and unconscious levels. I distinguish between a *dynamic-contemporaneous* and a *genetic-regressive* group level.

The former comprises the more readily observed momentary expressions of conscious needs and ego-adaptive patterns, group roles, network of attractions and repulsions, and group structure. The behavior here is primarily reactive to realistic group-situational factors, bringing into play the more external aspects of personality. The genetic-regressive level pertains to unconscious and preconscious motivations, defensive patterns, and conflicts—to such typical clinical phenomena as transference, countertransference, resistance, identification, or projection. At each of these levels, group and individual tensions of various depths and intensities are at work.

Each group member can thus perceive every other member and the therapist in widely varying ways—from the way they are in reality, to the most fantasied distortions arising from inner motivations, disturbances in ego functions, and group situational pressures. A fellow patient can at one time represent a peer, a realistic object of sympathy, empathy, or dislike. This same patient, in a deeper sense, could be viewed as a loved or hated transference object (sibling or parent) from any previous moment in the life history. Similarly, the group as a whole could be perceived on many levels—from peer group, through the family group, to the deepest symbolic ideations (for example, mother group).

The verbal and nonverbal communications in nondirective therapy groups are akin to free association and are subject to verbal and nonverbal interventions by the therapist and by the other group members, the latter in their role as peer therapists. The major therapeutic elements in group therapy reside in the opportunity to relive and rework earlier family and life experiences in a benign setting, to test reality, and to receive support from peers and from the group entity as a holding environment. In addition to these largely experiential elements, there are also the interventions aimed at "meaning attribution," ranging from clarifications through confrontations to interpretations of the unconscious motivational elements that underlie behavior.

My definition and description of group psychotherapy is designed to be juxtaposed to the following three additional categories of people-helping groups in mental health settings and in the community, each of which is broadly related yet specifically different. The first category is *therapeutic groups,* which comprises all group approaches (other than group therapy) utilized by human services personnel (not necessarily trained professionals) in inpatient or outpatient facilities. These might range from therapeutic community meetings in mental hospitals to waiting-list groups in outpatient clinics. The second category, *human development and training groups,* belongs more to the realm of affective and cognitive education. This category includes on one end of the continuum the many consciousness-raising and sensitivity groups open to the general public. On the other end of the continuum lie the varied training and organizational development enterprises that usually operate under three different auspices: (1) the laboratory method, with its T-group theory and practice, initiated in the 1940s in Bethel, Maine; (2) self-analytic groups employed in the human relations departments of universities; and (3) the A. K. Rice group relations conferences for professionals based largely on the group processing theories of W. R. Bion. The third category includes *self-help and mutual-help groups,* which are voluntary face-to-face group structures for the aid of people with common maladies and for the achievement of personal and social change. Some of the best-known examples here are Alcoholics Anonymous, Synanon, and Recovery.

This outline of people-helping groups is not meant to imply that they are inferior to group therapy, only that they are different. Only the need of a given client can suggest the optimum modality appropriate for the situation at hand. I have assumed a pluralistic position in relation to the controversy regarding the relative importance ascribed in group therapy to individual intrapsychic contexts, interpersonal contexts, and group-as-a-whole contexts. I also question the need for ascribing a theoretical primacy to any of these elements (which I view as a gestalt), except where a group therapist, guided by his or her view of what would be most curative, is moved to momentarily put stress on one or more of these elements in a planned intervention on behalf of an individual or of the group as an entity.

In this connection, the following (not necessarily all-inclusive) list of group therapist functions includes some that are primarily in the service of group maintenance as well as others that are specifically therapeutic in nature:

- Arranging the group's composition, time, meeting place, and remuneration procedures.
- Structuring the conduct of the sessions with reference to confidentiality, agenda, physical contact, use of free-associative productions, social interaction on the outside, and so on.
- Empathic acceptance and caring for each patient, coupled with a belief in the latter's potentiality for change.
- Encouraging the open expression of feelings and concerns.
- Fostering a climate of tolerance and acceptance of variance in feelings and behavior, coupled with a focus on self and on interpersonal scrutiny and awareness in which all group members are encouraged to participate.
- Controlling within acceptable limits the drive expression, tension, and anxiety level in individual patients.
- Controlling group manifestations in the interest of both individual patients and the maintenance of optimum group morale.
- Utilizing verbal interventions ranging from simple obser-

vations to psychoanalytic interpretations aimed at reality testing and at eliciting of meaning and of genetic connections.

Biography

Saul Scheidlinger, Ph.D., is professor of psychiatry (psychology) at the Albert Einstein College of Medicine and visiting lecturer in the Division of Child Psychiatry at Columbia University College of Physicians and Surgeons in New York City. He received his Ph.D. degree (1951) from New York University in clinical psychology. Scheidlinger is a past president of the American Group Psychotherapy Association and former editor of the *International Journal of Group Psychotherapy*. He has authored three books and more than seventy chapters and articles on group processes and community mental health. While adhering to a psychodynamic philosophy, he has pioneered the adaptation of classical group techniques to the realities of patients, especially those with socially deprived backgrounds.

Recommended Reading

Scheidlinger, S. (1980). *Psychoanalytic group dynamics: Basic readings.* New York: International Universities Press.

Scheidlinger, S. (1982). *Focus on group psychotherapy: Clinical essays.* New York: International Universities Press.

Scheidlinger, S. (1987). On interpretation in group psychotherapy: The need for refinement. *International Journal of Group Psychotherapy, 37,* 339–352.

Integrated Psychotherapy

John H. Gladfelter

Definition

Psychotherapy is a psychological craft practiced by a number of professional people for the amelioration of psychological (emotional and cognitive) distress and aiming for a cure of the distress of the soul. When practiced most effectively, it occurs with a group of distressed people present and becomes artful in design and appearance. Psychotherapy moves people toward autonomy and peace through a contractual arrangement between each person and the therapist. What differentiates this therapy from others is the partnership agreement for cure of the distressed person, the use of a variety of modalities (such as hypnosis, gestalt and behavioral techniques, Transactional Analysis, and redecision therapy) and the employment of a group setting as a context for support and protection as the individual changes.

Qualification Statement

Psychotherapy is a complex interpersonal craft made up of a myriad of skills in human relations. These skills are related to the ability to create an atmosphere, a feeling of trust, a sense of hopefulness, and a belief that something may happen that is beyond normal human interchange. Psychotherapy has little theoretical base in any of the existing psychological theories — analytic theory can perhaps explain a limited part of the dynamic process, but even it has little to say about why people change. I think that psychology is to therapy as botany is to woodworking — psychology explains nicely the structure, the function, and the processes of the human personality but says little of the craft of changing people. Psychotherapy, on the other hand, like woodworking, involves the intricate use of tools, skill and understanding in the use of the tools, and knowledge of the working characteristics of wood, nails, brackets, glue, and the like. A psychotherapist can bring out what is in the person or enable the emergence of what is there but cannot create something that is not present.

The goals of psychotherapy are built around the patient contracting with the therapist for changes that are possible and around validating and celebrating the human condition. There are complementary temporal goals that are therapeutic (but not psychotherapy) and as such make possible better relationships, an easier life both physically and emotionally, and satisfaction in everyday life. The goal of integrated psychotherapy is to enable the patient to find relief of suffering, meaning in existence, and a validation of the soul through change. When I refer to the soul I am going back to Freud's concept of the human spirit that has its base in the human body but is always more than, and always emerging from, its biological bounds.

The practice of integrated psychotherapy involves the use of a myriad of psychotherapy skills, such as those suggested by the work of Raymond Corsini (1981), where a wide range of psychotherapeutic skills is described. The therapist must learn to do what works with the patient—what gives symptomatic relief and what provides corrective and preventive skills. This means that after an evaluative process between therapist and patient the therapy contract is elected and agreed upon by both. After that point, the therapist begins using the skills of hypnosis, behavioral therapy, body work, psychoeducation, analysis, gestalt, redecision therapy, and whatever else is needed to fulfill the treatment contract. If the patient is depressed and wants cure of the depression, the therapist uses those skills with the patient that she or he believes will alleviate that depression. The patient may feel better and elect to discontinue the process before having changed and accepted the therapeutic benefit. It is the task of the therapist both to confront the patient with the values of change and, if necessary, to accept the patient's decision to terminate before change has occurred.

The context of the psychotherapy process is a group of patients. The group serves the function of providing support, encouragement, personal reflection, caring, interest, and an example for the change process. Each patient gets to watch, participate in, and experience the change process of each of the other group members and gets to explore verbally to the degree that they choose what they want to change and understand about themselves. The group experience also allows the patient to make changes of a highly significant sort by simply watching and experiencing the change process without verbalization.

The difference between psychotherapeutic change and psychotherapeutic benefit is large but also personal, and the psychotherapist must learn to respect and follow the needs of the patient.

Critique Statement

Psychotherapy has emerged as a full craft for changing people in the twentieth century as society has evolved from a survival society to an existence society. As less and less time is required for survival, humans have found greater amounts of time for a diversity of activities and experiences and have had the luxury of self-examination and the opportunity to contemplate existence. With such freedom has come the responsibility for self and others and the anxiety that attends such interpersonal responsibility. The craft of psychotherapy has developed to deal with the wide range of human foibles and pain and the wide range of human experience. Many interpersonal processes and experiences have healing properties and are important psychotherapeutic interventions for the easing of distress. That easing of distress does not, however, necessarily bring about change. I am reserving the word *psychotherapy* to mean the bringing about of change in both the internal and social psychological processes of the individual.

Integrated psychotherapy is an approach in which a therapist, using a variety of techniques, brings about change, working with individuals in a group setting to engage them in changing. The advantage of this approach is that the therapist can offer the patient a wide variety of options in the way of improving the quality of life and also provide symptomatic and situational relief without engaging in the change process. If, however, the patient elects to change, the therapist can use many of the same technical and interpersonal skills to enter into that therapeutic contract in the group.

The limits of integrated psychotherapy include the requirements for the therapist to have engaged in her or his own change process and to have trained in a wide range of treatment modalities. Psychotherapists are limited by their own personal preferences and acceptance of their limits of training and experience. Obtaining a full range of psychotherapeutic skills is as yet not possible in any one setting. This means that therapists who choose to master their craft will have lonely, lengthy, and unending adventure.

An advantage of the integrated psychotherapy approach is that the therapist is capable of offering a wider range of services to patients than would be available from traditionally trained psychotherapists. The therapist also is able to serve a wider range of clients by the nature of the diversity of skills available and the nontraditional orientation. Psychotherapists often find themselves limited by knowing only some kinds of therapy; by being able to work with only certain kinds of problems; or by being able to work with only certain class levels of patients.

A further advantage of the integrated approach is that the psychologist is in lifelong training and can attend more fully to personal change and growth in the self as a caring, moral, and autonomous human being. The search for meaning in theories of therapy or personality can become a sad, disappointing journey if it is seen as a way to do or implement the process of change. A theory of change will evolve out of the "doing" process in time and add to our competence in delivering the best services to patients. The need for premature closure has become stifling to the development of theory about change and has allowed a multitude of extraneous considerations to enter the arena of therapy, such as the cost of therapy, who should do it, and the political ramifications of insurance and health coverage.

Biography

John H. Gladfelter is a coordinator of studies at the Fielding Institute in Santa Barbara, California, and lives and is in private practice in Dallas, Texas. He received his Ph.D. degree (1957) from the University of Houston in clinical psychology. He is a diplomate in Clinical Psychology, a fellow of the American Group Psychotherapy Association, an approved supervisor in the American Association for Marriage and Family Therapy, and a level two Transactional Analyst in the International Transactional Analysis Association. He is teacher and trainer in a variety of psychotherapeutic modalities and travels extensively as a teacher and case consultant.

Reference

Corsini, R. J. (1981). *Handbook of innovative psychotherapies.* New York: Wiley.

Section 2
Modalities

Psychodrama

Zerka T. Moreno

Definition

Actional group psychotherapy and psychodrama rely less on
verbal exchange than on participatory interaction between the
group members, with the client in an enactment of real or fantasy
scenes important both in the client's history and contemporane-
ously. Psychotherapy in this sense has as its objective the elimination or easing of those mental and behavioral manifestations
that prevent the optimal use of all the faculties in both private
and social environments.

Qualification Statement

Sociometry does not view mental health as solely an intrapersonal matter but sees it instead as a totality made up of both
intra- and interpersonal factors. The healthy state exists when
there is "sociostasis," a balanced and functioning network of relationships in private, occupational, and social environments.

Disturbances in any of these three areas may adversely affect
the others. Therapy is aimed at working through and removing major barriers creating these difficulties and may include
treatment of the entire family or work group. Clients, therefore, are evaluated on their ability to deal with and be part of
a network of relationships. As Moreno (1934/1953, p. 3) stated,
"A truly therapeutic procedure cannot have less an objective than
the whole of mankind." This utopian ideal is not possible to
achieve, but on a modest scale we attempt to involve as many
aspects of the client's world as possible. Exploration of roles in

interaction with relevant others is done by diagrams and drama- tizations; clients are encouraged to map their own sociograms and to diagnose revealed imbalances. Correction of the percep- tion of self versus others may be carried out through role rever- sal with actual others (if available), with auxiliary egos (stand- in therapeutic actors or actresses), or with oneself.

Critique Statement

Many of the difficulties that can and do arise in group psy- chotherapy are related to the problem of confidentiality. There is a tendency for group members, especially in a small city or in the same professional or social network, to leak information about one another. There is no ideal solution to this; the best that can be done is to deal openly with any breach of confidence outside the group. Another difficulty is that of secret alliances (cliques or pairs) within the group itself. These, too, have to be brought to light and handled tactfully.

Criticism has also been leveled at the so-called tyranny of the group; it is undoubtedly a factor in some groups, and it is the responsibility of the therapist to monitor and confront it.

The advantages of this group approach include the overcom- ing or reducing of isolation, the possibility of human contact, a reorganization of the perception of self and others, a renewed or altered sense of self, and opportunities for changing the man- ner of dealing with others. The therapist's task is to balance con- frontation within the group and provide supportive guidance. In general, interactional therapists believe that purely verbal methods are inadequate approaches to the complex problems every human being faces.

Biography

Zerka T. Moreno is honorary president of the American So- ciety of Group Psychotherapy and Psychodrama and honorary board member of the International Association of Group Psy- chotherapy. Educated in Holland and England, Zerka Toeman became J. L. Moreno's student in 1941. In 1942, the Psycho- drama and Sociometric Institutes were opened in New York

City, and she was employed there as research assistant. Since then, she has made numerous contributions to the literature under both her maiden name and (after marrying J. L. Moreno) her married name. Starting in 1951, she accompanied her husband on his travels to Europe, including countries behind the iron curtain, and was largely responsible for helping to organize and administer the various organizations they jointly started, one of which is the International Association of Group Psychotherapy. She continues to work and travel abroad.

Recommended Reading

Malcolm, A. (1975). *The tyranny of the group.* Totowa, NJ: Littlefield, Adams & Co.
Moreno, J. L. (1946). *Psychodrama* (Vol. 1). Beacon, NY: Beacon House.
Moreno, J. L. (1966). Psychiatry of the twentieth century: Function of the universalia, time, space, reality and cosmos. *Group Psychotherapy, 19,* 146–158.
Moreno, J. L., & Moreno, Z. T. (1959). *Psychodrama* (Vol. 2). Beacon, NY: Beacon House.
Moreno, J. L., & Moreno, Z. T. (1975). *Psychodrama* (Vol. 3). Beacon, NY: Beacon House.

Reference

Moreno, J. L. (1953). *Who shall survive?* Beacon, NY: Beacon House. (Original work published 1934)

A Clinical Role Playing: Psychodramatic Psychotherapy

David A. Kipper

Definition

Psychotherapy through clinical role playing is the application of psychological knowledge through a systematic treatment procedure that involves the enactment of personal experiences with the aid of simulation techniques in the context of simulated conditions. The employment of such techniques and the setting of these conditions are designed to facilitate the emergence of the psychological processes associated with the attainment of the changes sought by the participants.

Qualification Statement

Clinical role playing is not a new form of psychotherapy. To be precise, it is a new conceptualization of the existing psychodramatic method and other role-playing and behavior rehearsal procedures. It is fitting, therefore, to characterize this undertaking as an attempt to provide the method of role playing with a rationale of its own and grant it an independent status exclusive of affiliation with any specific psychotherapeutic theories. The formulation of such an approach generates a wider acceptance of a psychological treatment based on role-playing portrayals and reduces its potential conflict with most of the currently held therapeutic modalities.

Awareness of the anomaly caused by the absence of such a conceptualization grew out of the realization that the advent of psychodrama, which was then thought to promote the use of role playing in psychotherapy, actually had the reverse effect. Originally invented by J. L. Moreno, the psychodramatic method always has been regarded as inseparable from his spontaneity-creativity theory (Moreno, 1964). The characterization of the method in such a fashion posed a conceptual conflict to many clinicians who subscribed to therapeutic theories other than that espoused by Moreno.

For those perturbed by the dilemma as well as for those who solved it by disregarding the theory and preserving the use of role playing, a new rationale justifying the application of these interventions had to be found. Indeed, recognizing this need, a set of principles was formulated with the explicit purpose of creating an independent conceptual frame of reference in the form of a *behavior simulation paradigm* for the use of what has become known as *clinical role playing* (Kipper, 1986).

The most important element of the rationale that gave rise to the paradigm was the definition of role playing as a specific form of *simulation*. Holding such a view led to two conclusions: that concrete portrayals of the issues and behaviors associated with the treated problem should be regarded as a valuable component of the therapeutic process, and that the very use of simulation ought to be therapeutically meritorious (Kipper, 1987).

Concretization ("enactment of personal experiences") enhances the meaningfulness of the presented issues because it offers optimal opportunities to express both the spontaneous, involuntary kind of communication and the symbolic, intentional kind. Thus, for therapists, concretization increases the likelihood that their responses will not be far removed from the client's own responses and experiences. For clients, it offers a *direct* way for addressing their difficulties. For the interactive process, it facilitates clarification of misunderstandings and promotes perceptual accuracies.

Another distinction ascribed to the therapeutic aspect of clinical role playing is its employment of "simulation techniques in the context of simulated conditions." The claim for such an inherent therapeutic propensity rests on the hypothesis that different categories of simulation conditions create different experiential (that is, phenomenological) states. These in turn facilitate the emergence of different psychological processes, which should produce different outcomes. Clinical observations and initial empirical data support the validity of this premise (Kipper, 1986).

The definition given above addresses clinical role playing as a "systematic" treatment procedure. This implies that the conduct of the therapeutic process is intentional and that the progression of the portrayed episodes (that is, the shift from one scene to another) follows certain rules. The rationale for this concerns providing adequate involvement in the enactments.

Finally, the stipulation that the method be based on "psychological knowledge" is not unique to clinical role playing. I believe that it is a requirement common to all psychotherapeutic endeavors.

Critique Statement

There are several interesting aspects of psychotherapy through clinical role playing that deserve mention. First, as already mentioned, its basic paradigm rests on the concept of simulation; a notion that can be incorporated into many therapeutic approaches. Second, the paradigm uses concepts and hypothesized relationships that are amenable to experimental research. Third, the method allows clients to experiment with different modes of behavior, decision making, and their realistic or fantasized aspirations without holding back for fear of their inevitable consequences in real life. In this regard, it represents a unique rehearsal-for-life laboratory. Clinical role playing offers a meaningful medium for completing unresolved issues and emotional conflicts. When used in a group therapy setting (the most prevalent application of clinical role playing), the involvement of other group members as auxiliaries for the various simulation techniques offers insights into the group dynamic and its sociometric structures.

An important limitation of clinical role playing is that it is, primarily, a *method* of application rather than a *theory* of human development or psychopathology. Therefore, in planning the course of the therapeutic intervention — its content and focus, the psychological processes to be addressed, and the goals to be targeted — one must rely on theories of personality and psychotherapy of one's own choice. Moreover, the method cannot serve as an exclusive form of psychotherapy. It may be used as the *main* psychotherapeutic thrust, occasionally supplemented by other therapeutic modalities rendered in the form of verbal treatments or other procedures. Alternatively, it may be introduced as an adjunct to other forms of treatment.

Finally, research has verified a number of predictions concerning the effectiveness of various components of the simulation procedure; for example, in reducing resistance and increasing disinhibition. But many other components still await empirical validations. Such information, once available, will most certainly uncover additional advantages as well as shortcomings associated with clinical role playing.

Biography

David A. Kipper is associate professor of psychology at Bar-Ilan University, Ramat-Gan, Israel. He received his Ph.D. degree (1969) from the University of Durham, England, in psychology. A clinical psychologist, he studied psychodrama under the late J. L. Moreno and was a postdoctoral fellow at the State University of New York at Stony Brook. He has been affiliated with the University of Chicago as the director of the Behavior Simulation Program and a visiting associate professor. He is a board-certified psychodrama trainer/practitioner and the president-elect of the American Society of Group Psychotherapy and Psychodrama. Kipper has published widely, including a recent book on clinical role playing. He also served as a coexecutive editor of the *Journal of Group Psychotherapy, Psychodrama and Sociometry*.

References

Kipper, D. A. (1986). *Psychotherapy through clinical role playing*. New York: Brunner/Mazel.

Kipper, D. A. (1987). On the definition of psychodrama: Another view. *Journal of Group Psychotherapy, Psychodrama and Sociometry, 40*, 164–168.

Moreno, J. L. (1964). *Psychodrama* (Vol. 1). New York: Beacon House.

Cognitive-Interpersonal Group Therapy

David M. Roth

Definition

The fundamental clinical goals of cognitive-interpersonal group treatment are the remediation of emotional and psychosocial distress. Conceptually, the practitioner believes these goals can be realized through the process of uncovering and correcting dysfunctional thinking and maladaptive relationship patterns. These therapeutic ends are attained through the theoretically guided use of cognitive-behavioral and relationship-enhancement skills. The therapy group, with its varied social stimuli, provides an optimal environment in which one can discover, test, reshape, and replace faulty beliefs and interactional styles.

Qualification Statement

A central premise of the cognitive-interpersonal orientation is that symptomatic distress is a manifestation of dysfunctional self-focused and socially focused beliefs. For example, the client who views himself as inadequate and others as disinterested is likely to experience an increased risk of becoming depressed. Years of scientific sleuthing have resulted in the identification of a compendium of core cognitive schemata underlying virtually every Axis I and Axis II entity in the *DSM-III-R*.

Irrational and self-defeating beliefs are likely to engender congruent maladaptive interpersonal behavior patterns. Hence, a second fundamental assumption of the cognitive-interpersonal model holds that both transient and longstanding disruptions of interpersonal attachment and affiliation further undermine one's emotional integrity. The individual who sees herself as inadequate and others as disinterested is unlikely to seek out reassurance, nurturance, and soothing from peers.

A third premise of this orientation is that dysfunctional interpersonal relationship patterns and cognitive schemata are apt to be self-perpetuating. Repeated maladaptive interpersonal interchanges not only fail to engender corrective feedback but may, in fact, elicit social reactions that reinforce core beliefs. The individual who feels inadequate is likely to engender parental directives from friends; the suspicious husband may promote secretiveness on the part of his wife; and clients who feel unlovable could find that they are being neglected by their therapist.

The therapy group is a wonderfully naturalistic environment in which individuals can address the interface between dysfunctional beliefs, maladaptive interpersonal relationships, and symptomatic distress. Within this context the depth, breadth, and complexity of intrapsychic processes and interpersonal relatedness can unfold. Over consecutive months of treatment, interactions with one's peers occur that reveal clinically significant cognitive and interactional material that never would have been provoked in individual therapy. Moreover, as longstanding self-defeating patterns are systematically evoked and challenged, the group offers a setting in which the interpersonal behaviors that have activated and maintained these patterns can be confronted and understood.

Expertise in the application of cognitive-behavioral techniques is a necessary, but not sufficient, condition for competent provision of cognitive-interpersonal therapy. A working knowledge of group process is also required. All too often, cognitive group therapy takes on the appearance of dyadic treatment conducted in the midst of a live and frequently bored audience.

The skillful interweaving of cognitive-behavioral practices and group-oriented interventions creates a powerful therapeutic force. Appropriately timed cognitive interventions can be applied at both the group and individual level. In the most basic cognitive-behavioral spirit, an individual client can be helped by group members and the therapist to develop a proficiency at identifying, testing, challenging, and modifying cognitive distortions and maladaptive interactional patterns. In addition to promoting skill acquisition and practice, the cognitive-interpersonal therapist can marshal group forces such as cohesion, altruism, and universality to further alleviate symptomatic distress. More-

over, this interpersonal milieu offers a growth-oriented and relatively safe place for experimenting with new and risky coping
skills, beliefs, and relationships. Analogously, the group can
identify, test, challenge, and modify its own dysfunctional norms
and rituals. For example, a group might generate hypotheses
about the scapegoating of its loudly self-proclaimed "inadequate"
member. Or it could draw upon standard assertion exercises
to facilitate the direct expression of anger toward more powerful members. Ultimately, each skillfully executed intervention
affects both the group and individual members.

Critique Statement

Interpersonal comparison is a standard feature of the therapy group. The practice allows members to vividly clarify the
relative advantages and disadvantages of their unique personal
attributes. The wisdom of the group reminds us that a given
attribute may be advantageous in one situation but not another.
Conceptual comparisons offer the researcher a tool for assessing the combined strengths and weaknesses of his or her particular orientation.

Cognitive-behavioral treatment has been traditionally conducted within the context of individual therapy. In its infancy,
the cognitive-behavioral counselor was a kind of teacher, im-
parting meaningful lessons in a didactic manner. Cognitive-
behavioral therapy has evolved into cognitive-interpersonal therapy with the critical realization that treatment occurs within the
context of a dyadic relationship. The teacher has matured and
now helps the student to utilize the therapeutic encounter as
another significant relationship in which central dysfunctional
beliefs and interactional patterns can be tested and corrected.

Nonetheless, the group, as a social microcosm, provides diagnostic and therapeutic opportunities that are not readily derived
from dyadic treatment. The diversity and number of social
stimuli activate a potpourri of beliefs and interactional patterns.
Therapists in the role of diagnosticians can observe significant
clinical events rather than learn about them through their clients'
frequently distorted reports. This bridge between therapy and

extratherapy environments promotes the generalizability of clinically engendered change. The group is a convenient and relatively safe place where one can clarify and correct social misperceptions. In fact, for many clients the group is the *only* intimate and secure social environment in which interpersonally oriented homework assignments can be conducted. The beliefs that one is alone in the world and that no one else can understand one's problems potentiate symptomatic distress. The inherent capacity of the group to promote cohesion and underscore the universality of existential issues is of considerable therapeutic value.

This same wealth of social stimulation may be too much to handle for certain clients with severe clinical and/or characterological disorders. Individuals struggling with such problems as paranoid, schizoid, and schizotypal personality disorders, incapacitating social phobias, and anhedonic depressions may be ill prepared to utilize the group. Some people have been too bruised, battered, or neglected over their lifetime to view the group as a safe holding environment. Many of these individuals never reach group therapy, while a sizeable subsample only get into a group after they have developed a deep, secure attachment with an individual therapist.

One final word of caution about the overzealous use of cognitive-interpersonal therapy: Symptomatic distress, disordered thinking, and impaired relationships are often the result of biochemical abnormalities. In cases such as the schizophrenic's decompensation or the manic episode, cognitive-interpersonal group treatment is a weak stepsister to pharmacotherapy. However, it should be considered once a client can maintain contact with reality.

Biography

David M. Roth is director of the Inpatient and Outpatient Eating Disorders Programs and Outpatient Affective Disorder Program at the Sheppard and Enoch Pratt Hospital in Baltimore, Maryland. He is also assistant clinical professor of medical psychology in the Department of Psychiatry at Johns Hopkins

Medical School. Roth received his Ph.D. degree (1977) from the University of Pittsburgh in clinical psychology. He has spoken widely on the topics of eating disorders, affective disorders, and cognitive therapy and has written numerous articles and chapters on these same topics. Roth has served as chair of the Maryland Governor's Task Force on Eating Disorders.

Recommended Reading

Beck, A. T., Rush, A. J., Shaw, B. F., & Emery, G. (1979). *Cognitive therapy of depression.* New York: Guilford.

Bowlby, J. (1982). *Attachment and loss: Vol. I. Attachment.* New York: Basic Books.

Burns, D. (1980). *Feeling good: The new mood therapy.* New York: William Morrow.

Roth, D., & Ross, D. (1987). *Short-term cognitive-behavioral group therapy for eating disorders.* Unpublished manuscript.

Roth, D., & Ross, D. (1988). Long-term cognitive-interpersonal group therapy for eating disorders. *International Journal of Group Psychotherapy, 38*(4), 491–510.

10

Hypnotherapy and Ericksonian Psychotherapy

Hypnotherapy is founded in technique and relies on a circum-scribed set of theoretical assumptions; a practitioner may adhere to any number of explicit personality theories, or even to none in particular, and yet utilize hypnotic technique effectively. The unifying theoretical assumption is that there is an unconscious mind that may be accessed and mobilized to produce psycho-logical relief, either by creating direct behavioral, affective, and/or symptomatic change, or by accessing highly charged, repressed information critical to problem resolution. Erickso-nian approaches expand on this foundation by asserting that the unconscious mind is perhaps the penultimate expert on the distressed individual and, whenever possible, should be utilized in directing the hypnotic experience. Although all aspects of client (and therapist) communication are important in hypnotic approaches, primary units-of-analysis are symbols and ambi-guity, especially in the Ericksonian approach, in which indirect techniques are used to stimulate and activate previously dor-mant strengths from within the patient.

Franz Anton Mesmer is often credited as the individual who first introduced medical hypnosis (Frankel, 1976). That distinc-tion brought Mesmer first fame and then abject disgrace when a special commission of the French Academy failed to validate his work. At first, hypnosis was seen as a force projected onto the passive subject by a powerful operator. However, this view was countered by early investigators. Both the English physician James Braid, who coined the term *hypnosis,* and the Portuguese priest Abbé Faria, recognized that the skill essential to developing a hypnotic state belongs more to the subject than to the hypnotist.

Just as acceptance of hypnosis cycled first positively and then negatively in Mesmer's time, so did its favor with Freud, who disliked the sexual connotation of the patient "giving" herself emotionally to the hypnotist and felt it unwise to indiscriminately remove symptoms. Freud's attitude may well account for the fact that through most of the early part of the twentieth century few therapists utilized clinical hypnosis (Crasilneck & Hall, 1975). Today's hypnotherapists owe a debt of gratitude to individuals like Clark Hull, Milton H. Erickson, Lewis Wolberg, Andre Weitzenhoffer, and Ernest Hilgard, who investigated, utilized, and legitimized hypnosis at a time when it was considered questionable.

The current chapter is divided into two sections: Ericksonian approaches and hypnotic approaches. The distinction between the two is simply whether the influence of Milton H. Erickson is present in or absent from the approach. It will be noted that the lion's share of this chapter is dedicated to Ericksonian approaches: The editors hope that this reflects the broad influence of Erickson rather than a sampling or editorial bias.

In the first selection of the Ericksonian section, Ernest Rossi presents a cogent conceptualization of the mind-body connection and describes a method of eliciting change. Stephen Lankton then discusses his strategic model and the processes common to both hypnosis and family therapy. Jeffrey Zeig addresses the nature of change in Ericksonian psychotherapy. Michael Yapko's directive approach utilizes the client's values, beliefs, and personal frame of reference in the context of a mutually responsive relationship. The paradoxical nature of psychotherapy is underscored in John Beahrs's strategic approach. Daniel Araoz's "OLD C" approach emphasizes a unique and total inner experience. Norma Barretta, Phillip Barretta, and Joseph

Bongiovanni collaborate on a discussion of hypnosis and neurolinguistic programming. Patterning is an essential part of David Gordon's approach, which is also based in neurolinguistic programming.

In the hypnotic approaches section, Helen and John Watkins collaborate on a discussion of an approach that utilizes psychoanalytic, cognitive, behavioral, and humanistic theory within the modality of hypnosis. D. Corydon Hammond describes an eclectic hypnotic model, and age-regressed clients confront traumatic events in Marian Kaplun Shapiro's "hypno-play therapy."

References

Crasilneck, H. B., & Hall, J. A. (1975). *Clinical hypnosis: Principles and applications.* New York: Grune & Stratton.

Frankel, F. H. (1976). *Hypnosis.* New York: Plenum.

Section 1
Ericksonian Approaches

Psychobiological Psychotherapy

Ernest L. Rossi

Definition

From a psychobiological perspective, psychotherapy is a means of accessing and therapeutically reframing the state-dependent mind-body processes that encode problems. Emotions, stress, and trauma associated with most life experiences release informational substances (messenger molecules) from many cells throughout the body that encode memory, learning, behavior, psychological complexes, and psychosomatic problems in a state-dependent manner; these same informational substances also regulate the body's biology at the cellular and genetic levels to modulate states of health and illness. We can utilize new process-oriented forms of psychotherapy to access these informational substances that serve as the communication link between mind and body to facilitate optimal levels of mind-body integration.

Qualification Statement

If we take the implications of recent psychobiological research to their logical conclusion, we may have a pragmatic resolution of the centuries-old Cartesian dualism of mind and body. The common denominator between mind and body is *information.* Life is a cybernetic process of information transduction. From our psychotherapeutic perspective, *mind can be defined as a process of self-reflective information transduction. Transduction* refers to the transformation or flow of information between the different modalities of experience such as words, metaphors, imagery, emotions, sensations, behavior, symptoms, and so on (Rossi, 1986c).

356

Most researchers believe that psychological experience and behavior are somehow encoded within the neural networks of the brain. What is really new is the idea that under the impact of stress (any form of emotional or novel experience), many information substances are released throughout the body. Many of these substances can reach the neural networks of the brain to encode our life experiences in a state-dependent manner; that is, what we remember, learn, and experience is dependent on the different psychological states encoded in the brain by informational substances. *The same informational substances that encode psychological experience simultaneously regulate the biology of cellular metabolism right down to the molecular-genetic level. These informational substances are the new bridge between mind and body.* Any life experience that upsets the stress-prone homeostatic processes that regulate health and illness therefore can be encoded throughout the mind-body on many levels by these information substances; sensation and perception, mood and behavior, psychological complexes and psychosomatic problems are linked by this common network of information transducting on the molecular level. From this psychobiological perspective, the goal of all forms of psychotherapy, from hypnosis and psychoanalysis to the cognitive, behavioral, and body therapies, may be recognized as different approaches to facilitating the many pathways of mind-body information flow (Erickson & Rossi, 1989; Rossi, 1980; Rossi & Ryan, 1986).

David Cheek and I recently published thirty specific three-step outlines that have evolved from Ericksonian hypnosis for facilitating the process of informational transduction in the resolution of mind-body problems ranging from the sexual, stress, and mood disorders of traditional psychosomatic medicine to the humanistically oriented processes of self-realization (Rossi & Cheek, 1988). Here is a very general three-step outline that most therapists can easily integrate within their own practice.

The first step is *accessing the source of the problem.* An obviously overworked physician in his mid-forties complained of migraine headaches, backaches, and a stiff neck that had generally worsened over the past few years. The first third of his initial session was spent simply listening as he poured out his conscious understanding of his problems. When, with a forlorn look he

finally paused for a breath, I simply held up my two hands (as
if holding a large rubber ball) and said: "Hold your hands up
like this, about eight inches apart. If your unconscious has some
understanding of the source and solution of these problems, you'll
find those hands coming together all by themselves. Otherwise,
you'll find them being pushed apart."

Incredulous at first, he became delighted as his hands moved
slowly together. He was obviously fascinated as he watched his
hands finally touch. I continued with: "And if your unconscious
is ready to provide you with the *necessary emotional understanding
of the sources of those problems so you can resolve them here and now,*
you'll find your eyes closing all by themselves." After a few blinks,
his eyes closed and his face relaxed as he spontaneously took
a deeper breath.

The second step is *therapeutically reframing a state-dependent problem.* I continued with: "And if your unconscious can now review
the entire history of those problems, privately within your own
mind, one of those hands will begin to slowly lower all by itself
with each significant memory that is reviewed." Slowly, one hand
lowered to his lap as a gamut of emotions moved across his face:
flushing, tears, and so forth. I added: *"Tune in with great sensitivity to all your symptoms and notice what changes take place as you continue to review all the significant memories."*

When his hand finally reached his lap, I said: "And if your
unconscious can help you make the inner and outer changes
required so you no longer need those symptoms, that other hand
will slowly move toward your lap with each change you see yourself making." As his hand moved down to his evident relief, I
added: *"Enjoy these more satisfactory emotional states that you will continue to experience as you make the right changes to transform your life."*

The third step is *facilitating continued self-healing.* When his hand
reached his lap, I asked if he was feeling comfortable, and he
nodded his head agreeably. I explained that there are periods
throughout the day when it is important to take a break and
relax like this in order to facilitate health. I concluded: "When
your unconscious and conscious minds know they can continue
with this inner healing, you'll find yourself awakening, feeling
refreshed and alert."

He "awakened" and confirmed that he was indeed symptom-free. He wondered if that was "some sort of hypnosis even though I was awake all the time?" I responded: "I don't know if it was hypnosis, or simply a process of emotional transformation whereby the information locked up in your symptoms has been transduced into insights that will enable you to make the appropriate changes in your life." I continued with a casual discussion of the "Ultradian healing response" (Rossi, 1982, 1986a, 1986b, 1986c; Rossi & Cheek, 1988) as a window of healing opportunity we all have available to us every hour and a half when we take a break to allow the autonomic, endocrine, immune, and neuropeptide systems to do their inner work. He wondered if that is really true, but he will do anything to maintain his well-being.

Critique Statement

There are three specific criticisms of the psychobiological approach:

1. We do not know enough about biology to relate it to mind and behavior.
2. Any attempt to reduce mind to biology and physics is fallacious.
3. Research on the relationship between informational substances and mind is still controversial, and there certainly is no research supporting the mind-gene connection as a plausible therapeutic approach with humans.

We do not know enough about biology. Most of the striking advances in science and therapeutics come from a synergistic merging of two or more fields of research. Most forms of psychotherapy today, however, are still locked in the phenomenological realm, just as were the founders of depth psychotherapy such as Janet, Freud, and Jung. The founders all recognized that psychological processes could not be divorced from the physiology of the body but acknowledged that the physiology of their day was not yet advanced enough to be related to the psycho-

logical. This is no longer the case. In fact, I would say that today the true innovators in psychology are coming from the ranks
of molecular biologists, who are discovering profound relationships between mind and molecule. To name just a few who must
be understood by any critic of the psychobiological approach:

- *James McGaugh,* a psychophysiologist, summarized in an
  authoritative paper (1983) more than a decade of research
  by a number of leading laboratories that established how
  hormones (information substances) released from the body
  during stress can modulate memory, learning, and behavior;
  that is, psychological states are dependent upon the presence
  or absence of these information substances that modulate
  the encoding of experience in the brain.
- *Francis O. Schmitt,* the pioneering molecular biologist who
  coined the phrase "informational substance," summarized
  a generation of research in his highly regarded paper (1984)
  on the molecular regulators of brain function. To use the
  computer metaphor, the informational substances may be
  regarded as the software that is continually changing during a creative interaction with the environment, while the
  nervous system is the relatively unchanging hardware.
- *Candace Pert,* chief of brain biochemistry at the National Institute of Mental Health, and her colleagues published a ground-
  breaking paper in 1985 on how the many neuropeptides (informational substances) can coordinate sensation, perception,
  emotion, and behavior (Pert, Ruff, Weber, & Herkenham,
  1985). These neuropeptides and their cellular receptors form
  a psychosomatic network that is regarded as the new informational network coordinating mind-body relationships.
- *Eric Kandel,* a research psychiatrist at Columbia University,
  has done pioneering work on the intracellular molecular processes of learning and their implications for clinical medicine (Kandel, 1987). Kandel has established how environmental stimuli are communicated to the cellular level by
  informational substances and are then converted to secondary messengers in the cell that can eventually turn on or
  off specific genes to modulate cellular metabolism.

Mind cannot be reduced to molecules. I have integrated the current zeitgeist of psychobiological research represented by these highly regarded pioneers into an overview of mind-body processes that I call the "mind-gene connection" (Rossi, 1986c, 1990; Rossi & Cheek, 1988). This, I believe, is the molecular basis of all forms of mind-body healing from the ancient shamanistic approaches of native societies to modern psychosomatic medicine. In retrospect, we can now understand how many of the fundamental processes of hypnotherapy and psychoanalysis such as dissociation, repression, psychological complexes, trauma, and stress can be understood within a more comprehensive mind-body framework. *This does not mean that we are reducing mind to molecule!* Quite to the contrary, for the first time we have a really scientific basis for exploring exactly how mind and mood can modulate matter, and vice versa. Psychology and biology are currently reveling in a new synergy, a new psychobiology that unites them through a true common denominator: the concepts of information and communication.

No research supports the mind-gene connection. This is a valid criticism. My psychobiological framework is a new synthesis of the *implications* of existing data; no direct tests of the mind-gene hypothesis have been conducted yet. I have recently outlined 128 research projects that are needed to evalute the relationship between mind and informational substances, down to the genetic level (Rossi & Cheek, 1988). I am already facilitating a few graduate students who are doing doctoral dissertations in this area, and I am eager to help anyone else.

The advantages of this psychobiological approach involve an obvious unification and higher-order understanding of life and therapeutics. Science in the nineteenth century fell into a Tower of Babel of specialization wherein scientists and scholars could hardly understand each other — much less the man on the street. The twentieth-century unification via the concept of *information* makes it possible for researchers in the most divergent fields to communicate comfortably with each other, as well as with clinicians and the body politic in general. We are all united in the common goal of facilitating our mutual well-being via enhanced processes of communication and self-realization.

Biography

Ernest L. Rossi is editor of *Psychological Perspectives: A Semi-Annual Review of Jungian Thought* and is currently in private practice in Malibu, California. He did graduate work in biochemistry before obtaining his Ph.D. degree in clinical psychology (Temple University, 1962). He studied psychosomatic medicine with Franz Alexander on a two-year postdoctoral U.S. Public Health Fellowship and is now a diplomate in clinical psychology. He is the author and editor of fifteen books in the areas of psychotherapy, dreams, and the psychobiology of mind-body healing. Rossi has extensive experience in Jungian analysis and has served on the certifying board of the C. G. Jung Institute of Los Angeles. He has written prolifically on the hypnotic approaches of Milton H. Erickson and is the coauthor (with Erickson) of four books. Additionally, Rossi has edited four volumes of Erickson's collected papers and coedited four volumes of Erickson's seminars, workshops, and lectures.

References

Erickson, M., & Rossi, E. (1989). *The February man: Evolving consciousness and identity in hypnotherapy.* New York: Brunner/Mazel.

Kandel, E. (Ed.). (1987). *Molecular neurobiology in neurology and psychiatry.* New York: Raven Press.

McGaugh, J. (1983). Preserving the presence of the past: Hormonal influences on memory storage. *American Psychologist, 38*(2), 161–173.

Pert, C., Ruff, M., Weber, R., & Herkenham, M. (1985). Neuropeptides and their receptors: A psychosomatic network. *Journal of Immunology, 135*(2), 820s–826s.

Rossi, E. (Ed.). (1980). *The collected papers of Milton H. Erickson on hypnosis* (4 vols.). New York: Irvington.

Rossi, E. (1982). Hypnosis and ultradian cycles: A new state(s) theory of hypnosis? *American Journal of Clinical Hypnosis, 25*(1), 21–32.

Rossi, E. (1986a). Altered states of consciousness in everyday life: The ultradian rhythms. In B. Wolman (Ed.), *Handbook of Altered States of Consciousness* (pp. 97–132). New York: Von Nostrand.

Rossi, E. (1986b). Hypnosis and ultradian rhythms. In B. Zilbergeld, M. Edelstein, & D. Araoz (Eds.), *Hypnosis questions and answers*. New York: Norton.

Rossi, E. (1986c). *The psychobiology of mind-body healing: New concepts of therapeutic hypnosis*. New York: Norton.

Rossi, E. (1990). Mind-molecular communication: Can we really talk to our genes? *Hypnos, 27,* 3–14.

Rossi, E., & Cheek, D. (1988). *Mind-body therapy: Methods of ideodynamic healing in hypnosis*. New York: Norton.

Rossi, E., & Ryan, M. (1986). *Mind-body communication in hypnosis: Vol. 3. The seminars, workshops, and lectures of Milton H. Erickson*. New York: Irvington.

Schmitt, F. (1984). Molecular regulators of brain function: A new view. *Neuroscience, 13,* 991–1001.

Ericksonian Strategic Therapy

Stephen R. Lankton

Definition

Psychotherapy is the branch of social science that makes a practical application of the principles of psychology, group dynamics, and sociology for the improvement of individual experience, social behavior, and performance. The practice often involves the reduction, or amelioration, of conflict and maladaptive patterns of cognitive, emotional, and individual and family behavior. The practice of psychotherapy or family therapy is primarily reliant upon verbal communication and may involve varying degrees of active involvement from either the therapist or the client, depending upon the specific approach being employed.

Qualification Statement

The Ericksonian strategic approach is a method of working with clients emphasizing common, even unconscious, natural abilities and talents. Therapy goals are built upon the intelligence and health of individuals. It works to frame change in ways that reduce resistance, reduce dependency upon therapy, bypass the need for insight, and allow clients to take full credit for changes.

Most problems are not viewed as internal pathologies but as the natural result of solving developmental demands in ways that do not fully work for the people involved. The Ericksonian strategic approach is distinctive in that it is associated with certain interventions upon which it relies heavily during extramural assignments and therapy sessions. These include skill building homework, paradoxical directives, ambiguous function assignments, indirect suggestions, hypnosis, reframing, metaphors, and therapeutic binds. These are not so much interventions as characteristic parts of the therapist's interactions with clients. As such they are used to motivate clients to actively participate in changing the way they live with themselves and others.

The rationale for strategic therapy, which credits Milton H. Erickson (1901–1980) as its ephemeris, is threefold. The main tenets affect the practice of therapy as well as the way in which problems and people are viewed. Problems are not seen as inside a person's head. Rather, there is a depathologizing of problems. Problems are thought to be the result of disordered interpersonal relations. Consequently, diagnosis is an activity that frames the presenting problem in terms of the developmental and interpersonal climate experienced by the individuals and their families. Likewise, therapy is directed toward making a creative rearrangement in relationships so that developmental growth is maximized. Accompanying the reduction of the pathology-oriented diagnosis is a corresponding reduction in so-called resistance.

Additionally, in strategic therapy, the therapist is active and is ultimately the one responsible for initiating therapeutic movement. This is accomplished by introducing material into the therapy session and by the use of extramural assignments. That is, therapy does not wait until clients spontaneously bring up material; rather, the therapist often sets the pace and challenges clients to grow and change.

Finally, strategic therapy is interested in getting clients moving. This movement will be in their lives outside the therapist's office, and the use of office time is directed to that end. Assignments are, of course, delivered in order to have clients carry out chosen acts between the sessions. Hypnotherapy and the use of anecdotes, metaphors, and indirect suggestions are designed to motivate clients during sessions to carry out new relational behaviors or congruently engage in the homework assignments. It is from the learning brought by new actions and not from insight or understanding that change develops. Consequently, a client's understanding or insight about a problem is not of central importance. The matter of central importance is the client's participation in new experiences and transactions that congeal developmentally appropriate relational patterns.

An Ericksonian approach to therapy, which can be considered a subcategory of strategic therapy, is centered upon an integration of family therapy and hypnotherapy. Often these areas are seen as extremes with little convergence. Although Erickson's approach grew in these two areas independently, there are philosophical underpinnings for an integrated approach in the work of Gregory Bateson, Heinz Von Foerster, and other epistemological thinkers who emphasize the need to depart from the linear causality essential to the medical model of therapy. Erickson's work, perhaps better than that of any other modern clinician, embodies this goal. The following psychological processes common to both hypnosis and family therapy delineate the notable differences and major strengths of an Ericksonian approach in this regard:

- *Nonpathology-based model.* Problems are seen to be a part of, and a result of, people's attempts to adapt to the changing needs of their family and social network. It is inaccurate and inconvenient to define an individual as having a problem "in his head." Rather, symptoms often are seen as the essentially natural mechanism that has been used to calibrate a system (for example, the family) that has made a particular adjustment to developmental demands.

- *Indirection.* Indirection concerns itself with helping an individual or members of a family discover talents and resources, options and answers, seemingly without the aid of the therapist.
- *Utilization.* This involves making use of common understandings and behaviors that clients bring to the office so that these may be a part of the motivation or reinforcements of therapy.
- *Action.* Clients are expected and encouraged to get into action related to the growth or change that is sought.
- *Strategic.* Therapists are active and take an instrumental role in setting or initiating the stages of therapy.
- *Future-oriented.* Therapy is directed to how clients will act and experience in the immediate present and future rather than being focused on what they did in the past or what they will do about what they did in the past.
- *Enchantment.* Therapy activity engages the mind and appeals to clients as a pleasant challenge.

Techniques used with an Ericksonian approach vary depending upon the case being treated, but several unique interventions are associated with the approach and had their origin in Erickson's practice. These include paradoxical assignments, ambiguous function assignments, skill-building assignments, therapeutic metaphors, anecdotes, conscious-unconscious dissociation, hypnotic induction, therapeutic binds, indirect suggestion, and reframing.

While diagnosis and assessment often are conducted in a conventional manner, the treatment plan usually involves shifting attention away from the identified problem or the identified patient. These techniques are used to help establish a conducive setting for therapy, establish rapport, elicit conscious and unconscious treatment contracts, and shift attention to strengths that are needed to carry out therapeutic assignments. Therapists do not usually construct artificial reinforcement paradigms to help build new behavior but rather rely upon the inherent reinforcements found in the natural satisfaction of living functionally and coping creatively with the pragmatic or profound aspects of one's developmental tasks. As these changes in developmentally appropriate relations are put into action, problems cease and satisfaction is found, or further diagnosis and treatment planning is formulated and carried out to that end.

Critique Statement

Specific advantages of the Ericksonian strategic approaches to therapy center around the flexibility of its treatment model. We see this element in two major arenas: the unique overall treatment of each case, and the ability to bypass or avoid the resistances to change that direct approaches often elicit. These two aspects will become more clearly important as we examine the major criticisms of the approach.

The major strength of the approach lies in its reliance upon careful observation of clients' methods of thinking, experiencing, and acting, and upon tailoring interventions to match the unique history and actions of the client moment by moment in each session. To the extent that this occurs, resistance is nonexistent or minimal, and client participation is high. It follows that applications of the approach make intervention possible with some of the historically most difficult client populations.

Certain criticisms naturally arise with this model, and these criticisms can be classified in the following three ways: (1) the paucity of research for the approach and the difficulties the approach provides to researchers; (2) difficulty in obtaining necessary skills, training, and supervision to bring practitioners to competency levels with the approach; and (3) possible concerns for the ethics of client manipulation or informed consent. These interrelated concerns are illustrated below.

Research paradigms are most easily applied to approaches that are redundant, use well-defined interventions, and conform to the epistemological view of linear causality. While this often has been a classical problem for the social science researcher, the more individualized an approach becomes, the greater will be the research problem.

An Ericksonian strategic approach aims at being scrupulously unique with each client and therefore does none of those things that would facilitate application of existing research paradigms.

Rather, each metaphor, each paradox, must be delivered with an ongoing sensitivity to the special needs of the listener (this is called the *utilization approach*). This need for a uniqueness during application eschews the redundant patterns that lend themselves to research. That is, a metaphor delivered in therapy to one individual at a certain time may elicit a grief reaction while the same metaphor at another time or to another individual is not likely to have the same result. This creates, of course, a difficulty in measuring the effect of a specific intervention. Likewise, interventions are changed slightly for each individual, and thus it is in the uniqueness rather than the commonality of the intervention that the therapeutic bond is made and from which the real efficacy of the approach arises.

Similarly, indirect suggestions for action (*indirection approach*) are used to elicit motivations. These will be carried out by individuals when they are closely matched to immediately existing behavior and experience (utilization). However, delivering those same suggestions to a group of individuals will not yield the same results for each person owing to the differences between their motivations, personal histories, degree of pain, and so on. Commonly, research paradigms are built upon generalizations about individuals, whereas the most successful Ericksonian approaches are built upon the uniqueness of individuals.

The participatory quality of the Ericksonian approach derives from an epistemological framework of circular organization known as recursion. This is radically opposed to the historical notion that observers have objective knowledge about a subject independent of themselves. The traditional medical model relies upon knowing that certain behaviors make the subject a "neurotic," a "borderline personality," and so on, and then giving medication to the individual to cure this internal pathology. An Ericksonian approach, on the other hand, recognizes that the perception of individuals is not based on an objective perspective. That is, therapists who speak the experiential language of a client will not find the client resistant, and therapists whose language is, for instance, psychiatric, will find all clients (except some psychiatrists) to be resistive. Hence, treating a person for being "resistive," "crazy," "antisocial," and so on, would be an epistemological error that comes from overlooking the role played by the participating (rather than observing) therapist and the social context. This epistemological difference, then, requires a research paradigm that is not based, as our current model is, upon linear causality (observer-based treatment).

This brings us to another difficulty: the question of consent. While it is easy to intellectualize about a different epistemological approach, in the moment-by-moment pragmatics of therapy we must be effective and accountable. Often effective intervention is done when resistance is lowest — a situation that often occurs when the limitations of conscious biases and beliefs are bypassed by means of indirect interventions.

Effective intervention with a bleeding arm does not require informed consent, although consent often can be easily obtained for such obvious troubles. In therapy, however, resistance is often created in situations involving personal growth into areas where clients have doubt or are fearful to proceed. For instance, standing up for one's own needs in the face of an intrusive parent, while necessary, may be easy to teach (and even to carry out) but may be met with much resistance and anxiety on the part of the client.

Requiring prior conscious consent before eliciting motivations for actions such as these may effectively stop therapy. In these situations, the Ericksonian approach frequently works from the knowledge that clients follow the suggestions that are most relevant for them and that prove to be in their best interest. Hence, an unconscious contract based on tacit or implicit approval can be obtained from a client and resistance springing from conscious insight and deliberation can be avoided. But once again, this may raise questions of ethics and informed consent as they have been viewed historically.

Related to this issue is the need for good training and supervision of Ericksonian strategic therapists and the difficulty inherent in measuring effectiveness of training and performance in the absence of easily obtainable and relevant research. Therapists in Ericksonian training must learn to be comfortable and confident, often with less verbal feedback than in other approaches. They must learn to rely upon highly trained and developed observation to a greater extent.

Independent of these criticisms, much excellent research is being done and published. And although no two interventions are alike, Ericksonian strategic therapy remains accountable because of its emphasis on pragmatic and reality-based goals for clients. Furthermore, despite the uniqueness of each intervention, well-specified protocols or intervention patterns exist, are becoming more widely known, and may provide the basis for further refinements on effectiveness and therapy outcome. Finally, as the profession continues to grow following the current trends created by the changing therapeutic paradigm, it is expected that the Ericksonian strategic approach will continue to flourish.

Biography

Stephen R. Lankton is a marriage and family therapist and adjunct assistant professor in the Department of Psychology, University of West Florida, Pensacola. He received his M.S.W. degree from the University of Michigan. Lankton is internationally recognized for his central role in the development and growth of Ericksonian approaches to family therapy and clinical hypnosis. As a teacher and author he has distinguished himself for his facility in bringing together many isolated, complex, and influential techniques of therapy and integrating these in a comprehensive system of therapy. He is the coauthor with his wife, Carol, of the acclaimed *The Answer Within: A Clinical Framework of Ericksonian Hypnotherapy* and *Enchantment and Intervention: An Ericksonian Framework for Family Therapy*. He previously authored *Practical Magic: A Translation of Basic Neuro-Linguistic Programming into Clinical Psychotherapy* and has edited, with Jeffrey Zeig, *Developing Ericksonian Psychotherapy: The State of the Arts*. He has recently completed an anthology of therapeutic metaphors with Carol Lankton entitled *Tales of Enchantment*.

Lankton was appointed as the founding editor of the *Ericksonian Monographs* (the official publication of the Milton H. Erickson Foundation) in 1983. His honors include being made full member of the Society for Clinical and Experimental Hypnosis and being selected as a fellow of the American Association for Marriage and Family Therapy. Additionally, he is an American Society for Clinical Hypnosis member, a clinical member of the International Transactional Analysis Association, and a member of the American Family Therapy Association and the International Society of Hypnosis. He has been an invited faculty member at the International and National Congresses on Ericksonian Approaches to Hypnosis and Psychotherapy, sponsored by the Milton H. Erickson Foundation, and has conducted hundreds of clinical workshops, lectures, demonstrations, and seminars throughout the world.

Ericksonian Psychotherapy

Jeffrey K. Zeig

Definition

Psychotherapy is an interpersonal, symbolic ritual, a significant emotional event (Massey, 1979), the injunction of which is: "By experiencing this drama, you will be able to make your life different." The therapist initiates the process of change by supplying a task (be it a gestalt technique, a strategic directive, family restructuring, a psychoanalytic interpretation, systematic desensitization, hypnosis, or even a medical prescription for a psychoactive drug), the covert implication of which is that salutary change (enhanced control) will be promoted by virtue of completing this procedure. Effective psychotherapists truly believe in the techniques of change they offer their patients. Personally, I use Ericksonian hypnotherapy because hypnosis is one of the best contexts for injunctively catalyzing change. In fact, Ericksonian psychotherapy can be described as the technology of accessing responsiveness to therapeutic injunctions in order to elicit previously dormant resources. Social influence is used to access resources for change.

Qualification Statement

Psychotherapy occurs whenever a change is made in the habitual pattern of behavior. The assignment for the therapist is to secure sufficient leverage to help the patient initiate the process of strategic change. This change may be negative or positive. A negative change in the problem can be therapeutic; as, for example, when a symptom prescription temporarily makes a problem worse. Any change can be built upon. Once the patient develops change, there can be a snowballing effect in a positive direction.

This position is based on two assumptions: (1) The unconscious mind tends to be benign and generally health seeking, and (2) the unconscious contains solutions to problems that can be brought into the foreground. Once the rigid sets of symptoms are disrupted, people attempt to move to more effective levels of functioning by accessing previously underutilized strengths.

Patients often present symptoms to therapists in the form of "I can't X," or "I never can X," or "I always X," where X is overcoming depression, flying in an airplane, having a good marriage, and so on. The implication is that patients are victimized by problems. Therefore, therapists provide injunctions that help patients elicit change in their sense of being victimized. The form becomes "I *can* X," which leads to "I *will* X." In some instances, the best possible result is "I will live happily in spite of X," as might be the case in dealing with a grief reaction.

The therapist fights fire with fire by presenting therapeutic maneuvers that have enough injunctive leverage to counteract the negative injunction of victimization that surrounds the symptom. Therapeutic tasks are often social symbol dramas designed to elicit previously dormant psychological and physiological resources, eliciting positive reassociations among the resources contained in subjective and/or social life. The patient is presumed to have a history that includes the building blocks of eventual change. For example, phobic patients have a history of relaxing. Socially inept people have a history that includes instances of good interpersonal contact. These resources may be dormant; that is, in the background. They can be elicited, however, through the therapist's directives, which appeal to the latent constructive history.

The job of the therapist in Ericksonian psychotherapy can be summarized as a five-step procedure that is conducted more simultaneously than sequentially:

1. Decide what to communicate to the patient.
2. Decide how to communicate it. Usually this entails being indirect, but it could be the presentation of any therapeutic maneuver.
3. Ascertain what the patient values; that is, the position the patient takes (Fisch, Weakland, & Segal, 1982).
4. Divide the solution into manageable steps. Each step may be initiated by a therapeutic intervention.
5. Present the intervention within a therapeutic sequence, tailoring the intervention to fit the patient's values. This usually entails a three-step procedure: Moving in small, directed Steps; Intervening; and Following Through. This procedure has been tabbed "SIFT" (Zeig, 1985).

For example, if the problem X is depression, the therapist can ponder "What is the opposite of X?" (or "How can the patient not be victimized by X?" if X is not easily modifiable, as in some cases of chronic pain). To the patient, the opposite of depression may be to be happy. Then the therapist can divide the idea of happiness into a number of component processes: being active, changing mood, being external, being oriented to the future, being positive about oneself and about others. Each one of these steps can be an idea to present to the patient; for example, through an indirect story or via a therapeutic directive, so that the patient can, to his or her own credit, elicit that state.

Having established a goal, the therapist ascertains what the patient values and utilizes those values; for example, the patient might value being adventuresome. The therapist can suggest to the adventuresome depressed patient the idea that an interesting adventure could be to be more aware of the external environment by noticing shapes in the clouds whenever he gets into the car. thereby tying together values and goals.

It is not enough to merely present the tailored suggestion: Suggestions must be sequenced. Essentially this is a method of moving in small steps while accessing motivation. The therapist paces where the patient is, works to disrupt rigid mind sets, and helps to elicit therapeutic goals.

In regard to how a therapeutic task is presented, a therapist can start by offering a direct intervention. If resistance is encountered, then the therapist invokes the rule that the amount of indirection to be used is directly proportional to the perceived resistance (Zeig, 1980). In the face of resistance, the therapist can provide the same idea in the form of an indirect injunction through the use of symbols, metaphors, therapeutic anecdotes, tasks, and so on.

This is psychotherapy by reciprocal association: The therapist finds the reciprocal (opposite) of the problem, divides this solution into manageable steps, and, using tailored indirect technique, associates the patient to the steps until enough associations exist to drive effective behavior (Zeig, 1985).

In conducting Ericksonian therapy, the practitioner concentrates on building responsiveness in order to access resources. Induction becomes a process of building responsiveness to minimal cues. For example, during hypnosis if the therapist says to the patient "Lift your arm," and the patient does so, that is not necessarily hypnosis. But if the therapist says, "I'd like you to realize in a way that is *handy* for you that hypnosis is an *uplifting* feeling in a way that you can find *right* for you," and then the patient lifts the right arm in dissociated response to the presented injunction, that is called hypnosis. In hypnosis, the therapist obscures the cues that elicit responses so that patient responses become increasingly autonomous. Once there is responsiveness to minimal cues, it is deemed that the patient is ready for influence — that the door to the constructive unconscious is opened. At this point, resistances have been disrupted and the patient is deemed amenable to change.

Then therapy becomes a process of providing catalysts to elicit dormant resources. The therapist presents associative techniques such as the interspersal method (Erickson, 1966), stories, metaphors, or tasks around which resources can crystallize. The job of the therapist is to appeal to the dormant history in the patient and to set up situations whereby the patient, to his or her own credit, can access hidden strengths and bring them to the foreground.

Critique Statement

Ericksonian therapy has been criticized as being manipulative, superficial, cult-oriented, nonresearchable, and "anti-insight." I will address each of these points in order.

Manipulation. Psychotherapy by its very nature is manipulation. The patient comes to the therapist to be manipulated. Psychotherapy is neither an equal relationship, nor an I-thou experience. Equal and profoundly human relationships happen outside of therapy. With the exchange of money, the patient contracts for the therapist to be an agent of social influence. This places the therapist in a one-up position, working on the patient. Interventions should be surgical, in that the therapist gets in and out of the patient's life as quickly as possible. (For further discussion of ethics, including informed consent, see Zeig, 1985.)

Superficial. Practitioners of long-term insight-oriented approaches criticize Ericksonian methods as superficial because Ericksonian psychotherapy is a symptom-oriented approach. However, as Ericksonian therapists work with a symptom, they expect a snowballing effect. Gaining competence over a symptom breaks patients out of rigid mind sets. Subsequently, there can be salutary reverberations into other aspects of the patient's life, including the patient's social system.

For the most part, Ericksonian therapists do not work to create a transference-free personality. Rather, therapists work with specific problems, helping patients to surmount blockages in their particular stages of life. This is a brief approach whereby patients can return to therapy intermittently throughout their life to deal with other specific concerns.

Cult. Milton Erickson was a charismatic figure. Unfortunately, there have been many people who have attempted to imitate him. Erickson was a firm believer in the importance of individuality, and he would not have appreciated imitation. He preferred that people develop their own unique styles.

Erickson's humanism and technical virtuosity attracted many luminaries, including Margaret Mead, Gregory Bateson, Aldous Huxley, Jay Haley, John Weakland, and Ernest Rossi — all of whom were intrigued by his power and presence. However, most of Erickson's followers have picked up on his individualism, developing their *own* perspectives and their own contributions to therapy. There is not an orthodoxy among Ericksonians as there was in other psychological movements in which a strong father figure was present.

Nonresearchability. There is a definite problem in researching Ericksonian approaches because the psychotherapy is tailored to the unique style of the individual. Rote standardized procedures are scorned: Erickson maintained that he invented a new therapy for each patient.

Erickson conducted extensive research into the nature of hypnosis and psychotherapy. However, his studies were more anthropological field experiments than the kind of empirical research that has predominated in contemporary psychology. Ericksonian approaches are a rather young branch of psychotherapy. It was only in 1980 that the term *Ericksonian* came into vogue. Many people are now working to research Ericksonian ideas and methods and to find a vehicle for quantifying some of Erickson's important contributions.

Anti-Insight. Psychological insight has been viewed as antithetical to the Ericksonian approach, which is seen as directed to stimulating the patient's unconscious and bypassing conscious understandings. Actually, insight can be used within Ericksonian methodologies: It is merely one of a number of health-promoting methods. If insight could be used to catalyze change, Erickson utilized it. More often, however, understanding **why** does not help people discover **how** to do things differently. In Ericksonian methods, insight is served as the dessert that follows change rather than as the main course. Change is independent of insight.

Biography

Jeffrey K. Zeig is director of the Milton H. Erickson Foundation in Phoenix, Arizona. Zeig received his Ph.D. degree

(1977) from Georgia State University and currently maintains an active private practice. In addition, he regularly conducts teaching seminars on Ericksonian psychotherapy around the world. Zeig has organized all of the yearly Erickson congresses and seminars since 1980, including the landmark 1985 Evolution of Psychotherapy Conference. He serves on the editorial boards of two foreign and three American journals, including the *Ericksonian Monographs*. Zeig has edited or coedited six books and coedited (with Stephen Lankton) four *Ericksonian Monographs.* He authored *Experiencing Erickson,* and a book about his work appears in Italian. His books have been translated into seven languages.

References

Erickson, M. H. (1966). The interspersal technique for symptom correction and pain control. *American Journal of Clinical Hypnosis, 3,* 198–209.

Fisch, R., Weakland, J. H., & Segal, L. (1982). *The tactics of change: Doing therapy briefly.* San Francisco: Jossey-Bass.

Massey, M. (1979). *The people puzzle: Understanding yourself and others.* Reston, VA: Reston Publishing.

Zeig, J. K. (Ed.). (1980). *A teaching seminar with Milton H. Erickson.* New York: Brunner/Mazel.

Zeig, J. K. (1985). Ethical issues in Ericksonian hypnosis: Informed consent and training standards. In J. K. Zeig (Ed.), *Ericksonian Psychotherapy: Vol. I. Structures* (pp. 459–473). New York: Brunner/Mazel.

Directive Psychotherapy

Michael D. Yapko

Definition

Psychotherapy is an art that emphasizes the utilization of a mutually responsive relationship between therapist and client for facilitating purposeful changes on multiple dimensions of client experience. Thus, psychotherapy is goal- and future-oriented, involving dynamic and individualized approaches that accept, acknowledge, and utilize individual strengths and frames of reference. Psychotherapy necessarily involves interrupting experiential patterns deemed dysfunctional and building adaptive patterns that yield desired outcomes.

Qualification Statement

Emphasizing psychotherapy as art deemphasizes psychotherapy as science. Since every therapy occurs in a specific context with numerous contextual variables in operation, it is ultimately impossible to separate technique from context. One clinician can duplicate the words and actions of another but will undoubtedly generate a different outcome simply by virtue of being a different individual. Psychotherapy is a subjectively conceived and operationalized process. While its success is determined by a number of variables (expectations, approach utilized, accuracy of assessment of key dynamics, and so forth), none are more significant than the quality of the relationship between therapist and client. While many therapies emphasize the role of a nonjudgmental and accepting demeanor by the therapist, it seems more important to go beyond acceptance in order to *utilize* the client's values, beliefs, memories, and other significant aspects of his or her personal frame of reference. Including the concept of a mutually responsive relationship in the definition of psychotherapy emphasizes an appreciation for the capacity of the therapist to influence the client for better or worse. Rather than imposing on the client the therapist's preferences or implying that approval is contingent on the client accepting the therapist's indirect suggestions to "be more like me," the therapist utilizes the relationship as a vehicle for the client to discover or develop abilities (or responses) on a variety of dimensions (both intraand interpersonal) for reasons that both parties *cooperatively* view as desirable and purposeful.

The focus is not on *why* the client developed as he or she did; that is, explaining the client's experience. Such explanations are viewed as irrelevant sidesteps in the forward-moving process of establishing a direction toward a desired goal and identifying the specific steps leading toward that goal. Insight, however, is *not* devalued or overlooked. Instead, underlying dynamics and root causes of a client's difficulties may be addressed at an unconscious level. Directive psychotherapy (including hypnotic and Ericksonian approaches) can be just as efficient in addressing and resolving underlying psychodynamics but differs in the lack of need to involve the conscious mind in doing so. By emphasizing the interruption of dysfunctional patterns (of thinking, feeling, and behaving) and the building of adaptive patterns, the client is able to make desired changes while maintaining choice as to whether conscious understanding is necessary or desirable. Emphasizing the all-important dimension of client choice is vital to the therapy. The therapist's use of deliberate treatment approaches to facilitate changes in patterns is based entirely on the client's needs and abilities and thus is client-centered.

Psychotherapy must be as multidimensional as the clients who seek it. Single-dimension interventions are not adept in responding to the systemic nature of human life; that is, the multiple components of one's self and one's world. For example, interventions can involve simultaneously altering patterns for the way one thinks, feels, and relates to others. The use of pattern-building experiences in hypnosis in conjunction with directives (various experiential task assignment structures) to be conducted out in the real world are the most common techniques associated with directive psychotherapy.

Generating the best (that is, the most productive, satisfying, and adaptive) choice in a given context is considered the most desirable goal of treatment. In order to achieve this, the client must be capable of developing flexibility in responding to his or her internal needs and life's external demands.

Critique Statement

Assuming a directive position as a psychotherapist is not without its risks. There is a sharp division among health professionals regarding the appropriateness of deliberately doing things to influence the course of treatment. The most common criticism aimed at directive therapists involves this issue. Should a therapist actively guide the client's growth or simply provide support while the client discovers his or her own direction? Critics often argue that the approach is manipulative—that is, clients are treated as if dehumanized chess pieces to be moved about on the therapist's game board. Critics further argue that the practice of directive therapy may be unethical because the client is not fully informed as to either the reasons for or the expected outcomes of treatment strategies (thus precluding a truly informed consent to treatment).

In fact, when directive approaches to therapy are used appropriately, they revolve so completely around the client's needs and abilities that no more person-centered an approach seems possible. Respecting the inherent integrity of the client is consistently required in order to facilitate positive gains. It is the clients who choose the direction or goal, and it is the clients who are fully accepted in terms of their personal frame of reference. Furthermore, the client is the controlling force in what does and does not get carried out in the therapy—just as in almost every other therapeutic modality. The main advantage of directive techniques is the emphasis on *experiential learning*—the acknowledgment that the most significant and memorable learnings occur in real-life contexts. Another advantage is the ability to address underlying dynamics through experiential learning rather than through insight. Such learnings are more multidimensional and are less prone to be restricted to new intellectual understandings only. While critics often dislike the emphasis on solutions and outcomes instead of on the growth process, they often fail to recognize that growth involves progressively developing new solutions to old problems. Rapidly solving dilemmas is reinforcing to the client, who simply wants to feel better at the earliest possible moment. Thus reinforced, the person is more likely and able to commit to treatment, increasing the likelihood of its longer-term benefits. The emphasis on brief treatment is also a great advantage, but only when brief therapy is appropriate. Unfortunately, therapists will often attempt brief therapy directives when longer-term therapy is indicated. Clearly, it is counterproductive to use directive tactics without an appreciation for those personal, interpersonal, and contextual variables that would preclude their effective use. Critics argue against the cookbook mentality they perceive in directive therapists—a valid concern that underscores the need for higher levels of awareness for indications and contraindications. In general, a strategy simply should not be used if *all* possible client responses to it are not potentially useful in the therapy.

Perhaps the greatest advantage of all is that a directive approach emphasizes to clients that they can be active in the treatment process rather than remain helpless victims of unknown forces who suffer while the therapist passively watches and listens.

Clients learn that they are not sick but only limited by a lack of awareness of better information or choices. Clients are powered by such an approach, contrary to what many critics believe. Developing positive potentials for participating fully in therapy and in life is the greatest benefit clients can hope to gain from therapy.

Biography

Michael D. Yapko is a clinical psychologist in private practice in San Diego, California, director of the Milton H. Erickson Institute of San Diego, and an international trainer in hypnotic and directive approaches to psychotherapy. He received his Ph.D. degree (1980) from the United States International

University. Yapko is author of *Trancework: An Introduction to Clinical Hypnosis, When Living Hurts: Directives for Treating Depression,* and numerous brief-therapy-related articles. He is editor of *Hypnotic and Strategic Interventions: Principles and Practice* and of the Milton H. Erickson Foundation newsletter. He is on the faculties of United States International University and National University in San Diego.

Strategic Self-Therapy

John O. Beahrs

Definition

Psychotherapy is a paradox in human relationships: a contractual process in which one individual, a professional therapist, intentionally uses knowledge and relationship skills in an attempt to effect change in another, the patient or client; in other words, to do to or for that person what he or she can only do for himself or herself. This raises the unresolved question of to what extent one person can and should be responsible for another.

Qualification Statement

All psychotherapies share this defining paradox, a therapist attempting what patients can literally only do for themselves. In behavioral therapies this is accomplished by mutually planned reinforcers. In interpersonal therapies, a game unfolds (Berne, 1966) in which (1) the therapist correctly puts the burden of responsibility on the patient but tacitly accepts the challenge of making, influencing, manipulating, or exhorting the desired change, while (2) the patient overtly accepts the goal of change while directing most life resources toward *defeating* such change. A transference relationship often becomes the therapeutic vehicle, with interpersonal boundaries sufficiently blurred that it is difficult to assess who has done what to or for whom and what has actually caused the change or failure to change. Western ethics support this game by its twofold charge on helping professionals: to be maximally effective and to respect their patients' autonomy as inviolate (Beahrs, 1986).

My favored approach, strategic self-therapy, is based on the threefold principles of limited intensity, rigorous differentiation of roles and boundaries, and contextual reframing as the vehicle for change (Beahrs, 1990). It shares the defining paradox of all psychotherapy, differing only in the degree to which interpersonal boundaries are explicitly defined and correctly enforced. A therapist maximizes impact by literally stating both *inability* to change the patient and *unwillingness* to even try; for example, "I wouldn't even if I could, because that would violate your birthright as an autonomous person free to make your own life choices and take responsibility for their consequences." The burden is placed on patients to chart their own course through graded self-therapy projects that define personal identity, direction, and values and then redefine and redirect discordant aspects of selfhood . . . all in search of a central focal point whose modification will lead to deep and enduring change at many levels. A guarantee of safety from their own destructive actions is the sole responsibility of patients and is a *precondition* for meaningful treatment as opposeed to its desired end result. A therapist is a catalyst or consultant, not a "doer to." Independent social systems serve as the primary crisis resource.

When a therapist does not try to change the patient, there is nothing for the patient to resist. The issue of change versus no change is then transferred from the level of psychopathology to that of a legitimate life dilemma or choice, the stuff of history and great literature. A symptom is now a legitimate skill (Beahrs, 1982), to be used or not toward specific life goals. The therapist has accomplished more by attempting less, and the patient has now changed due to personal efforts.

The paradox remains. If we assume that this change would not otherwise have occurred, then the therapist has still caused it in the full legal sense of causality . . . in apparent violation of the original and correct presumption that only patients can change themselves. This brings the focus to a central issue that will probably forever remain unresolved: *To what extent is one person responsible for the thoughts, feelings, impulses, and actions of another?*

Critique Statement

Hypnosis research provides a threefold scientific foundation for strategic self-therapy. First, consciousness and volition are complex (Hilgard, 1977), hence intrapsychic structure is real and a possible target for intervention (Freud, 1916/1966). Second, its *form* varies with the psychosocial context in which it is defined (Spanos, 1986). Finally, this context is manipulable by a variety of strategic approaches (Erickson, 1980). Contextual reframing is the reciprocal process of defining this context to imply maximum health and responsibility. Including both the patient's and the therapist's formulations as well as the patient's self-therapy activity, it may actually change the form of a patient's intrapsychic structure before the implementation of a more specific treatment plan. In strategic self-therapy, this is an ongoing process.

Research in progress demonstrates efficacy, efficiency, and safety. Also, therapeutic progress strongly correlates with the degree of patient self-therapy activity (Beahrs, 1990). Data on differential efficacy is not yet available. Contrasted with intensive psychodynamic psychotherapies, strategic self-therapy has two primary advantages: cost efficiency and safety. Even when the same time lapse is required for therapeutic change, strategic self-therapy is more cost-efficient by virtue of its lesser intensity. For patients with high regressive potential, like borderline and multiple personalities, it has proven exceptionally adept at stimulating growth while avoiding the vicious cycles of regressive dependency and acting out that plague intensive treatment. It may therefore be equally effective and significantly more safe for these patients.

Other patients may have the requisite coping skills for self-therapy (abstracting ability, motivation, and behavioral control) but be too demoralized to follow through unless they receive massive outside support. If these patients have adequate resources for a less efficient approach and are not likely to regress to an unacceptable degree, intensive treatment may be preferable here. Even when support takes priority to change, the conflicted transference that ensues can be used to help a patient identify and liberate himself or herself from maladaptive early life choices.

Another question applies to those patients so impaired that they truly cannot restrain violent impulses and therefore require outside control. Fortunately, this problem is far less common than often assumed and mainly applies to severe psychotic disorders now believed to have a primary biological defect. Strategic self-therapy, like intensive psychotherapy, is simply not appropriate for this group. The insanity defense, Western law's formalization of this issue, rarely succeeds for borderline or dissociative patients from whom violent actions are willful and directed, with intact capacity for restraint (Beahrs, 1988). For this latter group, whether strategic self-therapy can be safely implemented is a matter of patient choice.

All psychotherapy is ultimately self-therapy, supported by the observed correlation of therapeutic progress with patient self-therapy activity. Whether serving as a transference object, purveyor of information, or catalyst, the therapist has a primary task: to help shape the psychosocial context within which the patient defines himself or herself in a way that makes self-therapy more likely. Even when a patient's structure changes at the very outset, only the patient can be responsible for his or her actions. The paradox remains.

Biography

John O. Beahrs is associate professor of psychiatry at the Oregon Health Sciences University and works at the Portland Veterans Administration Outpatient Clinic. He received his M.D. degree (1969) from Stanford, has studied research hypnosis with Ernest R. Hilgard and clinical hypnosis with Milton H. Erickson, and is on the board of directors of the American Board of Medical Hypnosis. Author of three books and numerous papers, he is a three-time recipient of the Milton H. Erickson Award for writing on hypnosis from the American Society of Clinical Hypnosis. He lives in Portland with his wife, Claudette, and is also interested in the outdoors, photography, and music composition.

References

Beahrs, J. O. (1982). *Unity and multiplicity: Multilevel consciousness of self in hypnosis, psychiatric disorder and mental health.* New York: Brunner/Mazel.

Beahrs, J. O. (1986). *Limits of scientific psychiatry: The role of uncertainty in mental health.* New York: Brunner/Mazel.

Beahrs, J. O. (1988). *Spontaneous hypnosis in the forensic context.* Paper presented at the annual scientific meeting of the American Academy of Psychiatry and the Law, San Francisco.

Beahrs, J. O. (1990). Strategic self-therapy for personality disorders. Submitted to *Journal of Strategic and Systemic Therapies* and presented at annual scientific meeting, American Psychiatric Association, Montreal, Canada.

Berne, E. (1966). *Principles of group treatment.* New York: Grove Press.

Freud, S. (1966). In J. Strachey (Ed. and Trans.), *Introductory lectures on psychoanalysis.* New York: Norton. (Original work published 1916)

Hilgard, E. R. (1977). *Divided consciousness: Multiple controls in human thought and action.* New York: Wiley.

Rossi, E. (Ed.). (1980). *The collected papers of Milton H. Erickson on hypnosis.* New York: Irvington.

Spanos, N. P. (1986). Hypnotic behavior: A social-psychological interpretation of amnesia, analgesia, and "trance logic." *Behavior and Brain Science, 9,* 449–502.

The New Hypnosis

Daniel L. Araoz

Definition

Psychotherapy happens when a person with a problem (client) obtains the expert assistance of a therapist. Psychotherapy, then, is a therapist-planned interaction establishing a beneficial process for the client, who seeks to solve a personal, subjective problem. Using mostly words, a client-focused process is established activating right-hemispheric functioning in the client with inner, hypnotic experiences leading to second-order change. This happens at a time when the habitual mental resources of the client are insufficient to solve the problem. Rather than strive for change through rationality or external (behavioral) experiences, I do it through *vivencias,* or inner, hypnotic experiences.

Qualification Statement

Four elements constitute psychotherapy: client, problem, therapist, and process. The *client* recognizes that his or her habitual mental resources are insufficient to handle the present problem. This insufficiency leads him or her to seek expert assistance or psychotherapy to solve the problem. The *problem* is something in the client's life that is producing unhappiness and that the person wants (at least consciously) to change. A *therapist* is one especially trained to deal with the complexity of human change. To get involved purposely in the *process* of goal-oriented human change requires specialized preparation, both theoretical and practical, because clients, by definition, are in a vulnerable state at a time when the possibility of emotional harm is heightened.

The goal of psychotherapy, then, is change from problem to solution. The means to attain this goal are the special interventions of the therapist, selected to help the client utilize effectively his or her inner resources, which were previously untapped. A special intervention is the use of new hypnosis techniques leading to inner change.

Human change is either behavioral, without altering one's beliefs and convictions (first-order), or attitudinal, intrapersonal transformation, metanoia (second-order change). First-order change occurs because of coercion, convenience, or fear, as a means to obtain something else, and not out of inner certitude. Second-order change is the outcome of a *vivencia,* Spanish for "a unique and total (body and mind) inner experience of something (subjectively meaningful)" (Araoz & Negley-Parker, 1988, p. xx); a type of right-hemispheric thinking, hypnotic in nature. Psychotherapy, therefore, is the process which makes a *vivencia* possible. The *vivencia* is part of the second-order change, so much so that without a *vivencia* there is no possibility of second-order change either in psychotherapy or in ordinary life. Falling in love, religious conversion, acts of heroism or generosity are a few examples of this unique and total inner experience.

How does psychotherapy make a *vivencia* possible? What is my special intervention in psychotherapy to help people change internally? The answer is a heuristic model based on the two main characteristics of Erickson's approach. He was eminently client-centered and also respectfully interested in and concerned with the client's inner, subjective experience and his role in helping the client experience it. He considered this inner experience, the *vivencia,* to be essential for meaningful change. The OLD C paradigm (*o*bservation, *l*ead, *d*iscussion, *c*heck) provides a guideline for the therapist to work effectively, according to these Ericksonian principles of client-centeredness and personal experience.

The first step is careful *observation* of the client's nonconscious behavior. Three main areas are targeted to observe these behaviors: language style, important statements, and somatics. The therapist pays as much attention to these as to the content of the conversation. Language style includes any words, expressions, or figures of speech that can be translated into mental images. If the client states, "I can't stand it any more," this therapeutic model encourages the client to get in touch with the inner experience that the words used may reflect. Another area of observation is that of important statements that the client makes in the course of the conversation. Rather than to ask why he or she said for instance, "I know I have to do it," the OLD C goes first to the subjective experience by requesting the client to silently repeat this statement, paying attention to feelings and other internal dynamics awakened while these words resonate inside. The last area of observation is somatics, which includes any and all nonverbal behaviors occurring during the verbal exchange. By focusing on somatics, the client gets in touch with possible nonconscious meanings, motives, fears, hopes, and other feelings.

The second step, *lead,* is the utilization of those points of therapeutic entry observed by the therapist to facilitate the hypnotic experience. This is the main part of hypnotherapy, taking the longest time. The third step is a *discussion* of the two previous steps. Here an integration takes place between the hypnotic experience and reason; right- and left-hemispheric functions are integrated in a logical, objective, evaluative way so that they make sense to the client. The final step consists of a *check* to confirm the fact that the above-mentioned integration has taken place. This check is an invitation for the client to go back into hypnotic functioning in order to check whether his or her whole being is reacting positively to the decision made in the discussion step. If the inner response is positive, the current therapeutic issue is resolved. If it is not, the therapist again leads the client according to the areas of observation that the therapist utilizes as points of therapeutic entry, and so forth until the issue is resolved.

Critique Statement

The main objection to this method is that not all clients need second-order change. Many request help with behavioral problems like smoking or weight. The response to this is that the therapist uses differential treatment with the same skill involved in using differential diagnosis.

The advantage of my approach is that research keeps mount-
ing in its favor. Meichenbaum (1985), Barber (1985), and others
have offered data indicating that people change internally only
when they experience themselves differently; when they have
a chance to go through an internal, subjective reevaluation of
themselves. De Shazer (1988) and Watzlawick (1978) also provide evidence of this. What makes people change is not argument
and reason but an inner experience of themselves as changed.
Though this is not described in terms of hypnosis, this process
is hypnotic in the sense that it bypasses logic, giving people a
uniquely personal "in-sight" of themselves.

The benefit of my OLD C model is that it provides the therapist with an easy-to-follow outline of how to proceed. By taking seriously any manifestation of the nonconscious dynamics
of the client, the psychotherapist is able to lead her or him to
that inner experience and thus to second-order change.

Biography

Daniel L. Araoz is professor of mental health counseling and
director of the Post-Masters Program in Marriage and Family
Therapy at Long Island University, C.W. Post Campus. He
received his Ed.D. degree (1969) from Columbia University.
A psychologist in Illinois and Pennsylvania, he is also a diplo-
mate of the American Board of Professional Psychology, the
American Board of Psychological Hypnosis, and the American
Board of Family Psychology. He is a charter member of the
American Academy of Board-Certified Psychologists. His published books include *Hypnosis and Sex Therapy* (1982), *The New
Hypnosis* (1985), and (with Negley-Parker) *The New Hypnosis in
Family Therapy* (1988). He has authored more than fifty articles
or book chapters in professional publications. He has been president or an officer of, among others, the Academy of Psychologists in Marital, Sex and Family Therapy; the American Board
of Family Psychology; the New York Society of Clinical Hypnosis; and the Long Island chapter of the American Association for Marriage and Family Therapy, of which he is also an
approved supervisor. He is on the editorial boards of several

professional journals, among them the *American Journal of Family Therapy*, which he founded in 1973. His residence and office are in Malverne, New York.

Recommended Reading

Araoz, D. L. (1985). *The new hypnosis.* New York: Brunner/ Mazel.

Fisch, R., Watzlawick, P., Weakland, J. H., & Fisch, R. (1974). *Change: Principles of problem formation and problem resolution.* New York: Norton.

References

Araoz, D. L., & Negley-Parker, E. (1988). *The new hypnosis in family therapy.* New York: Brunner/Mazel.

Barber, T. X. (1985). Hypnosuggestive procedures as catalysts for psychotherapies. In S. J. Lynn & J. P. Garske (Eds.), *Contemporary psychotherapies: Models and methods.* Columbus, OH: Merrill.

de Shazer, S. (1988). *Clues.* New York: Norton.

Meichenbaum, D. (1985). Cognitive-behavioral therapies. In S. J. Lynn & J. P. Garske (Eds.), *Contemporary psychotherapies: Models and methods.* Columbus, OH: Merrill.

Watzlawick, P. (1978). *The language of change.* New York: Basic Books.

Psychotherapy: Understanding Negotiable Options

Norma Barretta,
Philip F. Barretta,
Joseph Bongiovanni

Definition

For whatever reason, the individual seeking therapy has temporarily lost an ability to be resourceful or to initiate optional behaviors. Psychotherapy, therefore, becomes a process of remediation and education wherein the therapist acts as a guide to assist the patient in establishing or reestablishing those states of resourcefulness that make change possible. The therapist serves not only as an empathetic confidant but also as a teacher providing skill learning at the conscious level and information at the unconscious level, enabling the patient to change less-than-optimal behaviors into functional, useful, and appropriate behaviors. It is not the purpose of therapy to re-create the individual along the lines of some master design, but rather to provide the tools necessary for that individual to re-create his or her own design replete with choice.

Qualification Statement

Traditional psychotherapy is a verbal delivery or exchange that seeks to justify the patient's nonfunctional behaviors by disclosure of an aggregation of past events in the patient's history. Conscious recovery of these events may or may not alleviate the unwanted behaviors. Length of therapy and levels of success may vary greatly depending upon a multiplicity of factors, not the least of which happen to be the resources (both emotional and physical) of the therapist and patient. The limitations of the traditional model rest primarily on two components: the collection of content information with no regard to the unconscious processing of that information and the lack of full recognition of the sensory modalities other than auditory.

It is our belief that in order to be as comprehensive and as expedient as possible, psychotherapy must utilize the full resources of the therapist and the patient by fully recognizing that valuable information is exchanged in both verbal and nonverbal formats and that the unconscious processing of that information is, in effect, the generator for all behaviors, whereas the content of the event itself is only a representation of how those behaviors have been utilized in a specific event. Hypnosis and neurolinguists provide the vehicle whereby therapy can be comprehensive and expedient. *It is not a matter of counting your words but of making your words count.*

The neurolinguistic model demands that the therapist utilize nonverbal, unconscious behavioral cues offered by the patient. These are a far more reliable source of information than verbalization alone can ever be, for language is slippery. (There are 172 meanings for the word *run* listed in the *Random House Unabridged Dictionary.*) Such linguistic ambiguity can only confound the therapist using the traditional format. On the other hand, nonverbal cues can be noted and calibrated by the observant therapist and therefore become a reliable gauge to guide therapeutic verbalizations to the hypnotized patient. In this way a precision becomes possible in which dramatic state changes can occur in relatively short periods of time. Since internal state is the director of external behavior, the patient now discovers *choice* and the possibility of change.

To paraphrase Marcus Aurelius: "I cannot control what the external environment provides, I only can manage my perception of it. Over this I have exquisite control."

The unconscious mind often continues to direct behavior based on old information that may or may not have been made up of healthy, appropriate, beneficial inputs from childhood. It is the task of the therapist to update and modify inputs from childhood that may be impairing functioning in the present. For

example, at age two a child is told, "You can't cross the street."
(A useful lie, actually, because if the child can walk, the child
can cross the street, albeit not safely.) Most children eventually learn to cross safely and update the information on their
own. Some don't. These are the ones who come to a therapist
at age thirty-two to cure their agoraphobia. The competent therapist updates the information at the unconscious level (either
metaphorically or in a formal hypnotic trance state) and then
teaches the patient some skills of resourcefulness to match the
update.

What about the resistant patient? In our framework, there
is no such thing—there is only inflexibility on the therapist's part.
So long as the therapist is able to vary responses to the patient,
always moving toward an ecological outcome, resistance will
not become an issue.

The flexible therapist will be creative and sensorily acute
enough to observe the patient's responses and will be able to
guide the patient into new ways of responding differently to old
stimuli, understanding all the while that negotiable options are
the optimal outcome that will help patients help themselves to
initiate and maintain the changes and choices that lead to optimal functioning.

Through verbal exchanges alone the patient may become
knowledgeable about dysfunctional behaviors with some insight
into those behaviors. And insight in and of itself may produce
change, but change without unconscious cooperation lacks the
component of purpose and the promise of permanence. Complete and comprehensive conscious-unconscious understanding
is not available through the single medium of nondirective conversation. To attempt to comprehend a patient's behavior in
this manner is to attempt to understand ballet by listening with
one's eyes closed and one's feet in leaden boots. Behavior is an
exquisite dance between the conscious and unconscious mind
in which life becomes a celebration or a lamentation. It is complex. It is circuitous. It must be invited into integrating both
conscious and unconscious processes so that the patient learns
to respond as a unified whole.

Critique Statement

The utilization of hypnosis and neurolinguistics is a respectful affirmation of the complexity of the human condition and a wondrous acknowledgment of the potential of the mind and spirit. While some proponents of traditional methods decry hypnosis and neurolinguistics as manipulative, it is well to point out that virtually *all* therapy is manipulative since its very nature requires a series of stimuli and responses between patient and therapist. In his book *The language of change,* Paul Watzlawick states, "One cannot not influence" (1978, p. 11). Therefore, the question for all psychotherapeutic models becomes: Is the manipulation respectful of the patient and for the benefit of the patient? Clearly this is not an issue in a model that is respectful of both the conscious and unconscious mind.

The power of this model is in its ability to expeditiously produce beneficial change in the conscious state of the patient through the patient's unconscious process. The emphasis is not on the ever elusive why of behavior but the far more concrete how and when. Because of the additional information provided by the observation of unconscious processing, dysfunctional behaviors can be replaced in a global sense, thus assuring ongoing states of resourcefulness capable of providing behavioral options well past the resolution of the initial presenting problem. Thus the patient is able to quickly learn skills that are useful beyond the confines of the therapy setting. Therefore, the learning is cumulative and generalizable.

This model supports the belief that the chief function of therapy is to provide guidance to change as respectfully, as comprehensively, and as expeditiously as possible. To that end the therapist works with the patient to determine exactly what change is needed and what the patient can provide in his or her own being to produce that change. The patient's own resources are engaged, prodded, updated, and amplified to work toward the desired state. Previous successful behavior in one area can be transplanted to another area where such experience is lacking. The patient learns to sustain internal nourishment, which is essential for new healthy growth, leafing off old unsuccessful behaviors to firmly root new ones. In this way the integrity of the patients is protected while they are encouraged to re-create their own world to their own choosing. Every means to protect the ecology is utilized, thus preempting resistance and virtually guaranteeing success.

In addition to installing successful strategies as replacements for unsuccessful ones, the patient learns to communicate more effectively at both conscious and unconscious levels. In this way the patient becomes better able to respond to reality and thus to avoid distortion or deletion of information from the environment. The patient becomes empowered through the enlistment of the personal unconscious process as a reliable and easily accessible ally. There comes a certain security in finally integrating the information that there is no enemy within.

There is an elegance in the hypnosis-neurolinguistic model because it utilizes the patient's own talents to realign the patient's own world. That is the highest form of respect.

Biographies

Norma Barretta is a clinical counseling psychologist specializing in the use of Ericksonian interventions and the techniques of neurolinguistic programming in psychotherapy. She received her Ph.D. degree (1970) from the University of Southern California and since 1971 has maintained a private practice in southern California. During the past sixteen years, along with her husband, Philip Barretta, she has provided training for thousands of professionals in Ericksonian hypnotherapy and neurolinguistic programming. A recurring faculty member for the American Society of Clinical Hypnosis (ASCH) and a core trainer for Grinder, DeLozier & Associates, she feels fortunate to have been among those who studied with Milton H. Erickson. Her professional affiliations include the American Psychological Association, ASCH, the Association for Humanistic Psychology (AHP), and the International Council of Psychologists (ICP).

Philip F. Barretta is a marriage and family therapist in private practice. He received his M.A. degree (1972) from California State University, Long Beach, and for the past sixteen years has worked with his wife, Norma Barretta, to make the techniques and innovations of Ericksonian hypnotherapy and the therapeutic applications of neurolinguistic programming available to professionals in training programs throughout the world. He feels most fortunate to have studied personally with Milton H. Erickson. He is a core trainer for Grinder, DeLozier & Associates and has been on the training faculty for the ASCH. He is also a member of the Southern California Society for Clinical Hypnosis. His personal affiliations include AHP, ICP, and the California Association of Marriage and Family Therapists.

Joseph A. Bongiovanni received his M.A. degree (1987) from Loyola Marymount University, Los Angeles, and is currently pursuing his doctorate in clinical evaluation at the Professional School of Psychological Studies at San Diego, California. He has had articles published in the *Association for Humanistic Psychology Newsletter* and *Movement News*. His background includes practitioner training in neurolinguistic programming and advanced Ericksonian hypnosis under John Grinder. His current focus is with children and childhood depression.

Recommended Reading

Andreas, S., & Andreas, C. (1987). *Change your mind and keep the change.* Moab, UT: Real People Press.

Bandler, R., Andreas, S., & Andreas, C. (Eds.). (1985). *Using your brain for a change.* Moab, UT: Real People Press.

Bandler, R., & Grinder, J. (1975). *The structure of magic: Vol. 1. A book about language and therapy.* Palo Alto, CA: Science and Behavior Books.

Bandler, R., & Grinder, J. (1976). *The structure of magic: Vol. 2. A book about communication and change.* Palo Alto, CA: Science and Behavior Books.

Bandler, R., & Grinder, J. (1979). *Frogs into princes: Neurolinguistic programming.* Moab, UT: Real People Press.

DeLozier, J., & Grinder, J. (1987). *Turtles all the way down: Prerequisites to personal genius.* Bonnie Doon, CA: Grinder, DeLozier & Associates.

Dilts, R., Grinder, J., Bandler, R., & DeLozier, J. (1980). *Neuro linguistic programming: Vol. 1. The study of the structure of subjective experience.* Cupertino, CA: Meta Publications.

Erickson, M., & Rossi, E. (1979). *Hypnotherapy: An exploratory casebook.* New York: Irvington.

Haley, J. (Ed.). (1967). *Advanced techniques of hypnosis and therapy: Selected papers of Milton Erickson, M.D.* New York: Grune & Stratton.

Haley, J. (1973). *Uncommon therapy.* New York: Norton.

Heller, S., & Steele, T. (1987). *Monsters and magical sticks, there's no such thing as hypnosis?* Phoenix, AZ: Falcon Press.

Laborde, G. Z. (1983). *Influencing with integrity: Management skills for communication and negotiation.* Palo Alto, CA: Syntony Publishing.

Laborde, G. Z. (1988). *Fine tune your brain: When everything's going right and what to do when it isn't.* Palo Alto, CA: Syntony Publishing.

Reference

Watzlawick, P. (1978). *The language of change.* New York: Basic Books.

Neurolinguistic Programming

David Gordon

Definition

The personal world is a latticework of beliefs held in place by the meaningful incidents, or *reference experiences,* in one's personal history. Psychotherapy is a process in which a person acquires new reference experiences that usefully alter his or her beliefs. A psychotherapeutic approach will be successful to the extent that the reference experiences it has to offer are appropriate and the techniques it has for delivering those reference experiences are effective for a particular client.

Qualification Statement

A therapeutic orientation based on modeling evolves out of the presupposition that "the map is not the territory," a notion most eloquently put forward by Alexander Korzybski. This presupposition (which explicitly underlies neurolinguistic programming and, I think, Milton Erickson's work as well) says that there is a real world but that the only way we know the world is through our subjective experience of it. Your experience of the world is filtered through not only the physiological biases of your sensory systems but also the layers of linguistic distinctions, cultural values, and personal beliefs. Taken together, these filters define your map. In terms of subjective experience, then, your map *is* your territory. Change the map and you change your world.

For the most part, our individual maps are comprised of our beliefs about who we are, how we work, what the world is, how it works, and so on. Therapeutic change, whether remedial or evolutionary, is a function of a change in beliefs (for instance, coming to believe that you can control your appetite or that you are a worthwhile person). Every psychotherapy operates by creating opportunities (and, in some cases, the necessity) for the client to change beliefs. (Even behavioral approaches are ultimately ineffective if there is no corresponding change in belief to maintain the changed behavior over time and across contexts.)

The question of change, then, comes down to how best to change beliefs. The particular beliefs you hold are the result of reference experiences you have had. It is experience that changes people. Talking about a problem is in and of itself ineffective in terms of change unless it creates an actual experiential context for the client that is sufficiently compelling to alter an old belief or install a new one. Therapies differ primarily with respect to the beliefs they attempt to inculcate in their clients and in the approaches and techniques they employ. The approaches and techniques a therapist uses shape and define the client's reference experiences while proceeding through that therapy. Most psychotherapies are so caught up in the delivery of their techniques that they lose sight of the intention those techniques are intended to fulfill, which is to provide the client with reference experiences that are appropriate for *that* individual and sufficiently compelling to alter that client's perspective. If the therapist is to be respectful, the focus needs to be on the client's map, not the therapist's map. If the therapist is to be consistently effective, the interaction must be directed toward creating reference experiences that will change the client's map, not toward trying to squeeze the client through the mold of the technique.

Critique Statement

Most of my criticisms regarding modeling as a basis for therapeutic intervention are reserved for the practitioners of this approach rather than for its effects on clients. Since it is not a technique-oriented approach, the emphasis is on the therapist, who must substitute personal cognitive and behavior skills for standard techniques. The most significant of these cognitive behaviors is patterning, which is the ability to discern within a person patterns of behavior, verbal representations, and thought processes. These patterns form the basis for formulating a model of the client within his or her world, and it is this model that the therapist must change. The ability to pattern, however, is an ability that does not seem to be easily learned. Those individuals who are already adept at patterning readily take to this therapeutic approach. Those who are not, however, find modeling mystifying and face a great deal of work if they are to eventually master the approach. It therefore requires a level of dedicated effort that is unacceptable (and perhaps inappropriate) for most people. One advantage of operating at the therapeutic level of patterns, however, is that it creates a situation of open-ended learning. That is, every new client teaches you something new about the variety of human subjective experience, rather than merely giving you additional content examples of already familiar problems.

There is an orientation at the core of this therapeutic approach that can be best summarized as: "Teach me how to be you." This is not the client's request, but the *therapist's*. Initially, the therapist's role is that of student. The goal is to discover how the client creates a subjective world. Once understood, the therapist can then move on to interventions at that level. This orientation is difficult for those therapists who feel that they must intervene immediately or who think there are right ways to think and behave. Such a therapist will, upon hearing the nature of the problem, "know" what the client needs in terms of a change and will, therefore, be anxious to get on with it. The advantage of the modeling approach, however, is that it is respectful of the fact that two people can manifest the same problem but have different patterns of cognition underlying that problem.

A potential hazard of this approach that should be noted is that it generates a tremendous amount of personal responsibility for one's experience and behavior. This is inherent in the notion that the map is not the territory. Emotions, behaviors, skills, and beliefs are no longer something that happen to you, but something you create (even if unintentionally). For many, the fact that they *can* change their experience and behavior becomes an injunction that they *must* and evolves into an ongoing burden of self-evaluation and self-manipulation. For others, this ability to choose remains simply that — the freedom to choose.

Biography

David Gordon is in private practice in Oakland, California. Gordon received his M.F.C.C. degree (1978) from Lone Mountain College in San Francisco. He is one of the pioneering co-developers of neurolinguistic programming. From the inception of the field, he has worked closely with Richard Bandler and John Grinder to help develop its content and shape its practice. As director of training of the seminal Division of Training and Research in Neurolinguistic Programming, Gordon was instrumental in developing credentialing programs for neurolinguistic programming across the United States. During the last few years he has been exploring the true potential of neurolinguistic programming as a basis for modeling human experience and behavior. Gordon has written five books on the subjects of neurolinguistic programming, metaphor, Ericksonian therapeutic interventions, and the structure of experience, as well as many articles, papers, and screenplays. He travels around the world conducting workshops on those topics.

Recommended Reading

Bandler, R., & Grinder, J. (1975). *The structure of magic* (Vol. 1). Palo Alto, CA: Science and Behavior Books.

Cameron-Bandler, L. (1985). *Solutions.* San Rafael, CA: FuturePace.

Cameron-Bandler, L., Gordon, D., & LeBeau, M. (1985). *The EMPRINT method: A guide to reproducing competence.* San Rafael, CA: FuturePace.

Cameron-Bandler, L., & LeBeau, M. (1986). *The emotional hostage.* San Rafael, CA: FuturePace.

Gordon, D., & Meyers-Anderson, M. (1981). *Phoenix: Therapeutic patterns of Milton H. Erickson.* Cupertino, CA: Meta Publications.

Korzybski, A. (1958). *Science and sanity.* Lakeville, CT: The International Non-Aristotelian Library Publishing Company.

Section 2
Hypnotic Approaches

Ego-State Therapy

Helen H. Watkins
John G. Watkins

Definition

Psychotherapy is a purposive interaction between two people, one of whom, called "the patient," has sought help from another, called "the therapist." Patients are suffering from some crippling or painful symptoms that have lessened their comfort and/or have interfered with their social adaptation to their world. They have entered into this interpersonal transaction with the therapist because they believe the therapist has professional training and knowledge that may be of help.

Qualification Statement

The essence of psychotherapy is the relationship between the two parties, aided by the psychological understanding and technical skill of the therapist. Each therapist operates within a theoretical frame of reference (such as psychoanalytic, behavioral, cognitive, or humanistic) that determines how he or she conceptualizes human nature and its maladjustments. Within this frame of reference the psychotherapist applies various procedures or interactions to assist the patient to relieve symptoms, improve adjustment, and encourage better interpersonal relationships with others. These procedures may be either actively interventionist or very client-centered such that the patient guides and controls the therapy. No one set of procedures has been found to be of help to all patients, but a close, interactive relationship between client and therapist seems to promote better understanding of the referring disorder and facilitate its amelioration.

In our approach we utilize a wide variety of procedures (psychoanalytic, cognitive, behavioral, and humanistic), often applied within the modality of hypnosis. We perceive hypnosis as an intensive interpersonal relationship experience that affords access to covert (unconscious) levels of personality functioning. Within a hypnotic state patients often are able to recall significant (and forgotten) life events, release bound or dissociated affects, and act upon constructive suggestions.

We conceptualize personality structure as being a multiplicity organized into various patterns of ego states, and we define an ego state as a body of behaviors and experiences bound together by some common principle and separated from other such entities by boundaries that are more or less permeable. In mood states the boundaries are permeable; in multiple personalities they are rigid and impermeable, restricting or almost eliminating communication between them. The rigidity of boundaries lies on a continuum. There are many degrees between mood states at one end of the continuum and true, overt multiple personalities at the other end.

Ego states can be hypnotically activated and the intrapersonal conflicts between them studied and resolved. Ego-state therapy uses group and family therapy techniques for the resolution of conflicts between the various ego states that constitute a "family of self" in a single individual.

Hypnoanalytic ego-state procedures, when applied within a close, interpersonal relationship with the "therapeutic self" of a resonant therapist, seem to result in general improvement by most patients—as evaluated by both therapist and patient.

Biographies

Helen H. Watkins is a psychologist on the staff of the University of Montana Counseling Center. She received her M.A. degree from the University of Montana in psychology. She has

gained increasing national recognition as an extremely sensitive and innovative psychotherapist. As the author or coauthor
of more than thirty-five publications and a fellow of the Society
for Clinical and Experimental Hypnosis, she has taught many
advanced classes and workshops both by herself and in collaboration with her husband, John G. Watkins. She has served on
the faculties of the International Graduate University of Switzerland, the Florida Institute of Technology, and the University of Montana.

John G. Watkins, professor emeritus, University of Montana,
has served as president of the Society for Clinical and Experimental Hypnosis, the American Board of Psychological Hypnosis, Division 30 of the American Psychological Association,
and the International Society of Hypnosis. He received his Ph.D.
degree from Columbia University in psychology. An accredited
psychoanalyst, he is the author of six books and more than a
hundred articles on psychotherapy, clinical hypnosis, personality theory, psychological testing, forensic psychology, dissociation, and ego-state therapy. With his wife and colleague, Helen
H. Watkins, he has given invited lectures and workshops at
many universities, medical schools, hospitals, and scientific meetings throughout the United States and in Europe, South
America, Asia, Australia, and New Zealand.

Recommended Reading

Watkins, J. G. (1978). *The therapeutic self.* New York: Human
    Sciences Press.
Watkins, J. G., & Watkins, H. H. (1979). The theory and prac-
    tice of ego-state therapy. In H. Grayson (Ed.), *Short Term Ap-
    proaches to Psychotherapy* (pp. 176–220). New York: Human
    Sciences Press.
Watkins, J. G., & Watkins, H. H. (1981). Ego-state therapy.
    In R. J. Corsini (Ed.), *Handbook of innovative psychotherapy* (pp.
    252–270). New York: Wiley.

Integrative Hypnotherapy

D. Corydon Hammond

Definition

Integrative hypnotherapy is a specialized type of psychother-apy wherein hypnosis is used to focus attention, facilitating ac-ceptance of ideas and enhancing motivation. This multidimen-sional, integrative approach incorporates methods from many hypnotic approaches, employing direct, indirect, and insight-oriented techniques to alter behavior, affect, physiological pro-cesses, imagery perceptions, cognitions, and internal dialogue. Hypnosis is used to explore unconscious functions, resolve histor-ical factors, and utilize unconscious resources. Self-hypnotic skill development enhances self-efficacy and provides self-management skills.

Qualification Statement

Integrative hypnotherapy is part of the emergent trend toward eclectic, comprehensive psychotherapy, tracing its roots to pio-neers like Thorne, Lazarus, and more recently Beutler, Pro-chaska, DiClemente, Norcross, and Hammond and Stanfield. Integrative hypnotherapy is in the best tradition of Milton Erick-son (Hammond, 1984, 1988c), who refused to be limited by a theoretical system, despite recent efforts to create an Erickso-nian theory and orientation.

Integrative hypnotherapy assumes that most problems have multiple determinants and emphasizes taking into account pa-tient individuality. It particularly builds on technical eclecticism (Lazarus, 1981; Hammond and Stanfield, 1977), encouraging the prescriptive use of techniques according to indications and contraindications derived empirically and by experimental validation rather than by theory. Integrative hypnotherapy is multidimensional (Lazarus, 1981) in emphasis, focusing on influencing "BASIC ID"—problematic behavior, affect, sensory-physical factors, imagery, cognitions, interpersonal-environmental context, and drugs or biological factors (Hammond & Stanfield, 1977).

Many hypnotherapists utilize a limited range of interventions. Integrative hypnotherapy seeks to utilize contributions from practitioners with many different emphases: authoritarian (Kroger, Hartland, LaScola, Erickson); indirect (Erickson, Rossi, Zeig, Thompson, Yapko, Gilligan); permissive (J. Barber, Rodger, Secter, Araoz); metaphoric (Erickson, Lankton, Barretta, Rosen, Barker, Gordon); direct-structured (Spiegel, Crasilneck, Wester, Soskis, Weitzenhoffer); analytic and insight-oriented (Cheek, LeCron, Wolberg, Watkins, Brown, Fromm, Edelstein, Diamond, Sacerdote, Wright, Barnett, Murray-Jobsis, Stein); behavioral (Clarke & Jackson, Kroger & Fezler, Dengrove, Lazarus, Cautela); non-state (T. X. Barber); cognitive (Lazarus, Ellis, Golden); meditative (Meares, Benson, Borysenko); guided imagery (Bresler, Rossman, Sheikh, Korn, Ahsen, Shorr); autogenic training (Jencks, Luther, Schultz); experimentalistic (Hilgard, Evans, Perry, Sheehan, Lynn, Orne); light trance (some Ericksonians); deep trance (Erickson, Sacerdote, Tart, Watkins, Wolberg, Hartland).

After the establishment of a therapeutic alliance (Hammond, Hepworth, & Smith, 1977), integrative hypnotherapy strategies and their associated techniques may include:

- *Unconscious exploration and enhancement of insight* (ideomotor exploration, inner adviser technique, guided imagery, hypnoprojective techniques).
- *Perceptual change* (posthypnotic suggestions, reframing, metaphors, ego strengthening, ego ideal technique, trance ratification, amnesia, time reorientation, time distortion).
- *Conflict resolution: intrapersonal* (ego-state therapy and negotiation, alternative need gratification, fusion of extremes technique) and *interpersonal* (age regression and abreaction, hypnodrama).

- *Abreaction and emotional facilitation* (age regression, affect bridge, abreaction, affect intensification).
- *Reduction and alteration of affect* (reframing, rational-emotional suggestions, affect tolerance, reconditioning techniques).
- *Behavioral control and facilitation* (posthypnotic suggestion, imaginal modeling and rehearsal, age progression).
- *Physiologic control and alteration* (anesthesia, hyperesthesia, vascular control).

Hypnotherapeutic strategies and techniques are selected according to patient needs, personality, preferences, expectations, dissociative capacity, hypnotic talents, nature of the problem, number of BASIC ID dimensions involved in the problem, whether the problem is situational and acute or ingrained and chronic, and whether the problem is a habit or has various etiologic factors and serves adaptive functions. The emphasis is on individualization of therapy. Reactance level—the degree to which the patient likes to have personal control and resists influence versus perceiving and seeking external control—is another important variable (Beutler, 1986). Reactance level helps determine the degree to which the therapist is indirect, permissive, and metaphoric versus direct, structured and even authoritarian. Therapist knowledge of patient hypnotic capacities is also important in determining the degree of direction versus indirection.

Critique Statement

Criticisms and Disadvantages

Research on effectiveness is lacking, and experimentally validated criteria do not exist for indications and contraindications and the matching of techniques with patient variables. For example, most recent research clearly shows a lack of differential effectiveness of indirect and permissive versus direct and authoritarian suggestions, although these interventions were not tailored to types of subjects (expectations, preferences, personalities, and reactance level). Thus, strategy and technique selection currently remain implicit and guided by empirical evidence and clinical experiences. Therapy is still largely an art and only embryonic in scientific development. Systematic and explicit guidelines need to be published concerning strategy and technique selection with different patients, and this process is currently under development (Hammond, 1990).

New, inexperienced clinicians will feel less secure without one approach to guide their actions with a more limited range of techniques. Integrative hypnotherapy requires a broader education and careful assessment and treatment planning rather than a seat-of-the-pants approach (Hammond & Stanfield, 1977; Hammond, 1985). Hypnotherapy in general also has limitations, not only with regard to the limits of hypnotic talent in individual patients, but particularly in systems and environmental intervention. Hypnosis is best integrated with broad-spectrum, eclectic psychotherapy.

Advantages

There are inadequacies and limitations with the individual hypnotic approaches advocated by different practitioners (for example, emphasizing primarily indirect and direct suggestions, metaphors, or exploratory and hypnoprojective techniques). Global theorizing is premature, and the field is moving away from individual theories toward validation of techniques and eclectic practice. In the field of psychotherapy, for example, behaviorism broadened in the last three decades to include cognitive factors, and rational therapy to include behavioral and emotive methods. Different schools have too often been viewed as competitors rather than contributors, with each operating on the one-true-light assumption. Thorne (1967) suggested that the emphasis on individual orientations is analogous to preferring a one-string violin when the entire spectrum of instruments is available.

Reality demands an eclectic approach in both hypnotherapy and psychotherapy. For this reason, 30–54 percent of various psychotherapists identify themselves as eclectic (Norcross, 1986), and most highly experienced therapists refuse to be limited by the blinders of a theoretical system (Norcross & Prochaska, 1982; Smith, 1982). Thus, integrative hypnotherapy is compatible with a trend toward integration in the field of psychotherapy in general that encourages greater flexibility and choice to meet the varied needs and personalities of patients. The application of the best concepts of eclectic psychotherapy to the specialty of hypnotherapy also allows hypnotherapy to be more easily integrated with a broad, eclectic psychotherapeutic approach. Furthermore, some research now suggests that lack of individualization results in destructive effects and that individualization of hypnosis is associated with positive outcomes. Although many give lip service to individualizing hypnosis, it is not individualization to treat everyone with indirect suggestions, or metaphors, or direct suggestions, or hypnoprojective techniques. There are many valuable methods to be gleaned from the work of highly diverse practitioners.

Biography

D. Corydon Hammond is an associate professor in physical medicine and rehabilitation and codirector of the Sex and Marital Therapy Clinic, University of Utah School of Medicine, and in private practice in Salt Lake City. He received his Ph.D. degree (1974) from the University of Utah and is a fellow of the American Society of Clinical Hypnosis and a member of the ASCH executive committee. He was the ASCH newsletter editor for more than five years, has chaired the ASCH annual workshops and the annual scientific meeting, and is the chair of the ASCH monthly regional workshops. He teaches workshops throughout the United States and Canada, and for three years he was president of the Utah Society of Clinical Hypnosis. Hammond is the abstracts editor for the *American Journal of Clinical Hypnosis,* has published four professional volumes (including *Learning Clinical Hypnosis* and *Hypnotic Induction and Suggestion,* available from ASCH), eleven chapters in books, and over two dozen professional journal articles. He is also an advisory editor and founding editorial board member of the *Ericksonian Monographs* and an invited presenter at the international congresses on Ericksonian approaches to hypnosis and psychotherapy. He is a certified American Association of Sex Educators, Counselors, and Therapists sex therapist and diplomate in marital and sex therapy, American Board of Family Psychology, as well as diplomate in clinical hypnosis, American Board of Psychological Hypnosis. Hammond also serves as an approved training supervisor for marital and family therapists in Utah.

Recommended Reading

Hammond, D. C. (1987). *Manual for self-hypnosis.* Des Plaines, IL: American Society of Clinical Hypnosis.
Hammond, D. C. (1988a). *Hypnotic induction and suggestion.* Des Plaines, IL: American Society of Clinical Hypnosis.
Hammond, D. C. (1988b). *Learning clinical hypnosis: An educational resources compendium.* Des Plaines, IL: American Society of Clinical Hypnosis.

References

Beutler, L. E. (1986). Systematic eclectic psychotherapy. In J. C. Norcross (Ed.), *Handbook of eclectic psychotherapy* (pp. 94–131). New York: Brunner/Mazel.
Hammond, D. C. (1984). Myths about Erickson and Ericksonian hypnosis. *American Journal of Clinical Hypnosis, 26,* 236–245.
Hammond, D. C. (1985). An instrument for utilizing client interests and individualizing hypnosis. *Ericksonian Monographs, 1,* 111–126.
Hammond, D. C. (1988c). Will the real Milton Erickson please stand up? *International Journal of Clinical and Experimental Hypnosis, 26,* 173–181.
Hammond, D. C. (1990). *Handbook of hypnotic suggestions and metaphors.* New York: Norton.
Hammond, D. C., Hepworth, D. H., & Smith, V. G. (1977). *Improving therapeutic communication.* San Francisco: Jossey-Bass.
Hammond, D. C., & Stanfield, K. (1977). *Multidimensional psychotherapy.* Champaign, IL: Institute for Personality and Ability Testing.

Lazarus, A. A. (1981). *The practice of multimodal therapy*. New York: McGraw-Hill.

Norcross, J. C. (1986). *Handbook of eclectic psychotherapy*. New York: Brunner/Mazel.

Norcross, J. C., & Prochaska, J. O. (1982). A national survey of clinical psychologists: Affiliations and orientations. *Clinical Psychologist, 35*(3), 4–6.

Smith, D. S. (1982). Trends in counseling and psychotherapy. *American Psychologist, 37*, 802–809.

Thorne, F. C. (1967). *Integrative psychology*. Brandon, VT: Clinical Psychology Publishing.

Hypno-Play Therapy

Marian Kaplun Shapiro

Definition

Psychotherapy is the process of restoring the lost self. As therapists, we do not try to shape particular results; instead, we try to create a safe and nurturant place in which clients can find what they have lost. To be a therapist is to be privileged to have assisted in this achievement.

Qualification Statement

No creature but the human being is physically unable to care for itself by the age of one. And no society expects the human child to be fully autonomous for a minimum of another eleven years. Even then, at least in contemporary Western culture, that human is still considered to be a child for six to twelve more years.

I think of adults as remarkable survivors because too often

in the process of growing up, characteristics innate to all humans and the specific uniqueness of each individual are pushed, pulled, prodded, cajoled, and sometimes brutally fashioned into the semblances consciously and unconsciously wished on them by the people closest to them and by the immediate and greater world in which they live. Children are little; adults are big. Children are dependent for a long time. What surprise that they comply, losing parts of themselves in the process. And what surprise that, becoming parents themselves, they raise a new generation of children to whom they bequeath their own experiences in the process of limitation.

Basically, however, I am an optimist, believing that it is not too late for adults to repair much of the psychological damage they suffered during their formative years. Granted that, especially when dealing with severe trauma, all damage cannot simply be excised, leaving the person pain-free. But I work from the assumption that impairment in living need not continue. The parent-child cycle of deficit can be interrupted. I have seen impressive results that indicate that my assumption reflects reality, not wishful fantasy.

Being a pragmatist, it seemed to me sensible to work from the following axiom: If possible, fix the problem where it occurred. As a hypnotherapist as well as a psychologist, I have therefore developed a method which I call *hypno-play therapy*. Hypno-play therapy is the deliberate use of play therapy with adults in an age-regressed hypnotic state. Hypnotherapists often work with the tool of age regression, in which the age-regressed client feels as he or she did at the age in question. Thus, when using hypno-play therapy, the client has the opportunity to enter therapy at the age at which the problem occurred, an age at which help was unavailable. This work can extend all the way down to infancy. It can be limited to particular periods, or expanded over a significant span, as in characterological work.

Critique Statement

The development of the self according to its inherent authenticity is an ideal with which few therapists today will argue. In a democratic culture, can we successfully defend a position in which *we* decide what is best and become Henry Higginses to a compliant crew of Elizas? At any rate, even if we have these tendencies — and who is there who has never tried to impose some "better" way on a client? — we will fail. A plant will not become a dog, no matter how much we think it would be better for that plant were it able to bark!

Neither hypnotherapy in general nor hypno-play therapy in particular is suitable or even applicable to all people or all issues. For some people, medication may be called for; as a humanist, I am appalled at those who uncritically eschew all biological interventions in the name of humanism. For others, methods including biofeedback, psychoanalysis, psychodrama, group therapy, psychodynamic psychotherapy — the myriad specialties in this great field — have much to offer to specific people in certain circumstances. If I could have but one of Aladdin's wishes it would be this: that we be committed to open-minded inquiry, that we take doctrine solely as the basis for new questions. In that way we will continue to inject ourselves and our profession with aliveness and bring the best that is possible to those who come to us with their problems.

Biography

Marian Kaplun Shapiro practices as a psychologist and hypnotherapist in Lexington, Massachusetts, and is also an adjunct member of the faculty of the Massachusetts School of Professional Psychology. She received her Ed.D. degree (1978) from Harvard University. An author of several journal articles in this and other fields, her book, *Second Childhood: Hypno-Play Therapy with Age-Regressed Adults,* appeared in 1988.

Recommended Reading

Shapiro, M. K. (1988a). Hypno-play therapy with adults: Theory, method, and practice. *American Journal of Clinical Hypnosis, 31*(1), 1–10.
Shapiro, M. K. (1988b). *Second childhood: Hypno-play therapy with age-regressed adults.* New York: Norton.

Jeffrey K. Zeig
W. Michael Munion

11

Defining Psychotherapy: Concluding Comments

In this concluding chapter, we will discuss some prior efforts to produce a general definition of psychotherapy that corresponds to the "family"-level definition offered in Chapter One; we will expand the taxonomy metaphor to explore the ecological niches into which our field has developed; and we will reexamine units-of-analysis.

Psychotherapy Defined

In Chapter One, we offered a generic (theory-nonspecific) definition of psychotherapy that was based on areas of convergence among the contributors to this volume. That definition was presented to provide a backdrop against which one could contrast the contributed approach-specific definitions. There have been a considerable number of efforts in the past to produce a viable definition of psychotherapy that would apply to all legitimate variants. "What is psychotherapy?" was addressed by Jerome Frank (1961/1973) in *Persuasion and healing.* He wrote:

> Since practically all forms of personal influence may affect a person's sense of well-being, the definition

415

of psychotherapy must of necessity be somewhat arbitrary. We shall consider as psychotherapy only those types of influence characterized by:

1. a trained, socially sanctioned healer, whose healing powers are accepted by the sufferer and by his social group or an important segment of it

2. a sufferer who seeks relief from the healer

3. a circumscribed, more or less structured series of contacts between the healer and the sufferer, through which the healer, often with the aid of a group, tries to produce certain changes in the sufferer's emotional state, attitudes, and behavior. All concerned believe these changes will help him. Although physical and chemical adjuncts may be used, the healing influence is primarily exercised by words, acts, and rituals in which sufferer, healer, and — if there is one — group participate jointly [pp. 2-3].

Julian Meltzoff and Melvin Kornreich (1970) offered the following definition:

Psychotherapy is taken to mean the informed and planful application of techniques derived from established psychological principles, by persons qualified through training and experience to understand these principles and to apply these techniques with the intention of assisting individuals to modify such personal characteristics as feelings, values, attitudes, and behaviors which are judged by the therapist to be maladaptive or maladjustive [p. 4].

Jules Masserman's definition of psychotherapy is quoted in Harry Garner's (1970) *Psychotherapy: Confrontation problem solving technique:*

Psychotherapy is the optimum utilization of every ethical means at the physician's command to help the patient understand that his previously neurotic patterns of behavior, though perhaps once suitable, are no longer either necessary or advantageous, while at the same time helping him to realize by subjective analysis, personal example, and progressive experience that more comprehensive adaptive and creative ways will also be found to be on the whole more pleasurable and profitable [p. 6].

In *The technique of psychotherapy,* Lewis Wolberg (1977) presented the following definition:

Psychotherapy is the treatment, by psychological means, of problems of an emotional nature in which a trained person deliberately establishes a professional relationship with the patient with the object of (1) removing, modifying, or retarding existing symptoms, (2) mediating disturbed patterns of behavior, and (3) promoting positive personality growth and development [p. 3].

Wolberg acknowledged other perspectives on this issue and therefore reprinted thirty-six separate definitions by noted practitioners. However, even considered collectively, they did not improve significantly on Wolberg's conceptualization.

Implicit in these generic definitions is a basic truth: Any definition derived from an overview is by nature ambiguous. For example, Masserman's definition stresses the importance of "understanding." But, more specifically, is this a modification in attitude, an emotional event, or a combination of both? To take another example, Frank's definition is inexact: It applies equally to the shaman and the psychiatrist.

Another situation compounds the problem of ambiguity: The psychotherapeutic field operates in a climate that encourages diversity and growth. When our field was in its infancy, psychoanalysis was the only accepted approach. Once behavioral and humanistic approaches challenged the exclusive dominance of psychoanalysis and established themselves by producing positive results, experts fostered additional theoretical developments and approaches. The resultant proliferation of approaches has taken place at an unchecked, almost exponential rate, resulting in further ambiguity about the parameters that determine what constitutes psychotherapy. Therefore, on the generic level, definitions of psychotherapy will have to become increasingly broad and ambiguous. On the practical level, as we shall see, the proliferation of therapy models carries its own set of consequences.

Ecological Niches

Little more than a century ago, Freud initiated his interest in the psychological aspects of medicine (Alexander and Selesnick, 1966). Since then, psychotherapy has evolved to occupy many niches in the human ecology. Such expansion may be expected in the infant stages of development in any field. In fact, expansion into previously uninhabited ecological niches — even those that seem hostile — is a quality inherent to both animal and vegetable species. For example, life exists at volcanic vents deep in the ocean where no light can penetrate; fish live in the frigid waters of the Antarctic. Under both normal and extreme situations, species thrive until they become supplanted by dominant competitors: 99.9 percent of all species that have ever existed no longer can be found on earth. To date, psychotherapy has been quite robust. It continues to proliferate unimpeded into many niches of human social life. However, because there have been few boundaries to psychotherapy's growth, the scope of the field remains ill-defined. Psychiatry began as a neurological discipline and spawned psychotherapy. Subsequently, psychotherapy moved into other disciplines, including psychology, social work, and educational counseling. Recently, psychotherapy has moved into business and even into the media. Moreover, psychotherapy has assumed other ecological niches and has merged with seemingly disparate disciplines to produce, for example, body therapies, music therapy, and art therapy. There has been an amalgamation of psychotherapy with philosophies of all types, especially existentialism and constructivism. Practitioners have expanded psychotherapy into the realm of spirituality to define the transpersonal approaches. Training standards also have changed and become less stringent. Paraprofessionals and nonprofessionals are trained by some experts to administer therapeutic practices. In addition self-help groups abound. Sprouting from a small, circumscribed seed, therapy has moved into a dominant place in the general ecosystem of helping relationships. No longer is it hidden. It is now an accepted part of postindustrial culture.

What is the result of this growth within the social ecosystem? To examine this effect, let us return to biology. It is nearly impossible to foresee the consequences of even apparently small changes in an ecosystem. For example, owing to a speech at the 1932 World Conference of Sugar Technologists in Puerto Rico, the cane toad (*Bufo marinus*), a native of Hawaii, was introduced into the Mulgrave River in Queensland, Australia, in an effort to disrupt the damage caused to the sugar industry by the cane beetle. The cane toad has thrived: Today it is estimated that, spreading out from the original eight introduction sites, the cane toad now inhabits more than 40 percent of the Queensland district. Unfortunately the cane toad never became an aggressive predator of the cane beetle. What it *has* done is to quickly become a dominant competitor to indigenous toads because of certain inherent abilities lacking in the endemic species. Local inhabitants give the toads mixed reviews: Some like them — some hate them. Contrasted with this is the case of the eucalyptus tree, which was imported to California from Australia because of its fast growth rate: It was to be used to produce railroad ties in the expanding West. This was a fine idea, but the wood proved to be far too soft for the intended purpose. However, there is not much reported negative effect from this intervention, and people seem to benefit from the eucalyptus and have already begun to think of it as a native plant, forgetting that it was an import.

Similarly, psychotherapy has continued to develop into the ecological niches of helping relationships at an alarming rate, and it has been difficult to assess the impact of this development with any confidence. While many initially unconventional

developments have proved to be quite beneficial, we believe that
unbridled proliferation of therapeutic approaches should be
regarded with a healthy skepticism. For example, one must
wonder about the value of psychotherapy as conducted by telephone on television talk shows and in some self-help groups.
Also, it is hoped that in evolving into ecological niches, psychotherapy won't crowd out other important relationships, such
as intimacy with family, friends, and religious advisers.

Just as it is important for us to attend to the niches into which
we have expanded and may yet expand, it is important to attend to the reality that we must share our domain with others.
For example, as E. Lakin Phillips pointed out in his contribution, researchers have observed natural attritional phenomena
within the field of psychology — a statistically significant portion
of all therapy terminates after a given number of contacts. Where
psychotherapy is conducted within the public health system, such
research can be used by politicians and administrators to delimit
service, which, in at least some cases, must be detrimental to
individuals who are exceptions to the statistical norm. Even
within the private sector, there is a very real threat that treatment may be dictated more by governmental regulation and
insurance policies than by client need. (Note, for example, how
many inpatient chemical dependency treatment programs re-
vamped to "complete" treatment in thirty days just when insurance companies put a thirty-day-ceiling on benefits.)

If, as a profession, we are to have credibility when we assert
that we are qualified to dictate treatment parameters and that
politicians, insurance underwriters, and other nonprofessionals
are not, then we must set rational limits in regard to what it
is that constitutes psychotherapy. The problem that confronts
us is the need to construct a meta-perspective of personality and
intervention that encompasses all that we have learned thus far
and that fosters growth and development in the field without
uncritically approving any method simply because it is new and
holds promise. Perhaps this will hinder proliferation and cause
some needed deceleration of growth. If the field fails to limit
itself, it may expand so much that it loses boundaries and becomes assimilated into general culture. This may not be bad;

the demise of psychotherapy through the psychologizing of the culture may ultimately make people more humanized in their interactions.

In regard to meta-perspective, there is a trend in the proliferation of psychotherapy that should be mentioned. As the field has evolved, eclecticism has prospered. There is a continuing reaction to competitive, pharisaical, single-theory perspectives. Norcross (1986) reports thirteen studies confirming that between 30 percent and 40 percent of contemporary practitioners favor the eclectic approach. This permits the therapist to "own" several sets of "lenses" to view the patient and the change process from multiple perspectives. Such flexibility has more assets than liabilities. It is also probable that a meta-perspective is most likely to emanate from this quarter.

Units-of-Analysis

In each chapter introduction, units-of-analysis were defined by the discipline (genus) versus the modality (species) or individual practitioners (subspecies). The astute reader will note that within each chapter, some individual practitioners attend to elements that range beyond those emphasized at the theoretical level. In some instances, the approach described might even appear to belong to an entirely different discipline. Recall that, with very few exceptions, contributors selected the discipline within which they deemed their work belonged. The apparent discrepancy between the basic theoretical parameters and the approaches described in some cases is an indication of how, once indoctrinated, one tenaciously identifies with a particular theory or format. In spite of such influences as changes owing to experience and the insinuation of the practitioner's persona into the therapy process, the work may continue to be identified as the indoctrinated discipline.

As stated earlier, the units-of-analysis described in individual approaches often ranged well beyond the parameters set forth in the theoretical formulation. The wide variety of theories and processes described in this book may each have validity, and, through the units-of-analysis, access specific aspects of the client.

We all have conscious and unconscious processes. We all behave, think, feel, relate, and wonder from time to time about
our place in the cosmos. These are all units-of-analysis because
they are facets of individuals. However, therapists often tend
to be doctrinaire rather than flexible in their description of what
constitutes the "correct" lens for their patients.

Therapeutic units-of-analysis are theoretically determined and
in practice become entry points. There is no such thing as therapeutic neutrality: We all have our own biases. The theoretical
orientation of the therapist is a lens that makes patient behavior
intelligible but also may delimit perception of the patient and
problem and thus impede the way in which therapy proceeds.
When that happens, it is time to remove the lens, because the
therapist has ceased to look at the patient and is fixated instead
on the "spectacles." The therapist, who encounters resistance
that cannot be overcome, is oriented to a model more than to
the person he or she encounters. It is essential to guard against
responding automatically to a given set of symptoms with a fixed
action pattern.

Conclusion

This book has been about perspectives within the field of psychotherapy. In the introductory chapter, we began with a medical metaphor that asserted that a person's perspective determines how a problem is conceptualized and, consequently, the
manner in which it is addressed. We offered a model describing units-of-analysis, which are essentially an interplay of theoretically determined lenses and the position that the therapist
takes (the therapist's personal proclivities regarding theory and
intervention). The unit-of-analysis model is merely a way to conceptualize and understand the diverse perspectives on psychotherapy assembled in this book.

Although in principle the unit-of-analysis model ought to apply only to species- and subspecies-level definitions, with genus-
and family-level definitions being determined by less subjective
parameters, the reality is that any definition at any level will
be influenced to some degree by the position the therapist takes.

The submitted definitions and qualifications are the strength and purpose of this book. Within these writings, the reader may discern the units-of-analysis utilized by the authors. The diversity among the approaches represented here is only an indication of the extent to which the practice of psychotherapy has evolved. The current climate encourages this growth and diversity. Rather than losing or inhibiting potentially important innovations, and within ethical limits, nearly any approach that appears to be effective is currently considered psychotherapy.

The rapid expansion within the field has meant the intrusion of therapy into domains previously inhabited strictly by nonpsychotherapeutic professionals (for example, spiritual leaders, friends, the media). We reviewed the cases of both the cane toad, which, if not malignant, is clearly not a wholly benign phenomenon, and the eucalyptus tree, which has been integrated into the California ecosystem with no apparent disruption. As editors and practitioners, we wonder whether the development of our field will have a negative or benign effect in the long run. Clearly, if development is not constrained from within the profession, then external forces such as insurance companies and government regulation will become an increasingly stronger influence.

In examining definitions of psychotherapy that address the practice collectively, we find that either they exclude some legitimate variants through parameters that are too stringent, or they are so general as to admit practices that may not be consonant with the goals, ethics, and standards of the mainstream psychotherapeutic community. It may be impossible to compose an encompassing definition of our field.

We believe that each of the approaches described in this book has something valuable to offer. The variance among the disciplines and modalities is as much a reflection of the underlying philosophy of practice or theory as it is a reflection of the individuality of the practitioner.

This position is echoed by the late Virginia Satir, who wrote the following response to our request that she participate in the *What Is Psychotherapy?* project:

> Psychotherapy is a name given to a process carried
> on between one or more persons called therapists,

and one or more persons called clients or patients,
which takes place in the context of human dysfunction and is aimed at creating change in a positive
direction. . . .

I cannot in good faith place myself in any of the
categories you listed [chapter titles]. My therapy
includes elements of all the therapies you mention.
I believe it is important that we stop categorizing
schools of approach and look at the individual practices within each of the approaches. From that point
of view, my therapy may differ from other therapies in that I am focused on the development of
health and think of all symptoms as barriers to
health. Therefore, I work at developing health,
which in turn then dissolves barriers.

References

Alexander, F. G., & Selesnick, S. T. (1966). *History of psychiatry:
    Evaluation of psychiatric thought and practice from prehistory to the
    present.* New York: Harper & Row.
Frank, J. D. (1973). *Persuasion and healing: A comparative study of
    psychotherapy.* Baltimore: Johns Hopkins University Press.
    (Original work published 1961)
Garner, H. (1970). *Psychotherapy: Confrontation problem solving tech-
    nique.* St. Louis, MO: W. H. Green.
Meltzoff, J., & Kornreich, M. (1970). *Research in psychotherapy.*
    New York: Atherton Press.
Norcross, J. C. (Ed.). (1986). *Handbook of eclectic psychotherapy.*
    New York: Brunner/Mazel.
Wolberg, L. R. (1977). *The technique of psychotherapy* (Part 1, 3rd
    Ed.). New York: Grune & Stratton.

Name Index

Subject Index

433